SELF-STUDY PROBLEMS/SOLUTIONS BOOK
VOLUME 2: CHAPTERS 15–25

INTERMEDIATE ACCOUNTING
NINTH EDITION

MARILYN F. HUNT, M.A., C.P.A.
University of Central Florida
Orlando, Florida

DONALD E. KIESO, Ph.D., C.P.A.
KPMG Peat Marwick Emeritus Professor of Accountancy
Northern Illinois University
DeKalb, Illinois

JERRY J. WEYGANDT, Ph.D., C.P.A.
Arthur Andersen Alumni Professor of Accounting
University of Wisconsin
Madison, Wisconsin

JOHN WILEY & SONS, INC.
NEW YORK • CHICHESTER • WEINHEIM
BRISBANE • SINGAPORE • TORONTO

ISBN 0-471-15898-4

Printed in the United States of America

10 9 8 7 6 5 4 3 2

Printed and bound by Bradford & Bigelow, Inc.

CONTENTS

PREFACE: To the Student

The purpose of this self-study tutorial is to help you to improve your success rate in solving accounting homework assignments and in answering accounting exam questions. For each chapter we provide you with:

OVERVIEW	To briefly introduce the chapter topics and their importance.
STUDY OBJECTIVES	To provide you with a learning framework. Explanations of these objectives also provide you with a summary of the major points covered in the chapter.
TIPS	To alert you to common pitfalls and misconceptions and to remind you of important terminology, concepts, and relationships that are relevant to answering specific questions or solving certain problems. To help you to understand the intricacies of a problematic situation and to tell you what to do in similar circumstances.
EXERCISES	To provide you with a selection of problems which are representative of homework assignments which an intermediate accounting student may encounter.
MULTIPLE CHOICE	To provide you with a selection of multiple-choice questions which are representative of common exam questions covering topics in the chapter.
PURPOSES	To identify the essence of each question or exercise and to link them to learning objectives.
SOLUTIONS	To show you the appropriate solution for each exercise and multiple-choice question presented.
EXPLANATIONS	To give you the details of how selected solutions were derived and to explain why things are done as shown.
APPROACHES	To coach you on the particular model, computational format, or other strategy to be used to solve particular problems. To teach you how to analyze and solve multiple-choice questions.

This book will be a welcome teaching/learning aid because it provides you with the opportunity to solve accounting problems in addition to the ones assigned by your instructor without having to rely on your teacher for solutions. Many of the exercises and questions contained herein are very similar to items in your intermediate accounting textbook; the difference is, the ones in this book are accompanied with detailed clearly-laid out solutions.

The use of the multiple choice questions in this volume and the related suggestions on how to approach them can easily increase your ability (and confidence in your ability) to deal with exam questions of this variety.

We are grateful to Jennifer Laudermilch of Coopers & Lybrand, Atlanta, Georgia, for her constructive suggestions and editorial comments. Also thanks to Chelsea Hunt, James S. Hunt, Annabelle Specie, and M.F. Specie for their assistance and support. Our appreciation to Mary Ann Benson who skillfully prepared the manuscript and performed the composition of this book.

Marilyn F. Hunt
Donald E. Kieso
Jerry J. Weygandt

HOW TO STUDY ACCOUNTING

The successful study of accounting requires a different approach than most other subjects. In addition to reading a chapter, applying the material through the completion of exercises or problems is necessary to develop a true and lasting understanding of the concepts introduced in the text chapter. The study of accounting principles is a combination of theory and practice; theory describes what to do and why, and practice is the application of guidelines to actual situations. We use illustrations (practice) to demonstrate how theory works and we use theory to explain why something is done in practice. Therefore, it is impossible to separate the two in the study of accounting.

Learning accounting is a cumulative process. It is difficult to master Chapter 4 until you are thoroughly familiar with Chapters 1-3, and so on. Therefore, it is imperative that you keep up with class assignments. And because accounting is a technical subject, you must pay particular attention to terminology.

Accounting is the language of business. It is an exciting subject that provides a challenge for most business majors. Your ultimate success in life may well depend on your ability to grasp financial data. The effort you expend now will provide rewards for years to come.

We encourage you to follow the four steps for study outlined below to give yourself the best possible chance for a successful learning experience and to make the most efficient use of your time. These steps provide a system of study for each new chapter in your text.

Step 1
- Scan the study objectives in the text.
- Scan the chapter (or chapter section) rather quickly.
- Glance over the questions at the end of the chapter.

This first step will give you an overview of the material to be mastered.

Step 2
- Read the assigned pages slowly.
- Use the marginal notes to review and to locate topics within each chapter.
- Study carefully and mark for later attention any portions not clearly understood.
- Pay particular attention to examples and illustrations.
- Try to formulate tentative answers to end-of-chapter questions.

During this phase, you will be filling in the "outline" you formed in Step 1. Most of the details will fall into place during this part of your study. The remaining steps are necessary, however, for a keen understanding of the subject.

Step 3
- Carefully read the **Overview, Learning Objectives,** and **Tips** sections of this *Self-Study* volume.
- Do the **Exercises** and **Cases** in the *Self-Study* that pertain to the same learning objectives as your homework assignments. Review the relevant **Illustrations** in this book.
- Do the **Multiple-Choice Type Questions** in the *Self-Study* that pertain to the same study objectives as your homework assignments.
- Refer back to the sections of the chapter in the text that you marked as unclear if any. It is likely that any confusion or questions on your part will have been cleared up through your work in the *Self-Study* book. If a section remains unclear, carefully reread it and rework relevant pages of the *Self-Study*.
- Repeat this process for each assigned topic area.

Step 4 • Write out formal answers to homework assignments in the text.

This step is crucial because you find out whether you can independently **apply** the material you have been studying to fresh situations. You may find it necessary to go back to the text and/or *Self-Study* to restudy certain sections. This is common and merely shows that the study assignments are working for you.

Additional comments pertaining to Step 3 and your usage of this *Self-Study* volume are as follows:

- The **Learning Objectives** and **Tips** sections, along with **Illustrations** will aid your understanding and retention of the material. **Exercises** provide examples of application of the text material. These should be very valuable in giving you guidance in completing homework assignments which are often similar in nature and content.

- The **Approach** stated for an exercise or question is likely the most valuable feature of this *Self-Study* volume because it tells you how to **think** through the situation at hand. This thought process can then be used for similar situations. It is impossible to illustrate every situation you may encounter. You can, however, handle new situations by simply applying what you know and making modifications where appropriate. Many students make the mistake of attempting to memorize their way through an accounting book. That too is an impossible feat. **Do not rely on memorization.** If this material is going to be useful to you, you must **think** about what you are reading and always be thinking of **why** things are as they are. If you know the reasoning for a particular accounting treatment, it will be much easier to remember that treatment and reconstruct it even weeks after your initial study of it.

- **Explanations** are provided for exercise and questions. These are very detailed so that you will thoroughly understand what is being done and why. These details will serve you well when you complete your homework assignments.

- Always make an honest effort to solve the exercises and answer the questions contained in this *Self-Study* volume **before** you look at the solutions. Answering the questions on your own will maximize the benefits you can expect to reap from this book.

- The **Multiple-Choice Type Questions** are self-tests to give you immediate feedback on how well you understand the material. Study the **Approaches** suggested for answering these questions in the *Self-Study*. Practice them when answering the multiple choice questions in the text. Apply them when taking examinations. By doing so, you will learn to calmly, methodically, and successfully process examination questions. This will definitely improve your exam scores.

- When you work an **Exercise** or **Case** in the *Self-Study* or in the text, always read the instructions **before** you read all of the given data. This allows you to determine what you are to accomplish. Therefore, as you now read through the data, you can begin to process it because you can determine its significance and relevance. If you read the data before the instructions, you are likely to waste your time because you will have to reread the facts once you find out what you are to do with them. Also, more importantly, you are likely to begin to anticipate what the problem is about, which will often cause you to do things other than what is requested in the question.

Good luck and best wishes for a positive learning experience!

CHAPTER 15

STOCKHOLDERS' EQUITY: CONTRIBUTED CAPITAL

OVERVIEW

A major source of assets of an entity is owners' equity. Owners' equity of a corporation is called **stockholders' equity** or **shareholders' equity** because the owners of the business hold shares of stock as evidence of their ownership claims. Stockholders' equity typically has two major classifications for reporting purposes: **contributed capital (paid-in capital)** and **retained earnings**. Contributed capital includes the subclassifications of **capital stock** and **additional paid-in capital**.

This chapter discusses the issuance of stock and the reacquisition of shares. When shares are reacquired and held in the treasury, two alternative generally accepted accounting methods are available for use: the cost method and the par value method. Although the cost method is more popular, the par value method is conceptually superior.

SUMMARY OF LEARNING OBJECTIVES

1. **Discuss the characteristics of the corporate form of organization.** Among the specific characteristics of the corporate form that affect accounting are: (1) influence of state corporate law; (2) use of the capital stock or share system; (3) development of a variety of ownership interests; (4) limited liability of stockholders; and, (5) formality of profit distribution.

2. **Identify the rights of stockholders.** In the absence of restrictive provisions, each share of stock carries the following rights: (1) to share proportionately in profits and losses; (2) to share proportionately in management (the right to vote for directors); (3) to share proportionately in corporate assets upon liquidation; and, (4) to share proportionately in any new issues of stock of the same class (called the preemptive right).

3. **Explain the key components of stockholders' equity.** Stockholders' or owners' equity is classified into two categories: contributed capital and earned capital. **Contributed capital (paid-in capital)** is the term used to describe the total amount paid in on capital stock; put another way, it is the amount advanced by stockholders to the corporation for use in the business. Contributed capital includes items such as the par value of all outstanding capital stock, and premiums less any discounts on issuance. **Earned capital (retained earnings)** is the capital that develops if the business operates profitably; it consists of all undistributed income that remains invested in the enterprise.

4. **Explain the accounting procedures for issuing shares of stock.** The accounting procedures involved in the issuance of different types of stock are: (1) **Par value stock:** Accounts required to be kept are (a) preferred stock or common stock; (b) paid-in capital in excess of par or additional paid-in capital; and, (c) discount on stock. (2) **No-par stock:** No-par stock with a stated value requires the same accounts to be kept as a par value stock. No-par stock with no stated value requires only a capital stock account (preferred stock or common stock). (3) **Stock**

sold on a subscription basis: Accounts required to be kept are (a) common stock subscribed or preferred stock subscribed, (b) paid-in capital in excess of par, and (c) subscriptions receivable. (4) **Stock issued in combination with other securities (lump sum sales):** The two methods of allocation available are (a) the proportional method; and, (b) the incremental method. (5) **Stock issued in noncash transactions:** When stock is issued for services or property other than cash, the property or services should be recorded at either the fair market value of the stock issued or the fair market value of the noncash consideration received, whichever is more clearly determinable.

5. **Identify the major reasons for purchasing treasury stock.** The reasons corporations purchase their outstanding stock are varied. Some major reasons are: (1) to meet employee stock compensation contracts or meet potential merger needs, (2) to increase earnings per share by reducing the shares outstanding, (3) to thwart takeover attempts or to reduce the number of stockholders, (4) to make a market in the stock, or (5) to contract (reduce) operations.

6. **Explain the accounting for treasury stock.** The cost method is generally used in accounting for treasury stock. This method derives its name from the fact that the Treasury Stock account is maintained at the cost of the shares purchased. Under the cost method, the Treasury Stock account is debited for the cost of the shares acquired and is credited for this same cost upon reissuance. The price received for the stock when originally issued does **not** affect the entries to record the acquisition and reissuance of the treasury stock.

7. **Describe the major features of preferred stock.** Preferred stock is a special class of shares that possesses certain preferences or features not possessed by common stock. The features that are most often associated with preferred stock issues are: (1) preference as to dividends, (2) preference as to assets in the event of liquidation, (3) convertible into common stock, (4) callable at the option of the corporation, and (5) nonvoting.

8. **Distinguish between debt and preferred stock.** With the right combination of features (i.e., fixed return, no vote, redeemable), a preferred stockholder may possess more of the characteristics of a creditor than those of an owner. Preferred shares generally have no maturity date, but the preferred stockholder's relationship with the company may be terminated if the corporation exercises its call privilege.

9. **Identify items reported as additional paid-in capital.** Items affecting the balance of total additional paid-in capital include: (1) premiums (discounts) on capital stock issued, (2) treasury stock transactions, (3) absorption of a deficit in a recapitalization or additional capital arising in recapitalizations or revisions in the capital structure (quasi-reorganization), (4) declaration of liquidating dividend, (5) additional assessments on stockholders, (6) conversion of convertible bonds or preferred stock, (7) declaration of a "small" (ordinary) stock dividend, and (8) retirement of stock.

10.* **Explain the par value method of accounting for treasury stock.** Under the par value method, the purchase of treasury shares is viewed as a constructive retirement of those shares. Inasmuch as the shares cannot be an asset, they must represent a retirement or at least a reduction of the outstanding stock. Because shares outstanding are shown at par, the reacquired shares must be carried at par to indicate the proper reduction in stock outstanding.

*This material is covered in Appendix 15-A in the text.

TIPS ON CHAPTER TOPICS

TIP: Paid-in capital is often called **contributed capital**. Additional paid-in capital is often called **additional contributed capital** or **paid-in capital in excess of par**. Although **capital surplus** is a term sometimes used for additional paid-in capital, it is not recommended terminology.

TIP: Stockholders are often called shareholders.

TIP: Make sure you understand the components of **total paid-in capital**, which include the capital stock accounts **plus** additional paid-in capital accounts.

TIP: **Capital stock** accounts include Common Stock, Preferred Stock, Common Stock Subscribed, Preferred Stock Subscribed, and Stock Dividends Distributable.

TIP: As you progress through this chapter, pay particular attention to the effect of the various transactions on total paid-in capital, retained earnings, and total stockholders' equity.

TIP: Additional paid-in capital can arise from many situations which include the following: the issuance of capital stock at a price above par, some treasury stock transactions, additional assessments on stockholders, the retirement of stock, the declaration of an ordinary (small) stock dividend, and the conversion of bonds to stock.

TIP: There is a tremendous amount of terminology relating to capital stock. You should have a clear understanding of all of the terms mentioned in this chapter before going on to subsequent chapters.

TIP: The **par value** of a stock is an arbitrary value assigned to a share of stock at the time of incorporation and is printed on the stock certificate. Par value usually has **no** direct relationship to the stock's issuance price or to its market value at any date subsequent to the issuance date.

TIP: The **par value** of a stock has legal significance because it establishes the amount of **legal capital**, which is an amount of owners' equity that must be maintained by the corporation for the protection of creditors.

TIP: The **market value** of a share of stock at a given point in time is the value at which the stock can be bought or sold.

TIP: **Premium** on capital stock is defined as an excess of issuance price over par for newly issued stock. In recording the issuance, this excess is often credited to an account called Premium on Capital Stock or Paid-in Capital in Excess of Par. Regardless of the account title, the premium amount is usually reported on the balance sheet by the caption Additional Paid-in Capital.

TIP: A no-par stock with a stated value is accounted for in a manner similar to stock with a par value; that is, the stated value is recorded in the capital stock account and an excess of the issuance price over stated value is recorded in an additional paid-in capital account. The entire proceeds from the issuance of a no-par stock with no stated value is recorded in the capital stock account.

TIP: When a corporation issues more than one class of capital stock, each additional paid-in capital account should specify the class of stock to which it relates. Although a separate account may be maintained in the general ledger for each source of additional paid-in capital, the balances of all additional paid-in capital accounts are typically summed and reported by a single amount on the balance sheet by the caption Additional Paid-in Capital.

TIP: When stock is issued in a noncash exchange, the historical cost principle is used to determine the issuance price. Thus, the exchange price is the fair value (cash equivalent) of the consideration given or the fair value of the consideration received, whichever is the more objectively determinable.

TIP: The receipt by a corporation of donated property from a city or other government entity to entice the company to do business in a locality represents a nonreciprocal transfer. A **nonreciprocal transfer** is to be recorded at the fair value of the property at the date of transfer. In this case, an account called Donated Capital should be credited. Donated Capital is classified as a separate element of stockholders' equity.

TIP: Memorize the definition of treasury stock: **Treasury stock** is a corporation's own stock that has been issued, fully paid, and subsequently reacquired, but not cancelled. Thus, treasury shares are issued shares but are not outstanding shares. Treasury stock is **not** an asset; rather it is a contraction of owners' equity.

TIP: Regardless of the method used to account for treasury stock, the **purchase** of treasury stock will cause owners' equity to **decrease** by the cost of the shares acquired; the **sale** of treasury stock will cause owners' equity to **increase** by the selling price of the shares sold. Although the net impact is the same under both methods, the choice of method will affect the individual stockholders' equity accounts involved in recording the transaction.

TIP: When the **cost method** is used to account for treasury stock, the Treasury Stock account is classified contra to the sum of all of the other stockholders' equity accounts, and its balance is the cost of the treasury shares held. When the **par value method** is used to account for treasury stock transactions, the Treasury Stock account is classified contra to the related capital stock account (such as Common Stock), and its balance is the par value of the treasury shares held.

TIP: The par value method of accounting for treasury stock views treasury stock as if it were temporarily retired and records the acquisition the same way a retirement is recorded except that the par value of the stock is charged to Treasury Stock rather than to the capital stock account used in recording the original issuance.

> **TIP:** Dividends in arrears are not to be reported as a liability. Dividends become a liability when they are declared. By definition, dividends in arrears are dividends on cumulative preferred stock which have been passed (not declared). Dividends in arrears should be disclosed, however, in the notes to the financial statements.

EXERCISE 15-1

Purpose: (L.O.4) This exercise will highlight the relationship between authorized, issued, outstanding, and subscribed shares.

The following data are available regarding the common stock of the Daffy Corporation at December 31, 1996:

Authorized shares	200,000
Unissued shares	60,000
Subscribed shares	5,000
Treasury shares	12,000

Instructions
Compute the number of outstanding shares.

Solution to Exercise 15-1

Authorized shares	200,000
Unissued shares	(60,000)
Issued shares	140,000
Treasury shares	(12,000)
Outstanding shares	128,000

Approach and Explanation: Write down the formula for determining the number of outstanding shares:

$$\text{Issued Shares} - \text{Treasury Shares} = \text{Outstanding Shares}$$

Fill in the data given. Authorized shares are either issued or unissued. Issued shares are either outstanding shares or treasury shares. The number issued can readily be computed in this situation. Treasury shares are issued shares but are not outstanding (in the hands of shareholders). Subscribed shares are not issued until they are fully paid so they are part of the unissued number.

ILLUSTRATION 15-1
TRANSACTIONS AFFECTING ADDITIONAL PAID-IN CAPITAL (L.O.9)

Additional paid-in capital is a classification of accounts (like current assets is another classification). Therefore, there is no one account titled "additional paid-in capital"; rather, there are numerous individual accounts within that classification (such as Premium on Common Stock, Paid-in Capital in Excess of Par from Treasury Stock, and Paid-in Capital in Excess of Par). However, for illustrative purposes, the basic transactions affecting additional paid-in capital are expressed in T-account form below:

Additional Paid-in Capital

1. Discounts on capital stock issued.	1. Premiums on capital stock issued.
2. Sale of treasury stock below cost (when the cost method is used).	2. Excess of subscription price over par value of subscribed stock.
3. Absorption of a deficit in a recapitalization (quasi-reorganization).*	3. Forfeitures of stock subscriptions.
4. Declaration of a liquidating dividend.	4. Sale of treasury stock above cost (when the cost method is used).
5. Retirement of stock which was originally issued at a price above par.	5. Additional capital arising in recapitalizations or revisions in the capital structure (quasi-organizations).
	6. Additional assessments on stockholders.
	7. Conversion of convertible bonds (or preferred stock).
	8. Declaration of a "small" (ordinary) stock dividend.
*Discussed in Chapter 16.	9. Retirement of stock at a price below its original issuance price.

CASE 15-1

Purpose: (L.O.4) This case will review the proper accounting procedures for stock subscriptions and the issuance of no par stock.

Problems may be encountered in accounting for transactions involving the stockholders' equity section of the balance sheet.

Instructions
(a) Describe how to account for the subscription of common stock at a price in excess of the par value of the common stock.
(b) Describe how to account for the issuance for cash of common stock with no par value at a price in excess of the stated value of the common stock.
(c) Describe the two methods of accounting for the costs of the initial issuance of stock.

(AICPA Adapted)

Solution to Case 15-1

(a)   The subscription of common stock at a price in excess of the par value of the common stock is accounted for at the date of subscription as follows:

- Stock Subscriptions Receivable is debited for the subscription price of the common stock.

- Common Stock Subscribed is credited for an amount representing the par value of the common stock that will be issued when the stock subscription is collected.

- An additional paid-in capital account is credited for the excess of the subscription price of the common stock over its par value.

(b)   The issuance for cash of common stock with no par value at a price in excess of the stated value of the common stock is accounted for as follows:

- Cash is debited for the proceeds from the issuance of the common stock.

- Common Stock is credited for the stated value of the common stock.

- An additional paid-in capital account is credited for the excess of the proceeds from the issuance of the common stock over its stated value.

(c)   The two primary methods of accounting for initial stock issuance costs (such as attorneys' fees, underwriters' fees and commissions, expenses of printing and mailing certificates and registration statements, filing fees, and costs of advertising the issue) are:

- Treat issue costs as a reduction of additional paid-in capital. This treatment is based on the premise that issue costs are unrelated to corporate operations and thus are not properly chargeable to expense; issue costs are viewed as a reduction of proceeds of the financing activity.

- Treat issue costs as an organization cost that is capitalized and classified as an intangible asset and amortized to expense over an arbitrary time period not to exceed 40 years. This treatment is based on the premise that amounts paid in as invested capital should not be violated, and that issue costs benefit the corporation over a long period of time or so long as the invested capital is utilized.

EXERCISE 15-2

Purpose: (L.O.4) This exercise will illustrate how to record selected transactions related to the issuance of capital stock.

On February 1, 1999, Bimini Bay Corporation received authorization to issue 400,000 shares of $10 par value common stock and 100,000 shares of $50 par value preferred stock. The following transactions occurred during 1999:

Feb. 24   Issued 100,000 shares of common stock for cash at a price of $18 per share.

Feb. 28   Issued 50,000 shares of common stock in exchange for a group of modular warehouses.

Mar. 2   Received a plot of land as a donation from the city of Gainesville as an inducement to bring the business to this community. The land has a market value of $220,000.

Mar. 5   Sold 20,000 shares of Bimini Bay preferred stock at $51 each.

Mar. 23   Sold a package of shares for $1,340,000. The package consisted of 20,000 shares of Bimini Bay common stock and 20,000 shares of Bimini Bay preferred stock. The market value of the preferred was $51 per share, and the market value of the common was $18 per share at this date.

Mar. 28   Received subscriptions for 30,000 shares of common stock at $18 per share. Collected a down payment of 20% of the subscription price.

Apr. 15   Collected 50% of the subscription price from the subscribers.

Apr. 30   Collected the balance from the subscribers of 28,000 shares and issued the related stock. The remaining subscribers (2,000 shares) defaulted. The subscription agreement provides that the corporation will refund only the amount collected in excess of 20% of the subscription price.

Nov. 4   Issued 20,000 shares of common stock at $24 per share.

Nov. 14   Sold a package of shares for $1,510,000. The package consisted of 20,000 shares of Bimini Bay common stock and 20,000 shares of Bimini Bay preferred stock. The market value of the common stock was $24 at this date; however, no recent quote on the preferred stock could be found.

Instructions

Prepare the journal entries to record the transactions listed above.

Solution to Exercise 15-2

February 24

Cash (100,000 x $18)..	1,800,000	
Common Stock (100,000 x $10).............................		1,000,000
Paid-in Capital in Excess of Par—Common		
(100,000 x $8)...		800,000

February 28

Warehouses (50,000 x $18)......................................	900,000	
Common Stock (50,000 x $10)...............................		500,000
Paid-in Capital in Excess of Par—Common		
(50,000 x $8)..		400,000

March 2

Land	220,000	
Donated Capital..		220,000

March 5

Cash (20,000 x $51)..	1,020,000	
Preferred Stock (20,000 x $50).............................		1,000,000
Paid-in Capital in Excess of Par—Preferred		
(20,000 x $1)..		20,000

March 23

Cash.	1,340,000	
Discount on Preferred Stock ($1,000,000 - $990,434)............	9,566	
Preferred Stock (20,000 x $50).............................		1,000,000
Common Stock (20,000 x $10)...............................		200,000
Paid-in Capital in Excess of Par—Common		
($349,566 - $200,000)...................................		149,566

Computations:

20,000 x $18	=	$ 360,000	fair value of common
20,000 x $51	=	1,020,000	fair value of preferred
		$ 1,380,000	total fair value

$$\frac{\$360,000}{\$1,380,000} \times \$1,340,000 = \underline{\$349,566} \text{ allocated to common}$$

$$\frac{\$1,020,000}{\$1,380,000} \times \$1,340,000 = \underline{\$990,434} \text{ allocated to preferred}$$

March 28

Subscriptions Receivable (30,000 x $18)	540,000	
Common Stock Subscribed (30,000 x $10)		300,000
Paid-in Capital in Excess of Par—Common		
(30,000 x $8)		240,000

> **TIP:** In accounting for stock subscriptions, additional paid-in capital is increased at the date the subscriptions (contracts) are received, not when the related cash is received.

Cash (20% x 30,000 x $18)	108,000	
Subscriptions Receivable		108,000

April 15

Cash (50% x 30,000 x $18)	270,000	
Subscriptions Receivable		270,000

April 30

Cash (30% x 28,000 x $18)	151,200	
Subscriptions Receivable		151,200

Common Stock Subscribed (28,000 x $10)	280,000	
Common Stock		280,000

Common Stock Subscribed (2,000 x $10)	20,000	
Paid-in Capital in Excess of Par—Common (2,000 x $8)	16,000	
Cash (2,000 x 50% x $18)		18,000
Subscriptions Receivable (2,000 x 30% x $18).............		10,800
Paid-in Capital from Defaulted Subscriptions		
(2,000 x 20% x $18).......................................		7,200

November 4

Cash (20,000 x $24)...	480,000	
Common Stock (20,000 x $10)		200,000
Paid-in Capital in Excess of Par—Common		
(20,000 x $14)..		280,000

November 14

Cash	1,510,000	
Preferred Stock (20,000 x $50)...............................		1,000,000
Paid-in Capital in Excess of Par—Preferred		
($1,030,000* - $1,000,000)...............................		30,000
Common Stock (20,000 x $10)		200,000
Paid-in Capital in Excess of Par—Common		
(20,000 x $14)..		280,000

*20,000 x $24 = $480,000 market value of common
  $1,510,000 - $480,000 = $1,030,000 allocated to preferred

Explanation:

Feb. 24   The **issuance of stock in exchange for cash** is recorded by crediting stockholder equity accounts for the amount of the cash consideration received ($1,800,000). The par value ($10) per share is entered into the related capital stock account, and the excess of the issuance price over par value per share ($8) is recorded in the related additional paid-in capital account. When more than one class of stock is authorized, any additional paid-in capital amounts are properly identified to indicate the related class of stock.

Feb. 28   The **issuance of stock in exchange for noncash assets** requires an application of the historical cost principle. The asset and the stock are to be recorded at the fair value of the consideration given (the stock) or the fair value of the consideration received (warehouses), whichever is the more clearly determinable. Because some shares of common were issued only four days earlier at $18 per share, the February 24 transaction provides good evidence of the fair value (cash equivalent value) of the stock issued on February 28. No mention of the fair value of the warehouses is made.

Mar. 2   The **receipt of a nonmonetary asset as a gift** represents a nonreciprocal transfer which is to be recorded at the fair value of the asset transferred. Assets donated to the corporation by a governmental entity to entice the company to conduct business in the locality are recorded by credits to Donated Capital.

Mar. 5   In recording the **issuance of preferred shares for cash**, the par value of the preferred shares issued is placed in a capital stock account for that class of stock. The amount received in excess of par is an element of additional paid-in capital; the account title clearly indicates the related class of stock. The account title "Premium on ... Stock" is sometimes used to record the excess of issuance price over par.

Mar. 23   When **shares of two classes of stock are sold for one lump sum** and the fair value of each class of security is known, the lump sum received is allocated between the two classes of securities on a proportional basis; that is, based on the relative fair values of the securities involved. Thus, a ratio is developed for each security, and that ratio is equal to the total fair value of the particular shares in question divided by the total fair value of all of the shares in the transaction. Therefore, 26.087% ($360,000 ÷ $1,380,000) of the proceeds are allocated to stockholder equity accounts attributable to common stock, and 73.913% ($1,020,000 ÷ $1,380,000) of the proceeds are allocated to the issuance price of the preferred stock. Because the proceeds attributable to the preferred stock ($990,434) are less than the par value of the preferred shares being sold ($50 x 20,000 shares), the preferred shares are being issued at a total discount of $9,566. The Discount on Preferred Stock account is a negative component of additional paid-in capital.

Mar. 28   The **receipt of a subscription contract** is recorded by a debit to a receivable account for the total contract (subscription) price, a credit to a stock subscribed account for the par value of the subscribed stock, and a credit to an additional paid-in capital account for the excess of the subscription price over par of the subscribed shares. Thus, additional paid-in capital increases at the date the subscription contract is received. The partial collection increases Cash and reduces the Subscriptions Receivable account. The Common Stock Subscribed account is classified as a capital stock account; it has a balance only from the date of receipt of the subscription contract until the date the last collection is made on the contract. The Subscriptions Receivable account is classified as a contra stockholders' equity account, similar to the presentation of treasury stock when the cost method is used.

Apr. 15 The **collection of cash from subscribers** increases assets (cash). It also increases total stockholders' equity by reducing the contra account—Subscriptions Receivable.

Apr. 30 The **collection of additional cash from subscribers** is recorded in the same manner as previous collections. The **issuance of the subscribed shares** reduces one capital stock account (Common Stock Subscribed) and increases another capital stock account (Common Stock) by the same amount. The default is recorded by removing the subscription price of the related shares from the accounts; the Common Stock Subscribed account is debited for the par value of the shares and the Paid-in Capital in Excess of Par account is debited for the excess of the subscription price over par. Cash is credited for the amount refunded. Subscriptions Receivable is credited with the unpaid balance. The portion of the subscription price paid by the defaulting subscribers but not refunded to them is credited to an additional paid-in capital account (Paid-in Capital from Defaulted Subscriptions).

Nov. 4 The **issuance of stock for cash** increases assets and total stockholders' equity by the issuance proceeds. The par value of the issued shares is recorded in a capital stock account, regardless of the issuance price. An additional paid-in capital account is debited or credited (whichever is appropriate) for the difference between the total proceeds and the total par value of the shares.

Nov. 14 In a situation where **more than one class of securities are issued in a lump sum issuance**, and the market value of all classes of securities is **not** determinable, the incremental method may be used. The market value of the securities is used as a basis for those classes that are known (market value for common stock, in this case) and the remainder of the lump sum is allocated to the class for which the market value is **not** known (preferred stock, in this case).

ILLUSTRATION 15-2
COST METHOD OF ACCOUNTING FOR TREASURY STOCK (L.O.6)

When treasury stock is purchased:
1. Cash is credited for the cost of the treasury shares acquired.
2. Treasury Stock is debited for the cost of the treasury shares acquired.

When treasury stock is sold:
1. Cash is debited for the selling price of the treasury shares sold.
2. Treasury Stock is credited for the cost of the treasury shares sold.
3. The selling (reissuance) price of the treasury shares is compared with the cost of those shares:
   a. An excess of selling price over cost is credited to Paid-in Capital from Treasury Stock.
   b. An excess of cost over selling price is debited to any additional paid-in capital account related to previous treasury stock transactions or retirements of stock in the same class. When the balances in Paid-in Capital from Treasury Stock and Paid-in Capital from Retirements are exhausted, Retained Earnings is debited for the remainder.*

> *An alternate treatment often applied in practice is as follows: The excess of cost over the reissuance price is charged to Paid-in Capital in Excess of Par for a pro rata amount per share of any premium on the original issuance of the stock, and any remaining excess is charged to Paid-in Capital from Treasury Stock (to the extent of its balance) and then to Retained Earnings.

ILLUSTRATION 15-3
JOURNAL ENTRIES FOR RECORDING
TREASURY STOCK TRANSACTIONS USING THE COST METHOD (L.O.6)

Assume that the following transactions occur in chronological order and that there are no prior balances in any additional paid-in capital accounts.

1. **1,000 shares of $10 par stock are sold for $13 per share.**

Cash	13,000	
Common Stock		10,000
Paid-in Capital in Excess of Par		3,000

2. **100 treasury shares are acquired for $11 each.**

Treasury Stock	1,100	
Cash		1,100

3. **10 treasury shares are sold at $14 each.**

Cash	140	
Treasury Stock		110
Paid-in Capital from Treasury Stock		30

4. **10 treasury shares are sold at $6 each.**

Cash	60	
Paid-in Capital from Treasury Stock	30	
Retained Earnings	20	
Treasury Stock		110

5. **All 80 remaining treasury shares are retired.**

Common Stock	800	
Paid-in Capital in Excess of Par	240	
Treasury Stock		880
Paid-in Capital from Retirement of Common		
Stock		160

TIP: The accounts and amounts used to record the original issuance of shares are used to record the retirement of the same shares.

TIP: When the **cost method** is used to account for treasury stock transactions, a "gain on the sale of treasury stock" is an expression used to indicate that treasury stock was sold for a price in excess of the treasury stock's cost; a "loss on the sale of treasury stock" refers to treasury stock which is sold for a price that is less than the cost of the treasury shares. For example, transaction #3 above results in a "gain" of $3 ($14 - $11) per share and transaction #4 results in a "loss" of $5 ($11 - $6) per share.

ILLUSTRATION 15-3 (Continued)

> **TIP:** When a corporation engages in treasury stock transactions, a gain or loss is **never** reported on the income statement because a corporation cannot have an accounting gain or loss when dealing with the owners of the business in their capacity of being owners of the business. The purchase and sale of treasury stock are capital transactions; there is no element of income in a capital transaction.
>
> **TIP:** Treasury stock transactions can sometimes **reduce** retained earnings but can **never increase** retained earnings.
>
> **TIP:** Regardless of the method used to account for treasury stock, most state corporate laws require that retained earnings be appropriated (restricted) in the amount of the cost of treasury stock acquired.

EXERCISE 15-3

Purpose: (L.O.6,9,10) This exercise will illustrate how the components of stockholders' equity should be reported in the balance sheet.

Bobbit Corporation's charter authorizes 200,000 shares of $20 par value common stock, and 50,000 shares of 6% cumulative and nonparticipating preferred stock, par value $100 per share.

The corporation engaged in the following stock transactions between the date of incorporation and December 31, 1999:

(1) Issued 40,000 shares of common stock for $1,920,000.
(2) Issued 10,000 shares of preferred stock in exchange for machinery valued at $1,120,000.
(3) Took subscriptions for 5,000 shares of common stock and collected 30% of the subscription price of $50 per share.
(4) Purchased 1,000 shares of common stock at $46 per share for the treasury. The cost method was used to record the transaction.
(5) Sold 500 shares of treasury stock for $51 per share.

At December 31, 1999, Bobbit's retained earnings balance was $2,200,000. State law requires that the amount of retained earnings available for dividends be restricted by an amount equal to the cost of treasury shares held.

Instructions
Prepare the stockholders' equity section of the balance sheet in good form.

Solution to Exercise 15-3

Bobbit Corporation
PARTIAL BALANCE SHEET
December 31, 1999

Stockholders' equity
  Preferred stock, $100 par; 6% cumulative and
    nonparticipating; 50,000 shares authorized;
    10,000 shares issued and outstanding $1,000,000
  Common stock, $20 par; 200,000 shares authorized,
    40,000 shares issued, 39,500 shares outstanding   800,000
  Common stock subscribed; 5,000 shares   100,000
  Additional paid-in capital:
    From preferred stock $ 120,000
    From common stock   1,270,000
    From treasury stock   2,500   1,392,500
      Total paid-in capital   3,292,500
  Retained earnings (restricted in the amount of
    $23,000 cost of treasury stock held)   2,200,000
      Total paid-in capital and retained earnings   5,492,500
  Less: Cost of 500 treasury common shares $ 23,000
    Stock subscriptions receivable   175,000   198,000
      Total stockholders' equity $ 5,294,500

Approach: Reconstruct the journal entries for the transactions and post those entries to T-accounts. Use the resulting balances in the accounts to prepare the stockholders' equity section of the balance sheet at December 31, 1999.

Explanation:

(1) Cash 1,920,000
    Common Stock (40,000 x $20)............... 800,000
    Paid-in Capital in Excess of Par—Common
      ($1,920,000 - $800,000) 1,120,000

(2) Machinery 1,120,000
    Preferred Stock (10,000 x $100)......... 1,000,000
    Paid-in Capital in Excess of Par—Preferred
      ($1,120,000 - $1,000,000) 120,000

(3) Subscriptions Receivable (5,000 x $50) 250,000
    Common Stock Subscribed (5,000 x $20).............. 100,000
    Paid-in Capital in Excess of Par—Common
      (5,000 x $30)................. 150,000

    Cash (30% x $250,000)................. 75,000
      Subscriptions Receivable................. 75,000

(4) Treasury Stock—Common (1,000 x $46)......... 46,000
    Cash. 46,000

(5)	Cash (500 x $51)	25,500	
	Treasury Stock—Common (500 x $46)		23,000
	Paid-in Capital from Treasury Stock		
	($25,500 - $23,000)		2,500

A restriction on retained earnings can be reported by parenthetical note in the retained earnings caption on the balance sheet, by footnote, or by formal appropriation of retained earnings (see Chapter 16). A restriction on retained earnings does **not** affect the total balance of retained earnings; it merely makes a portion of retained earnings unavailable to serve as the basis of a dividend declaration.

Preferred Stock			Common Stock	
	(2) 1,000,000			(1) 800,000

Common Stock Subscribed		Paid-in Capital in Excess of Par--Preferred	
	(3) 100,000		(2) 120,000

Paid-in Capital in Excess of Par--Common		Paid-in Capital from Treasury Stock	
	(1) 1,120,000		(5) 2,500
	(3) 150,000		
	Bal. 1,270,000		

Stock Subscriptions Receivable		Treasury Stock--Common	
(3) 250,000	(3) 75,000	(4) 46,000	(5) 23,000
Bal. 175,000		Bal. 23,000	

CASE 15-2

Purpose: (L.O.4,9) This case examines the major classifications within the stockholders' equity section of the balance sheet.

Stockholders' equity is an important element of a corporation's balance sheet.

Instructions

Identify and discuss the general categories of stockholders' equity (capital) for a corporation. Enumerate specific sources included in each general category.   (AICPA Adapted)

Solution to Case 15-2

The general categories of a corporation's capital are:
- Paid-in capital or contributed capital (capital stock **plus** additional paid-in capital).
- Retained earnings.

Contributed capital represents the amounts paid in for all classes of shares of stock and the amounts capitalized by order of the corporation's board of directors. Included in contributed capital is legal capital, which is usually the aggregate par value or stated value of the shares issued. Legal capital is usually not subject to withdrawal; it is intended to protect corporate creditors. Contributed capital also includes other amounts in addition to the legal capital. These amounts are generally referred to as additional paid-in capital and include the following:

- Premiums on capital stock issued (excess of issuance price over par or stated value).
- Excess of subscription price over par value of subscribed stock.
- Forfeitures of stock subscriptions.
- Excess of proceeds from reissuing treasury stock over its cost when using the cost method of accounting for treasury stock.
- Quasi-reorganization.
- Assessments on stockholders.
- Conversion of convertible bonds or preferred stock to common stock.
- Declaration of small (ordinary) stock dividend.
- Reacquisition and retirement of outstanding shares at an amount below their original issuance price.

Retained earnings are the accumulated net earnings of a corporation in excess of any net losses from operations and dividends (cash or stock). Total retained earnings should also include prior-period adjustments as direct increases or decreases and may include certain appropriations. These appropriations of retained earnings are restrictions on retained earnings, making a portion of the balance unavailable to serve as a basis for dividends. These restrictions may arise as a result of a restriction in a bond indenture or other formal agreement or they may be created at the discretion of the board of directors.

> **TIP:**   Another component of stockholders' equity, called "donated capital," will appear on the balance sheet of a corporation that has received a donation of assets (such as land) from a governmental entity as an inducement for the corporation to conduct operations in that municipality. The assets and donated capital are recorded at the fair value of the assets received by donation.

> **TIP:** The following items may appear as separate adjunct components in the stockholders' equity section of the balance sheet:
> (1) unrealized holding gains on available-for-sale securities held as an investment.
> (2) accumulated foreign currency translation adjustments.
>
> **TIP:** The following items may appear as separate contra components in the stockholders' equity section of the balance sheet:
> (1) unrealized holding losses on available-for-sale securities.
> (2) accumulated foreign currency translation adjustments.
> (3) excess of additional pension liability over unrecognized prior service cost.
> (4) guarantees of employee stock option plan (ESOP) debt.
> (5) unearned or deferred compensation related to employee stock award plans.
> (6) amounts owed to a company by employees for loans to buy company stock.
> (7) balance of stock subscriptions receivable.

ILLUSTRATION 15-4
PAR VALUE METHOD OF ACCOUNTING FOR TREASURY STOCK (L.O.11)

When treasury stock is purchased:
1. Cash is credited for the cost of the treasury shares acquired.
2. Treasury Stock is debited for the par value (or stated value) of the treasury shares acquired.
3. Paid-in Capital in Excess of Par (or Stated Value) is debited for the pro rata (per share) amount of any excess of original issuance price over par value (or stated value).
4. The acquisition cost of the treasury shares is compared with the original issuance price (amount received at the time of their original issuance):
    a. An excess of the original issuance price over the acquisition price of the treasury stock is credited to Paid-in Capital from Treasury Stock.
    b. An excess of the acquisition cost over the original issuance price is charged (debited) to Retained Earnings.

When treasury stock is sold:
1. Cash is debited for the selling price of the treasury shares sold.
2. Treasury Stock is credited for the par value (or stated value) of the treasury shares sold.
3. The selling price is compared with par value (or stated value):
    a. An excess of selling price over par (or stated value) is credited to Paid-in Capital in Excess of Par (or Stated Value).
    b. An excess of par (or stated value) over selling price is debited to Paid-in Capital from Treasury Stock (to the extent of the balance of that account) and to Retained Earnings when that balance is exhausted.

ILLUSTRATION 15-5
JOURNAL ENTRIES FOR RECORDING TREASURY STOCK TRANSACTIONS — A COMPARISON OF THE PAR VALUE METHOD WITH THE COST METHOD (L.O.6,11)

Assume that the following transactions occur in chronological order and that there are no prior balances in any additional paid-in capital accounts.

1. **1,000 shares of $10 par stock are sold for $13 per share.**

Cash	13,000	
Common Stock		10,000
Paid-in Capital in Excess of Par		3,000

2. **100 treasury shares are acquired for $11 each.**

Cost Method

Treasury Stock	1,100	
Cash		1,100

Par Value Method

Treasury Stock	1,000	
Paid-in Capital in Excess of Par	300	
Cash		1,100
Paid-in Capital from Treasury Stock		200

3. **10 treasury shares are sold at $14 each.**

Cost Method

Cash	140	
Treasury Stock		110
Paid-in Capital from Treasury Stock		30

Par Value Method

Cash	140	
Treasury Stock		100
Paid-in Capital in Excess of Par		40

4. **10 treasury shares are sold at $6 each.**

Cost Method

Cash	60	
Paid-in Capital from Treasury Stock	30	
Retained Earnings	20	
Treasury Stock		110

Par Value Method

Cash	60	
Paid-in Capital from Treasury Stock	40	
Treasury Stock		100

5. **All 80 remaining treasury shares are retired.**

Cost Method

Common Stock	800	
Paid-in Capital in Excess of Par	240	
Treasury Stock		880
Paid-in Capital from Retirement of Common Stock		160

Par Value Method

Common Stock	800	
Treasury Stock		800

ILLUSTRATION 15-5 (Continued)

6.   100 treasury shares are acquired for $14 each.

Cost Method		Par Value Method	
Treasury Stock....................	1,400	Treasury Stock.................	1,000
Cash............................	1,400	Paid-in Capital in Excess	
		of Par............................	300
		Retained Earnings.............	100
		Cash.........................	1,400

> **TIP:**   The **par value method** of accounting for treasury stock transactions is sometimes called the **stated value method.**
>
> **TIP:**   When using the **par value method**, a "gain on a treasury stock transaction" is an expression used to indicate that treasury stock was purchased for a price that is less than the stock's original issuance price; a "loss on a treasury stock transaction" is an expression which refers to treasury stock that was purchased for a price that is more than the stock's original issuance price. For example, transaction #2 above results in a "gain" of $2 ($13 - $11) per share and transaction #6 results in a "loss" of $1 ($14 - $13) per share.
>
> **TIP:**   Recall from **Illustration 15-2** and **Illustration 15-3** that when the **cost method** is used to account for treasury stock transactions, a "gain on the sale of treasury stock" is an expression used to indicate that treasury stock was sold for a price in excess of the treasury stock's cost; a "loss on the sale of treasury stock" refers to treasury stock which is sold for a price that is less than the cost of the treasury shares. For example, transaction #3 above results in a "gain" of $3 ($14 - $11) per share and transaction #4 results in a "loss" of $5 ($11 - $6) per share.

EXERCISE 15-4

Purpose: (L.O.6, 11) This exercise will illustrate the use of both the cost and the par value methods of accounting for treasury stock transactions under a variety of price relationships.

LaToya Corporation reported the following stockholder equity items at December 31, 1998:

Common Stock, $10 par	$ 350,000
Paid-in Capital in Excess of Par	70,000
Retained Earnings	710,000
Total Stockholders' Equity	$ 1,130,000

During 1999, LaToya had the following treasury stock transactions:
1. Purchased 1,000 shares at $15 per share.
2. Purchased 1,000 shares at $13 per share.
3. Sold 1,000 shares at $11 per share.
4. Sold 1,000 shares at $14 per share.
5. Purchased and immediately retired 1,000 shares at $16 per share.

Instructions
(a) Prepare the journal entries for the treasury stock transactions listed above assuming the cost method is used. Apply a FIFO approach in determining the cost of treasury shares sold.
(b) Prepare the journal entries for the treasury stock transactions listed above assuming the par value method is used.

Solution to Exercise 15-4

(a)   **Cost Method**

1. Treasury Stock (1,000 x $15).............................	15,000	
Cash...		15,000
2. Treasury Stock (1,000 x $13).............................	13,000	
Cash...		13,000
3. Cash (1,000 x $11)..	11,000	
Retained Earnings...	4,000	
Treasury Stock (1,000 x $15)		15,000
4. Cash (1,000 x $14)..	14,000	
Treasury Stock (1,000 x $13)		13,000
Paid-in Capital from Treasury Stock		1,000

5.   Common Stock (1,000 x $10)............................   10,000
      Paid-in Capital in Excess of Par (1,000 x $2).......   2,000*
      Retained Earnings...   4,000
          Cash (1,000 x $16)......................................   16,000

*$350,000 Common Stock balance ÷ $10 par = 35,000 shares issued
$70,000 PIC in Excess of Par balance ÷ 35,000 shares = $2 original
issuance premium per share

Approach and Explanation: Follow the guidelines listed in **Illustration 15-2** and the examples in **Illustration 15-3**. An explanation for each entry above is as follows:

1.   Treasury Stock is debited for the cost of the treasury shares acquired.

2.   Treasury Stock is debited for the cost of the treasury shares acquired.

3.   Cash is debited for the selling price of the treasury shares sold. Treasury Stock is credited for the cost of the treasury shares sold. The excess of the cost over the selling price of the treasury shares is to be charged to Paid-in Capital from Treasury Stock or Paid-in Capital from Retirements to the extent that these accounts have balances that came from previous transactions involving stock of the same class. In this scenario, there is no balance in either of these accounts so the entire excess is charged to Retained Earnings.

      An acceptable alternative would be to debit Paid-in Capital in Excess of Par for $2,000 and to debit Retained Earnings for $2,000. Additional paid-in capital can be charged for the pro rata amount per share of any original issuance premium. (The original issuance premium was an average of $2 per share.) Then Paid-in Capital from Treasury Stock is to be debited to the extent of its balance. The $2 premium per share can be computed as follows:

          $350,000 Common Stock balance ÷ $10 par = 35,000 shares issued
          $70,000 PIC in Excess of Par balance ÷ 35,000 shares = $2 per share

4.   Cash is debited for the selling price of the treasury shares sold. Treasury Stock is credited for the cost of the treasury shares sold. The excess of the selling price over the cost of the treasury shares is to be credited to Paid-in Capital from Treasury Stock.

5.   A retirement of stock is to be handled in a manner similar to the par value method of handling the purchase of treasury stock except that the capital stock account will be debited rather than Treasury Stock. Thus, the amounts recorded for the original issuance of the stock are removed from the accounts (debit Common Stock for $10 per share and debit Paid-in Capital in Excess of Par for $2 per share). The excess of the retirement price ($16 per share) over the original issuance price ($12 per share) is charged to Retained Earnings. An alternative treatment would be to reduce additional paid-in capital arising from previous reissuances or retirements of treasury stock of the same class before reducing Retained Earnings. Because Paid-in Capital from Treasury Stock ($1,000) is insufficient to absorb the $4,000 excess in this situation, the remainder ($3,000) would be charged to Retained Earnings.

(b)   **Par Value Method**

1.   Treasury Stock (1,000 x $10)................................   10,000
      Paid-in Capital in Excess of Par (1,000 x $2).......   2,000*
      Retained Earnings..   3,000
            Cash (1,000 x $15).......................................   15,000

2.   Treasury Stock (1,000 x $10)................................   10,000
      Paid-in Capital in Excess of Par (1,000 x $2).......   2,000*
      Retained Earnings..   1,000
            Cash (1,000 x $13).......................................   13,000

3.   Cash (1,000 x $11)...   11,000
            Treasury Stock (1,000 x $10)......................   10,000
            Paid-in Capital in Excess of Par..................   1,000

4.   Cash (1,000 x $14)...   14,000
            Treasury Stock (1,000 x $10)......................   10,000
            Paid-in Capital in Excess of Par..................   4,000

5.   Common Stock...   10,000
      Paid-in Capital in Excess of Par..........................   2,000*
      Retained Earnings..   4,000
            Cash...   16,000

*$350,000 Common Stock balance ÷ $10 par = 35,000 shares issued
$70,000 PIC in Excess of Par balance ÷ 35,000 shares = $2 original
issuance premium per share

Approach and Explanation: Follow the guidelines listed in **Illustration 15-4**. An explanation for each entry above is as follows:

1.   Cash is credited for the purchase price of the shares. Treasury Stock is debited for the par value of the treasury shares acquired. The original issuance premium related to the reacquired shares is removed from additional paid-in capital. The excess of the cost of treasury shares over the original issuance price is charged to Retained Earnings.

2.   Same as #1 immediately above.

3.   Cash is debited for the selling price of the shares. Treasury Stock is credited for the par value of the treasury shares sold. An excess of selling price over the par value of treasury shares is recorded in a manner similar to an original issuance premium; thus, Paid-in Capital in Excess of Par is credited for this excess.

4.   Same as #3 immediately above.

5.   Cash is credited for the retirement price of the shares. The amounts used in recording the original issuance are removed from the accounts. The excess of the retirement price over the original issuance price is charged to Retained Earnings.

ANALYSIS OF MULTIPLE-CHOICE TYPE QUESTIONS

QUESTION

1.   (L.O.4) Common stock is sold on a subscription basis. Paid-in Capital in Excess of Par should be credited for the excess of the subscription price over par at the date the:
a.   stock is authorized.
b.   subscription contracts are received.
c.   cash is received.
d.   stock is issued.

Explanation: At the date the subscription is received, Stock Subscriptions Receivable is debited for the sales (subscription) price, Common Stock Subscribed is credited for the par (or stated value), and Paid-in Capital in Excess of Par (or Stated Value) is credited for the excess of selling price over par (or stated value). At the date the stock is authorized, there is usually no formal journal entry. When cash is received, Cash is debited and Stock Subscriptions Receivable is credited. When the stock is issued, Common Stock Subscribed is debited for the par (or stated value) and Common Stock is credited for the same amount. (Solution = b.)

QUESTION

2.   (L.O.4,9) The Tom Powell Corporation has 10,000 shares of $10 par common stock authorized. The following transactions took place during 1999, the first year of the corporation's existence:
- Sold 1,000 shares of common stock for $18 per share.
- Issued 1,000 shares of common stock in exchange for a patent valued at $20,000.
- Reported net income of $7,000.

At the end of Tom Powell's first year, total paid-in capital amounted to:
a. $8,000.
b. $18,000.
c. $20,000.
d. $28,000.
e.   none of the above.

Approach and Explanation: (1) Write down the components of paid-in capital: (a) balances of capital stock accounts, and (b) balances of additional paid-in capital accounts. (2) Reconstruct the journal entries for the transactions listed and post those entries to T-accounts. (3) Compute the balances of the relevant accounts. (4) Sum the relevant account balances.

Cash	18,000	
Common Stock...		10,000
Premium on Common Stock...		8,000
Patent	20,000	
Common Stock...		10,000
Premium on Common Stock...		10,000
Income Summary..	7,000	
Retained Earnings..		7,000

Common Stock			Premium on Common Stock		
		10,000			8,000
		10,000			10,000
	Bal.	20,000		Bal.	18,000

Common stock	$ 20,000
Additional paid-in capital	18,000
Total paid-in capital	$ 38,000

(Solution = e.)

> **TIP:** The account title "Premium on Common Stock" is another name for Paid-in Capital in Excess of Par.

QUESTION
3.   (L.O.3,7) Which of the following rights does a preferred stockholder normally possess?
   a.   right to vote
   b.   right to receive a dividend before a common shareholder
   c.   preemptive right
   d.   right to participate in management

Explanation: A preferred stockholder usually has a preference over common stockholders as to dividends and as to distribution of assets upon liquidation. A preferred stockholder normally has to forego other rights because of the preference described above. The rights the preferred stockholder normally forgoes are the right to participate in management (right to vote on operational and financial decisions) and the preemptive right. A common stockholder normally has the right to vote and the preemptive right (right to maintain the same percentage ownership when additional shares of common stock are issued). (Solution = b.)

QUESTION

4.   (L.O.4) Which of the following represents the total number of shares that a corporation may issue under the terms of its charter?
   a.   authorized shares
   b.   issued shares
   c.   unissued shares
   d.   outstanding shares
   e.   treasury shares

Approach and Explanation: Explain the meaning of each of the terms used as answer selections. Choose the one that matches the stem of the question. Issued shares (ones the corporation has issued to date) **plus** unissued shares (shares that have not been issued yet but may be issued in the future in accordance with the terms of the charter) **equals** total authorized (approved) shares. Outstanding shares are the issued shares which are now in the hands of the public. Treasury shares are issued shares which are not outstanding at the present time. (Solution = a.)

QUESTION

5.   (L.O.5) Treasury shares are:
   a.   shares held as an investment by the treasurer of the corporation.
   b.   shares held as an investment of the corporation.
   c.   issued and outstanding shares.
   d.   unissued shares.
   e.   issued but not outstanding shares.

Approach and Explanation: Write down the definition of treasury stock. Treasury stock is a corporation's own stock that has been issued, fully paid for, and reacquired by the corporation but **not** retired (cancelled). Treasury shares are shares that have been issued previously (so are not unissued) but are not outstanding now, as they have been subsequently reacquired by the company. Treasury shares refer to a company's own shares so they cannot be an investment. A company cannot own itself. The acquisition of treasury stock represents a contraction of capital (owners' equity) rather than the acquisition of an asset. (Solution = e.)

> **TIP:**   If and when treasury shares are formally retired, they revert back to an unissued status.

QUESTION

6.   (L.O.4) If common stock with a par value is issued by a closely-held corporation for noncash assets, the amount to be recorded as paid-in capital related to this transaction is determined by the:
   a.   fair market value of the noncash assets received.
   b.   par value of the stock issued.
   c.   legal value of the stock issued.
   d.   book value of the noncash assets on the seller's books.

Approach and Explanation: Recall that any time assets are acquired, the historical cost principle is applied; that is, the assets are to be recorded at historical cost. Cost is measured by the fair market value (cash equivalent value) of the consideration given or the fair market value of the consideration received, whichever is the more objectively determinable. Assuming equipment with a fair value of $70,000 is received in exchange for stock of a closely-held corporation with a par value of $20,000, the journal entry to record the transaction would be as follows:

Equipment..	70,000	
Common Stock..		20,000
Paid-in Capital in Excess of Par Value.....................		50,000

Notice that two paid-in capital accounts (one capital stock account and one additional paid-in capital account) are affected. The increase in total paid-in capital is $70,000. (Solution = a.)

QUESTION

7. (L.O.7) Preferred stock which can be returned to the corporation and exchanged for common stock at the option of the shareholder is referred to as:
   a. cumulative preferred stock.
   b. convertible preferred stock.
   c. participating preferred stock.
   d. callable preferred stock.

Approach and Explanation: Holders of **convertible preferred stock** may, at their option, exchange their preferred shares for common stock at a predetermined ratio. Holders of **cumulative preferred stock** are entitled to receive dividends in arrears before any dividends can be paid to common stockholders; dividends in arrears refers to a passed dividend. Thus, dividends not paid in any year on cumulative preferred must be made up in a later year before any profits can be distributed to common stockholders. Holders of **participating preferred stock** share ratably with common stockholders in any dividend distributions beyond the preferred stock's annual preference. With **callable preferred stock**, the issuing corporation can call or redeem at its option the outstanding preferred shares at specified future dates and at stipulated prices. (Solution = b.)

QUESTION

8. (L.O.6) Assume the cost method is used to account for treasury stock. A "gain" on the sale of treasury stock should be classified as an:
   a. extraordinary item on the income statement.
   b. element of other income on the income statement.
   c. increase in additional paid-in capital.
   d. increase in retained earnings.

Explanation: When the cost method is used, a "gain" on the sale of treasury stock refers to the disposition of treasury stock at a price in excess of cost. This excess is recorded as a credit to Paid-in Capital from Treasury Stock. Selections "a" and "b" are incorrect because treasury stock transactions are capital transactions and capital transactions do not give rise to components of income determination. Answer selection "d" is incorrect because, regardless of the method used, treasury stock transactions can sometimes reduce retained earnings but may **never** increase retained earnings. (Solution = c.)

QUESTION

9.   (L.O.4,10) The balance of the Stock Subscriptions Receivable account should be classified:
   a.   as a current asset.
   b.   contra to common stock.
   c.   contra to retained earnings.
   d.   contra to the sum of paid-in capital and retained earnings.

Explanation: The balance of the Stock Subscriptions Receivable account is best classified contra to the subtotal of paid-in capital plus retained earnings. (Solution = d.)

QUESTION

10.   (L.O.6,10) Which of the following transactions will cause a net decrease in total additional paid-in capital?
   a.   The sale of treasury stock at a price in excess of cost when the cost method is used.
   b.   The purchase of treasury stock at a price in excess of par value but less than the original issuance price when the par value method is used.
   c.   The purchase of treasury stock at a price in excess of par value but less than the original issuance price when the cost method is used.
   d.   The sale of treasury stock at a price in excess of cost and in excess of par when the par value method is used.

Approach and Explanation: Write down the entry for each transaction described. Carefully analyze the debits and credits within each entry to determine the entry's net effect on total additional paid-in capital. The entries and analyses would be as follows:

a.   Cash . . . .   Selling Price
         Treasury Stock....................................   Cost
         Paid-in Capital from Treasury Stock ...   Difference

Additional paid-in capital is increased by the excess of the selling price over the cost of the treasury shares.

b.   Treasury Stock ....   Par
      Paid-in Capital in Excess of Par ....   Issuance Premium
         Cash ....   Cost
         Paid-in Capital from Treasury Stock ...   Difference

Because the cost is in excess of par, the debit to Paid-in Capital in Excess of Par is greater than the credit to Paid-in Capital from Treasury Stock. Additional paid-in capital is decreased by the "issuance premium" and increased by the "difference." Thus, the net effect on additional paid-in capital is a decrease.

c.   Treasury Stock ....   Cost
        Cash . . . .   Cost

This transaction has no effect on additional paid-in capital.

d.   Cash . . . .   Selling Price
        Treasury Stock....................................   Par
        Paid-in Capital in Excess of Par ....   Difference

This transaction increases additional paid-in capital.

(Solution = b.)

CHAPTER 16

STOCKHOLDERS' EQUITY: RETAINED EARNINGS

OVERVIEW

The term **earnings** refers to net income for a period. The term **retained earnings** refers to accumulated earnings. That is, retained earnings is the total of all amounts reported as net income since the inception of the corporation less the sum of any amounts reported as net losses and dividends declared since the inception of the corporation. Thus, distributions of corporate profits to stockholders reduce retained earnings.

A corporation may distribute cash, noncash assets, or additional shares of the corporation's own stock to its owners in the form of dividends. A distribution of assets may represent a distribution of income or a return of invested capital. A distribution of a corporation's own stock results in capitalizing retained earnings. Corporate distributions and appropriations of retained earnings (which are restrictions on the amount of retained earnings available as a basis for declaration of future cash, property, and stock dividends) are discussed in this chapter.

SUMMARY OF LEARNING OBJECTIVES

1. **Describe the policies used in distributing dividends.** The state incorporation laws normally provide information concerning the legal restrictions related to the payment of dividends. Corporations rarely pay dividends in an amount equal to the legal limit. This is due, in part, to the fact that assets represented by undistributed earnings are used to finance future operations of the business. If a company is considering declaring a dividend, two preliminary questions must be asked: (1) Is the condition of the corporation such that the dividend is **legally permissible**? (2) Is the condition of the corporation such that a dividend is **economically sound**?

2. **Identify the various forms of dividend distributions.** Dividends are of the following types: (1) cash dividends, (2) property dividends, (3) scrip dividends (instead of paying a dividend now, the corporation has elected to pay it at some future date; the scrip issued to stockholders as a dividend is merely a special form of note payable), (4) liquidating dividends (dividends based on capital other than retained earnings are sometimes described as liquidating dividends), (5) stock dividends (the nonreciprocal issuance by a corporation of its own stock to its stockholders on a pro rata basis).

3. **Explain the accounting for small and large stock dividends.** Generally accepted accounting principles require that the accounting for small stock dividends (less than 20 or 25%) be based on the fair market value of the stock issued. When a small stock dividend is declared, Retained Earnings is debited for the fair market value of the stock to be distributed. The entry includes a credit to Common Stock Dividend Distributable for the par value times the number of dividend shares, with any excess credited to Paid-in Capital in Excess of Par. Between the declaration date and the date of issuance, common stock dividend distributable is reported as a capital stock item in the stockholders' equity section of the balance sheet. If the number of shares to be issued

in the dividend exceeds 20 or 25% of the shares outstanding (large stock dividend), Retained Earnings is debited only for the par value of the dividend shares, and no additional paid-in capital is recorded.

4.   **Distinguish between stock dividends and stock splits.** A stock dividend is a capitalization of retained earnings that results in a reduction in retained earnings and a corresponding increase in certain contributed capital accounts. The par value per share and total stockholders' equity remain unchanged with a stock dividend. Also, all stockholders retain their same proportionate share of ownership in the corporation. A stock split results in an increase or decrease in the number of shares outstanding, with a corresponding proportional decrease or increase in the par or stated value per share. No accounting entry is required for a stock split. Similar to a stock dividend, stockholders' equity remains unchanged. A stock split is usually intended to improve the marketability of the shares by reducing the market price of the stock being split.

5.   **Explain the effect of different types of preferred stock dividends.** Dividends paid to shareholders are affected by the dividend preferences of the preferred stock. Preferred stock can be: (1) cumulative or noncumulative; and, (2) fully participating, partially participating, or nonparticipating.

6.   **Identify the reasons for appropriating retained earnings.** An appropriation of retained earnings serves to restrict for a specific purpose the payout of retained earnings. In general, the major reason for retained earnings appropriations is the corporation's desire to reduce the basis upon which dividends are declared (unappropriated credit balance in retained earnings). This desire may stem from (1) legal restrictions, (2) contractual restrictions, (3) existence of possible or expected loss, and (4) protection of working capital position.

7.   **Explain accounting and reporting for appropriated retained earnings.** To establish an appropriation of retained earnings, a corporation prepares a journal entry, debiting Unappropriated Retained Earnings and crediting a specific appropriations account (for example, Retained Earnings Appropriated for Sinking Fund). The entry is confined to stockholders' equity accounts and does not directly affect corporate assets or liabilities. The only way to dispose of an appropriation of retained earnings is to reverse the entry that created the appropriation. Appropriations of retained earnings are more often disclosed in the notes to the financial statements as an alternative to making a formal entry against retained earnings.

8.   **Indicate how stockholders' equity is presented and analyzed.** The stockholders' equity section of a balance sheet includes capital stock, additional paid-in capital, and retained earnings. Additional items that might also be presented are treasury stock and accumulated comprehensive income. A statement of stockholders' equity is often also presented. Common ratios used in this area include rate of return on common stock equity, payout ratio, price earnings ratio, and book value per share.

9.*   **Describe the accounting for a quasi-reorganization.** A corporation that has accumulated a large debit balance (deficit) in retained earnings may, under the laws of certain states, enter into a process known as a quasi-reorganization. This procedure consists of the following steps: (1) All assets are revalued at appropriate current values so the company will not be burdened with excessive inventory or fixed asset valuations in following years. Any loss on revaluation increases the deficit. (2) Paid-in or other types of capital must be available or must be created, at least equal in amount to the deficit. If no such capital exists, it is created through donation of outstanding stock, or by some similar means. (3) The deficit is then eliminated by a charge against paid-in capital (usually additional paid-in capital). In addition to the steps above, a quasi-reorganization requires: (1) approval by stockholders, (2) fair and unbiased valuation of assets, (3) a zero balance in retained earnings at the conclusion of the reorganization, (4) the date of the quasi-reorganization shown with retained earnings for the succeeding 10 years, and (5) balance sheet disclosure of the amount of the deficit eliminated, for 3 years.

  *This material appears in Appendix 16-A in the text.

TIPS ON CHAPTER TOPICS

TIP: **Stockholders' equity** is often referred to as **capital**. In accounting for stockholders' equity, the emphasis is on the source of capital. **Retained earnings** is sometimes called **earned capital** because it is the portion of stockholders' equity which has been generated by the entity's operations. **Paid-in capital** is often called **contributed capital** or **invested capital** because it arises from owner contributions. Contributed capital includes capital stock accounts and additional paid-in capital accounts.

TIP: A preferred stock's preference as to dividends is usually expressed as a percentage of the par or stated value; sometimes, the preference is expressed in terms of dollars.

TIP: Retained earnings represents a source of corporate assets. The balance of the Retained Earnings account at any point in time reflects the total unspecified assets which have been obtained through profitable operations of the reporting entity. The balance of the Retained Earnings account has **no** direct relationship to the amount of cash held by the entity; a corporation can have a large balance in the Cash account and a small balance in Retained Earnings or a small balance in Cash and a large balance in Retained Earnings.

TIP: There are three dates associated with the declaration of any dividend: (1) the declaration date, (2) the date of record, and (3) the date of payment (or distribution). A journal entry is required at the date of declaration and at the date of payment.

TIP: Dividends are **not** an expense; they do not meet the definition of expense. Dividends are a distribution of income, not a determinant of income. In recording the declaration of any dividend (except for a liquidating dividend), the accountant may use a temporary account called Dividends Declared, rather than debiting the Retained Earnings account directly. At the end of the period, in the closing process, the balance of the Dividends Declared account is closed directly to the Retained Earnings account.

TIP: The declaration of a cash dividend reduces working capital; the payment of a previously declared (and unrecorded) cash dividend has no effect on working capital. Unless otherwise indicated, Dividends Payable will require a cash payment to settle the obligation.

TIP: A property dividend (dividend payable in assets of the corporation other than cash) is an example of a nonreciprocal transfer of nonmonetary assets. *APB Opinion No. 29* requires that a nonreciprocal transfer of nonmonetary assets be recorded at the fair value of the assets transferred. Thus, any difference between the transferred asset's fair value and its carrying amount is to be recognized as a gain or a loss.

TIP: A **liquidating dividend** is a distribution to stockholders from invested capital. Thus, a liquidating dividend results in a reduction of paid-in capital (usually additional paid-in capital) and does not affect retained earnings. A stockholder's investment in the corporation is reduced, but maybe not eliminated, by this type of dividend. If a dividend is only **partially liquidating**, both paid-in capital and retained earnings are reduced.

TIP: Although a stock dividend results in a reduction in retained earnings, it also causes an increase in paid-in capital by the same amount. There is **no change in total stockholders' equity** when a stock dividend is declared or distributed.

TIP: The term **capitalization of retained earnings** refers to the process of transferring an amount from retained earnings to paid-in capital. Stock dividends result in the capitalization of retained earnings. Thus, stock dividends are declared as a means of informing stockholders that assets arising from past income will be retained in the business rather than distributed as dividends to the stockholders.

TIP: The amount of retained earnings to be capitalized for a stock dividend depends on whether or not the issuance of the dividend shares is expected to have a material effect on the market price per share of stock. If a material effect is **not** expected, the market price at the date of declaration is used; if a material effect is expected, the par value is used. Generally, when the number of shares in the dividend are equal to 20% or less of the number of shares currently outstanding, the dividend is called a **small or ordinary stock dividend**, and no material effect on market price per share is expected. When the number of shares in the dividend are equal to 25% or more of the number of shares currently outstanding, the dividend is called a **large stock dividend** or a **stock split-up effected in the form of a dividend**, and a material effect will likely occur.

TIP: The account title, Stock Dividend Payable, is a poor title for Stock Dividend Distributable. The word "payable" implies it is a liability; however, it is **not** a liability because there is no associated debt that must later be paid by the use of cash or other assets or services. Stock Dividend Distributable is a capital stock account and, therefore, is to be reported as an element of paid-in capital. This account only has a balance for the short period of time between the date of declaration and the date of distribution of the dividend.

TIP: If a journal entry involves an appropriated retained earnings account (debit or credit), the other half of the entry (debit or credit) has to be Retained Earnings (unappropriated).

TIP: An appropriation of retained earnings does **not** affect the total retained earnings balance; it does **not** affect net income or any other major financial statement figure. An appropriation merely transfers an amount from unappropriated retained earnings to appropriated retained earnings. Since appropriated and unappropriated balances are added to obtain total retained earnings, no change occurs in total retained earnings. An appropriation of retained earnings is merely a manner of disclosure of a restriction on retained earnings. Restrictions may be disclosed by parenthetical note or in the notes to the financial statements without formal appropriations through the accounts.

TIP: Recall from your study of Chapter 4 that when a company has reported components of other comprehensive income, an item called Accumulated Other Comprehensive Income (or Loss) is to be reported as a separate component of stockholders' equity. It is usually the last item displayed in the stockholders' equity section of the balance sheet; it may be a positive or a negative element of stockholders' equity. A number of items may be included in the Accumulated Other Comprehensive Income (Loss) caption. Among these items are "foreign currency translation adjustments" (covered in advanced accounting), "unrealized holding gains and losses for available-for-sale securities" (covered in Chapter 18), "excess of additional pension liability over unrecognized prior service cost" (covered in Chapter 21), "guarantees of employee stock option plan (ESOP) debt," "unearned or deferred compensation related to employee stock award plans," and others.

TIP: All changes during a period in all stockholders' equity accounts should be disclosed. Disclosure of such changes may take the form of a separate **statement of stockholders' equity** (sometimes called the statement of changes in stockholders' equity or the stockholders' equity statement) or may be made in the other general purpose financial statements or the notes thereto. A popular format for the presentation of changes in stockholders' equity items is illustrated in the **Solution to Exercise 16-5** in this self-study volume.

TIP: If the return on common stockholders' equity is greater than the return on assets, the interest rate on debt is less than the average return on total assets; hence, the entity is **favorably trading on the equity.** However, if the cost of debt exceeds the return on total assets, the return on common stockholders' equity will be less than the return on total assets; hence, the entity will be **unfavorably trading on the equity.**

ILLUSTRATION 16-1
DETERMINING HOW TO RECORD A DISTRIBUTION OF STOCK (L.O.3,4)

When a corporation distributes additional shares of its own stock to its existing stockholders for no consideration, the accountant must record the distribution as one of the following, whichever is appropriate: (1) a small stock dividend, (2) a large stock dividend, or (3) a stock split. The following flowchart will provide guidance in determining the proper treatment.

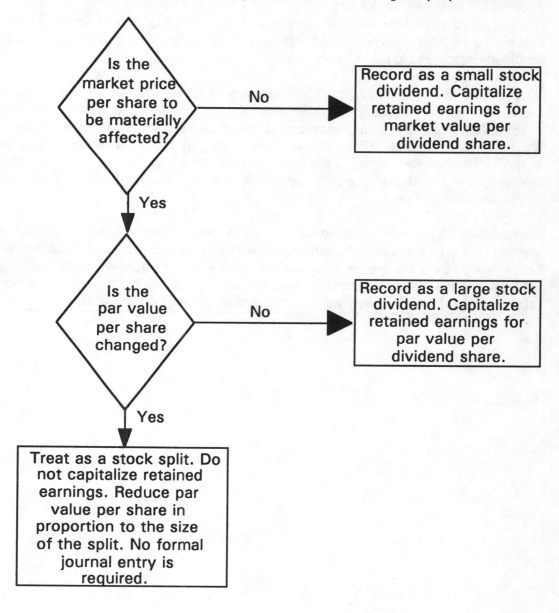

ILLUSTRATION 16-2
JOURNAL ENTRIES FOR RECORDING DIVIDENDS AND SPLITS (L.O.3,4)

Cash Dividend

Data The board of directors declares a cash dividend of $100,000.

Date of Declaration
Retained Earnings (or Cash Dividends Declared) 100,000
   Dividends Payable 100,000

Date of Record No entry.

Date of Payment
Dividends Payable 100,000
   Cash 100,000

Property Dividend

Data Dave Jones Corporation declares a property dividend on March 1 to be distributed to stockholders on April 15. The property is an investment in shares of Bonnie Corporation and has a carrying value of $11,000. The market value of the Bonnie shares is $14,000 on March 1 and $14,900 on April 15.

Date of Declaration
Investments in Securities 3,000
   Gain on Appreciation of Securities 3,000

Retained Earnings (or Property
   Dividends Declared) 14,000
     Property Dividends Payable 14,000

Date of Record No entry.

Date of Payment
Property Dividends Payable 14,000
   Investments in Securities 14,000

TIP: Any change in the fair value of the property between the date of declaration and the date of payment of the dividend is ignored.

ILLUSTRATION 16-2 (Continued)

Liquidating Dividend

Data   Harker Corporation declares a liquidating dividend of $4,000.

Date of   Additional Paid-in Capital*..   4,000
Declaration   Dividends Payable..   4,000

*One of a number of additional paid-in capital accounts may be used, depending on the relevant state law, such as Paid-in Capital in Excess of Par or Paid-in Capital from Treasury Stock.

Date of   No entry.
Record

Date of   Dividends Payable..   4,000
Payment   Cash   4,000

Small Stock Dividend

Data   D & E Henry Corporation has 100,000 shares of $10 par common stock outstanding on March 1, 1999. On March 2, the board of directors declares a 10% stock dividend distributable on April 4 to stockholders of record on March 16. The market price per share of common is $24 on March 2, $23 on March 16, and $25 on April 4.

Date of   Retained Earnings (or Stock Dividend Declared)   240,000
Declaration   Common Stock Dividend Distributable...............   100,000
                   Paid-in Capital in Excess of Par   140,000
                       (10% x 100,000 = 10,000 shares)
                       (10,000 shares x $24 = $240,000)
                       (10,000 shares x $10 par = $100,000)
                       ($240,000 - $100,000 = $140,000)

Date of   No entry.
Record

Date of   Common Stock Dividend Distributable   100,000
Distribution   Common Stock..   100,000

ILLUSTRATION 16-2 (Continued)

Large Stock Dividend

Data   JJH Corporation has 100,000 shares of $10 par common stock outstanding on March 1, 1999. On March 2, the board of directors declares a 40% stock split-up effected in the form of a dividend. The par value per share is unchanged. The dividend shares are to be distributed on April 3 to stockholders of record on March 15. The market price per share of common stock is $24 on March 2, $15 on March 15, and $16 on April 3.

Date of Declaration

Retained Earnings (or Stock Dividend Declared)	400,000	
Common Stock Dividend Distributable...............		400,000
(40% x 100,000 = 40,000 shares)		
(40,000 x $10 par = $400,000)		

Date of Record   No entry.

Date of Distribution

Common Stock Dividend Distributable	400,000	
Common Stock		400,000

Stock Split

Data   Howell Cove Corporation has 100,000 shares of $10.00 par common stock outstanding on March 1, 1999. On March 2, the board of directors declares a 4-for-1 stock split. The par value per share is to be reduced to $2.50. The split is to be effective April 2 for shareholders of record on March 13.

Date of Declaration   No entry.

Date of Record   No entry.

Date of Distribution   No entry. Par value per share is reduced from $10.00 to $2.50. The number of shares outstanding is increased proportionally from 100,000 to 400,000. The balance of Common Stock remains at $1,000,000 (400,000 x $2.50).

EXERCISE 16-1

Purpose: (L.O.2,3,4) This exercise will review the effects of various types of distributions to stockholders.

Instructions

For each transaction listed across the top of the following matrix, indicate the effect on each of the items listed down the left side of the matrix. Use a "+" to indicate an increase, a "-" to indicate a decrease, and a "NE" for no effect.

TRANSACTION

ITEM	Declaration of a cash dividend	Payment of a previously recorded cash dividend	Declaration & payment of a property dividend	Declaration & payment of a liquidating dividend	Declaration & distribution of a small stock dividend	Declaration & distribution of a large stock dividend	Stock Split
Working capital							
Assets							
Total capital stock							
Total additional paid-in capital							
Retained earnings							
Total stock-holders' equity							
Par value per share							
Total number of shares outstanding							

Solution to Exercise 16-1

TRANSACTION

ITEM	Declaration of a cash dividend	Payment of a previously recorded cash dividend	Declaration & payment of a property dividend	Declaration & payment of a liquidating dividend	Declaration & distribution of a small stock dividend	Declaration & distribution of a large stock dividend	Stock Split
Working capital	–	NE	–	–	NE	NE	NE
Assets	NE	–	–	–	NE	NE	NE
Total capital stock	NE	NE	NE	NE	+	+	NE
Total additional paid-in capital	NE	NE	NE	–	+	NE	NE
Retained earnings	–	NE	–	NE	–	–	NE
Total stock-holders' equity	–	NE	–	–	NE	NE	NE
Par value per share	NE	NE	NE	NE	NE	NE	–
Total number of shares outstanding	NE	NE	NE	NE	+	+	+

Approach: Write down the journal entry(ies) associated with each situation. (Refer to **Illustration 16-2** to check your entries.) Take the accounts in each entry and examine their individual effects on each of the items listed.

CASE 16-1

Purpose: (L.O.3,4) This case will compare and contrast a large stock dividend with a small stock dividend.

Stock splits and stock dividends may be used by a corporation to change the number of shares of its stock outstanding.

Instructions

(a)   Explain what is meant by a stock split effected in the form of a dividend.

(b)   From an accounting viewpoint, explain how a stock split effected in the form of a dividend differs from an ordinary stock dividend.

(c)   Explain how and why a stock dividend which has been declared but not yet issued should be classified in a statement of financial position.

(AICPA Adapted)

Solution to Case 16-1

(a)   A stock split effected in the form of a dividend is a distribution of corporate stock to present stockholders in proportion to each stockholder's current holdings which can be expected to cause a material decrease in the market value per share of stock. Usually a distribution in excess of 20% to 25% of the number of shares previously outstanding would cause a material decrease in market value; a 40% stock dividend, a 50% stock dividend, and a 100% stock dividend are examples.

(b)   Usually a stock split will call for the reduction of the par value per share; whereas, a stock dividend will leave the par value per share unchanged. A stock split effected in the form of a dividend is like a dividend in that it does not affect the par value per share; it is like a split in its effect on the market value per share.

A stock split effected in the form of a dividend is accounted for similarly to an ordinary stock dividend in that retained earnings is capitalized. The difference is, retained earnings is charged for the market value of the dividend shares in an ordinary stock dividend but is charged only for the par value of the dividend shares in a stock split effected in the form of a dividend. A stock split does not involve any transfer of retained earnings to paid-in capital; rather, the par value per share is changed in proportion to the multiple of issued shares.

(c)   A declared but unissued stock dividend should be classified as part of corporate capital rather than as a liability in a statement of financial position. A stock dividend affects only capital accounts; that is, retained earnings are decreased and contributed capital is increased. Thus, there is no debt to be paid, and, consequently, there is no severance of corporate assets when a stock dividend is distributed. Furthermore, stock dividends declared can be revoked by a corporation's board of directors any time prior to issuance. Finally, the corporation usually will formally announce its intent to issue a specific number of additional shares, and these shares must be reserved for this purpose.

EXERCISE 16-2

Purpose: (L.O.2,3,4) This exercise will allow you to practice recording various types of dividends.

Scotty Corporation has the following stockholder equity items at December 31, 1998:

Common stock, $10 par, 200,000 shares authorized, 80,000 shares issued	$ 800,000
Premium on common stock	2,400,000
Retained earnings	28,500,000
Total paid-in capital and retained earnings	31,700,000
Less treasury stock, 2,000 shares at cost	24,000
Total stockholders' equity	$ 31,676,000

Instructions

Assume each of the transactions listed below is **independent** of the others unless otherwise indicated. Dividends are declared only on outstanding shares of stock. Record the following transactions at the beginning of 1999:

1. Declared a cash dividend of $.50 per share.
2. Paid the dividend declared in "1" above.
3. Declared a property dividend. Inventory with a cost of $160,000 and a market value of $200,000 is to be distributed.
4. Distributed the property for the dividend described in "3" above.
5. Declared a 5% stock dividend when the market value was $14 per share.
6. Distributed the shares for the stock dividend described in "5" above.
7. Declared a liquidating dividend of $.10 per share.
8. Distributed the dividend described in "7" above.
9. Declared a 100% stock dividend when the market value was $14 per share.
10. Distributed the dividend described in "9" above.
11. Declared a 2:1 stock split.

Solution to Exercise 16-2

1.	Retained Earnings (or Cash Dividends Declared)..................	39,000	
	Dividends Payable		39,000
	(80,000 issued - 2,000 treasury = 78,000 outstanding shares)(78,000 outstanding shares x $0.50 = $39,000)		
2.	Dividends Payable	39,000	
	Cash..		39,000

3.   Inventory..   40,000
          Gain on Appreciation of Inventory.................................   40,000
          ($200,000 market value - $160,000 cost = $40,000)

    Retained Earnings (or Property Dividends Declared)...............   200,000
          Property Dividends Payable.....................................   200,000

4.   Property Dividends Payable...   200,000
          Inventory   200,000

5.   Retained Earnings (or Stock Dividend Declared)....................   54,600
          Common Stock Dividend Distributable   39,000
          Premium on Common Stock.......................................   15,600
          (5% x 78,000 outstanding shares =
           3,900 dividend shares)
          (3,900 shares x $14 market value = $54,600)
          (3,900 shares x $10 par value = $39,000)

6.   Common Stock Dividend Distributable..................................   39,000
          Common Stock...   39,000

7.   Premium on Common Stock   7,800
          Dividends Payable   7,800
          ($.10 x 78,000 outstanding shares = $7,800)

8.   Dividends Payable   7,800
          Cash..   7,800

9.   Retained Earnings (or Stock Dividend Declared)....................   780,000
          Common Stock Dividend Distributable   780,000
          (100% x 78,000 shares outstanding =
           78,000 dividend shares)
          (78,000 x $10 par = $780,000)

10.   Common Stock Dividend Distributable..................................   780,000
          Common Stock...   780,000

11.   No entry required except for a memorandum type entry. The par value per share is reduced to one-half of what it was (from $10 per share to $5 per share) and the number of shares are doubled. Thus, the authorized number increases to 400,000, the issued number increases to 160,000, and the number of treasury shares increases to 4,000 shares.

ILLUSTRATION 16-3
STEPS IN ALLOCATING DIVIDENDS TO
PREFERRED AND COMMON STOCKHOLDERS (L.O.5)

Step 1: Assign arrearage to preferred, if any.
If there are any dividends in arrears, the amount of arrearage is first allocated to the preferred stockholders. The remaining amount of dividends to be allocated is computed. (If the amount declared is not enough to cover the arrearage, all dividends declared go to preferred holders, the remaining arrearage is computed for disclosure, and the rest of the steps are not performed.)

Step 2: Assign current period preference to preferred.
The amount of the preferred stockholders' current year preference is computed and that amount is allocated to the preferred stockholders. The remaining amount of dividends to be allocated is computed. (If the dividends declared are not enough to cover the preferred's current year preference, all of the dividends declared are allocated to the preferred stockholders, the remaining arrearage is computed for disclosure, and the rest of the steps are not performed.)

Step 3: Assign common an equal percentage dividend.
An amount of dividends to common stockholders to "match" the "percentage-on-par" dividend given to preferred (for current year preference only) is computed. If the remaining amount of dividends is sufficient to cover this "matching process," the amount of "matching" is allocated to common and the remaining amount of dividends is the amount in which both preferred and common will "participate." (If the amount declared is not enough to "match" the preferred, whatever is available after the preferred get their portion as calculated in steps "1" and "2" is allocated to common.)

Step 4: Assign the participation amount to preferred and common.
If the preferred stock is nonparticipating, any remaining dividends are assigned to the common stockholders. If the preferred stock is participating, the amount of dividends available for "participation" is allocated between preferred and common based on an "equal percentage on par basis." That percentage is determined by dividing the amount of dividends available for participation by the sum of the aggregate par value of the preferred and the aggregate par value of the common.

Step 5: Total the amounts allocated and compute per share amounts.
The amounts from the previous steps are added for each class. The total amount allocated to preferred stockholders and to common stockholders is often expressed on a per share basis. To calculate the amount per share, divide the total dividends allocated to the class by the number of outstanding shares in that class.

EXERCISE 16-3

Purpose: (L.O.5) This exercise will illustrate the allocation of dividends when a corporation has both preferred stock and common stock outstanding.

Charlie B. Daly Corporation has the following stock outstanding without any changes for years 1998, 1999, and 2000.

50,000 shares of $10 par, 4% preferred	$ 500,000
200,000 shares of $5 par common	1,000,000
	$ 1,500,000

Dividends are declared as follows:

1998	$15,000
1999	$50,000
2000	$72,000

Instructions

Compute the amount of dividends (total and per share) to be allocated to the preferred stockholders and the common stockholders for each of the three years under each of the **independent** assumptions below:

(a)   The preferred stock is noncumulative and nonparticipating.
(b)   The preferred stock is cumulative and nonparticipating.
(c)   The preferred stock is cumulative and participating.

Solution to Exercise 16-3

Approach: Compute the preferred's current year preference (50,000 shares x $10 par x 4% = $20,000) and the amount to "match" the common holders (200,000 shares x $5 par x 4% = $40,000). Then use the steps listed in **Illustration 16-3** to solve.

(a)

		Preferred	Common	Total
1998:	Total to distribute			$15,000
	Step 1:			
	Step 2: Less than preference	$15,000		$15,000
	Step 3:			
	Step 4:			
	Step 5:	$15,000	$ -0-	$15,000
	÷ by	50,000	200,000	
	=	$ .30	$ .00	
1999:	Total to distribute			$50,000
	Step 1:			
	Step 2: 4% x $500,000	$20,000		$20,000
	Step 3: Remainder		$30,000	30,000
	Step 4:			
	Step 5:	$20,000	$30,000	$50,000
	÷ by	50,000	200,000	
	=	$ .40	$ .15	
2000:	Total to distribute			$72,000
	Step 1:			
	Step 2: 4% x $500,000	$20,000		$20,000
	Step 3: 4% x $1,000,000		$40,000	40,000
	Step 4: Remainder		12,000	12,000
	Step 5:	$20,000	$52,000	$72,000
	÷ by	50,000	200,000	
	=	$ .40	$ .26	

(b)

		Preferred	Common	Total
1998:	Total to distribute			$15,000
	Step 1:			
	Step 2: Less than preference	$15,000		$15,000
	Step 3:			
	Step 4:			
	Step 5:	$15,000	$ -0-	$15,000
	÷ by	50,000	200,000	
	=	$ .30	$ .00	
1999:	Total to distribute			$50,000
	Step 1: $20,000 - $15,000	$ 5,000		$ 5,000
	Step 2: 4% x $500,000	20,000		20,000
	Step 3: Remainder		$25,000	25,000
	Step 4:			
	Step 5:	$25,000	$25,000	$50,000
	÷ by	50,000	200,000	
	=	$ .50	$ .125	
2000:	Total to distribute			$72,000
	Step 1:			
	Step 2: 4% x $500,000	$20,000		$20,000
	Step 3: 4% x $1,000,000		$40,000	40,000
	Step 4: Remainder		12,000	12,000
	Step 5:	$20,000	$52,000	$72,000
	÷ by	50,000	200,000	
	=	$ .40	$ .26	

(c)

		Preferred	Common	Total
1998:	Total to distribute			$15,000
	Step 1:			
	Step 2: Less than preference	$15,000		$15,000
	Step 3:			
	Step 4:			
	Step 5:	$15,000	$ -0-	$15,000
	÷ by	50,000	200,000	
	=	$ .30	$ .00	
1999:	Total to distribute			$50,000
	Step 1: $20,000 - $15,000	$ 5,000		$ 5,000
	Step 2: 4% x $500,000	20,000		20,000
	Step 3: Remainder		$25,000	25,000
	Step 4:			
	Step 5:	$25,000	$25,000	$50,000
	÷ by	50,000	200,000	
	=	$ .50	$ .125	

> **TIP:** Notice that in performing step 3, the remaining dividends ($25,000) are not sufficient in amount to allocate a "matching" dividend to the common stockholders (4% x $1,000,000 > $25,000)

		Preferred	Common	Total
2000:	Total to distribute			$72,000
	Step 1:			
	Step 2: 4% x $500,000	$20,000		$20,000
	Step 3: 4% x $1,000,000		$40,000	40,000
	Step 4: To participate at .8%*	4,000	8,000	12,000
	Step 5:	$24,000	$48,000	$72,000
	÷ by	50,000	200,000	
	=	$ .48	$ .24	

$$\frac{\text{*Amount to participate}}{\text{Total par}} = \frac{\$12,000}{\$1,500,000} = .008 \text{ or } .8\%$$

.008 x $500,000 = $4,000 allocated to preferred
.008 x $1,000,000 = $8,000 allocated to common

> **TIP:** Notice that in 2000 under assumption (c) that the common stockholders receive a total dividend that is equal—percentage wise on par—to the dividend received by the preferred stockholders ($.48 ÷ $10 = 4.8%; $.24 ÷ $5 = 4.8%). This happens when the three following conditions are met:
> (1)   The preferred stock is fully participating.
> (2)   There are enough dividends declared to reach the point where both classes "participate."
> (3)   There are no dividends in arrears.

ILLUSTRATION 16-4
REASONS FOR APPROPRIATION OF RETAINED EARNINGS (L.O.7)

1. **Legal restrictions:** some state laws restrict retained earnings to the extent of the cost of treasury shares held.

2. **Contractual restrictions:** bond indentures frequently contain a requirement that retained earnings in specified amounts be appropriated each year during the life of the bonds.

3. **Existence of possible loss:** an appropriation might be established for an estimated loss (due to a contingency) whose level of likelihood is reasonably possible and, therefore, is not great enough to warrant accrual of the loss. (Examples would include losses due to lawsuits and losses due to unfavorable contractual obligations.)

4. **Protection of working capital position:** an appropriation may be prompted by a decision to finance a building with internal financing (example is Appropriation for Plant Expansion) or to communicate the desire of the board of directors to maintain a strong current position.

EXERCISE 16-4

Purpose: (L.O.7) This exercise will illustrate the use of formal appropriations of retained earnings through the accounts.

On December 15, 1998 the directors of Doc Swartz Corporation voted to appropriate $80,000 of retained earnings and to retain in the business assets equal to the appropriation for use in expanding the corporation's factory building. This was the fifth of such appropriations; after it was recorded, the stockholders' equity section of Doc Swartz's balance sheet appeared as follows:

Stockholders' equity:		
Common stock, $10 par value, 400,000 shares authorized, 300,000 shares issued and outstanding		$ 3,000,000
Paid-in capital in excess of par		3,800,000
Total paid-in capital		6,800,000
Retained earnings:		
Unappropriated	$2,800,000	
Appropriated for plant expansion	400,000	
Total retained earnings		3,200,000
Total stockholders' equity		$10,000,000

On January 8, 1999 the corporation entered into a contract for the construction of the factory addition for which the retained earnings were appropriated. On September 5, 1999, the addition was completed and the contractor was paid the contract price of $322,500.

On December 11, 1999 the board of directors voted to return the balance of the Retained Earnings Appropriated for Plant Expansion account to Unappropriated Retained Earnings. They also voted a fifty-cent cash dividend per share, payable on January 23, 2000 to the stockholders of record on January 15, 2000. The dividend was paid per the board's resolution. The corporation's stock was selling at $46 in the market on December 14, 1999. Doc Swartz reported net income for 1998 of $525,000 and for 1999 of $600,000.

Instructions

(a)   Prepare the appropriate journal entries for Doc Swartz Corporation from the information above (December 15, 1998 to January 23, 2000, inclusive).

(b)   Prepare the stockholders' equity section of the balance sheet for Doc Swartz at December 31, 1999 in proper form.

Solution to Exercise 16-4

(a) | 12/15/98 | Unappropriated Retained Earnings .... | 80,000 | |
|---|---|---|---|
| | Retained Earnings Approp. for Plant | | |
| | Expansion.. | | 80,000 |
| | | | |
| 12/31/98 | Income Summary... | 525,000 | |
| | Unappropriated Retained Earnings .... | | 525,000 |
| | | | |
| 9/5/99 | Factory Building.. | 322,500 | |
| | Cash... | | 322,500 |
| | | | |
| 12/11/99 | Retained Earnings Approp. for Plant Expansion .... | 400,000 | |
| | Unappropriated Retained Earnings .... | | 400,000 |
| | | | |
| | Unappropriated Retained Earnings .... | 150,000 | |
| | Dividends Payable... | | 150,000 |
| | (300,000 x $.50 = $150,000) | | |
| | | | |
| 12/31/99 | Income Summary.. | 600,000 | |
| | Unappropriated Retained Earnings .... | | 600,000 |
| | | | |
| 1/23/00 | Dividends Payable... | 150,000 | |
| | Cash... | | 150,000 |

(b)   Stockholders' Equity:

Common stock, $10 par value, 400,000 shares authorized, 300,000 shares issued and outstanding	$ 3,000,000
Paid-in capital in excess of par	3,800,000
Total paid-in capital	6,800,000
Retained earnings	4,175,000*
Total stockholders' equity	$ 10,975,000

*$3,200,000 + $525,000 - $150,000 + $600,000 = $4,175,000.

EXERCISE 16-5

Purpose: (L.O.8) This exercise will illustrate the preparation of a statement of stockholders' equity.

On January 1, 1999, Huseman Corporation had the following stockholders' equity balances:

Common Stock ($1 stated value)	$ 300,000
Paid-in Capital in Excess of Stated Value	710,000
Retained Earnings	390,000
Accumulated Other Comprehensive Income	30,000
Treasury Stock (3,000 shares)	6,000

During 1999, the following occurred:
- Issued 50,000 shares of common stock at $3 per share.
- Declared a $70,000 cash dividend.
- Purchased 1,000 shares of treasury stock at $2 per share.
- Declared and distributed a 5% stock dividend when the market value was $3 per share.
- Earned net income for the year of $200,000
- Reported an unrealized holding loss on available-for-sale securities, net of tax, $8,000.

Instructions
Prepare a statement of stockholders' equity for the year ending December 31, 1999.

Solution to Exercise 16-5

Huseman Corporation
STATEMENT OF STOCKHOLDERS' EQUITY
For the Year Ended December 31, 1999

	Total	Compre-hensive Income	Retained Earnings	Accumulated Other Com-prehensive Income	Common Stock ($1 Stated Value)	Paid-in Capital in Excess of Stated Value	Treasury Stock
Balance January 1	$1,424,000		$390,000	$30,000	$300,000	$710,000	$(6,000)
Issued 50,000 shares of common stock at $3	150,000				50,000	100,000	
Declared a $70,000 cash dividend	(70,000)		(70,000)				
Purchased 1,000 shares for treasury at $2	(2,000)						(2,000)
Declared & distributed a 5% stock dividend			(51,900)		17,300	34,600	
Net income for year	200,000	$200,000	200,000				
Other Comprehensive Income	(8,000)	(8,000)		(8,000)			
Balance, December 31	$1,694,000	$192,000	$468,100	$22,000	$367,300	$844,600	$(8,000)

> **TIP:** Notice how the columns on this statement foot (add down) and crossfoot (add across).

Explanation: A corporation is to disclose all changes that took place in all stockholder equity items during the reporting period. A convenient and effective way of meeting that requirement is to present a statement of stockholders' equity (sometimes called a stockholders' equity statement). When this statement is presented, it replaces the statement of retained earnings because it contains all the information that a statement of retained earnings would contain plus data regarding changes in other components of stockholders' equity.

The computations for the stock dividend are as follows:

350,000 shares issued - 4,000 treasury shares = 346,000 shares outstanding.
346,000 shares outstanding x 5% = 17,300 dividend shares.
17,300 shares x $3 market value = $51,900 decrease in Retained Earnings.
17,300 shares x $1 stated value = $17,300 increase in Common Stock.
17,300 shares x ($3 - $1) = $34,600 increase in additional paid-in capital.

> **TIP:** It can readily be determined that the Huseman Corporation uses the cost method to account for treasury stock; the balance of the Treasury Stock account exceeds the par value of the treasury shares. Thus, the balance of the Treasury Stock account must represent the cost of the treasury shares held.

ILLUSTRATION 16-5
RATIOS FOR ANALYSIS OF STOCKHOLDERS' EQUITY (L.O.8)

The following four ratios use stockholders' equity amounts to evaluate a company's profitability and long-term solvency.

1. **Rate of return on common stock equity.** This widely used ratio measures profitability from the common stockholders' viewpoint. This ratio shows how many dollars of net income were earned for each dollar invested by the owners. The ratio is computed as follows:

$$\text{Rate of return on common stock equity} = \frac{\text{Net income - preferred dividends}}{\text{Average common stockholders' equity}^a}$$

[a]The par value of preferred stock is deducted from total stockholders' equity to arrive at the amount of common stock equity used in this ratio.

> **TIP:** When the rate of return on common stock equity is greater than the rate of return on total assets, the company is said to be "trading on the equity at a gain" or "favorably trading on the equity." **"Trading on the equity"** describes the practice of using borrowed money at fixed interest rates or issuing preferred stock with constant dividend rates in hopes of using the assets obtained (by use of the money from the borrowing or issuance of preferred stock) in such a way that the rate of return on the assets exceeds the rate of interest or dividends. If this can be done, the capital obtained from bondholders or preferred stockholders earns enough to pay interest or dividends and to leave a margin for the common stockholders. When this condition exists, trading on the equity is profitable.

2. **Payout ratio.** The payout ratio is the relationship of cash dividends to net income; it is a measure of profitability. The ratio is computed for common stockholders as follows:

$$\text{Payout ratio} = \frac{\text{Cash dividends}}{\text{Net income less preferred dividends}}$$

> **TIP:** Some investors look for a stock that has a payout ratio sufficiently high to provide a good yield on the stock; other investors view the potential appreciation in the market value of the stock as more important than the prospect of high dividends.

> **TIP:** Another closely watched ratio is the **dividend yield** which is computed by dividing the cash dividend per share by the market price of the stock. This ratio affords investors of some idea of the rate of return that will be received in cash dividends from their investment.

3. **Price earnings (P/E) ratio.** This ratio is often highlighted by an analyst in discussing the investment possibility of a given enterprise. It is computed by dividing the market price of the stock by its earnings per share. This ratio is computed as follows:

$$\text{Price earnings ratio} = \frac{\text{Market price of stock}}{\text{Earnings per share}}$$

TIP:	The P/E ratio is often referred to as a "multiple."
TIP:	When one company has a P/E ratio significantly different than the P/E ratio of another company, the reason for this difference is linked to several factors; relative risk, stability of earnings, trends in earnings, and the market's perception of the company's growth potential.

4. **Book value per share.** The book value or **equity value per share** of stock is a much-used basis for evaluating the net worth of a corporation. Book value per share of stock is the amount each share would receive **if** the company were liquidated on the basis of amounts reported on the balance sheet. The ratio loses much of its relevance if the valuations on the balance sheet do not approximate fair market value of the assets. Assuming no preferred stock is outstanding, the ratio is as follows:

$$\text{Book value per share} = \frac{\text{Common stockholders' equity}}{\text{Outstanding shares}}$$

TIP:	To compute the book value per share of common stock when there is preferred stock also outstanding, use the following steps:

	Step 1: Compute the total book value of preferred stock by multiplying the book value per share of preferred stock by the number of preferred shares outstanding. The book value per share of preferred is one of the following (listed in order of preference):
	  a. Liquidation value of preferred plus dividends in arrears.
	  b. Call or redemption price of preferred plus dividends in arrears.
	  c. Par value of preferred plus dividends in arrears.

	Step 2: Compute the total book value of common stock by deducting the total book value of preferred stock from total stockholders' equity.
	Step 3: Compute the book value per share of common stock by dividing the total book value of common stock by the number of common stock shares outstanding.

EXERCISE 16-6

Purpose: (L.O.9) This exercise will illustrate the proper procedures to be employed in a quasi-reorganization.

The following facts pertain to the Kelliher Corporation at December 31, 1999:
1.   Retained earnings has a negative balance of $30,000.
2.   The cost of inventory exceeds its market value by $12,000.
3.   The carrying value of plant assets exceeds their market value by $28,000.
4.   There are 3,000 shares of common stock outstanding with a par value of $100 per share.
5.   There is no additional paid-in capital.

Future prospects for successful operations are good. In order to eliminate the deficit (negative retained earnings balance), a quasi-reorganization is effected. The par value of the stock is reduced to $50 per share and the number of common shares outstanding is unchanged.

Instructions
(a)   Record all of the journal entries related to this quasi-reorganization.
(b)   Explain what must be disclosed for retained earnings after the quasi-reorganization.

Solution to Exercise 16-6

Approach: Follow the three easy steps listed below.

Step 1:   **Revalue all assets to appropriate current values.** Any resulting gain or loss is credited or charged to Retained Earnings.

Step 2:   **Create additional paid-in capital, if necessary.** Additional paid-in capital, at least equal to the deficit, must be available or must be created.

Step 3:   **Charge additional paid-in capital for the amount of the deficit.** This eliminates the negative balance in retained earnings.

(a)   **ENTRIES:**

Step 1: Retained Earnings	40,000	
Inventory		12,000
Plant Assets		28,000
Step 2: Common Stock	150,000	
Additional Paid-in Capital		150,000

[To reduce the par value per share from $100 to $50; 3,000 x ($100 - $50) = $150,000]

Step 3: Additional Paid-in Capital   70,000
        Retained Earnings   70,000
          ($30,000 + $40,000 = $70,000)

(b)   After a quasi-reorganization, the retained earnings must be "dated" in subsequent reports for a period of approximately 10 years to show the amount and the date of the quasi-reorganization. Assuming Kelliher's retained earnings balance is $11,000 on December 31, 2001, these disclosures at that balance sheet date would be:

Retained earnings since January 1, 2000, when a deficit of
    $30,000 was eliminated through a quasi-reorganization   11,000

TIP: A quasi-reorganization is often called a **fresh start**.

TIP: For SEC companies, the amount of the writeup of assets is limited to an amount sufficient to offset decreases in other assets. Therefore, there should be no net asset writeup in a quasi-reorganization.

ANALYSIS OF MULTIPLE-CHOICE TYPE QUESTIONS

QUESTION
1.   (L.O.3) What effect does the declaration and distribution of a 30% stock split-up effected in the form of a dividend have on the following?

	Retained Earnings	Total Paid-in Capital	Total Stockholders' Equity
a.	Decrease	Increase	No Effect
b.	Decrease	No Effect	No Effect
c.	Decrease	No Effect	Decrease
d.	No Effect	No Effect	No Effect

Approach and Explanation: Write down the journal entries for the declaration and distribution of a large stock dividend. Analyze the accounts in each entry separately to determine the impact on the three items requested.

The journal entry to record the declaration will reduce retained earnings and increase stock dividend distributable (a component of total capital stock and, therefore, a component of total paid-in capital) by the par value multiplied by the number of shares to be distributed in the dividend. That entry will **decrease retained earnings** and **increase total paid-in capital** by identical amounts, and thus have **no effect on total stockholders' equity**. The entry to record the distribution will reduce the dividend distributable balance (one capital stock account) and increase the common stock account (another capital stock account). Thus, the distribution entry will have **no effect** on any total within the major classifications of stockholders' equity. (Solution = a.)

QUESTION

2. (L.O.3,4) A 300% stock dividend will have the same impact on the number of shares outstanding as a:
    a. 2-for-1 stock split.
    b. 3-for-1 stock split.
    c. 4-for-1 stock split.
    d. 5-for-1 stock split.

Approach and Explanation: Set up an example with numbers. For instance, assume we begin with 10,000 shares outstanding. A 300% stock dividend (or stock split-up effected in the form of a dividend) will mean 30,000 new shares will be distributed and there will then be 40,000 total shares outstanding. A 2-for-1 split will cause 10,000 shares to be replaced by 20,000. A 3-for-1 split will result in 30,000 total shares. A 4-for-1 split will cause the 10,000 shares to be replaced by 40,000 shares. The example proves that a 300% stock dividend (shares are increased **by** 300%) has the same effect on the number of shares outstanding as does a 4-for-1 split (each share is replaced with four shares). (Solution = c.)

QUESTION

3. (L.O.3) Pat Trim Corporation declared a stock dividend of 10,000 shares when the par value was $1 per share, the market value was $5 per share, and the number of shares outstanding was 200,000. How does the entry to record this transaction affect retained earnings?
    a. No effect
    b. $10,000 decrease
    c. $40,000 decrease
    d. $50,000 decrease

Approach and Explanation: Analyze the data to determine the size of the stock dividend. Prepare the journal entry to record the declaration of the stock dividend and analyze the entry's effect on retained earnings. Comparing the 10,000 dividend shares to the 200,000 outstanding shares prior to the dividend yields a 5% relationship; thus, the stock dividend is an ordinary (small) stock dividend. An ordinary stock dividend is recorded by transferring retained earnings equal to the market value of the dividend shares to paid-in capital. Therefore, 10,000 shares multiplied by $5 means retained earnings is to be charged for $50,000. (Solution = d.)

QUESTION

4. (L.O.2) Barney's Corporation has an investment in 1,000 shares of Phil Jones Corporation common stock with a cost of $29,000. These shares are used in a property dividend to stockholders of Barney's. The property dividend is declared on March 23 and scheduled to be distributed on April 30 to stockholders of record on April 15. The market value per share of Phil Jones stock is $42 on March 23, $44 on April 15, and $45 on April 30. The net effect of this property dividend on retained earnings is a reduction of:
    a. $29,000.
    b. $42,000.
    c. $44,000.
    d. $45,000.

Approach and Explanation: Write down the journal entries involved in accounting for this dividend. Examine each account in the entries for its effect on retained earnings. Summarize the results. The entries and their effects on retained earnings (RE) would be as follows:

			Effect on RE
3/23 Investments in Securities	13,000		-0-
Gain on Appreciation of Securities		13,000	↑ $13,000
[($42 x 1,000) - $29,000 = $13,000]			
Retained Earnings	42,000		↓ 42,000
Property Dividends Payable		42,000	-0-
4/30 Property Dividends Payable	42,000		-0-
Investments in Securities		42,000	-0-
Net effect on retained earnings =			↓ $29,000
			(Solution = a.)

> **TIP:** Although a property dividend gets recorded at the **fair value** of the asset to be distributed, retained earnings is decreased by the **carrying value** of the asset due to the recognition of the increase or decrease in the fair value of the asset (this increase or decrease goes through net income, which is closed into retained earnings).

QUESTION

5.   (L.O.7) The balance of the Retained Earnings account represents:
   a.   cash set aside for specific purposes.
   b.   the earnings for the most recent accounting period.
   c.   the balance of unrestricted cash on hand.
   d.   the total of all amounts reported as net income since the inception of the corporation minus the sum of any amounts reported as net loss and dividends declared since the inception of the corporation.

Approach and Explanation: Define retained earnings and select the answer that most closely matches that definition. Retained earnings is net income retained in a corporation. Retained earnings is often referred to as earnings retained for use in the business. Thus, net income (earnings for a period) increases the balance of retained earnings. Distributions of earnings to stockholders (owners) are called dividends; they reduce the balance of retained earnings. (Solution = d.)

QUESTION

6.   (L.O.2) The declaration and payment of cash dividends by a corporation will result in a(an):

a.   increase in Cash and an increase in Retained Earnings.
b.   increase in Cash and a decrease in Retained Earnings.
c.   decrease in Cash and an increase in Retained Earnings.
d.   decrease in Cash and a decrease in Retained Earnings.

Approach and Explanation: Prepare the journal entries required to record the declaration and payment of a cash dividend. Separately analyze each debit and credit to determine the effect on the balance of Cash and on the Retained Earnings account. Assuming cash dividends of $10,000 are declared, the entries and analysis are as follows:

At the date of declaration:			Effect
Retained Earnings	10,000		Decrease in Retained Earnings
Dividends Payable		10,000	Increase in current liabilities

At the date of payment:			Effect
Dividends Payable	10,000		Decrease in current liabilities
Cash		10,000	Decrease in Cash

The net effect of the declaration and payment of a cash dividend is to reduce retained earnings (and, thus, total stockholders' equity) and Cash (and, thus, total assets). (Solution = d.)

QUESTION

7.   (L.O.2) The net effect of the declaration and payment of a liquidating dividend is a decrease in:

a.   retained earnings and a decrease in total assets.
b.   total paid-in capital and a decrease in total assets.
c.   total paid-in capital and an increase in retained earnings.
d.   total stockholders' equity and an increase in liabilities.

Explanation: A dividend based on paid-in capital (rather than retained earnings) is termed a **liquidating dividend**, because the amount originally paid in by stockholders is being reduced or "liquidated." (Solution = b.)

QUESTION
8.   (L.O.4) A 4-for-1 stock split will cause a decrease in:
    a.   total assets.
    b.   total stockholders' equity.
    c.   retained earnings.
    d.   the par value per share.

Explanation: A stock split involves the issuance of additional shares of stock to existing stockholders according to the number of shares presently owned. A stock split does **not** result in the capitalization of any retained earnings; rather, the par value per share is reduced in proportion to the increase in shares. Thus, in a 2-for-1 split, the number of shares are doubled and the par value per share is cut in half. Whereas with a 4-for-1 stock split, the number of total shares is four times what the number was before the split and the par value per share after the split is 1/4 of the par value per share before the split. Assets are not affected. (Solution = d.)

QUESTION
9.   (L.O.8) Seminole Raiders Corporation recently discontinued paying insurance coverage and is now self-insured. In the company's ledger there is an account titled "Appropriation for Self-Insurance." In preparing a balance sheet, this account preferably will be classified as a(an):
    a.   liability.
    b.   offset to Cash Surrender Value of Insurance.
    c.   positive component of retained earnings.
    d.   deferred credit.

Explanation: Uninsured losses are to be charged entirely to expense (or loss) in the period in which they are sustained. Recognition can be given to contingent losses in periods other than their incurrence, however, by appropriation of retained earnings. (Solution = c.)

QUESTION
10.   (L.O.8) A corporation has two classes of stock outstanding. The return on common stock equity is computed by dividing net income:
    a.   minus preferred dividends by the number of common stock shares outstanding at the balance sheet date.
    b.   plus interest expense by the average amount of total assets.
    c.   by the number of common stock shares outstanding at the balance sheet date.
    d.   minus preferred dividends by the average amount of common stockholders' equity during the period.

Explanation: The return on common stock equity is computed by dividing the amount of earnings applicable to the common stockholders' interest in the company by the average amount of common stockholders' equity during the period. The amount of earnings applicable to the common stockholders is the amount of net income for the period less the dividends declared on preferred stock during the period. (Solution = d.)

QUESTION

11.   (L.O.9) A corporation with a $4,000,000 deficit undertakes a quasi-reorganization on August 1, 1999. Certain assets will be written down by $800,000 to their present market value. Liabilities will remain unchanged. The par value of the stock will be reduced by 50%. Common stock is $6,000,000 and additional paid-in capital is $3,000,000 before the quasi-reorganization. How will the entries to accomplish these changes on August 1, 1999 affect the following?

	Contributed Capital	Retained Earnings	Total Stockholders' Equity
a.	Increase	Decrease	No Effect
b.	Decrease	Increase	Decrease
c.	Decrease	Increase	No Effect
d.	No Effect	Increase	Increase

Approach and Explanation: Write down the entries to record the procedures involved in the quasi-reorganization. Carefully analyze the effect of each debit and credit on the items requested.

The entries would be as follows:

(a)	Retained Earnings	800,000	
(b)	Assets		800,000
(c)	Common Stock	3,000,000	
(d)	Additional Paid-in Capital		3,000,000
(e)	Additional Paid-in Capital...	4,800,000	
(f)	Retained Earnings..		4,800,000

The effects of the entries are as follows (using the reference letters above):

	Contributed Capital	Retained Earnings	Total Stockholders' Equity
(a)	No Effect	Decrease $800,000	Decrease $800,000
(b)	No Effect	No Effect	No Effect
(c)	Decrease $3,000,000	No Effect	Decrease $3,000,000
(d)	Increase $3,000,000	No Effect	Increase $3,000,000
(e)	Decrease $4,800,000	No Effect	Decrease $4,800,000
(f)	No Effect	Increase $4,800,000	Increase $4,800,000
Totals	Decrease $4,800,000	Increase $4,000,000	Decrease $800,000

(Solution = b.)

TIP: Contributed capital is synonymous with paid-in capital; this includes capital stock accounts **and** additional paid-in capital accounts.

CHAPTER 17

DILUTIVE SECURITIES AND EARNINGS PER SHARE

OVERVIEW

During the past three to four decades, many corporations have engaged in heavy merger activity. These business combinations have utilized an increasing amount of dilutive securities such as convertible bonds, convertible preferred stocks, and stock warrants. The accounting procedures for each of these are discussed in this chapter.

Earnings per share (EPS) is typically the most widely quoted financial ratio. The computation of earnings per share is complicated by situations where dilutive securities, as well as common stock, are outstanding. EPS computations are also discussed in this chapter.

SUMMARY OF LEARNING OBJECTIVES

1. **Describe the accounting for the issuance, conversion, and retirement of convertible debt securities.** The method for recording convertible bonds at the date of issuance follows that used to record straight (nonconvertible) debt issues. Any discount or premium that results from the issuance of convertible bonds is amortized assuming the bonds will be outstanding to maturity. If bonds are converted into other securities, the principal accounting problem is to determine the amount at which to record the securities exchanged for the bond. Two possible methods of determining the issuance price of the stock could be used: (1) the market value approach or (2) the book value approach. The book value method is generally used in practice. Under GAAP, the retirement of convertible debt is considered a debt retirement, and the difference between the carrying amount of the retired convertible debt and the cash paid should result in a charge or credit to income.

2. **Explain the accounting for convertible preferred stock.** When convertible preferred stock is converted, the book value method is employed; Preferred Stock and any related Paid-in Capital in Excess of Par are debited, and Common Stock and Paid-in Capital in Excess of Par (if any excess exists) are credited.

3. **Contrast the accounting for stock rights issued to existing shareholders and stock warrants issued with other securities.** *Stock rights:* No entry is required when rights (warrants) are issued to existing stockholders. Only a memorandum entry is needed to indicate the number of rights issued to existing stockholders and to ensure that the company has additional unissued stock registered for issuance in case the rights are exercised. *Stock warrants:* The proceeds from the sale of debt securities with detachable stock warrants should be allocated between the two securities. Warrants that are detachable can be traded separately from the debt, and, therefore, a market value can be determined. The two methods of allocation available are the proportional method and the incremental method. Nondetachable warrants do not require an allocation of the proceeds between the debt securities and the warrants. The entire proceeds are recorded as debt.

4.   **Describe the accounting for stock compensation plans under GAAP.** Companies are given a choice in the recognition approach to stock compensation; however, the FASB encourages adoption of the fair value method. Using the fair value approach, total compensation expense is computed based on the fair value of the options (that are expected to vest) on the grant date. Under the intrinsic value approach, total compensation cost is computed as the excess of the market price of the stock over the option price on the date when both the number of shares to which employees are entitled and the option or purchase price for those shares are known. Under both the fair and intrinsic value methods, compensation expense is recognized in the periods in which the employee performs the services.

5.   **Explain the controversy involving stock compensation plans.** When first proposed, there was considerable opposition to the recognition provisions contained in the fair value approach, because that approach could result in substantial compensation expense that was not previously recognized. Corporate America, particularly the small, high technology sector, was quite vocal in its opposition to the proposed standard. They believed that they would be placed at a competitive disadvantage with larger companies that can withstand higher compensation charges. In response to this opposition, which was based primarily on economic consequences arguments, the FASB decided to encourage, rather than require, recognition of compensation cost based on the fair value method and require expanded disclosures.

6.   **Compute earnings per share in a simple capital structure.** When a company has both common and preferred stock outstanding, the current year preferred stock dividend is subtracted from net income to arrive at income available to common stockholders. The formula for computing earnings per share is net income less preferred stock dividends divided by the weighted average of shares of common stock outstanding.

7.   **Compute earnings per share in a complex capital structure.** A complex capital structure requires a dual presentation of earnings per share, each with equal prominence on the face of the income statement. These two presentations are referred to as basic earnings per share and dilutive earnings per share. Basic earnings per share is based on the number of weighted average common shares outstanding (i.e., equivalent to EPS for a simple capital structure). Diluted earnings per share indicates the dilution of earnings per share that would have occurred if all potential issuances of common stock that would have reduced earnings per share had taken place.

8.*   **Explain the accounting for various stock option plans under APB Opinion No. 25.** (1) *Incentive stock option plans:* The market price and exercise price on the grant date must be equal. Because there is no compensation expense, there is no allocation problem. (2) *Nonqualified stock option plans:* Compensation is the difference between the market price and exercise price on the grant date. Compensation expense is allocated by the straight-line method during the service period. (3) *Stock appreciation rights:* The compensation is measured by the difference between market price and exercise price on the exercise date. The compensation expense is allocated by the percentage approach over the service period, then marked to market. (4) *Performance-type plan:* Compensation is measured by the market value of shares issued on the exercise date. Compensation expense is allocated by the percentage approach over the service period, then marked to market.

*This material is covered in Appendix 17-A in the text.

9.**   **Compute earnings per share in a complex situation.** For diluted EPS, (1) determine, for each potentially dilutive security, the per share effect assuming exercise/conversion; (2) rank from most dilutive to least dilutive; (3) recalculate EPS starting with the most dilutive, and continue adding securities until EPS increases (is antidilutive).

**This material is covered in Appendix 17-B in the text.

TIPS ON CHAPTER TOPICS

TIP: Convertible bonds are sometimes referred to as debt with nondetachable stock warrants. All proceeds from the issuance of convertible debt are recorded in liability accounts; none of the proceeds is allocated to the conversion feature.

TIP: A **stock right** is defined as a privilege extended by a corporation to acquire additional shares of its capital stock. A **stock warrant** is defined as the physical evidence of stock rights. The warrant specifies the number of rights conveyed, the number of shares to which the rightholder is entitled, the exercise price, and the exercise period. Although the terms "stock right" and "stock warrant" have distinct meanings, they are often used interchangeably; thus, "to record the issuance of stock rights" means the same thing as "to record the issuance of stock warrants."

TIP: When bonds are issued with detachable warrants, the amount of proceeds to be allocated to the warrants is to be determined as follows:

$$\frac{\text{Market Value of Warrants}}{\begin{array}{c}\text{Market Value of Warrants +}\\ \text{Market Value of Bonds}\\ \text{Ex-warrants (without warrants)}\end{array}} \times \text{Total Proceeds} = \begin{array}{c}\text{Amount to be Recorded}\\ \text{for Warrants (Paid-in}\\ \text{Capital)}\end{array}$$

The remainder of the proceeds are to be attributed to the debt instrument. The amount allocated to the bonds can be independently verified by using the formula above and substituting the market value of the bonds in the numerator of the fraction.

TIP: By use of the formula in the **TIP** immediately above, the proceeds from the issuance of **bonds with detachable stock warrants** are allocated between the bonds and the stock warrants based on the relative market values of the two securities. This is sometimes referred to as the **proportional method**. If the market value of the bonds ex-warrants is not known or not determinable, the warrants are recorded at their market value and the remaining proceeds are allocated to the debt. This latter approach is sometimes called the **incremental method**.

TIP: When accounting for convertible bonds and bonds issued with detachable warrants, follow the basic recording rules for bonds discussed in Chapter 14 (see your *Self-Study Problems/Solutions Book*). These include:

1. Record the par (face) amount of the bonds issued in the Bonds Payable account.

2. Record an excess of issuance price over par for the bonds in the Premium on Bonds Payable account; record an excess of par over issuance price in the Discount on Bonds Payable account.

3. Record debt issuance costs in an asset account to be amortized over the life of the bonds.

4.   Remove all related amounts from the accounts when the debt is extinguished. The net carrying amount of the debt is eliminated from the accounts when the debt is settled.

TIP: An options market exists that works similarly to the stock market. For example, an investor may purchase a share of Amex stock for $120 per share or he may purchase an option to buy Amex stock. Assume the option allows the holder to buy Amex stock for $122 anytime within the next six months. This type of option is created by the marketplace, not by Amex. Therefore, the Amex Corporation is not involved with accounting for this type of security. In this chapter, the only type of options addressed are employee stock options which are granted by the related corporation.

TIP: A **dilutive security** is a security which would reduce earnings per share (EPS) if it became common stock. An **antidilutive security** is one which would result in an increase in the amount reported as EPS or a decrease in the amount reported as a net loss per share.

TIP: In computing diluted EPS, any antidilutive security is to be excluded. This means that a convertible bond will be assumed to be converted to common stock for the purposes of computing diluted EPS **if** the effect of that assumption is dilutive. The convertible bond will **not** be assumed to be converted in computing EPS **if** the effect of that assumption is antidilutive.

TIP: Assume a corporation has no discontinued operations, no extraordinary item, and no cumulative effect of a change in accounting principle. If the corporation has a **loss per share** result from the basic EPS formula, any and **all assumptions will be antidilutive**; therefore, a single EPS presentation will be made. A loss per share can result in the basic formula for the following conditions:

1.   Corporation has a net loss on its income statement for the period.

2.   Corporation has net income for the period but the amount of preferred dividends for the period exceeds the amount of net income.

3.   Corporation has a net loss and preferred stock dividends (this situation results in a large negative numerator for the EPS ratio).

EXERCISE 17-1

Purpose: (L.O.1) This exercise will illustrate how to record the issuance of convertible debt and its subsequent conversion to common stock.

Oviedo Oatmeal Corporation has 300,000 shares of its $10 par value common stock outstanding on January 1, 1999 when it issues convertible bonds. The debt issue is comprised of 1,000 bonds at $1,000 par with a 20-year term and a 10% stated interest rate. Each bond is sold at 101 and is convertible into 20 shares of common stock. Oviedo Oatmeal incurs costs of $80,000 related to the issue. The straight-line method is to be used to amortize any related premium or discount. An underwriter advises the issuer that the bonds would likely have sold for 99 without the conversion feature.

Instructions

(a)   Record the issuance of the convertible bonds on January 1, 1999.

(b)   Explain why a portion of the issuance proceeds is or is not allocated to the conversion feature.

(c)   Record the conversion of 50% of the bonds on January 1, 2001, assuming the book value method is used.

(d)   Ignoring part (c), record the conversion of 50% of the bonds on January 1, 2001, assuming the market value method is used, and the common stock is selling for $52 per share on that date.

(e)   Record the additional entry required on January 1, 2001 if 500 additional shares of common stock are issued by Oviedo Oatmeal as an inducement for conversion in either part (c) or part (d) above.

(f)   Record the additional entry required on January 1, 2001 if costs of $21,000 are incurred in administering (but not inducing) the conversion that takes place in part (c) or in part (d) above.

Solution to Exercise 17-1

(a)   Cash   930,000
        Unamortized Bond Issue Costs...   80,000
            Bonds Payable   1,000,000
            Premium on Bonds Payable   10,000
                ($1,000 x 1,000 = $1,000,000 par)
                ($1,000,000 x 101% = $1,010,000 issuance price)
                ($1,010,000 - $80,000 = $930,000 net proceeds)
                ($1,010,000 - $1,000,000 = $10,000 premium)

> **TIP:**   No portion of the proceeds from the issuance of convertible debt should be allocated to the conversion feature; therefore, **none** of the proceeds should be recorded as paid-in capital. Thus, convertible bonds do not affect paid-in capital until they are converted to stock.

(b)   No portion of the proceeds from the issuance of convertible debt is allocated to the conversion feature for accounting purposes because *APB Opinion No. 14* indicates that the conversion option is inseparable from the debt security.

(c)

Bonds Payable (50% x $1,000,000)	500,000	
Premium on Bonds Payable (50% x $10,000 x 18/20)	4,500	
Unamortized Bond Issue Costs		36,000
(50% x $80,000 x 18/20)		
Common Stock...		100,000
(50% x 1,000 bonds x 20 shares x $10 par)		
Paid-in Capital in Excess of Par (Difference)...................		368,500*

*Par value of bonds converted (50% x 1,000 x $1,000)	$ 500,000
Related unamortized premium (50% x $10,000 x 18/20)	4,500
Book value of bonds converted	504,500
Unamortized bond issue costs (50% x $80,000 x 18/20)	(36,000)
Net book value of bonds converted	468,500
Par value of stock issued (50% x 1,000 bonds x	
20 shares x $10 par)	(100,000)
Additional paid-in capital recorded	$ 368,500

Explanation: The net book value of bonds payable is removed from the accounts and that net amount is recorded in appropriate stockholder equity accounts. No gain or loss is recorded.

> **TIP:**   The **book value method** of recording the conversion of bonds payable to common stock simply removes the net book value of the bonds from debt accounts and records that amount in appropriate stockholder equity accounts. **No gain or loss is recorded** when the book value method is used.
>
> **TIP:**   Recall from Chapter 14 that **book value** is synonymous with **carrying value** and **carrying amount**.

(d)

Bonds Payable (50% x $1,000,000)	500,000	
Premium on Bonds Payable (50% x $10,000 x 18/20)	4,500	
Loss on Redemption of Bonds Payable....................................	51,500*	
Unamortized Bond Issue Costs		36,000
(50% x $80,000 x 18/20)		
Common Stock (50% x 1,000 x 20 x $10)		100,000
Paid-in Capital in Excess of Par		420,000
[(50% x 1,000 x 20 x $52) - $100,000 par]		

*Net book value of bonds converted [see (c) above]	$ 468,500
Market value of stock issued upon conversion	
(50% x 1,000 x 20 x $52)	(520,000)
Gain (loss) on redemption of bonds	$ (51,500)

Explanation: The stock issued is recorded at its fair value. An excess of the fair value of the consideration given (stock issued) over the net carrying value of the liability settled is recorded as a loss.

> **TIP:** The **market value method (approach)** of recording the conversion of bonds payable to common stock is often called the **fair value method** or **fair market value approach**. It is so named because it uses the market price of either the common stock or the bonds to record the common stock issued upon conversion of the bonds. A gain or loss on extinguishment of debt is recognized for the difference between the market price used and the net book value (net carrying value) of the debt. An excess of the market value of the stock (recorded by credits in the journal entry for the conversion) over the net book value of the bonds (removed by a net debit in the conversion entry) results in a loss (recorded by a debit); an excess of the net book value of the bonds over the market value of the stock results in a gain (recorded by a credit).

(e) Debt Conversion Expense (500 x $52) 26,000
    Common Stock (500 x $10) 5,000
    Paid-in Capital in Excess of Par [500 x ($52 - $10)] 21,000

Explanation: When an additional payment is needed to make bondholders convert, the payment is for a service (bondholders converting at a given time) and should be reported as an expense. The additional payment is called a **sweetener** to induce conversion; it should be recognized as an expense of the current period at an amount equal to the fair value of the additional securities or other consideration given.

(f) Paid-in Capital in Excess of Par.. 21,000
    Cash 21,000

Explanation: If the administrative costs of conversion are viewed to be costs of issuing the stock, treatment similar to any other stock issuance costs is used, which will mean a charge to additional paid-in capital in this case. When a corporation is in the process of initial formation, stock issuance costs can either be charged to additional paid-in capital (as is shown in this solution) or to a deferred cost account (such as organization costs), which is to be classified as an intangible asset and amortized over an arbitrary time period. If the costs are viewed as connected with an inducement to convert, they should be expensed in the current period.

EXERCISE 17-2

Purpose: (L.O.2) This exercise will illustrate how to account for convertible preferred stock.

Roy Rogers Corporation has 1,000 shares of $50 par 6% convertible preferred stock outstanding at December 31, 1999. Each share was issued in a prior year at $54. The preferred stock is convertible into $10 par common stock.

Instructions

(a)   Record the conversion of 100 shares of preferred stock if one share of preferred is convertible into four shares of common.

(b)   Record the conversion of 100 shares of preferred if the conversion ratio is 6:1.

Solution to Exercise 17-2

(a)   Convertible Preferred Stock (100 x $50)............................... 5,000
      Paid-in Capital in Excess of Par—Preferred (100 x $4) 400
          Common Stock (100 x 4 x $10) 4,000
          Paid-in Capital in Excess of Par—Common..................... 1,400
          [100 x ($54 - $40)]

(b)   Convertible Preferred Stock (100 x $50)............................... 5,000
      Paid-in Capital in Excess of Par—Preferred (100 x $4) 400
      Retained Earnings [100 x 6 x $10 - (100 x $54)]...................... 600
          Common Stock (100 x 6 x $10) 6,000

Approach: Use the following guidelines to record the conversion of preferred stock to common stock:

1.   No gain or loss is recorded. This is a capital transaction. A corporation cannot record an accounting gain or loss when dealing with its stockholders in their capacity of being owners of the business.

2.   The amount originally recorded (at issuance) in the Convertible Preferred Stock account and a related additional paid-in capital account is removed from those accounts and recorded in the Common Stock account and a related additional paid-in capital account. As usual, the par amount goes in the Common Stock account and any excess goes in an additional paid-in capital account.

3.   If the par value of the common stock exceeds the recorded value of the preferred, the difference is charged to retained earnings (or some states allow for a charge to additional paid-in capital from other sources).

EXERCISE 17-3

Purpose: (L.O.3) This exercise reviews the accounting rules for the issuance of stock rights to existing stockholders.

Hot Videos Corporation wished to raise additional capital. One right was distributed for each of the 100,000 shares of stock outstanding. Four rights and $30 cash were required to purchase one new share of $10 par value common stock. Ninety percent (90%) of the rights were exercised and the rest expired three weeks after their issuance. The market value of the stock was $32 per share at the date the rights were distributed and $35 per share at the date the rights were exercised.

Instructions
(a)   Explain the most likely reason for the distribution of the stock rights to existing stockholders. Why are these rights good for a very limited time period?
(b)   Record the issuance of the rights.
(c)   Record the exercise of the rights.
(d)   Record the expiration of the rights.

Solution to Exercise 17-3

(a)   The existing stockholders likely have the preemptive right (privilege to purchase newly issued shares in proportion to their holdings before the new issuance); thus, they must have the first opportunity to acquire new shares. The distribution of the rights (warrants) is a way to administer that opportunity. The rights have a short life because the corporation is anxious to sell the new shares to somebody; if the existing stockholders do not wish to buy them, they are offered to the general public.

(b)   Only make a memorandum entry at the grant (issuance) date. The corporation has received no consideration; no exchange has taken place; there are no proceeds to allocate.

(c)   Cash 675,000*
      Common Stock (22,500 x $10)   225,000
      Paid-in Capital in Excess of Par   450,000
        ($675,000 - $225,000)

        *100,000 x 90% = 90,000 rights exercised
         90,000 rights ÷ 4 = 22,500 common stock shares issued
         22,500 shares x $30 = $675,000 proceeds

> **TIP:**   When the rights are exercised, the issuance of the stock is recorded as any other stock issuance. At this date, assets and owners' equity are increased by the amount of the proceeds received.

(d)   Only make a memorandum entry at the expiration date.

EXERCISE 17-4

Purpose: (L.O.3) This exercise will review the accounting procedures for the issuance of debt securities with detachable warrants.

A new issue of 1,000 bonds was sold at 102.5 on January 1, 1999. Each bond had a face amount of $1,000 and one detachable warrant attached. One warrant allowed the holder to purchase 10 shares of $10 par common stock at $43 per share. The market value of the common stock at January 1, 1999 was $46. Shortly after issuance of the bonds and warrants, quotes were 98.5 for a bond ex-warrant and $48 for a common stock warrant. A few months later, 800 warrants were exercised. Two years later, the remaining 200 warrants expired.

Instructions
(a)   Record the issuance of the 1,000 bonds with detachable warrants.
(b)   Record the exercise of 800 warrants.
(c)   Record the expiration of 200 warrants.
(d)   Indicate the effect of each of the entries [(a), (b), and (c)] above on (1) assets, (2) total paid-in capital, and (3) number of common stock shares outstanding. State the direction and amount of each effect.
(e)   Explain how the journal entry for part (a) would differ if the market value of a bond ex-warrant was unknown.

Solution to Exercise 17-4

(a)   Cash (1,000 x $1,000 x 102.5%)   1,025,000
      Discount on Bonds Payable...   22,628[b]
          Bonds Payable (1,000 x $1,000)   1,000,000
          Paid-in Capital—Stock Warrants ....   47,628[a]

$$^a\frac{\$48,000}{\$48,000 \; + \; \$985,000} \times \$1,025,000 = \$47,628 \text{ amount to allocate to warrants}$$

[b]$1,025,000 total proceeds - $47,628 allocated to the warrants
      = $977,372 allocated to the bonds.
  $1,000,000 face amount of bonds - $977,372 carrying value of bonds
      = $22,628 to record for discount on bonds payable.

Explanation: The proportional method is used; thus, the proceeds are allocated to the two securities based on their relative market values. The amount to be allocated to the warrants is determined by the formula:

$$\frac{\text{MV Warrants}}{\text{MV Warrants} \; + \; \text{MV Bonds Ex-Warrants}} \times \frac{\text{Total}}{\text{Proceeds}} = \frac{\text{Paid-in Capital}}{\text{To Record}}$$

The remaining proceeds are recorded in bond accounts (the par value of the bonds always goes in the Bonds Payable account). The $22,628 excess of the bonds' par value over the proceeds allocated to the bonds [$1,000,000 - ($1,025,000 - $47,628) = $22,628] represents a discount on the bonds.

> **TIP:** Recall from your study of bonds payable that a bond's price is quoted in terms of a percentage of its par value. Carefully compute the bond's price before proceeding with the formula in this exercise. A very common error would be to use $98.50 for the price of one bond in this situation rather than the **correct** price of $985.00 (98.5% of $1,000 par = $985.00).
>
> **TIP:** Warrant prices are quoted like stock prices—in terms of dollars.
>
> **TIP:** When using the proportional method, the amount determined for allocation to the warrants should be close (but usually **not** equal) to the market value of the warrants. In part (a) of this problem, $47,628 is close to $48,000 (1,000 x $48); therefore, the amount determined by the formula is reasonable.

(b)

Cash (800 x 10 x $43)..	344,000	
Paid-in Capital—Stock Warrants (800/1,000 x $47,628)	38,102	
Common Stock (800 x 10 x $10)		80,000
Paid-in Capital in Excess of Par		302,102*

*Cash proceeds from exercise (800 warrants x 10 shares each x $43 exercise price)	$ 344,000
Amount recorded on the books for the warrants exercised (800 warrants exercised out of 1,000 outstanding = 80%; 80% x $47,628)	38,102
Total consideration received for stock issued	382,102
Par value of stock issued (800 x 10 x $10)	(80,000)
Excess of consideration received over par for stock issued upon exercise of warrants	$ 302,102

> **TIP:** The number of shares of stock obtainable upon the exercise of one warrant does **not** effect the computations and recording in part (a) [issuance date of bonds plus warrants] but it **does** effect the computations in part (b) [exercise date of the warrants].

(c)

Paid-in Capital—Stock Warrants ($47,628 - $38,102)..............	9,526	
Paid-in Capital from Expired Stock Warrants....................		9,526

(d)   Effect on:

	(1) Assets	(2) Total Paid-in Capital	(3) Number of Common Shares Outstanding
(a)	Increase $1,025,000	Increase $47,628	No effect
(b)	Increase $344,000	Increase $344,000	Increase 8,000
(c)	No effect	No effect	No effect

(e)   The incremental method would be used. Thus, the market value of the warrants would be used to record the warrants and the remaining proceeds would be recorded in debt accounts. The entry would be as follows:

Cash (1,000 x $1,000 x 102.5%)	1,025,000	
Discount on Bonds Payable..	23,000	
Bonds Payable (1,000 x $1,000)		1,000,000
Paid-in Capital—Stock Warrants (1,000 x $48)		48,000

ILLUSTRATION 17-1
ACCOUNTING FOR STOCK COMPENSATION PLANS (L.O.4)

The following guidelines pertain to accounting for a stock option, purchase, or award plan:

1.   The consideration that a corporation receives for stock issued through a stock option, purchase, or award plan consists of cash or other assets, if any, plus services received from the employee.

2.   Compensation for services should be measured by either the (1) **intrinsic value method** or (2) **fair value method.** APB Opinion No. 25 prescribed the intrinsic value method. Issued more recently, *SFAS No. 123* allows use of the intrinsic value method but encourages use of the fair value method. Using the **intrinsic value method**, the compensation for services (compensation cost) is measured by the excess of the quoted market price of the stock at the measurement date less the amount, if any, that the employee is required to pay. Using the **fair value method,** an option pricing model is used to compute the fair value (at the grant date) of the stock-based compensation paid to employees for their services. *SFAS No. 123* requires that when the intrinsic value method is used, the entity must disclose in a note to the financial statements the pro-forma net income and earnings per share (if presented by the company), as if it had used the fair value method.

3.   When using the intrinsic value method, the measurement date for determining compensation cost is the first date on which both the following are known:
      (a)   the number of shares that an individual is entitled to receive, and
      (b)   the option or purchase price, if any.

4.   Compensation cost should be recognized as an expense of one or more periods in which an employee performs services (often called **the service period**). The grant or award may specify the periods, or the periods may be inferred from the terms or from the past pattern of grants or awards. Unless otherwise specified, the service period is the vesting period—the time between the grant date and the vesting date. The vesting date is the date the employee's right to receive or retain shares of stock or cash under the award is no longer contingent upon the employee remaining in the service of the employer.

> **TIP:**   Although the measurement date for a stock option plan may be the date of grant, sometimes it is later. If the measurement date is later than the date of grant, the employer corporation should record compensation expense each period from the date of grant or award to the measurement date based on the quoted market price of the stock at the end of each period. Adjustment to this estimate may be needed in a later period.
>
> **TIP:**   Assume a stock option plan provides for the company's president to obtain 1,000 shares of common stock between January 1, 1999 and January 1, 2001 at a price equal to 20% of the market price at the date of exercise. The measurement date for this plan will be the date of exercise; the option price is unknown until the options are exercised.

EXERCISE 17-5

Purpose: (L.O.4) This exercise will illustrate the application of the intrinsic value method in accounting for a compensatory stock option plan. It will also examine how application of the fair value method differs from that of the intrinsic value method.

Worldwise Corporation granted options for 10,000 shares of its $10 par value common stock to certain executives on January 1, 1999, when the stock was selling for $52 per share. The options stipulate a price of $44 per share for the stock and must be exercised between January 1, 2001 and December 31, 2003, at which time they expire. The options state that the service period is January 1, 1999 through December 31, 2000. An option pricing model determined that, at the date of grant, the estimated fair value of these options was $500,000. The intrinsic value method is used in accounting for stock options.

Instructions

(a)   Compute the total compensation cost.

(b)   Explain when the compensation cost should be recognized as an expense.

(c)   Prepare the journal entries for the following (items 3 and 4 are independent assumptions):

   (1)   To record the issuance of the options (grant of options) on January 1, 1999.

   (2)   To record compensation expense, if any. Date the entry(s). Assume all employees remain employed by the corporation.

   (3)   To record the exercise of the options, assuming all of the options were exercised on the earliest possible date, January 1, 2001.

   (4)   To record the expiration of the options, assuming all of the options were **not** exercised because the market price fell below the exercise price before January 1, 2001 and stayed below that level for the balance of the option period.

(d)   Explain how your entries for part (c) would differ if the fair value method was used rather than the intrinsic value method.

Solution to Exercise 17-5

(a)   Using the intrinsic value method, the total compensation cost is measured by the excess of the market value of the stock over the option price at the date of measurement. The measurement date for this particular plan is the grant date because both the number of shares under option and the option price are known at that date. The total compensation cost is computed as follows:

Market value of the stock at the measurement date	$ 52
Option price	(44)
Compensation cost per share subject to option	8
Shares obtainable upon exercise of options	x 10,000
Total compensation cost	$ 80,000

TIP: The **option price** is often called the **exercise price.**

(b)   The compensation cost should be recognized as an expense in the periods the employees perform services for which the option is granted. This **service period** is either stated in the plan or inferred. In this case, the stated service period is from the date of grant (January 1, 1999) to December 31, 2000. Thus, the compensation cost will be recognized evenly over that two-year period. $80,000 ÷ 2 years = $40,000 per year.

> **TIP:** When answering exam questions over this subject, use the service period stated, if one is clearly indicated. If it is not stated, indicate the period you assume to be the service period (choose from date of grant to the vesting date or to the date the options first become exercisable **or** from the date of grant to the date the options expire). If the question is of the multiple-choice type and you cannot write in your assumption, use the amount of time from the date of grant to the date the options become exercisable as the service period. If your resulting solution does not match one of the answer selections, redo your computations using the time span from the date of grant to the date the options expire as the service period. Your new solution should now match one of the answer selections given.

(c)   **(1)**   **January 1, 1999**
No entry

(2)   **December 31, 1999**

Compensation Expense	40,000	
Paid-in Capital—Stock Options		40,000

December 31, 2000

Compensation Expense	40,000	
Paid-in Capital—Stock Options		40,000

(3)   **January 1, 2001**

Cash (10,000 x $44)	440,000	
Paid-in Capital—Stock Options	80,000	
Common Stock (10,000 x $10)		100,000
Paid-in Capital in Excess of Par		420,000

> **TIP:** The entry to record the exercise of the options is **not** affected by the date the exercise takes place. Thus, this same entry would record the exercise if it took place on December 31, 2003. If there is a situation in which the options are exercised prior to the end of the service period (therefore, **prior** to the date the total compensation cost has been charged to expense), an unearned compensation cost account is charged. The balance of this Unearned Compensation Cost account is classified as a contra stockholders' equity item.

(4)   **December 31, 2003**

Paid-in Capital—Stock Options	80,000	
Paid-in Capital from Expired Stock Options		80,000

> **TIP:** The fact that a stock option is never exercised does not nullify the propriety of recording the cost of services received from executives and attributable to the stock option plan. Compensation expense is, therefore, not adjusted upon expiration of the options. However, if a stock option is forfeited because an employee fails to satisfy a service requirement (e.g., leaves employment), the estimate of compensation expense recorded in the current period should be adjusted (as a change in estimate). This change in estimate would be recorded by debiting Paid-in Capital—Stock Options and crediting Compensation Expense, thereby decreasing compensation expense in the period of forfeiture.

(d)   If the fair value of the method was used, the journal entries would be as follows:

(1)   **January 1, 1999**
       No entry

(2)   **December 31, 1999**
       Compensation Expense 250,000
           Paid-in Capital—Stock Options   250,000

                              December 31, 2000
       Compensation Expense 250,000
           Paid-in Capital—Stock Options   250,000

(3)   **January 1, 2001**
       Cash.. 440,000
       Paid-in Capital—Stock Options 500,000
           Common Stock   100,000
           Paid-in Capital in Excess of Par   840,000

                              December 31, 2003
(4)   Paid-in Capital—Stock Options 500,000
           Paid-in Capital from Expired Stock Options.................   500,000

ILLUSTRATION 17-2
STEPS IN COMPUTING EARNINGS PER SHARE (EPS) (L.O.6,7,9)

Step 1:   **Compute the weighted average number of common stock shares outstanding.**

A.   When common shares are issued for assets during the period, weight them according to the length of time in the period the stock is outstanding in relation to the total time in the period.

B.   When common shares are issued in connection with a stock split or stock dividend declared during the period, give retroactive treatment to these shares. Give retroactive treatment even if the stock dividend or split is declared after the end of the period (but before the financial statements are published). Restate EPS in financial statements for prior periods presented.

> **TIP:**   See **Illustration 17-3** for a short-cut method of computing the weighted-average number of common stock shares outstanding.

Step 2:   **Compute basic EPS (EPS before any assumptions or adjustments).**

$$\text{Basic Formula: } \frac{\text{Net Income - Preferred Dividends}}{\text{Weighted- Average Number of Common Shares Outstanding}}$$

The numerator should be the income available to common stockholders which is net income minus preferred stock dividend requirements. Thus, in the numerator, deduct the preferred dividends actually declared. If the preferred stock is cumulative, deduct the preferred's current year preference as to dividends, even if no dividends were declared. Dividends in arrears for prior years have no effect on the current year's basic EPS calculation.

> **TIP:**   Dividends declared and/or paid during the year on common stock have no effect on this computation.
>
> **TIP:**   If there is a net loss rather than a net income, the amount of the loss is increased by the preferred dividends.

Step 3:   **Compute diluted earnings per share.**

A.   The basic formula is adjusted as follows:

$$\frac{\text{Net Income - Preferred Dividends} \pm \text{Adjustments}}{\text{Weighted Average Number of Common Shares Outstanding +}\atop\text{Weighted Average Number of Potential Common Shares}}$$

ILLUSTRATION 17-2 (Continued)

B.   Treatment of convertibles: Use the **if converted** method.

1.   Assume the convertible is converted to common stock, if the effect of that assumption is dilutive.

> **TIP:**   Dilution (dilutive) is a reduction in earnings per share. **Antidilution (antidilutive)** is an increase in earnings per share amounts or a decrease in loss per share amounts.
>
> **TIP:**   A quick test to determine if a convertible debt instrument is antidilutive is as follows: if the amount of interest net of taxes per common share obtainable upon conversion exceeds basic EPS, the effect is antidilutive.
>
> **TIP:**   A quick test to determine if a convertible preferred stock is antidilutive is as follows: if the amount of preferred dividends per common share obtainable on conversion exceeds basic EPS, the effect is antidilutive.

2.   For a convertible preferred, add back the preferred dividends (that had been deducted in the basic formula) in the numerator and add an appropriate weighted average number of potential common shares (assumed to be outstanding) in the denominator of the diluted EPS formula.

3.   For convertible debt, add back interest and deduct tax savings due to interest in the numerator and add an appropriate weighted average number of potential common shares in the denominator.

> **TIP:**   In using the "if converted" method for a convertible bond, interest expense is added back in the numerator of the EPS formula and the related tax effect is deducted. In using the "if converted" method for a convertible preferred stock, preferred dividends are added back in the numerator (because they were deducted in the numerator of the basic formula); however, there is **no** related tax effect because preferred dividends are not a tax deductible item.

4.   Assume the conversion takes place at the beginning of the period for which EPS is being calculated or at the date of the issuance of the convertible, whichever is later (more recent).

5.   If there is a scale of conversion rates, use the rate that is the most advantageous from the standpoint of the security holder.

C.   Treatment of options and warrants:

1.   Assume the options and warrants are exercised if the effect of that assumption is dilutive.

ILLUSTRATION 17-2 (Continued)

> **TIP:** An option or warrant is dilutive if the average market price of the common stock during the period is greater than the exercise price of the option or warrant.

2. Use the **treasury stock method**. Assume that the proceeds (from the exercise of the options or warrants) are used to purchase treasury stock at the **average market price** for the period. Thus, shares will be added to the EPS denominator because of the assumed exercise, and then a smaller number of shares will be deducted from the denominator because of the assumed purchase of treasury stock. Weight the resulting **net** number of common equivalent shares according to the time they are assumed to be outstanding.

3. Assume the exercise occurs at the beginning of the period or at the date of the issuance of the options or warrants, whichever is the later.

D. Treatment of contingent issuance agreements.

1. Common stock contingently issuable with the only condition being the mere passage of time should be assumed to be outstanding for computing diluted EPS.

2. Common stock contingently issuable upon condition of the attainment or maintenance of a level of earnings should be considered outstanding in computing diluted EPS **if** that level is currently being attained.

3. Common stock contingently issuable upon condition of the attainment of a market price level should be considered outstanding shares **if** that level is met at the end of the current year.

> **TIP:** An entity with a **simple capital structure,** that is, one with only common stock outstanding, must report **basic-per-share** amounts for income from continuing operations and for net income on the face of the income statement. An entity with a **complex capital structure** (i.e., a structure with one or more potentially dilutive securities outstanding) must report **basic and diluted per share** amounts for income from continuing operations and for net income on the face of the income statement with equal prominence.
>
> **TIP:** Securities such as options, warrants, convertible bonds, convertible preferred stock, or contingent stock agreements are referred to as "potential common stock" or "potentially dilutive securities."

ILLUSTRATION 17-2 (Continued)

TIP: The computation of diluted EPS should not assume conversion, exercise, or **contingent issuance** of securities that would have an **antidilutive** effect on earnings per share. Shares issued on actual conversion, exercise, or satisfaction of certain conditions for which the underlying potential common shares were antidilutive shall be included in the computation as outstanding common shares from the date of conversion, exercise, or satisfaction of those conditions, respectively. In determining whether potential common shares are dilutive or antidilutive, each issue or series of issues of potential common shares should be considered separately rather than in the aggregate.

TIP: Convertible securities may be dilutive on their own but antidilutive when included with other potential common shares in computing diluted EPS. To reflect maximum potential dilution, each issue or series of issues of potential common shares shall be considered in sequence from the most dilutive to the least dilutive. That is, dilutive potential common shares with the lowest "earnings per incremental share" shall be included in diluted EPS before those with a higher earnings per incremental share. (Options and warrants generally will be included first because use of the treasury stock method does not impact the numerator of the computation.)

TIP: An entity that reports a discontinued operation, an extraordinary item, or the cumulative effect of an accounting change in a period should use income from continuing operations (adjusted for preferred dividends) as the "control number" in determining whether those potential common shares are dilutive or antidilutive. That is, the same number of potential common shares used in computing the diluted per-share amount for income from continuing operations should be used in computing all other reported diluted per-share amounts even if those amounts will be antidilutive to their respective basic per-share amounts.

For example, assume that Corporation A has income from continuing operations of $2,400, a loss from discontinued operations of $(3,600), a net loss of $(1,200), and 1,000 common shares and 200 potential common shares outstanding. Corporation A's basic per-share amounts would be $2.40 for continuing operations, $(3.60) for the discontinued operations, and $(1.20) for the net loss. Corporation A would include the 200 potential common shares in the denominator of its diluted per-share computation for continuing operations because the resulting $2.00 per share is dilutive. (For illustrative purposes, assume no numerator impact of those 200 potential common shares.) Because income from continuing operations is the control number, Corporation A also must include those 200 potential common shares in the denominator for the other per-share amounts, even though the resulting per-share amounts [$(3.00) per share for the loss from discontinued operation and $(1.00) per share for the net loss] are antidilutive to their comparable basic per-share amounts; that is, the loss per-share amounts are less.

TIP: Including potential common shares in the denominator of a diluted per-share computation for continuing operations always will result in an antidilutive per-share amount when an entity has a *loss* from continuing operations or a *loss* from continuing operations available to common stockholders (that is, after any preferred dividend reductions). Although including those potential common shares in the other diluted per-share computations may be dilutive to their comparable basic per-share amounts, no potential common shares should be included in the computation of any diluted per-share amount when a loss from continuing operations exists, even if the entity reports net income.

ILLUSTRATION 17-3
SHORT-CUT METHOD FOR COMPUTING WEIGHTED AVERAGE
NUMBER OF COMMON STOCK SHARES OUTSTANDING* (L.O.6)

Step 1: Begin with the number of common shares outstanding at the beginning of the period. Assume they were outstanding the entire year; multiply the number by 12/12 to get an equivalent amount. Enter the equivalent amount in the Weighted Average column.

Step 2: Take the first transaction that occurred during the year that changed the number of shares outstanding and properly adjust the balance in the Weighted Average column.
   a. **If shares were issued for assets, weight the new shares** by multiplying them by a fraction. The numerator of the fraction is the number of months in the period the shares were outstanding; the denominator is the number of months in the year. Add this equivalent amount in the Weighted Average column; arrive at a new balance.
   b. **If shares were issued in a stock dividend or a stock split, retroactively adjust for these shares** by taking an appropriate multiple of the existing balance in the Weighted Average column. Ignore the date of the stock dividend or split; the multiple is determined by the size of the stock dividend or split. Arrive at a new balance.
   c. **If shares were acquired as treasury stock or retired by the corporation, weight** the shares for the time they were **not** outstanding and deduct this equivalent amount from the existing balance. Arrive at a new balance.

Step 3: Take each of the other transactions that occurred during the year that changed the number of common shares outstanding and properly adjust the balance in the Weighted Average column as shown in Step 2 above. Handle each transaction in order of date.

EXAMPLE:

Data:	January 1, 1999	100,000 shares were outstanding.
	April 1, 1999	Issued 40,000 shares for cash.
	June 1, 1999	Declared a 40% stock dividend.
	October 1, 1999	Declared a 2-for-1 split.
	December 1, 1999	Issued 60,000 shares for cash.

*The reporting period is assumed to be one year.

ILLUSTRATION 17-3 (Continued)

Computation:

Date		Weighted Average
1/1/99	100,000 x 12/12 =	100,000
4/1/99	40,000 x 9/12 =	30,000
	New balance	130,000
6/1/99	40% stock dividend	x 140%**
	New balance	182,000
10/1/99	2-for-1 split	x 2***
	New balance	364,000
12/1/99	60,000 x 1/12	5,000
	New balance	369,000

**The appropriate multiple for a stock dividend is 100% plus the percentage used in the dividend. Thus, 100% + 40% dividend = 140% as the multiplier.

***The appropriate multiple for a stock split is the size of the split. Thus, for a 2-for-1 split, multiply by 2.

> **TIP:** Notice how the computation for the weighted-average number of common stock shares outstanding for the period differs from the computation for the actual number of common stock shares outstanding at the end of the period. The number of common stock shares actually outstanding at December 31, 1999 can be computed as follows:
>
> | Date | | Actual Shares |
> |------|------|------|
> | 1/1/99 | Balance | 100,000 |
> | 4/1/99 | Issued for assets | 40,000 |
> | | New balance | 140,000 |
> | 6/1/99 | 40% stock dividend | 56,000 |
> | | New balance | 196,000 |
> | 10/1/99 | 2:1 split | 196,000 |
> | | New balance | 392,000 |
> | 12/1/99 | Issued for assets | 60,000 |
> | | New balance | 452,000 |
>
> **TIP:** Assume that in addition to the transactions listed above, a 10% stock dividend was declared on January 7, 2000, before the financial statements for 1999 were issued. The weighted average number of common stock shares outstanding for purposes of computing EPS for 1999 would be 405,900 (369,000 x 110% = 405,900) and the actual number of common stock shares outstanding to be reported on the balance sheet at December 31, 1999 would be 452,000.

EXERCISE 17-6

Purpose: (L.O.6) This exercise will apply the guidelines for computing the weighted average number of common stock shares outstanding.

When the number of common stock shares varies during the year, the weighted average number of common stock shares outstanding must be calculated before the EPS can be computed.

Listed below are the details regarding common stock shares outstanding for four different companies:

1. Michael Jackson Corporation had 100,000 shares of common stock outstanding on January 1, 1999. On March 1, 1999, 6,000 shares of common stock were issued for cash.

2. Jimmy Buffet corporation had 100,000 shares of common stock outstanding on January 1, 1999. On March 1, 6,000 shares of common stock were issued for cash. On July 1, a 4-for-1 split was declared.

3. Emmy Lou Harris Corporation had 100,000 shares of common stock outstanding on January 1, 1999. On March 1, 1999, 6,000 shares of common stock were reacquired by the corporation.

4. Elton John Corporation had 100,000 shares of common stock outstanding on January 1, 1999. On March 1, 1999, 6,000 shares of common stock were issued for cash. On June 1, 1999, a 10% stock dividend was declared. On December 1, 1999, 12,000 shares of common stock were issued for cash.

Instructions
(a) Compute the weighted average number of common stock shares outstanding for 1999 (to be used to compute EPS) for **each** of the **independent** situations above.
(b) Compute the number of common stock shares outstanding to be reported on the balance sheet at December 31, 1999 for Elton John Corporation (situation 4).

Solution to Exercise 17-6

(a) **Approach and Explanation:** Use the short-cut method explained in **Illustration 17-3**.

	Date		Weighted Average
1.	1/1/99	100,000 x 12/12 =	100,000
	3/1/99	6,000 x 10/12 =	5,000
		New balance	105,000

> **TIP:** The weighted average calculation for common stock shares uses the same concept that is applied in computing equivalent units of production for a manufacturing firm. In the situation above, the computation indicates that having 6,000 shares outstanding for ten months of the year is equivalent to having 5,000 shares outstanding for twelve months. The weighted average number of shares outstanding is sometimes referred to as equivalent shares.

	Date		Weighted Average
2.	1/1/99	100,000 x 12/12 =	100,000
	3/1/99	6,000 x 10/12 =	5,000
		New balance	105,000
	7/1/99	4-for-1 split	x 4
		New balance	420,000
3.	1/1/99	100,000 x 12/12 =	100,000
	3/1/99	(6,000) x 10/12 =	(5,000)
		New balance	95,000
4.	1/1/99	100,000 x 12/12 =	100,000
	3/1/99	6,000 x 10/12 =	5,000
		New balance	105,000
	6/1/99	10% stock dividend	x 110%
		New balance	115,500
	12/1/99	12,000 x 1/12 =	1,000
		New balance	116,500

> **TIP:** If you want, you can prove the answer of 116,500 by a more complex procedure as follows:
>
> | Dates Outstanding | Actual Shares[a] | Restatement | Fraction | Weighted Shares |
> |-------------------|-----------------|-------------|----------|-----------------|
> | 1/1/99 to 2/28/99 | 100,000 | 1.1 | 2/12 | 18,333 |
> | 3/1/99 to 5/31/99 | 106,000 | 1.1 | 3/12 | 29,150 |
> | 6/1/99 to 11/30/99 | 116,600 | | 6/12 | 58,300 |
> | 12/1/99 to 12/31/99 | 128,600 | | 1/12 | 10,717 |
> | | | | | 116,500 |
>
> [a]See solution to part (b) for computations.

A stock dividend or a stock split requires retroactive restatement of shares for the computation of EPS. A 10% stock dividend causes a 10% increase in the number of shares outstanding. Therefore, to restate the number of shares outstanding at a certain date in the past as to give retroactive effect to a subsequently declared 10% stock dividend, the old number of shares is multiplied by 110% (which is 1.1 in decimal form).

> **TIP:** When shares are issued for assets, they are weighted for the number of months they are outstanding in relation to the number of months in the period for which EPS is being computed. When shares are issued in a stock dividend or a stock split, they are **not** weighted; rather, retroactive adjustment is made for these additional shares in the weighted average shares calculation. The reason for the difference in treatment is that when assets are received, the entity has more resources and, therefore, an opportunity to increase the net income figure by earning a rate of return on those new assets for the months the new resources are available. When shares are issued in connection with a stock dividend or stock split, there are no new resources and, therefore, no changes in net income. In order for EPS figures for successive periods for a company to be meaningful, they must all be based on the rearranged capital structure; therefore, stock dividends and stock splits must be handled retroactively. This **retroactive treatment** causes adjustment to the weighted average shares computation for EPS **for all periods presented**. Therefore, when the financial statements for a prior period are republished in comparative statements, the EPS amounts for the prior period are to be restated for all stock dividends and stock splits occurring subsequent to the prior period. Thus, a stock dividend declared in 1999 calls for retroactive restatement of the 1998 EPS figure when the 1998 income statement is republished in 1999 for comparative purposes.

(b)

Date		Actual Shares
1/1/99	Balance	100,000
3/1/99	Issued for assets	6,000
	New balance	106,000
6/1/99	10% stock dividend	10,600
	New balance	116,600
12/1/99	Issued for assets	12,000
	New balance	128,600

EXERCISE 17-7

Purpose: (L.O.7) This exercise will illustrate the application of the treasury stock method.

Ronald Tsang Corporation had 200,000 shares of common stock outstanding during 1999. On January 1, 1999 40,000 stock options were granted. Each option entitles the holder to purchase one share of common stock at $40. The options become exercisable in 2001. Net income for 1999 was $400,000. The average market price of stock during 1999 was $50; the closing market price was $54.

Instructions

(a)   Compute the amount(s) that Ronald Tsang Corporation should report for earnings per share for 1999.

(b)   Explain how your answer(s) to Part (a) would change if the options were issued on April 1, 1999 rather than January 1, 1999.

Solution to Exercise 17-7

(a)   **Explanation and Approach:** Follow the steps for computing EPS as outlined in Illustration 17-2.

Step 1:   **Compute the weighted average number of common stock shares outstanding.**
There were no changes in the 200,000 shares of common stock outstanding during 1999. Therefore, the weighted average is <u>200,000</u> shares.

Step 2:   **Compute basic EPS before any assumptions** (basic formula without adjustment).

$$\frac{\$400,000 - \$0}{200,000} = \underline{\$2.00}$$

Step 3:   **Compute diluted earnings per share.**
- Use the treasury stock method for the options.
- Use the quick test to determine if these options are dilutive. Compare the option price and the current market price. The option price ($40) is less than the average market price ($50), so the options will have a dilutive effect on EPS.
- Adjust the basic formula:

$$\frac{\$400,000 - \$0}{200,000 + 40,000^a - 32,000^b} = \underline{\$1.92}$$

[a]Number of shares to be issued upon exercise of options.
[b]Number of shares that could be purchased for the treasury at $50 (average market price for the period) per share from the proceeds of the exercise of the options:
40,000 x $40 = $1,600,000 proceeds
$1,600,000 ÷ $50 = 32,000 assumed treasury shares

> TIP: Notice the incremental number of shares calculated by use of the treasury stock method is 8,000 in this example (40,000 - 32,000). If the average market price was less than the option price, the number of assumed treasury shares would exceed the number of shares assumed issued upon exercise of the options, and the result would be to decrease the denominator from the figure used in the basic formula. That decrease in the denominator would have an antidilutive effect on EPS; therefore, the exercise of the options would **not be** assumed in that circumstance. **Never make assumptions in computing diluted EPS that are antidilutive.**

> TIP: Notice why the treasury stock method is so named; the proceeds from the assumed exercise of stock options are assumed to be used for the purchase of treasury stock.

Ronald Tsang Corporation should report a dual presentation for 1999 as follows:

$2.00 basic earnings per share, and
$1.92 diluted earnings per share

(b)   The exercise of the options would be assumed to have taken place on April 1 rather than at the beginning of the year. Therefore, the assumed shares in the denominator would have to be weighted as follows:

$$9/12 \ (40,000 - 32,000) = 6,000$$

Therefore, the computation for diluted EPS would then be:

$$\frac{\$400,000}{200,000 \ + \ 6,000} = \underline{\$1.94} \text{ diluted EPS.}$$

EXERCISE 17-8

Purpose: (L.O.7,9) This exercise will illustrate the proper treatment of convertible securities in the EPS computations.

The following data pertain to the Star Trek Corporation at December 31, 1999:

Net income for the year	$1,600,000
6% convertible bonds issued at par in a prior year, convertible into 200,000 shares of common stock	$3,000,000
8% convertible, cumulative, preferred stock, $100 par, issued in a prior year (each share is convertible into 6 shares of common)	$2,000,000
Common stock, $10 par, issued in prior years	$6,000,000
Additional paid-in capital	$3,400,000
Retained earnings	$5,200,000
Tax rate for 1999	40%

There were no changes during 1999 in the number of common stock shares, preferred stock shares, or convertible bonds outstanding. There is no treasury stock held.

Instructions
(a)   Compute the basic earnings per share for 1999.
(b)   Compute the diluted earnings per share for 1999.
(c)   Explain whether a dual presentation should be presented for EPS for 1999.

Solution to Exercise 17-8

(a) $2.40 (See Step 2 below.)

(b) $1.86 (See Step 3 below.)

(c)   Yes, a dual presentation must be reported in 1999 because the corporation has some dilutive securities outstanding.

> **TIP:** Whenever a situation involves the EPS computation(s), follow the steps (in order) listed in **Illustration 17-2**. By using this organized approach to these situations, you are less likely to overlook guidelines that may affect your solution.

Approach and Explanation:

Step 1: **Compute the weighted average number of common stock shares outstanding.** There were no changes in the number of common shares outstanding during 1999. There are no treasury shares; thus, the number of shares outstanding is equal to the number of shares issued. The number of common shares issued can be computed by:

$$\$6,000,000 \div \$10 \text{ par} = 600,000 \text{ shares}$$

Step 2: **Compute basic EPS (before any assumptions).**

$$\frac{\$1,600,000 - \$160,000^a}{600,000} = \underline{\$2.40}$$

^{a}8% x $2,000,000 par = $160,000 preferred dividends.

> **TIP:** Recall that with cumulative preferred stock, the preferred's current year preference as to dividends is deducted in the basic EPS formula, whether or not the dividends were declared.

Step 3: **Compute diluted earnings per share.**

$$\frac{\$1,600,000 - \$160,000 + \$180,000^a - \$72,000^b + \$160,000}{600,000 + 200,000 + 6(20,000)^c} = \underline{\$1.86}$$

^{a}6% x $3,000,000 par = $180,000 interest expense.
^{b}$180,000 interest x 40% tax rate = $72,000 tax effect of interest.
^{c}$2,000,000 par ÷ $100 per share = 20,000 shares of preferred issued.

> **TIP:** Notice why the "if converted method" is so named; the earnings per share computation assumes conversion of the convertible securities.

When there is more than one potentially dilutive security outstanding, the steps for computing diluted earnings per share are as follows:

1. Determine, for each dilutive security, the per share effect assuming exercise/conversion.
2. Rank the results from step 1 from smallest to largest earnings effect per share; that is, rank the results from most dilutive to least dilutive.
3. Beginning with the earnings per share based upon the weighted average of common shares outstanding ($2.40 in this problem), recalculate earnings per share by adding the smallest per share effects from step 2. If the results from this recalculation are less than $2.40, proceed to the next smallest per share effect and recalculate earnings per share. This process is continued so long as each recalculated earnings per share is smaller than the previous amount. The process will end either because there are no more securities to test or a particular security maintains or increases earnings per share (is antidilutive).

> **TIP:** This means that dilutive potential common stock with the lowest "earnings per incremental share" will be included in diluted EPS before those with a higher "earnings per incremental share."

The 3 steps are now applied to the Star Trek Corporation. The Star Trek Corporation has two securities (6% and 8% convertible bonds) that could reduce EPS.

The first step in the computation of diluted earnings per share is to determine a per share effect for each potentially dilutive security.

Step 1: Determine the per share effect of each dilutive security.
Convertible bonds:

Interest expense for year (6% x $3,000,000)	$180,000
Income tax reduction due to interest (40% x $180,000)	72,000
Interest expense avoided (net of tax)	$108,000
Number of additional common shares issued assuming conversion of bonds	200,000

Per share effect:

$$\frac{\text{Incremental Numerator Effect: } \$108,000}{\text{Incremental Denominator Effect: } 200,000 \text{ shares}} = \underline{\$.54}$$

Convertible preferred stock:

Dividend requirement on cumulative preferred (20,000 shares X 8% X $100)	$160,000
Income tax effect (dividends are not a tax deduction)	none
Dividend requirement avoided	$160,000
Number of additional common shares issued assuming conversion of preferred (6 x 20,000 shares)	120,000

Per share effect:

$$\frac{\text{Incremental Numerator Effect:}\quad \$160{,}000}{\text{Incremental Denominator Effect:}\ 120{,}000\ \text{shares}} = \underline{\$1.33}$$

Step 2: Rank the results from Step 1.

The ranking of the two potentially dilutive securities is as follows (lowest earnings per incremental share to the largest):

	Effect Per Share
1. 6% convertible bonds	$.54
2. 8% convertible preferred	1.33

Step 3: Determine diluted earnings per share.

The next step is to determine earnings per share giving effect to the ranking above. Starting with the earnings per share of $2.40 computed previously, add the incremental effects of the options to the original calculation, as follows:

6% Convertible Bonds

Numerator from previous calculation	$1,440,000
Add: Interest expense avoided (net of tax)	108,000
Total	$1,548,000
Denominator from previous calculation (shares)	600,000
Add: Number of common shares assumed issued upon assumed	
conversion of bonds	200,000
Total	800,000
Recomputed earnings per share ($1,548,000 ÷ 800,000 shares)	$1.94

Since the recomputed earnings per share is reduced (from $2.40 to $1.94), the effect of the 6% bonds is dilutive.

Next, earnings per share is recomputed assuming the conversion of the 8% preferred stock. This is shown below:

8% Convertible Preferred

Numerator from previous calculation	$1,548,000
Add: Dividend requirement avoided	160,000
Total	$1,708,000
Denominator from previous calculation (shares)	800,000
Add: Number of common shares assumed issued upon conversion	
of preferred stock	120,000
Total	920,000
Recomputed earnings per share ($1,708,000 ÷ 920,000 shares)	$1.86

Since the recomputed earnings per share is reduced, the effect of the 8% convertible preferred is dilutive. Diluted earnings per share is $1.86.

ILLUSTRATION 17-4
SUMMARY OF COMPENSATION PLANS (L.O. 8)

A summary of some compensation plans and their major characteristics is provided as follows:

Type of Plan	Measurement Date	Measurement of Compensation	Allocation Period	Allocation Method
Incentive stock option				
APB Opinion No. 25	Grant	Market price less exercise price	N/A (no compensation expense)	N/A (no compensation expense)
SFAS No. 123	Grant	Option pricing model	Service	Straight-line
Nonqualified stock option				
APB Opinion No. 25	Grant	Market price less exercise price	Service	Straight-line
SFAS No. 123	Grant	Option pricing model	Service	Straight-line
Stock appreciation rights				
APB Opinion No. 25	Exercise	Market price less exercise price	Service	Percentage approach for service period, then mark to market.
SFAS No. 123	Grant	Option pricing model	Service	Straight-line
Performance-type plan				
APB Opinion No. 25	Exercise	Market value of shares issued	Service	Percentage approach for service period, then mark to market.
SFAS No. 123	Exercise	Market value of shares issued	Service	Percentage approach for service period, then mark to market.

ANALYSIS OF MULTIPLE-CHOICE TYPE QUESTIONS

QUESTION

1. (L.O.1) For the purpose of inducing conversion, a corporation with convertible bonds increases the number of common shares into which this debt may be converted. Upon conversion, the fair value of the additional shares given should be reported as:
   a. an expense of the current period.
   b. an extraordinary item.
   c. a direct reduction of owners' equity.
   d. a deferred expense.

Explanation: When an issuer offers some form of additional consideration (cash, other assets, or common stock), called "sweetener," to induce conversion of convertible debt, *SFAS No. 84* requires that the sweetener be recognized as an expense equal to the fair value of the additional securities or other consideration given. (Solution = a.)

QUESTION

2.   (L.O.1) The Goodings Corporation issued 1,000 8% convertible bonds with a face value of $1,000 each at a price of 102. An underwriter advised the corporation that without the conversion feature, the bonds could not have been issued at a price above 99. At the date of issuance, the amount to be recorded as paid-in capital attributable to the conversion feature is:

a. $0.
b. $10,000.
c. $20,000.
d. $30,000.

Approach and Explanation: State the rule related to accounting for the issuance of convertible bonds. All proceeds received from the issuance of convertible debt are to be recorded in liability accounts; none of the proceeds is to be allocated to the conversion feature under current generally accepted accounting principles. The journal entry to record the issuance of these bonds is no different than the recording of bonds without the conversion feature. That entry would be as follows for the bonds in question:

Cash 1,020,000		
Bonds Payable...		1,000,000
Premium on Bonds Payable..		20,000

(Solution = a.)

QUESTION

3.   (L.O.3) A corporation issues bonds with detachable warrants. The amount to be recorded as paid-in capital is preferably:
a.   zero.
b.   calculated by the excess of the proceeds over the face amount of the bonds.
c.   equal to the market value of the warrants.
d.   based on the relative market values of the two securities involved.

Explanation: When both the market value of a warrant and the market value of a bond ex-warrant are known, the proportional method is to be employed; hence, the proceeds are allocated to the warrant (paid-in capital) and the debt instrument (liabilities), based on the relative market values of the warrants and bonds. The incremental method (answer section "c") would be appropriate in this case if the market value of the bonds ex-warrants is not known. Answer section "a" (zero) is appropriate only if the warrants are nondetachable (another way of referring to convertible debt instruments). (Solution = d.)

QUESTION

4.   (L.O.3) The distribution of stock rights to existing common stockholders will increase paid-in capital at the:

	Date of Issuance of the Rights	Date of Exercise of the Rights
a.	Yes	Yes
b.	Yes	No
c.	No	Yes
d.	No	No

Approach and Explanation: Quickly reconstruct and review the journal entries involved in accounting for stock rights. Analyze the effect of each entry on paid-in capital. At the date of issuance of the rights, there is no debit and credit entry; thus, no effect on paid-in capital. At the date of exercise, assets and paid-in capital increase by the exercise price multiplied by the number of related shares. (Solution = c.)

QUESTION

5.   (L.O.4) Stock options allowing selected executives to acquire 10,000 shares of $1 par common stock are granted on January 1, 1999. The market price at January 1, 1999 is $22. The option price is $10. The options are for services to be performed over four years from the date of grant. The options become exercisable on January 1, 2001 and expire on December 31, 2003. The amount of compensation cost related to these options to be charged to expense for 1999 (assuming the intrinsic value method is used) is:
   a. $0.
   b. $24,000.
   c. $30,000.
   d. $60,000.
   e. $120,000.

Approach and Explanation: (1) Compute the total compensation cost. It is the excess of the market price over the option price at the measurement date. The date of grant is the measurement date in this situation. Therefore, ($22 - $10) x 10,000 shares = $120,000 total compensation cost. (2) Determine the service period—span of time over which the employees are to provide services in exchange for the options. It is clearly stated in this plan that the service period is the four years 1999, 2000, 2001, and 2002. (3) Divide total compensation cost ($120,000) by the service period (4 years) to arrive at $30,000 per year. (Solution = c.)

QUESTION

6.   (L.O.4) On January 1, 1999 Stewart Chandler, Inc. granted stock options to officers and key employees for the purchase of 1,000 shares of the company's $1 par common stock at $20 per share as additional compensation for services to be rendered over the next two years. The options are exercisable during a four-year period beginning January 1, 2001 by grantees still employed by Stewart Chandler. The market price of Stewart Chandler's common stock was $26 per share at the date of grant. Assuming the intrinsic value method is used, the journal entry to record the compensation expense related to these options for 1999 would include a credit to the Paid-in Capital— Stock Options account for:
   a. $26,000.
   b. $20,000.
   c. $6,000.
   d. $3,000.
   e. $1,000.

Approach and Explanation: Reconstruct the journal entry to record the compensation expense for 1999. It would be as follows:

Compensation Expense...	3,000	
Paid-in Capital—Stock Options		3,000

The total compensation cost is determined by the excess of the market price of the stock ($26) over the option price ($20) at the measurement date multiplied by the number of shares subject to being issued (1,000 shares). The measurement date is the grant date in this case, because both the number of shares (1,000) and the exercise price ($20) are known at the date of grant. The total compensation cost is allocated to the periods included in the service period (two years). $6,000 ÷ 2 = $3,000. (Solution = d.)

QUESTION

7.   (L.O.6,7) Tempo, Inc. had 200,000 shares of common stock issued and outstanding at December 31, 1998. On July 1, 1999 an additional 200,000 shares were issued for cash. Tempo also had stock options outstanding at the beginning and end of 1999 which allow the holders to purchase 60,000 shares of common stock at $20 per share. The average market price of Tempo's common stock was $15 during 1999. The market price of Tempo's common stock was $25 at December 31, 1999. What is the number of shares that should be used in computing diluted earnings per share for the year ended December 31, 1999?

a.   400,000
b.   300,000
c.   360,000
d.   415,000
e.   320,000
f.   280,000

Approach and Explanation: Use the treasury stock method to compute the number of shares to be used in determining diluted EPS. **However**, only make assumptions about the exercise of stock options when those assumptions are **not** antidilutive. A quick test to determine whether these options are dilutive or antidilutive is to compare the average market price ($15) with the option price ($20). The market price is **not** higher; therefore, the assumed exercise of stock options in applying the treasury stock method when computing EPS will have an antidilutive effect. Therefore, no assumptions should be made. Only the weighted average actual outstanding shares should be used in computing EPS in this situation.

Jan. 1 Shares outstanding: 200,000 x 12/12   =   200,000
July 1   Issued for assets: 200,000 x 6/12   =   100,000
            Weighted average shares outstanding =   300,000   (Solution = b.)

TIP: You could calculate EPS using the basic formula and calculate diluted EPS assuming the exercise of the options and application of the treasury stock method. Because this would entail an assumption of $1,200,000 proceeds being used to buy back stock at $15 (average market price) per share, this would result in making adjustments to the denominator as follows:

- Add 60,000 shares because of assumed exercise of options.
- Deduct 80,000 shares because of assumed purchase of treasury stock with $1,200,000 proceeds from assumed exercise of options.

The net result of these assumptions is a **decrease** in the number of shares used to calculate diluted EPS, which indicates an antidilutive effect on EPS. Thus, these assumptions should **not** be made in the scenario described in this question.

QUESTION

8.   (L.O.6,7) Refer to the facts of Question 7 above. If the average market price of Tempo's common stock was $25 rather than $15 during 1999, what is the number of shares that should be used in computing diluted earnings per share for the year ended December 31, 1999?

a.   330,000
b.   448,000
c.   412,000
d.   320,000
e.   348,000
f.   312,000

Approach and Explanation: Use the treasury stock method to compute the number of shares to be used in determining diluted EPS. The weighted average number of shares actually outstanding is 300,000 (see Explanation to Question 7 above for this computation). The average market price of the common stock ($25) should be used in determining the number of assumed treasury stock shares in computing diluted EPS. The average market price ($25) of Tempo's common stock exceeds the option price ($20); thus the effect of assuming the exercise of the options and purchase of treasury stock with the assumed proceeds is dilutive. Thus, the computation of the number of shares used in computing diluted EPS is as follows:

Weighted average actual shares outstanding	300,000
Shares assumed issued upon exercise of options	60,000
Assumed shares purchased for the treasury ($1,200,000 ÷ $25)	(48,000)
Shares used for denominator of diluted EPS	312,000
	(Solution = f.)

TIP: A comparison of 312,000 shares (determined by use of the treasury stock method) with the weighted average number of common stock shares actually outstanding (300,000) indicates a dilutive effect on EPS.

QUESTION

9.   (L.O.6) Peter Wong Corporation had net income reported for 1999 of $880,000. During 1999 dividends of $120,000 were declared on preferred stock and $200,000 were declared on common stock. There were no changes in the 200,000 shares of common stock or the 40,000 shares of preferred stock outstanding during 1999. There were no potentially dilutive securities outstanding. The earnings per share to be reported for 1999 is:

a. $4.40.
b. $3.80.
c. $3.67.
d. $2.80.
e.   none of the above.

Approach and Explanation: Write down the basic EPS formula. Solve using the data in this question.

$$\frac{\text{Net Income - Preferred Stock Dividends}}{\text{Weighted Average Number of Common Shares Outstanding}}$$

$$\frac{\$880,000 - \$120,000}{200,000} = \underline{\$3.80}$$

(Solution = b.)

QUESTION
10. (L.O.7) A convertible bond issue should be included in the diluted earnings per share computation as if the bonds had been converted into common stock, if the effect of its inclusion is:

	Dilutive	Antidilutive
a.	Yes	Yes
b.	Yes	No
c.	No	Yes
d.	No	No

Explanation: A convertible security is a potentially dilutive security. All potentially dilutive securities should be included in the diluted EPS computation, if the effect of inclusion is dilutive. **No** antidilutive assumptions are to be made in computing diluted EPS. (Solution = b.)

QUESTION
11. (L.O.6) At December 31, 1998 Opal Company had 200,000 shares of common stock and 5,000 shares of 8%, $100 par value cumulative preferred stock outstanding. No dividends were declared on either the preferred or common stock in 1998 or 1999 On February 10, 2000, prior to the issuance of its financial statements for the year ended December 31, 1999, Opal declared a 100% stock split on its common stock. Net income for 1999 was $480,000. In its 1999 financial statements, Opal's 1999 earnings per common share should be:
    a. $2.40.
    b. $2.20.
    c. $2.00.
    d. $1.20.
    e. $1.10.
    f. $1.00.

Explanation:

$$\frac{\$480,000 - 5,000(8\% \times \$100)}{200,000 \times 2} = \underline{\$1.10}$$

Dividends on **cumulative** preferred stock are deducted in the numerator, whether declared or not. However, only the current year's preference is used; dividends in arrears for prior years do not affect the EPS computation. Stock dividends and stock splits are given retroactive treatment for all periods presented, even if they occur after the end of the current year, but before the financial statements are issued. (Solution = e.)

CHAPTER 18

INVESTMENTS

OVERVIEW

Oftentimes an entity has cash that is temporarily in excess of its immediate needs. That cash should be invested wisely so that it produces income while being a ready source of funds. Sometimes an entity invests in the stocks and bonds of other entities for long-term purposes. Accounting for both short-term (temporary) and long-term investments is discussed in this chapter.

SUMMARY OF LEARNING OBJECTIVES

1.   **Identify the three categories of debt securities and describe the accounting and reporting treatment for each category.** (1) **Held-to-maturity debt securities** are carried and reported at amortized cost. (2) **Trading debt securities** are valued for reporting purposes at fair value, with unrealized holding gains or losses included in net income. (3) **Available-for-sale debt securities** are valued for reporting purposes at fair value, with unrealized holding gains or losses reported as other comprehensive income and as a separate component of stockholders' equity.

2.   **Identify the categories of equity securities and describe the accounting and reporting treatment for each category.** The degree to which one corporation (investor) acquires an interest in the common stock of another corporation (investee) generally determines the accounting treatment for the investment. Long-term investments by one corporation in the common stock of another can be classified according to the percentage of the voting stock of the investee held by the investor. Refer to **Illustration 18-3** for a summary of the accounting and reporting for equity securities by category.

3.   **Explain the equity method of accounting and compare it to the fair value method for equity securities.** Under the equity method, a substantive economic relationship is acknowledged between the investor and the investee. The investment is originally recorded at cost but is subsequently adjusted each period for changes in the net assets of the investee. That is, the investment's carrying amount is periodically increased (decreased) by the investor's proportionate share of the earnings (losses) of the investee and decreased by all dividends received by the investor from the investee. Under the fair value method, the equity investment is reported by the investor at fair value each reporting period irrespective of the investee's earnings or dividends paid to the investor. The equity method is generally applied to investment holdings between 20% and 50% of ownership, whereas the fair value method is generally applied to holdings below 20%.

4.   **Describe the disclosure requirements for investments in debt and equity securities.** Unrealized holding gains or losses for the current period related to available-for-sale securities should be reported in other comprehensive income and the aggregate balance of net unrealized holding gains or losses should be reported in accumulated comprehensive income on the

balance sheet. A reclassification adjustment is necessary when realized gains or losses are reported as part of net income but also are shown as part of other comprehensive income in the current or in previous periods. Trading securities should be reported at aggregate fair value as current assets. Individual held-to-maturity and available-for-sale securities are classified as current or noncurrent, depending upon the circumstances. For available-for-sale and held-to-maturity securities, a company should describe: aggregate fair value, gross unrealized holding gains, gross unrealized holding losses, amortized cost basis by type (debt and equity), and information about the contractual maturity of debt securities. For the income statement, a company must disclose information about realized gains and losses and changes in unrealized holding gains and losses. In addition, proceeds from sales and the basis on which cost is determined should be reported.

5.   **Discuss the accounting for impairments of debt and equity investments.** Impairments of debt and equity securities are losses in value that are determined to be other than temporary, are based on a fair value test, and are charged to income.

6.   **Describe the accounting for transfers of investment securities between categories.** Transfers of securities between categories of investments are accounted for at fair value, with unrealized holding gains or losses treated in accordance with the nature of the transfer.

7.*   **Explain the accounting entries to record the transfer of securities.** Entries are required to be made to recognize holding gains or losses, if any, when transfers of financial instruments are made between categories.
         *This material is covered in Appendix 18-A in the text.

8.**   **Make the computations and prepare the entries necessary to record a change from or to the equity method of accounting.** When changing from the equity method to the fair value method, the cost basis for accounting purposes is the carrying amount used for the investment at the date of change. The new method is applied in its entirety once the equity method is no longer appropriate. When changing to the equity method, a retroactive adjustment of the carrying amount, of results of current and past operations, and of retained earnings is necessary to restate the accounts as if the equity method had been in effect during all of the periods in which the investment was held.
         **This material is covered in Appendix 18-B in the text.

9.***   **Discuss the special issues that relate to accounting for investments.** The special issues that relate to investments are: recognizing revenue from investments in equity securities; recognizing dividends received in shares of stock (stock dividends and stock splits); allocating cost between stocks and stock rights; accounting for changes in the cash surrender value of life insurance; and accounting for assets set aside in special funds.
         ***This material is covered in Appendix 18-C in the text.

10.****   **Identify the general rules for accounting and reporting of financial instruments.** Derivatives are assets or liabilities and should be reported in the financial statements. Fair value is the most relevant measure for financial instruments and fair value is the only relevant measure for derivatives. Special accounting for items designated as being hedged should be provided only for qualifying transactions.
         ****This material is covered in Appendix 18-D in the text.

TIPS ON CHAPTER TOPICS

TIP: An investment may be classified as a current asset (if it is a short-term investment) or as a noncurrent asset (if it is a long-term investment). For an investment in available-for-sale securities to be classified as a **current asset**: (1) it should be readily marketable, and (2) there should be a lack of management intent to hold it for long-term purposes.

TIP: Included in the long-term investment classification are the following: (1) long-term receivables, (2) long-term investments in stocks and bonds and stock rights of other entities, (3) restricted funds, (4) cash surrender value of life insurance, and (5) land held for future plant site.

TIP: When there is a price decline in a debt or equity security held as an investment, assume the decline is temporary unless otherwise indicated.

TIP: Changes in the valuation account for investment securities classified as trading should be included in the determination of **net income** of the period in which they occur. The amount of increase or decrease in the valuation account for investment securities classified as available-for-sale should be reported as a component of **other comprehensive income**; the amount of accumulated changes in this valuation account should be included in the equity section of the balance sheet and shown separately there as part of Accumulated Other Comprehensive Income.

TIP: The cost of an investment includes its purchase price and all other costs necessary to acquire the investment. Thus, the cost of an investment in stock or bonds is likely to include broker commissions and incidental fees.

TIP: Although premiums and discounts on investments in debt securities classified as current assets need not be amortized (because of the immaterial effect of doing so), premiums and discounts on investments in debt securities classified as long-term (noncurrent) assets should be amortized. The **effective interest method** is the prescribed method; however, the **straight-line method** is often justifiably used based on the immaterial difference between its results and the effect of the preferable method. Other names for the **effective interest method** include **present value method**, **compound interest method**, **effective yield method**, **yield method**, **interest method**, and the **effective method**.

TIP: **Accumulation of bond investment discount** is another way of referring to amortization of discount on bonds held as an investment.

TIP: If the effective interest method of amortization is used to account for an investment in bonds, the following relationships will exist:
1. The interest rate is constant each period.
2. The interest revenue is an increasing amount each period if the bond is purchased as a discount (because a constant rate is applied to an increasing carrying amount each period).
3. The interest revenue is a decreasing amount each period if the bond is purchased at a premium (because a constant rate is applied to a decreasing carrying amount each period).
4. The amount of amortization increases each period because the difference between the effective interest revenue and the cash interest widens each period.

TIP: Review **Illustration 14-2** for formats for common computations involving bonds payable. Think about how those same formats can be used to apply to computations involving an investment in bonds; the major difference is that the investor has an asset (rather than a liability) and interest revenue (rather than interest expense). Also, the investor lacks unamortized debt issue costs and will have a gain (rather than a loss) if the redemption price is higher than the bond's carrying value.

TIP: Review **Illustration 14-3** for the graph to depict interest patterns for bonds. Notice how that graph can be used to solve questions relating to bonds held as an investment; simply change interest expense to interest revenue when using the graph from an investor's viewpoint.

TIP: When the accounting period ends on a date other than an interest date, the amortization schedule for a bond investment is unaffected by this fact. That is, the schedule is prepared and computations are made according to the bond interest periods, ignoring the details of the accounting period. The interest revenue amounts shown in the amortization schedule are then apportioned to the appropriate accounting period(s). As an example, if the interest revenue for the six months ending April 30, 1999 is $120,000, then $40,000 of that amount would go on the income statement for the 1998 calendar year and $80,000 of it should be reflected on the income statement for the 1999 calendar year.

TIP: An investor who owns only a small percentage of the outstanding shares of stock of an investee should use the fair value method to account for the investment. If additional shares are purchased over time, the investor may find that at some point it is appropriate to change to the equity method. This change should be given retroactive treatment; that is, a catch up adjustment is recorded directly to the Retained Earnings account and to the Investment account to reflect balances that would exist if the equity method had been used in all prior periods during which this investment had been held.

TIP: A payment for an insurance premium is recorded by a credit to Cash for the amount paid, a debit to Cash Surrender Value of Life Insurance for the increase in that value during the period and a debit to Life Insurance Expense for the difference.

TIP: If cash is set aside for a special purpose, Cash is reduced and a fund account (restricted cash) is increased. An appropriation of retained earnings does **not** by itself establish a fund. Regardless of the composition of the assets in the fund, the entire balance of the fund should be reported as a noncurrent asset (in the Long-term Investments section) on the balance sheet as long as the fund is earmarked for a long-term purpose.

TIP: The amount reported for a sinking fund is affected by (1) additions or withdrawals to the fund, (2) earnings on assets in the fund, (3) gains or losses on the disposal of assets in the fund, (4) unrealized holding gains or losses on debt and equity securities contained in the fund, and (5) expenses of operating the fund.

TIP: In a general sense, **financial instruments** are defined as cash, an ownership interest in an entity, or a contractual right to receive or deliver cash or another financial instrument on potentially favorable or unfavorable terms. By this definition, traditional assets and liabilities such as accounts and notes receivable, accounts and notes payable, investment in debt and equity securities, and bonds payable are considered financial instruments. But the definition also includes many innovative and complex financial instruments such as futures, options, forwards, swaps and caps.

These innovative financial instruments are referred to as **derivative financial instruments** (or just simply "derivatives") because their value is derived from the value of some underlying asset, (i.e., stocks, bonds, or commodities) or is tied to a basic indicator (i.e., interest rates, Dow-Jones averages). The following are some of the most common financial instruments.

Traditional	Derivatives
Accounts receivable and payable	Interest-rate swaps and options
Corporate bonds and notes	Currency futures and options
Municipal bonds	Stock-index futures and options
Treasury bonds, bills, and notes	Caps, floors, and collars
Bank certificates of deposit	Commodity futures and options
Mortgages	Swaptions and leaps
Currencies	Collateralized mortgage obligations

ILLUSTRATION 18-1
SUMMARY OF INVESTMENTS IN
DEBT AND EQUITY SECURITIES (L.O. 1 THRU 4)

Investments in the stocks of other companies are often referred to as investments in **equity securities** or stock investments. Investments in the bonds of other companies are often referred to as investments in **debt securities** or debt investments.

The major categories for investments in debt and equity securities and their reporting treatments are summarized below.

Category	Balance Sheet	Income Statement
Trading (debt and equity securities)	Investments are shown at fair value. Current assets.	Interest and dividends are recognized as revenue. Unrealized holding gains and losses are included in income. Gains and losses from sale are included in income.
Available-for-Sale (debt and equity securities)	Investments are shown at fair value in current or long-term assets. Unrealized holding gains and losses are recognized in other comprehensive income and as a separate component of stockholders' equity.	Interest and dividends are recognized as revenue. Unrealized holding gains and losses are **not** included in net income; they are reported as other comprehensive income. Gains and losses from sale are included in net income.
Held-to-Maturity (debt securities)	Investments are shown at amortized cost (unrealized holding gains and losses are not recognized). Current or long-term assets.	Interest is recognized as revenue. Gains and losses from sale are included in income.
Equity method and/or Consolidation (equity securities)	Investments are carried at cost, are periodically adjusted by the investor's share of the investee's earnings or losses, and are decreased by all dividends received from the investee. Classified in long-term assets.	Revenue is recognized to the extent of the investee's earnings or losses reported subsequent to the date of investment (adjusted by amortization of the difference between cost and underlying book value). Gains and losses from sale are included in income.

ILLUSTRATION 18-1 (Continued)

TIP:	Investments in debt securities and investments in equity securities that are accounted for by the cost method (as opposed to the equity method) are categorized as follows:
Trading securities:	Debt and equity securities held with the intention of selling them in a short period of time (generally less than a month); held to generate income on short-term price swings.
Held-to-maturity securities:	Debt securities that the investor has the intent and ability to hold to maturity.
Available-for-sale securities:	Debt and equity securities that are not classified as trading or held-to-maturity; securities that may be sold in the future.

ILLUSTRATION 18-2
USE OF A SECURITIES FAIR VALUE ADJUSTMENT ACCOUNT (L.O.1,2)

The only time an accountant records an entry affecting the Securities Fair Value Adjustment (Trading) account or the Securities Fair Value Adjustment (Available-for-Sale) account is in the adjusting process at the end of an accounting period. Thus, when securities are purchased and/or sold during the period, the accountant **ignores** the related valuation account and its contents. The balance of a valuation account should be adjusted as needed at the end of the period by performing the following three easy steps for the related portfolio (after recording permanent impairments for any individual securities):

Step 1:   **Determine the total fair value:** Determine the aggregate fair value of the portfolio. This amount gets reported in the balance sheet.

Step 2:   **Determine the desired balance in the related valuation account:** Compute the difference between the aggregate cost and the aggregate fair value of the portfolio at the balance sheet date.

Step 3:   **Determine the amount of adjustment required:** Compare the result of Step 2 with the existing balance in the valuation account (which is the result of entries in previous periods, if any, and a reclassification adjustment, if any). The difference is the required adjustment (either increase or decrease in the valuation account).

TIP: Investments in debt and equity securities which are classified as trading or available-for-sale are initially recorded at cost, but they are to be reported at fair value at a balance sheet date. The writeup or writedown of such an investment will be accomplished by the use of a valuation account; thus, original cost information is preserved in the investment account.

TIP: If a decline in fair value is judged to be other than temporary for a security classified as available-for-sale or held-to-maturity, the cost basis of the individual security shall be written down to fair value as a new cost basis (thus, the investment account rather than the valuation account is credited). The amount of the writedown shall be accounted for as a realized loss and included in net income. The new cost basis is not changed for subsequent recoveries in fair value. Subsequent temporary changes in the fair value of an available-for-sale security are to be included in the separate component of equity.

TIP: Temporary price declines and subsequent recoveries of market value affect net income **only if** they relate to trading securities. Permanent price declines (impairments) affect net income regardless of which classification the related securities are in.

ILLUSTRATION 18-2 (Continued)

TIP: The journal entry to record an increase in the fair value of securities held as an investment would be as follows:

      Securities Fair Value Adjustment   xxx

           Unrealized Holding Gain or Loss   xxx

The entry to adjust the valuation account for the trading securities classification is the same as the entry to adjust the valuation account for the available-for-sale classification; however, a change in the valuation account for the trading securities classification goes through earnings, whereas a change in the valuation account for the available-for-sale classification does **not** get reported in the net income figure; rather it is reported as a component of other comprehensive income which is transferred to a separate component of stockholders' equity called Accumulated Other Comprehensive Income.

TIP: For the available-for-sale classification, notice that the balance of the Securities Fair Value Adjustment account will **always** be equal in amount to the balance of the Unrealized Holding Gain or Loss—Equity account (because they are both real accounts and are always involved in an entry to adjust the portfolio to fair value). However, for the trading classification, the balance of the Securities Fair Value Adjustment account will **rarely** be equal in amount to the balance of the Unrealized Holding Gain or Loss—Income account for the current period (because the adjustment account is a real account and the other account is a nominal account).

TIP: Market value is usually used as a measure of fair value for investments in debt and equity securities.

TIP: The accounts, Gain on Sale of Securities, Loss of Sale of Securities, Unrealized Holding Gain or Loss—Income, and Loss on Impairment, are to be classified as "other revenues, gains, expenses, and losses" on the multiple-step format for an income statement.

TIP: The balance of an investment account and its related valuation account are often combined and reported net on a balance sheet.

TIP: Significant net realized and net unrealized gains and losses that arise after the balance sheet date may be disclosed in the notes to the financial statements; they should **not** be reflected in the body of the statements.

TIP: If an investor purchases a security and later sells it for less than the security's cost, the investor has a **realized loss** (loss on sale of investment). If the market price of a security changes while an investor holds the security, changes in the market price (fair value) are referred to as **unrealized holding gains and losses.** Thus, if an investor purchased a security for $1,000 and the fair value is $700 at the balance sheet date, the investor has an unrealized holding loss of $300. If the security is one which is to be reported at fair value on the balance sheet, the writedown of the investment is accomplished by the use of a valuation account (Securities Fair Value Adjustment); thus, original cost information is preserved in the investment account.

ILLUSTRATION 18-2 (Continued)

The journal entry to record the decline in the fair value of the investment if the security is classified as trading is as follows:

```
Unrealized Holding Gain or Loss—Income.................................    XX
        Securities Fair Value Adjustment (Trading)......................           XX
```

The effects of this entry on the basic accounting equation and on net income are as follows:

$$A = L + OE \quad NI$$
$$\downarrow \qquad \downarrow \quad \downarrow$$

The journal entry to record the decline in fair value if the security is classified as available-for-sale is as follows:

```
Unrealized Holding Gain or Loss—Equity ....................................    XX
        Securities Fair Value Adjustment (Available-for-Sale)........           XX
```

The effects of this entry on the basic accounting equation and on net income are as follows:

$$A = L + OE \quad NI$$
$$\downarrow \qquad \downarrow \quad NE$$

A = Assets	L = Liabilities	OE = Owners' Equity
NI = Net Income	NE = No Effect	

From the above, you can see that changes in the valuation account (Securities Fair Value Adjustment) for investment securities classified as trading are included in the determination of net income of the period in which they occur. The amount of increase or decrease in the valuation account for investment securities classified as available-for-sale shall be reported as a component of other comprehensive income; the amount of accumulated changes in this valuation account are included in the equity section of the balance sheet and shown separately there as part of Accumulated Other Comprehensive Income.

ILLUSTRATION 18-3
ACCOUNTING AND REPORTING FOR
EQUITY SECURITIES BY CATEGORY (L.O.2, 3)

The accounting and reporting for equity securities depends upon the level of influence and the type of security involved, as shown below:

Category	Valuation	Unrealized Holding Gains or Losses	Other Income Effects
Holdings less than 20%[a]			
1. Available-for-sale	Fair value	Recognized in other comprehensive income and as a separate component of stockholders' equity.	Dividends declared; gains and losses from sale.
2. Trading	Fair value	Recognized in net income.	Dividends declared; gains and losses from sale.
Holdings between 20% and 50%[b]	Equity	Not recognized.	Proportionate share of investee's net income or net loss (adjusted for amortization of the difference between cost and the underlying book value); gains and losses from sale.
Holdings more than 50%[c]	Consolidation	Not recognized.	Not applicable.

[a]Unless there is evidence to the contrary, the investor is assumed to have only a little or no influence over the investee.

[b]Unless there is evidence to the contrary, the investor is assumed to have significant influence over the investee.

[c]The investor has a controlling interest in the investee.

EXERCISE 18-1

Purpose: (L.O.1) This exercise will quickly review the process of determining the required year-end entry to adjust the valuation account for an investment in debt securities classified as available-for-sale.

Nevercrash Airlines has a portfolio of marketable debt securities classified as available-for-sale securities, the first of which was acquired in 1998. The aggregate cost and fair value of the securities contained in that investment portfolio for five balance sheet dates are as follows:

Date	Aggregate Cost	Aggregate Fair Value	Net Unrealized Gains (Losses)
12/31/98	$ 142,000	$ 138,000	$ (4,000)
12/31/99	159,000	143,000	(16,000)
12/31/00	172,000	163,000	(9,000)
12/31/01	190,000	203,000	13,000
12/31/02	190,000	184,000	(6,000)

Instructions

At each balance sheet date, determine the following:

(a)   Reported value for the portfolio.

(b)   Desired balance in the related valuation account and indicate whether the desired balance is a debit or a credit.

(c)   Amount of adjustment required to the related valuation account and indicate whether the required adjustment to the related allowance account is a debit or credit.

Solution to Exercise 18-1

	(a)		(b)		(c)	
12/31/98	$138,000	FV	$ 4,000	credit	$ 4,000	credit
12/31/99	143,000	FV	16,000	credit	12,000	credit
12/31/00	163,000	FV	9,000	credit	7,000	debit
12/31/01	203,000	FV	13,000	debit	22,000	debit
12/31/02	184,000	FV	6,000	credit	19,000	credit

Explanation: Investments in debt securities which are classified as available-for-sale are initially recorded at cost, but they are to be reported at fair value at a balance sheet date. The writeup or writedown of the investment is accomplished by the use of a valuation account. A debit balance in a valuation account is needed when fair value exceeds cost; a credit balance in the valuation account is needed when cost exceeds fair value. The desired balance in the valuation account is the amount by which aggregate cost differs from aggregate fair value at the particular balance sheet date. The balance of the valuation account is adjusted, as needed, at each balance sheet date.

TIP: Apply the steps in **Illustration 18-2** in solving this exercise.

TIP: The portfolio in this exercise may be classified as a current asset or a noncurrent asset. The responses in this exercise are not affected by whether it is a current or noncurrent classification.

ILLUSTRATION 18-4
RECLASSIFICATION ADJUSTMENTS FOR
AVAILABLE-FOR-SALE SECURITIES (L.O.4)

As indicated in Chapter 4, changes in unrealized holding gains and losses related to available-for-sale securities are reported as part of other comprehensive income. Companies have the option to display the components of other comprehensive income (1) in a combined statement of income and comprehensive income, (2) in a separate statement of comprehensive income that begins with net income, or (3) in a statement of stockholders' equity.

The reporting of changes in unrealized gains or losses in comprehensive income is straightforward unless securities are sold during the year. In this situation, double counting results when realized gains or losses are reported as part of net income but also are shown in other comprehensive income as unrealized holding gains or losses in the period in which they arose (in the current period or in previous periods). Adjustments are to be made to avoid this double counting. Those realized gains must be deducted (or realized losses must be added) through other comprehensive income of the period in which they are included in net income to avoid including them in comprehensive income twice. These adjustments are referred to as **reclassification adjustments.**

> **TIP:** Net income for a period is closed to Retained Earnings. The total of other comprehensive income for a period is transferred to a separate component of stockholders' equity on the balance sheet called Accumulated Other Comprehensive Income. If the reporting entity has had more than one type of transaction reported as other comprehensive income, it must disclose accumulated balances for each classification in that separate component of stockholders' equity; this disclosure can be made on the face of the balance sheet, in a statement of stockholders' equity, or in the notes that accompany the financial statements.

EXERCISE 18-2

Purpose: (L.O.2) This exercise will review the accounting for investments in available-for-sale equity securities.

At December 31, 1997, Ed & Kay Hastings Company had no investments. One equity security is purchased for $34,680 on November 15, 1998; commission costs on the purchase amount to $320. At December 31, 1998, a balance sheet date, the fair value of that security is $32,000. At December 31, 1999, the security is still held and the fair value is $40,000. The security is classified as available-for-sale in noncurrent assets. On January 15, 2000, the security is sold for a price of $42,800.

Instructions

(a) Prepare the journal entry for the purchase of the security on November 15, 1998.
(b) Prepare the appropriate adjusting entry on December 31, 1998.
(c) Describe what will appear on the 1998 financial statements with regard to this investment.
(d) Prepare the appropriate adjusting entry on December 31, 1999.
(e) Describe what will appear on the 1999 financial statements with regard to this investment.
(f) Prepare the journal entry to record the sale of the investment on January 15, 2000.
(g) Prepare the appropriate adjusting entry on December 31, 2000.
(h) Describe what will appear on the 2000 financial statements with regard to this investment.

Solution to Exercise 18-2

(a) **November 15, 1998**

Available-for-Sale Securities	35,000	
Cash ($34,680 + $320)		35,000

(b) **December 31, 1998**

Unrealized Holding Gain or Loss—Equity	3,000	
Securities Fair Value Adjustment (Available-for-Sale)		3,000

(c) The investment will be reported at a net amount of $32,000 ($35,000 - $3,000) in the long-term investment section of the balance sheet at December 31, 1998. The unrealized holding loss of $3,000 is reported as a component of other comprehensive income (loss) and as a separate item in the stockholders' equity section of the balance sheet at December 31, 1998. Because, in this case, that item has a debit balance, it appears as a reduction of stockholders' equity.

(d) **December 31, 1999**

Securities Fair Value Adjustment (Available-for-Sale)	8,000	
Unrealized Holding Gain or Loss—Equity		8,000

(e)   The investment will be reported at the fair value of $40,000 ($35,000 cost plus $5,000 excess of fair value over cost reflected in the Securities Fair Value Adjustment account) on the balance sheet at December 31, 1999. The increase in market price of $8,000 during the period is reported as a positive component of other comprehensive income during the period. The net unrealized holding gain of $5,000 appears as Other Accumulated Comprehensive Income — a separate credit item in the stockholders' equity section of the balance sheet at December 31, 1999 (thus, it increases the total stockholders' equity balance).

(f)   **January 15, 2000**
Cash   42,800
        Available-for-Sale Securities   35,000
        Gain on Sale of Securities ($42,800 - $35,000)   7,800

(g)   **December 31, 2000**
Unrealized Holding Gain or Loss—Equity...   5,000
        Securities Fair Value Adjustment (Available-for-Sale)...........   5,000

Explanation: There is no investment held at December 31, 2000 and no need for a valuation account; hence, its entire balance is eliminated. The adjusting entry also eliminates the $5,000 balance in the related stockholders' equity account. This $5,000 entry also contains the amount of the reclassification adjustment.
(See Illustration 18-4).

(h)   There will be no investment and no separate component of stockholders' equity related to unrealized holding gains or losses on the December 31, 2000 balance sheet. The income statement for 2000 will reflect a $7,800 realized gain on sale of securities ($42,800 net selling price - $35,000 cost) in the "other revenues and gains" section of a multiple-step income statement. There will be a $5,000 reclassification adjustment shown as a deduction in other comprehensive income for 2000.

Approach: Follow the steps listed in **Illustration 18-2**.

> **TIP:** Some accountants would report the increase in market value during 2000 (selling price of $42,800 less fair value $40,000 at last balance sheet date = $2,800) as a component of other comprehensive income. If this is done, the reclassification adjustment described above must be increased by that same amount ($2,800) to $7,800.

EXERCISE 18-3

Purpose: (L.O.1,2) This exercise will review the accounting for an investment in trading securities.

On December 27, 1999, Dave Alexander Company purchased the following three securities for a trading portfolio:

Security	Cost
A	$ 12,000
B	20,000
C	30,000
Total	$ 62,000

On December 31, 1999, the three securities were still held and the respective fair values were as follows:

Security	Fair Value
A	$ 13,500
B	18,000
C	34,000
Total	$ 65,500

The three securities were all sold on January 2, 2000 for the following amounts:

Security	Sales Price
A	$ 13,500
B	18,000
C	34,000
Total	$ 65,500

No more trading securities were held or acquired.

Instructions

(a)   Prepare all journal entries related to these securities.

(b)   Describe what will appear on the financial statements for 1999 with regard to these securities. Assume a calendar year reporting period.

(c)   Describe what will appear on the financial statements for 2000 with regard to these securities.

Solution to Exercise 18-3

(a)   **December 27, 1999**

Trading Securities	62,000	
Cash		62,000

December 31, 1999

Securities Fair Value Adjustment (Trading)	3,500	
Unrealized Holding Gain or Loss—Income		3,500

January 2, 2000

Cash	65,500	
Trading Securities		62,000
Gain on Sale of Securities		3,500

December 31, 2000

Unrealized Holding Gain or Loss—Income	3,500	
Securities Fair Value Adjustment (Trading)		3,500

(b)   The securities will be reported at the fair value of $65,500 ($62,000 cost plus $3,500 excess of fair value over cost reflected in the securities fair value adjustment account) in the current asset section of the balance sheet at December 31, 1999. An unrealized holding gain of $3,500 will be reported in the "other revenues and gains" section of the income statement for the year ending December 31, 1999.

(c)   There are no securities reported on the balance sheet at December 31, 2000. The gain on sale of securities of $3,500 is reported in the "other revenues and gains" section of the income statement and the $3,500 unrealized holding loss is reported in the "other expenses and losses" section of the income statement for the year ending December 31, 2000.

> **TIP:**   Notice that the realized gain on sale of $3,500 during 2000 is offset by the unrealized loss of $3,500 (caused by the necessary adjustment of the valuation account). There was a net profit or gain of $3,500 from this investment and it was recognized during the period (1999) in which there was an increase in the fair value rather than in the period of sale.

EXERCISE 18-4

Purpose: (L.O.1,2) This exercise will illustrate how to account for investments in trading and available-for-sale securities.

Accolades Cruise Company has two investment portfolios at the December 31, 1999 balance sheet date. The securities contained in these portfolios are all equity securities and were purchased during 1999, Accolades' first year of operations. None of the investments are accounted for by the equity method. No investments were sold during 1999. Details are as follows:

Trading Portfolio

	December 31, 1999		
	Cost	Market	Difference
Stock of ABC Co.	$100,000	$ 80,000	$(20,000)
Stock of DEF Co.	70,000	92,000	22,000
Stock of GHI Co.	60,000	50,000	(10,000)
Total	$230,000	$222,000	$(8,000)

Available-for-Sale Portfolio--Long-term

December 31, 1999

	Cost	Market	Difference
Stock of JKL Co.	$140,000	$153,000	$13,000
Stock of MNO Co.	120,000	135,000	15,000
Stock of PQR Co.	150,000	121,000	(29,000)
Stock of STU Co.	160,000	136,000	(24,000)
Total	$570,000	$545,000	$(25,000)

Instructions

(a) Prepare the appropriate adjusting entry(s) at December 31, 1999.

(b) Explain how the data will be displayed on the balance sheet. Also, explain what will appear and where on the combined statement of comprehensive income for the year ending December 31, 1999. (Assume at the balance sheet date, Accolades has a balance of $600,000 in its Common Stock account, $400,000 in its Retained Earnings account, and $0 in Accumulated Comprehensive Income. Also, assume net income for 1999 is $92,000.)

(c) Assuming the stock of DEF Co. is sold for $94,000 on January 7, 2000 and the stock of STU Co. is sold for $141,000 on January 8, 2000, prepare the journal entries to record these sales and explain what will appear and where on the combined statement of comprehensive income for the year ending December 31, 2000.

SOLUTION TO EXERCISE 18-4

(a) Unrealized Loss—Income   8,000

       Securities Fair Value Adjustment (Trading)   8,000

    Unrealized Loss—Equity..   25,000

       Securities Fair Value Adjustment (Available-for-Sale)   25,000

Explanation: Investments in marketable equity securities are to be accounted for by the equity method if the investor has significant influence over the investee. When the equity method is inappropriate, the securities are accounted for by the cost method and are reported at fair value. With this latter method, the securities are first grouped into one of two portfolios: the trading portfolio or the available-for-sale portfolio. Each portfolio is to be reported at fair value. Thus, the total market value of the trading portfolio at the balance sheet date ($222,000) is compared with the total cost of the trading portfolio ($230,000) to determine the balance needed in the related valuation (market adjustment) account. If market value is lower than cost, a credit balance is needed in the valuation account for the excess of cost over market ($8,000 in this case). Thus, the market adjustment account is credited and an unrealized loss account is debited. The same comparison is made for the available-for-sale portfolio. The journal entry to establish a valuation account for the available-for-sale portfolio looks very similar to the journal entry to establish a valuation account for the trading portfolio but a major difference lies in the reporting of the unrealized loss (or gain) account [see part (b) of this exercise].

(b)
Balance Sheet

Current assets
    Trading securities, at fair value $222,000

Investments
    Available-for-sale securities, at fair value $545,000

Stockholders' equity
    Common stock $ 400,000
    Retained earnings   600,000
       Total paid-in capital and retained earnings   1,000,000
    Accumulated other comprehensive income
        Unrealized gains (losses) on securities   (25,000)
       Total stockholders' equity $ 975,000

Income Statement

Income from operations $100,000
Other expenses and losses:
    Unrealized loss on valuation of trading
       marketable equity securities   (8,000)
Net income   92,000
Other comprehensive income
    Unrealized holding loss   (25,000)
Comprehensive income $ 67,000

Explanation: Changes in the valuation account for the trading portfolio of marketable securities go through net income but changes in the valuation account for an available-for-sale portfolio are reflected as a component of other comprehensive income and as a separate component in stockholders' equity (i.e. in a contra stockholders' equity account in this case).

> **TIP:** If there had been transactions involving the available-for-sale securities in prior periods, the amount of unrealized holding gains or losses reflected in accumulated other comprehensive income on the balance sheet would very likely be unequal to the amount of unrealized holding gains or losses running through the other comprehensive income section of the combined statement of comprehensive income for the current period.

(c)
                           January 7, 2000
Cash   94,000
       Stock Investments—Trading   70,000
       Gain on Sale of Investments   24,000

January 8, 2000

Cash	141,000	
Loss on Sale of Investments..	19,000	
Stock Investments—Available-for-Sale		160,000

The sale of an investment (short-term or long-term) at a price other than its cost will result in a realized gain or loss to be reported in the Other Revenues and Gains or Other Expenses and Losses section of a multiple-step income statement. Thus, the $24,000 gain will be reported in the Other Revenues and Gains section and the $19,000 loss will be reported in the Other Expenses and Losses section of Accolades' income statement for the year of 2000. It is permissible to net the realized gains and losses for a period, in which case Accolades would report a gain of $5,000 in the Other Revenues and Gains classification on its income statement for the year of 2000.

TIP: The valuation account is not involved in recording the purchase or sale of securities during the period. The valuation account is adjusted **only** at the end of an accounting period.

TIP: Because $22,000 of the above $24,000 realized gains associated with DEF stock was reported as an unrealized holding gain in the prior year (as a part of net income and, therefore, a component of comprehensive income for 1999) and a loss of $24,000 ($160,000 - $136,000) was reported as an unrealized holding loss in the prior year (as a part of other comprehensive income for 1999), reclassification adjustments are to be made to avoid double counting these items in comprehensive income. These reclassification adjustments will result in the following being reported in a combined statement of comprehensive income for the year of 2000:

Net income	?
Other comprehensive income:	
Total holding gains or losses arising during	
the period	?
Reclassification adjustment for gains included	
in net income	(22,000)
Reclassification adjustment for losses included	
in net income	24,000
Comprehensive income	$?

EXERCISE 18-5

Purpose: (L.O.1) This exercise will review the accounting procedures appropriate for an investment in debt securities classified as available-for-sale or held-to-maturity.

A five-year $100,000 bond with a 7% stated interest rate and a 5% yield rate is purchased on December 31, 1998 for $108,660. The bond matures on December 31, 2003. Interest is to be received at the end of each year. The following amortization schedule reflects interest to be received, interest revenue, amortization of bond premium, and amortized cost of the bond investment at year end.

Date	Stated Interest	Effective Interest	Amortization	Amortized Cost
12/31/98				$108,660
12/31/99	$ 7,000	$ 5,433	$1,567	107,093
12/31/00	7,000	5,354	1,646	105,447
12/31/01	7,000	5,272	1,728	103,719
12/31/02	7,000	5,186	1,814	101,905
12/31/03	7,000	5,095	1,905	100,000
Totals	$35,000	$26,340	$8,660	

The following presents a comparison of the amortized cost and market value (assumed) of the bond at year end.

Date	Amortized Cost	Market Value	Difference
	$108,660	$108,660	
12/31/98	107,093	106,000	$(1,093)
12/31/99	105,447	107,500	2,053
12/31/00	103,719	105,500	1,781
12/31/01	101,905	103,000	1,095
12/31/02	100,000	100,000	0
12/31/03			

Instructions

(a)   Record the journal entries at December 31, 1998, December 31, 1999, and December 31, 2000, assuming the bond is classified as held-to-maturity.

(b)   Assuming the bond is classified as held-to-maturity, describe what will be reflected in the income statement and balance sheet prepared at December 31, 1999 and December 31, 2000 with regard to this investment.

(c)   Record the journal entries at December 31, 1998, December 31, 1999, and December 31, 2000, assuming the bond is classified as available-for-sale.

(d)   Assuming the bond is classified as available-for-sale, describe what will be reflected in the income statement and balance sheet prepared at December 31, 1999 and December 31, 2000 with regard to this investment.

(e)   Assuming the bond is classified as held-to-maturity, prepare the journal entry to record the sale of the investment if it is sold on January 2, 2001 for $107,250.

(f)   Assuming the bond is classified as available-for-sale, prepare the journal entry to record the sale of the investment if it is sold on January 2, 2001 for $107,250.

Solution to Exercise 18-5

(a)
December 31, 1998

Held-to-Maturity Securities	108,660	
Cash		108,660

> **TIP:** Although the issuer of the bonds sets up a separate account for premium or discount on bonds, an investor typically does **not** set up a separate account; rather, any discount or premium is reflected in the investment account.

December 31, 1999

Cash	7,000	
Interest Revenue		5,433
Held-to-Maturity Securities		1,567

December 31, 2000

Cash	7,000	
Interest Revenue		5,354
Held-to-Maturity Securities		1,646

(b) The bond investment would be reported in the long-term investment section of the balance sheet at amortized cost of $107,093 at December 31, 1999 and $105,447 at December 31, 2000. Interest revenue of $5,433 would be reported in the income statement for the year ending December 31, 1999 and interest revenue of $5,354 would be reported in the income statement for the year ending December 31, 2000. Interest revenue is classified as "other revenue" on a multiple-step income statement.

> **TIP:** Only debt securities can be classified as held-to-maturity because only debt securities have a maturity date; equity securities do not have a maturity date. Held-to-maturity debt securities are always reported at amortized cost. Held-to-maturity securities are always a noncurrent asset classification (long-term investments) unless their maturity date is within one year of the balance sheet date; then they are classified as a current asset.

(c)
December 31, 1998

Available-for-Sale Securities	108,660	
Cash		108,660

December 31, 1999

Cash	7,000	
Interest Revenue		5,433
Available-for-Sale Securities		1,567
Unrealized Holding Gain or Loss—Equity	1,093	
Securities Fair Value Adjustment (Available-for-Sale)		1,093

December 31, 2000

Cash	7,000	
Interest Revenue		5,354
Available-for-Sale Securities		1,646

Securities Fair Value Adjustment (Available-for-Sale).................	3,146[a]	
Unrealized Holding Gain or Loss—Equity		3,146

> [a]$107,500 market value - $105,447 amortized cost = $2,053 debit balance
> desired in valuation account.
> $2,053 debit balance desired + $1,093 credit balance existing = $3,146
> debit adjustment required for the valuation account.

(d)   An investment in an available-for-sale security is reported in the current asset or long-term investment section of the balance sheet at fair value at a balance sheet date. It is a current asset classification if the item is readily marketable and if there is a lack of management intent to hold on to it for a long-term purpose; otherwise, it is classified as a long-term investment. The investment in this exercise would be reported at the fair value of $106,000 at December 31, 1999 and $107,500 at December 31, 2000. An unrealized loss of $1,093 would be shown as a negative item (loss) in other comprehensive income and as a separate component of stockholders' equity (Accumulated Other Comprehensive Income) at December 31, 1999; an unrealized gain of $3,146 would be shown as a positive item in other comprehensive income and a net unrealized gain of $2,053 would be shown as a separate component of stockholders' equity at December 31, 2000. Interest revenue of $5,433 would be reported in the income statement for the year ending December 31, 1999 and interest revenue of $5,354 would be reported in the income statement for the year ending December 31, 2000.

(e)
January 2, 2001

Cash	107,250	
Held-to-Maturity Securities		105,447[a]
Gain on Sale of Securities...		1,803

> [a]$108,660 - ($1,567 + $1,646) = $105,447 balance

(f)
January 2, 2001

Cash	107,250	
Available-for-Sale Securities		105,447
Gain on Sale of Securities...		1,803

> **TIP:** At the end of 2001, there would no longer be any need for the valuation account, so the following entry would be made:
>
> | Unrealized Holding Gain or Loss—Equity .... | 2,053 | |
> |---|---|---|
> | Securities Fair Value Adjustment (Available-for-Sale)... | | 2,053 |

> **TIP:** The realized gain of $1,803 from the sale of the investment will be reported in the "other revenues and gains" section of the income statement for the year ending December 31, 2001. The $2,053 would be reflected as a debit type reclassification adjustment in other comprehensive income. This adjustment is needed to "back out" the net cumulative unrealized gains reflected in other comprehensive income in the current and prior years related to this security. This is appropriate because the realized gain of $1,083 is a component of net income this period and we don't want duplication of reported gains and losses (see **Illustration 18-4**).

EXERCISE 18-6

Purpose: (L.O.1) This exercise will review the factors involved in computing interest revenue using the straight-line method of amortization for bonds purchased at a discount between interest payment dates.

Tennie Pumps Corporation purchased bonds to be held as a long-term investment; they are classified as held-to-maturity. Tennie uses the straight-line method of amortization, reversing entries where appropriate, and a calendar year reporting period. Other facts are as follows:

Par value of bonds	$300,000
Stated rate of interest	10%
Purchase price	$287,960
Purchase date	March 1, 1999
Interest payment dates	January 1 and July 1
Maturity date	January 1, 2005

Instructions
(a)   Compute the interest revenue to be reported on the income statement for the year ending December 31, 1999.
(b)   Compute the interest revenue to be reported on the income statement for the year ending December 31, 2000.
(c)   Compute the interest revenue to be reported on the income statement for the year ending December 31, 2001.

> **TIP:** Recall that the straight-line method of amortization is not a generally acceptable accounting method. It can be used and not be considered a departure from GAAP when the results of its use are not materially different from the results of using the preferable effective interest method of amortization. This problem assumes an immaterial difference exists.

Solution to Exercise 18-6

Approach: Draw a T-account. Make all the entries that would be reflected in the Interest Revenue account for the period in question.

(a)

Interest Revenue			
3/1/99	5,000	7/1/99	15,000
		12/31/99	15,000
		12/31/99	1,720
		12/31/99 Bal.	26,720

Explanation:

3/1/99   **Payment of accrued interest at date of purchase.** A purchaser of bonds must pay the seller any interest accrued between the last interest payment date and the purchase date. This amount can be debited to the Interest Revenue account or to the Interest Receivable account on the purchaser's books. This solution assumes the former.

$300,000 x 10% = $30,000 interest per year.
$30,000 ÷ 12 = $2,500 interest per month.
$2,500 x 2 = $5,000 accrued interest at 3/1/99.

7/1/99   **Receipt of interest at interest payment date.** A full six months interest is received every interest payment date. Because the accrued interest at 3/1/99 was recorded in the revenue account, the entire receipt on 7/1/99 can be credited to the revenue account.

$2,500 x 6 months = $15,000.

12/31/99   **Accrual of interest at year end.** Six months have passed since the last interest receipt.

$2,500 x 6 months = $15,000.

12/31/99   **Amortization of discount for the year.** The discount is to be amortized over the 70 months that are between the purchase date (March 1, 1999) and the maturity date (January 1, 2005). Ten months of amortization pertain to 1999 (March 1 to December 31).

$300,000 - $287,960 = $12,040 discount.
$12,040 ÷ 70 months = $172 amortization per month.
$172 x 10 months = $1,720 amortization for 1999.

(b)

Interest Revenue			
1/1/00 Reversing	15,000	1/1/00	15,000
		7/1/00	15,000
		12/31/00	15,000
		12/31/00	2,064
		12/31/00 Bal.	32,064

Explanation:

1/1/00   **Reversal of last period's accrual.** The reversal causes a debit to the Interest Revenue account.

1/1/00   **Receipt of interest at interest payment date.** $2,500 x 6 months = $15,000.

7/1/00   **Receipt of interest at interest payment date.** $2,500 x 6 months = $15,000.

12/31/00 **Accrual of interest at year end.** $2,500 x 6 months = $15,000.

12/31/00 **Amortization of discount for the year.** $172 x 12 months = $2,064.

(c) $32,064.   Same explanation and solution as for part (b) of this exercise.

EXERCISE 18-7

Purpose: (L.O.1) This exercise will illustrate (1) the computations and journal entries for a bond investment purchased at a discount and (2) the accounting procedures required when the bond investment is sold prior to the bond's maturity date.

John and Martha Hitt Company purchased bonds to be held to maturity. The following details pertain:

Face value	$100,000.00
Stated interest rate	7%
Yield rate	10%
Maturity date	January 1, 2002
Date of purchase	January 1, 1999
Interest receipts due	Annually on January 1
Method of amortization	Effective interest
Purchase price	$92,539.95

Instructions

(a)   Compute the amount of purchase premium or discount.

(b)   Prepare the journal entry for the purchase of the bonds. Do not record the premium or discount separately in the accounts.

(c)   Prepare the amortization schedule for these bonds.

(d)   Prepare all of the journal entries (subsequent to the purchase date) for 1999 and 2000 that relate to these bonds. Assume the accounting period coincides with the calendar year. Assume reversing entries are not used.

(e)   Prepare the journal entry to record the sale of the bonds, assuming they are sold on January 1, 2001 for $102,000.00. Assume the sale occurs immediately after the annual interest receipt.

Solution to Exercise 18-7

(a)

Face value	$100,000.00
Purchase price	92,539.95
Discount on investment in bonds	$ 7,460.05

(b)

January 1, 1999

Held-to-Maturity Securities...	92,539.95	
Cash.		92,539.95

Explanation: The discount of $7,460.05 is reflected in the investment account because the instructions indicate the discount is not to be shown separately in the accounts. If a separate account were to be used, the entry would have included a debit to Held-to-Maturity Securities for $100,000.00, a credit to Discount on Held-to-Maturity Securities for $7,460.05, and a credit to Cash for $92,539.95.

(c)

Date	7% Stated Interest	10% Interest Revenue	Discount Amortization	Carrying Value
1/1/99				$ 92,539.95
1/1/00	$ 7,000.00	$ 9,254.00	$ 2,254.00	94,793.95
1/1/01	7,000.00	9,479.40	2,479.40	97,273.35
1/1/02	7,000.00	9,726.65[a]	2,726.65	100,000.00
	$ 21,000.00	$ 28,460.05	$ 7,460.05	

[a]Includes rounding error of $.69.

Explanation: Stated interest is determined by multiplying the par value ($100,000) by the contract rate of interest (7%). Interest revenue is computed by multiplying the carrying value at the beginning of the interest period by the effective interest rate (10%). The amount of discount amortization for the period is the excess of the interest revenue over the stated interest (cash interest) amount. The carrying value at an interest receipt date is the carrying value at the beginning of the interest period plus the discount amortization for the interest period.

> **TIP:** The amount of interest revenue of $9,479.40 appearing on the "1/1/01" receipt line is the amount of interest revenue for the interest period ending on that date. Thus, in this case, $9,479.40 is the interest revenue for the twelve months preceding the date 1/1/01 which would be the calendar year of 2000.
>
> **TIP:** Any rounding error should be plugged to (included in) the interest revenue amount for the last period. Otherwise, there would be a small balance left in the Investment in Bonds account after the bonds are extinguished.
>
> **TIP:** Notice that the total interest revenue ($28,460.05) over the three-year period equals the total cash interest ($21,000.00) plus the total purchase discount ($7,460.05). Thus, you can see that the purchase discount represents an additional amount of interest to be recognized over the time the bonds are held.

(d)	12/31/99	Held-to-Maturity Securities	2,254.00	
		Interest Receivable	7,000.00	
		Interest Revenue		9,254.00

Explanation: This entry records (1) the accrual of interest for twelve months, and (2) the amortization of discount for the first twelve months the bonds are held. This compound entry could be replaced with two single entries to accomplish the same objectives. The first entry would include a debit to Interest Receivable and a credit to Interest Revenue for $7,000.00. The second entry would include a debit to Held-to-Maturity Securities and a credit to Interest Revenue for $2,254.00. The two entry approach is sometimes easier to employ when reversing entries are used because the first of the two single entries can be reversed, but the second of the two single entries (the one to record the amortization of discount or premium) should **never** be reversed.

	1/1/00	Cash	7,000.00	
		Interest Receivable		7,000.00
	12/31/00	Held-to-Maturity Securities	2,479.40	
		Interest Receivable	7,000.00	
		Interest Revenue		9,479.40
(e)	1/1/01	Cash	7,000.00	
		Interest Receivable		7,000.00
		Cash	102,000.00	
		Held-to-Maturity Securities		97,273.35[a]
		Gain on Sale of Securities		4,726.65[b]

> [a]($92,539.95 + $2,254.00 + $2,479.40
> = $97,273.35 carrying amount)
> [b]($102,000.00 - $97,273.35
> = $4,726.65 gain)

TIP: Gains or losses on the sale of investments are to be classified in the "other revenues, gains, expenses, and losses" section of a multiple-step income statement. They very rarely meet the criteria to be classified as an extraordinary item.

EXERCISE 18-8

Purpose: (L.O.3) This exercise will allow you to compare the results of using the fair value and equity methods of accounting for an investment in stock.

On January 1, 1999, Magic Johnson Corporation acquired 100,000 of the 400,000 outstanding shares of common stock of Wilt Chamberlain Corporation as a long-term investment at a cost of $50 per share. The fair value and the book value of the investee's net assets were both $20,000,000 at January 1, 1999. Wilt Chamberlain Corporation paid a cash dividend of $2.00 per common share on September 5, 1999 and reported net income of $1,400,000 for the year ending December 31, 1999. The market value of the Wilt Chamberlain stock was $47 at December 31, 1999.

Instructions

(a)   Assuming Magic Johnson does **not** exercise significant influence over the investee, determine the following:

   (1)   Amount to report as investment (dividend) revenue for the year ending December 31, 1999.
   (2)   Amount to report as the carrying value of the investment at December 31, 1999.

(b)   Assuming Magic Johnson **does** exercise significant influence over the investee, determine the following:

   (1)   Amount to report as investment revenue for the year ending December 31, 1999.
   (2)   Amount to report as the carrying value of the investment at December 31, 1999.

Solution to Exercise 18-8

Approach: Mentally reconstruct the journal entries to record the transactions above. Draw T-Accounts for the investment and the investment revenue accounts. Enter the amounts as they would be posted to those accounts.

(a)   (1) $200,000.
       (2) $4,700,000.

Available-for-Sale Securities		Dividend Revenue	
1/1/99 $5,000,000^1			9/5/99 $200,000^2

   ^{1}100,000 shares x $50 = $5,000,000.
   ^{2}100,000 shares x $2 = $200,000.

Explanation: Because the investor does not exert significant influence over the investee, the investor should use the fair value method (as opposed to the equity method) to account for the investment. The investment should be reported at fair value at each balance sheet date. At December 31, 1999, the market value ($47 x 100,000 = $4,700,000) is lower than the cost ($50 x 100,000 = $5,000,000) of the shares held; thus a valuation account with a $300,000 credit balance is needed.

> **TIP:** In general, investments accounted for under the **fair value method** are maintained in the investment account at acquisition cost until partially or entirely liquidated. (A writedown of cost is appropriate when [a] a dividend received represents a liquidating dividend, or [b] operating losses of the investee significantly reduce its net assets and greatly impair its earning potential.) A valuation account (Securities Fair Value Adjustment) is used to record the difference between cost and fair (market) value so that the investment in stock is reported at fair value at each balance sheet date. Cash dividends received from the investee are usually recorded as dividend revenue. However, when the dividends received by the investor in periods subsequent to the purchase exceed the investor's share of the investee's earnings for the same periods, the dividends are to be accounted for as a return of capital; thus, the investor is to record a reduction of the investment's carrying value rather than revenue.

(b) (1) $350,000.
     (2) $5,150,000.

Investment in Wilt Chamberlain Stock				Revenue From Investment		
1/1/99	5,000,000	9/5/99	200,000[3]		12/31/99	350,000[4]
12/31/99	350,000[4]					
12/31/99 Bal.	5,150,000				12/31/99 Bal.	350,000

[3]100,000 shares x $2 = $200,000.
[4]100,000 ÷ 400,000 = 25% ownership; 25% x $1,400,000 = $350,000.

Explanation: The investor should use the equity method when the investment allows the investor to exercise significant influence over the investee. The investor recognizes its proportionate share of the investee's earnings by a debit to the investment account and a credit to investment revenue. When the investee distributes earnings, the investor records an increase in cash and a decrease in the carrying value of the investment. Because the cost of the investment was equal to the carrying value of the investee's underlying net assets, there is no amortization to be considered (which would affect investment revenue and the investment account balance) in this case. The market value of the shares at the balance sheet date is not relevant when the equity method is used.

> **TIP:** Under the **equity method**, the investment is originally recorded at cost and then subsequently adjusted by the investor's **proportionate share** of the investee's earnings and dividend payments. Income earned by the investee results in investment revenue and an increase in the investment account on the books of the investor. An investee's net loss or dividend payments reduce the investment account. When the investor acquires the stock at a price unequal to the book value of the investee's underlying net assets, the investor must amortize the difference between the investor's cost and the investor's proportionate share of the underlying book value of the investee at the date of acquisition. This amortization affects investment revenue and the investment account balance.

EXERCISE 18-9

Purpose: (L.O.3) This exercise will illustrate how to use the equity method of accounting for an investment in stock.

Deloitte Corporation acquired 30% of the 1,000,000 outstanding shares of Touche Corporation on January 1, 1999 for $3,240,000 when the book value of the net assets of Touche totaled $9,600,000. At January 1, 1999 Touche's plant assets, having a remaining life of ten years, had a fair value which exceeded book value by $700,000.

Touche Corporation reported net income of $1,600,000 for 1999 and $2,000,000 for 2000. Touche paid dividends of $400,000 on December 6, 1999 and $500,000 on December 5, 2000.

Instructions

(a) Prepare all journal entries for Deloitte Corporation for 1999 and 2000 that relate to this investment.

(b) Indicate the amount that should appear as investment income on Deloitte's income statement for (1) the year ending December 31, 1999, and (2) the year ending December 31, 2000.

(c) Indicate the amount that should appear as the balance of Deloitte's investment on: (1) the balance sheet at December 31, 1999, and (2) the balance sheet at December 31, 2000.

Solution to Exercise 18-9

(a)

1/1/99	Investment in Touche Company Stock	3,240,000	
	Cash..		3,240,000
12/6/99	Cash	120,000	
	Investment in Touche Company Stock........		120,000
	(30% x $400,000 = $120,000)		
12/31/99	Investment in Touche Company Stock	480,000	
	Revenue from Investment............................		480,000
	(30% x $1,600,000 = $480,000)		
	Revenue from Investment.................................	21,000	
	Investment in Touche Company Stock........		21,000
	(30% x $700,000 = $210,000; $210,000 ÷ 10 years = $21,000)		
	Revenue from Investment.................................	3,750*	
	Investment in Touche Company Stock........		3,750

*Computations:

Total book value of net assets of investee at 1/1/99	$9,600,000
Investor's percentage	30%
Book value of investor's share of investee's net assets	2,880,000
Cost of investment	3,240,000
Excess cost over book value of underlying net assets	360,000
Portion attributable to excess fair value over book value of net identifiable assets ($700,000 x 30% = $210,000)	(210,000)
Portion attributable to an unidentifiable asset (unrecorded goodwill)	150,000
	÷ 40 years
Annual amortization of goodwill	$ 3,750

12/5/00	Cash..	150,000	
	Investment in Touche Company Stock........		150,000
	(30% x $500,000 = $150,000)		

12/31/00	Investment in Touche Company Stock................	600,000	
	Revenue from Investment..........................		600,000
	(30% x $2,000,000 = $600,000)		
	Revenue from Investment.................................	21,000	
	Investment in Touche Company Stock........		21,000
	(30% x $700,000 = $210,000; $210,000 ÷ 10 years = $21,000)		

12/31/00	Revenue from Investment.................................	3,750	
	Investment in Touche Company Stock........		3,750
	(Same computation for annual amortization of goodwill as for 1999 above)		

Explanation: The equity method is an accrual method of accounting for an investment in stock. A portion of the investee's earnings is recorded as income by the investor in the same time period the investee earns it. Dividends received are recorded as a recovery of investment, not as income. (To record dividends as income would "double count" the amount already recorded as a share of the investee's earnings.)

The excess of the investor's cost over the carrying value of the underlying net assets on the investee's books must be determined and amortized. In this exercise, a portion ($210,000) of that excess is due to the fact that the investee has identifiable assets whose fair values are in excess of their carrying values; this portion should be amortized by the investor over the remaining life of the underlying assets (10 years in this case). The remaining excess cost over book value ($150,000) is attributed to an unidentifiable and unrecorded asset—goodwill. Because there is no indication of an amortization period to be used for goodwill, the maximum period of forty years is assumed to be appropriate.

(b)   (1) $455,250 for the year ending December 31, 1999.
       (2) $575,250 for the year ending December 31, 2000.

Approach: Post the amounts from the entries in part (a) to a T-account to solve.

Revenue from Investment

12/31/99	21,000	12/31/99	480,000
12/31/99	3,750		
12/31/99 To close	455,250	12/31/99 Balance	455,250
12/31/00	21,000	12/31/00	600,000
12/31/00	3,750		
		12/31/00 Balance	575,250

(c)   (1) $3,575,250 at December 31, 1999.
       (2) $4,000,500 at December 31, 2000.

Approach: Post the amounts from the entries in part (a) to a T-account to solve.

Investment in Touche Company

1/1/99	3,240,000	12/6/99	120,000
		12/31/99	21,000
12/31/99	480,000	12/31/99	3,750
12/31/99 Balance	3,575,250		
12/31/00	600,000	12/5/00	150,000
		12/31/00	21,000
		12/31/00	3,750
12/31/00 Balance	4,000,500		

EXERCISE 18-10

Purpose: (L.O.6) This exercise will apply the proper accounting procedures for reclassification of securities.

The Moylan Corporation has the following securities at December 31, 1998, a balance sheet date:

Trading Securities

	Cost	Fair Value	Net Unrealized Gain (Loss)
U.S. government bonds	$ 110,000	$ 103,000	$ (7,000)

Available-for-Sale Securities

	Cost	Fair Value	Net Unrealized Gain (Loss)
Equity securities	$ 174,000	$ 195,000	$ 21,000
Corporate bonds	150,000	168,000	18,000

All securities were purchased during 1998.

Instructions

(a)   Assume that on January 1, 1999 Moylan decides to transfer its equity securities to the trading portfolio. Prepare the journal entry(ies) necessary to record this transfer.

(b)   Assume that on January 1, 1999 Moylan decides to transfer its U.S. government bonds to the available-for-sale portfolio. Prepare the journal entry necessary to record this transfer.

(c)   Assume that on January 1, 1999 Moylan decides to transfer its corporate bonds to a held-to-maturity portfolio. Prepare the journal entry(ies) necessary to record this transfer.

Solution to Exercise 18-10

(a)   Unrealized Holding Gain or Loss—Equity 21,000
            Unrealized Holding Gain or Loss—Income 21,000

Trading Securities 195,000
      Available-for-Sale Securities 174,000
      Securities Fair Value Adjustment (Available-for-Sale) 21,000

Explanation: The equity securities are transferred to the trading security category at fair value, which establishes the new cost basis of that security. When this transfer occurs, the unrealized holding gain of $21,000 reflected in stockholders' equity related to the equity securities is eliminated by recognizing the unrealized gain in income of

1999. The cost of the securities ($174,000) is removed from the Available-for-Sale Securities account and the balance of the Securities Fair Value Adjustment account related to these securities is eliminated. A reclassification adjustment is needed to reflect a charge of $21,000 in other comprehensive income because the $21,000 reflected as a realized gain in net income of the current period (1999) also had been included in other comprehensive income as an unrealized holding gain in the prior period (1998) in which the holding gain arose. The $21,000 is deducted through comprehensive income in 1999 (which is the same year the $21,000 gain is included in net income) to avoid including it in comprehensive income twice.

(b)   Available-for-Sale Securities... 103,000
      Securities Fair Value Adjustment (Trading)...................................   7,000
           Trading Securities   110,000

Explanation: The U.S. government bonds are transferred to the available-for-sale category at fair value, which is the new cost basis of the security. When this transfer occurs, stockholders' equity and net income are not affected. The $7,000 net unrealized loss that was recognized in income in 1998 is not reversed. The trading securities account for these bonds and the related fair value adjustment account are eliminated.

(c)   Held-to-Maturity Securities... 150,000
      Securities Fair Value Adjustment (Held-to-Maturity)......................... 18,000
           Available-for-Sale Securities   150,000
           Securities Fair Value Adjustment (Available-for-Sale)...........   18,000

Explanation: The corporate bonds are transferred to the held-to-maturity category at fair value at the date of transfer. Upon transfer, the carrying value in the balance sheet and the net unrealized holding gain of $18,000 reported in stockholders' equity will remain the same. In this case, both the Securities Fair Value Adjustment (Held-to-Maturity) balance of $18,000 and the Unrealized Holding Gain—Equity of $18,000 (a stockholders' equity account that is one possible component of the classification Accumulated Other Comprehensive Income) are to be amortized over the remaining life of the bonds.

TIP:	Refer to **Illustration 18-5** for a summary of guidelines in accounting for transfers of securities from one category to another.

ILLUSTRATION 18-5
INVESTMENTS—ACCOUNTING FOR
TRANSFERS BETWEEN CATEGORIES (L.O.6)

Type of Transfer	Measurement Basis	Impact of Transfer on Stockholders' Equity	Impact of Transfer on Net Income
Transfer from Trading to Available-for-Sale*	Security transferred at fair value at the date of transfer, which is the new cost basis of the security.	None.	None (The unrealized gain or loss at the date of transfer will have already been recognized in income and should not be reversed).
Transfer from Available-for-Sale to Trading*	Security transferred at fair value at the date of transfer, which is the new cost basis of the security.	The unrealized gain or loss at the date of transfer carried as a separate component of stockholders' equity is reversed.	The unrealized gain or loss at the date of transfer is recognized in net income.
Transfer from Held-to-Maturity to Available-for-Sale*	Security transferred at fair value at the date of transfer.	The separate component of stockholders' equity is increased or decreased by the unrealized gain or loss at the date of transfer.	None (The unrealized holding gain or loss will be included in other comprehensive income).
Transfer from Available-for-Sale to Held-to-Maturity	Security transferred at fair value at the date of transfer.	The unrealized gain or loss at the date of transfer carried as a separate component of stockholders' equity is amortized over the remaining life of the security.	None

Statement No. 115 states that these types of transfers should be rare.

EXERCISE 18-11

Purpose: (L.O.9) This exercise will illustrate the proper accounting for the receipt of stock dividends and stock rights.

At January 1, 1999 Nickolodeon Corporation held the following available-for-sale securities classified as long-term investments. (Neither qualify for use of the equity method.)

	Cost
50,000 shares of Universal Studios Corp.	$ 1,650,000
30,000 shares of Hard Rock Cafe Corp.	1,050,000

The following transactions took place during 1999:
1. January 3, 1999: Received a cash dividend of $1.00 per share from Universal.
2. May 1, 1999: Received a 10% stock dividend from Universal.
3. June 5, 1999: Sold 10,000 shares of Universal for $35 per share.

4. July 1, 1999: Received one stock right for every share of Hard Rock Cafe stock held. The rights stipulate that four rights and $33 can be used to purchase one new share of common stock. The market value of the stock was $37 per share and the market value of the rights was $1.50 per right at this date.
5. July 19, 1999: Sold 10,000 of the stock rights received on July 1 for $1.75 per right.
6. July 30, 1999: Exercised 18,000 of the stock rights received on July 1.
7. October 1, 1999: Allowed the remaining 2,000 stock rights to elapse.
8. November 1, 1999: Sold 5,000 shares of Hard Rock Cafe stock for $39 per share. The FIFO method is used.

Instructions

(a) Prepare the journal entries to record each of the transactions listed above.
(b) Determine the investor's book value per share of the stock acquired on July 30, 1999.

Solution to Exercise 18-11

(a) 1. Cash.. 50,000
            Dividend Revenue 50,000
                (50,000 shares x $1 = $50,000)

2. Memorandum entry:
    Received 5,000 shares of Universal Studios stock in connection with a 10% stock dividend. This reduces the carrying value per share from $33 to $30 per share.

$$\frac{\$1,650,000 \text{ total cost}}{55,000 \text{ total shares}} = \$30 \text{ per share}$$

Explanation: If an investor in equity securities receives a **stock dividend**, no income is recorded and the carrying amount of the total investment remains unchanged. However, the carrying value per share of stock held is reduced.

3. Cash (10,000 x $35).. 350,000
            Available-for-Sale Securities.................................... 300,000
            Gain on Sale of Stock ($350,000 - $300,000) 50,000

4. Available-for-Sale Securities (Stock Rights)...................... 40,908
            Available-for-Sale Securities................................ 40,908

$$\frac{30,000(\$1.50)}{30,000(\$1.50) + 30,000(\$37)} \times \$1,050,000 = \text{cost of rights}$$

$$\frac{\$45,000}{\$45,000 + \$1,110,000} \times \$1,050,000 =$$

$$3.896\% \times \$1,050,000 = \$40,908$$

$$\$40,908 \div 30,000 \text{ rights} = \$1.3636 \text{ cost per right}$$

Explanation: When an investor receives **stock rights** for no consideration, the cost of the investment in stock must be allocated to the rights and to the stock based on the relative market values of the securities involved. The following formula can be used:

$$\frac{\text{Market Value of Rights}}{\text{Market Value of Rights + Market Value of Stock Ex-Rights}} \times \frac{\text{Total}}{\text{Cost}} = \frac{\text{Amount to}}{\text{Allocate to Rights}}$$

5. Cash (10,000 x $1.75).. 17,500
   Available-for-Sale Securities (Stock Rights)............   13,636
      (10,000 x $1.3636)
   Gain on Sale of Stock Rights.................................   3,864
      ($17,500 - $13,636)

6. Available-for-Sale Securities 173,045
   Available-for-Sale Securities (Stock Rights)............   24,545
      (18,000 x $1.3636)
   Cash 148,500*

   *18,000 ÷ 4 = 4,500 shares;
    4,500 shares x $33 exercise price = $148,500

7. Loss on Expiration of Stock Rights.................................. 2,727
   Available-for-Sale Securities (Stock Rights)............   2,727
      ($40,908 - $13,636 - $24,545 = $2,727)
      (or 2,000 x $1.3636 = $2,727)

8. Cash (5,000 x $39)... 195,000
   Available-for-Sale Securities...................................   168,182*
   Gain on Sale of Stock ($195,000 - $168,182)   26,818

*Initial cost of 30,000 shares	$ 1,050,000
Amount of cost allocated to stock rights	(40,908)
Amount of cost allocated to 30,000 shares	1,009,092
Number of shares in first lot	÷ 30,000
Cost per share held in first lot	33.6364
Shares sold	x 5,000
Cost of shares sold	$ 168,182

(b) Transaction 6: $173,045 cost ÷ 4,500 shares = $38.4544 per share.

ANALYSIS OF MULTIPLE-CHOICE TYPE QUESTIONS

QUESTION

1.   (L.O.1) At December 31, 1998, Bithlo Corporation reported the following for its portfolio of investment in marketable debt securities:

Investment in bonds, at cost	$ 400,000
Less securities fair value adjustment	39,000
	$ 361,000

At December 31, 1999 the market value of the portfolio was $389,000. The cost remained at $400,000. Under what circumstances would Bithlo report a $28,000 credit on its income statement for 1999 as a result of the increase in the market price of the investment in 1999?

a.   When the security is classified in the trading category.
b.   When the security is classified in the available-for-sale category.
c.   When the security is classified in the held-to-maturity category.
d.   No circumstances would call for such a credit of $28,000 on the 1999 income statement.

Approach and Explanation: Quickly review the guidelines in accounting for an investment in debt securities; they are:

Trading category: Report at fair value on the balance sheet. Changes in fair value are reported on the income statement.

Available-for-sale category: Report at fair value on the balance sheet. Changes in fair value are reflected in a separate component of stockholders' equity rather than as a component of income.

Held-to-maturity category: Report at amortized cost on the balance sheet. Changes in fair value are ignored. (Solution = a.)

QUESTION

2.   (L.O.2) ABC Studios holds four available-for-sale equity securities at December 31, 1999. They are all classified as long-term investments. All securities were purchased in 1999. The portfolio of securities appears as follows at December 31, 1999:

	Cost	Market Value	Difference
Barbara Walters Corp.	$100,000	$ 80,000	$(20,000)
Harry Reasoner Corp.	220,000	230,000	10,000
David Brinkley Corp.	210,000	150,000	(60,000)
Hugh Downs Corp.	140,000	145,000	5,000
Totals	$670,000	$605,000	$(65,000)

Assuming the decline in the market value of David Brinkley Corp. stock is considered to be other than temporary, the amounts of realized loss and unrealized loss to report as a component of net income for the year ending December 31, 1999 are:

	Realized Loss	Unrealized Loss
a.	$60,000	$5,000
b.	$60,000	$0
c.	$0	$65,000
d.	$0	$60,000

Explanation: A decline in fair value that is other than temporary is referred to as an **impairment**. Regardless of the category in which the security is classified, the security is written down to fair value. The amount of the writedown is accounted for as a realized loss and, therefore, included in net income. The fair value at the date of writedown is used as a new cost basis for the security. Temporary changes in the fair value of securities in the available-for-sale category are reflected as a component of other comprehensive income and in a separate stockholders' equity account rather than a component of net income. Thus, the $60,000 reduction in market value of David Brinkley Corp. stock is recorded as an impairment (charge to the income statement as a realized loss) and the remaining net unrealized loss [($20,000) + $10,000 + $5,000 = ($5,000)] is reported as a component of other comprehensive income and as a separate component of stockholders' equity and **not** a component of net income. (Solution = b.)

> **TIP:** If the same facts above were for securities classified in the trading category, the answer would be "a" because the temporary changes in fair value of a trading portfolio are recognized as an element of net income.

QUESTION

3. (L.O.1) The market value of Security A exceeds its cost, and the market value of Security B is less than its cost at a balance sheet date. Both securities are held as investments in debt securities; Security A is classified as trading and Security B is classified as available-for-sale. How should each of these assets be reported on the balance sheet?

	Security A	Security B
a.	Market value	Market value
b.	Amortized cost	Amortized cost
c.	Amortized cost	Market value
d.	Market value	Amortized cost

Approach and Explanation: Mentally review the accounting requirements for debt securities. They are summarized in **Illustration 18-1**. Investments in debt and equity securities classified as trading or available-for-sale are to be reported at fair value. Market value, if one is available, is used as a measure of fair value. Investments in debt securities classified as held-to-maturity are to be reported at amortized cost. (Solution =a.)

QUESTION

4.   (L.O.2) During 1998, Colquitt Company purchased 4,000 shares of Eichner Corp. common stock for $63,000 as an available-for-sale investment. The fair value of these shares was $60,000 at December 31, 1998. Colquitt sold all of the Eichner stock for $17 per share on December 3, 1999, incurring $2,800 in brokerage commissions. Colquitt Company should report a realized gain on the sale of stock in 1999 of:

a. $8,000.
b. $5,200.
c. $5,000.
d. $2,200.

Explanation: The gain is computed as follows:

Selling price ($17 x 4,000 shares)	$ 68,000
Cost of sale—commissions	(2,800)
Net proceeds (or net selling price)	65,200
Cost	63,000
Realized gain on sale	$ 2,200

(Solution = d.)

> **TIP:** The valuation account balance existing at the end of 1998 would have no effect on this computation.

QUESTION

5.   (L.O.1) An investor purchased bonds with a face amount of $100,000 between interest payment dates. The investor purchased the bonds at 102, paid incidental costs of $1,500, and paid accrued interest for three months of $2,500. The amount to record as the cost of this long-term investment in bonds is:

a. $100,000.
b. $102,000.
c. $103,500.
d. $106,500.

Explanation: The cost is determined as follows:

Purchase price (102% x $100,000 par)	$ 102,000
Incidental costs to acquire	1,500
Total acquisition cost of investment	$ 103,500

The cost of an investment includes its purchase price and all incidental costs to acquire the item, such as brokerage commissions and taxes. Any accrued interest is to be recorded by a debit to Interest Receivable or by a debit to Interest Revenue; it is **not** an element of the investment's cost. Accrued interest increases the cash outlay to acquire an investment but does not increase the investment's cost. (Solution = c.)

QUESTION

6.   (L.O.2) On its December 31, 1998 balance sheet, Simpson Company appropriately reported a $4,000 credit balance in its Securities Fair Value Adjustment (Available-for-Sale) account. There was no change during 1999 in the composition of Simpson's portfolio of marketable equity securities held as available-for-sale securities. The following information pertains to that portfolio:

Security	Cost	Fair value at 12/31/99
A	$ 50,000	$ 65,000
B	40,000	38,000
C	70,000	50,000
	$160,000	$153,000

What amount of unrealized loss on these securities should be included in Simpson's shareholders' equity section of the balance sheet at December 31, 1999?

a. $0
b. $3,000
c. $4,000
d. $7,000

Explanation: The Securities Fair Value Adjustment (Available-for-Sale) account would be increased by $3,000 to a $7,000 credit balance; hence the Unrealized Holding Gain or Loss account would be also adjusted to a $7,000 debit balance. The Unrealized Holding Gain or Loss account is reported as a separate line item in stockholders' equity; it reflects the net unrealized loss of $7,000 on this portfolio ($160,000 cost - $153,000 fair value = $7,000). It is one possible component of Accumulated Other Comprehensive Income. (Solution = d.)

QUESTION

7.   (L.O.3) An investor has a long-term investment in stocks. Regular cash dividends received by the investor are recorded as:

	Fair Value Method	Equity Method
a.	Income	Income
b.	A reduction of the investment	A reduction of the investment
c.	Income	A reduction of the investment
d.	A reduction of the investment	Income

Approach and Explanation: Write down the journal entry to record the receipt of cash dividends (other than liquidating dividends) under both the fair value and equity methods. Observe the effects of the entries. Find the answer selection that correctly describes those effects.

Fair Value Method			Equity Method		
Cash	XX		Cash	XX	
Dividend Revenue		XX	Investment in Investee Stock		XX

(Solution = c.)

QUESTION
8. (L.O.6) A debt security is transferred from one category to another. Generally acceptable accounting principles require that for this particular reclassification (1) the security be transferred at fair value at the date of transfer, and (2) the unrealized gain or loss at the date of transfer currently carried as a separate component of stockholders' equity be amortized over the remaining life of the security. What type of transfer is being described?

a. transfer from trading to available-for-sale
b. transfer from available-for-sale to trading
c. transfer from held-to-maturity to available-for-sale
d. transfer from available-for-sale to held-to-maturity

Approach: Mentally review the accounting requirements for transfers from one investment category to another. Refer to **Illustration 18-5** for a summary of these requirements. (Solution = d.)

QUESTION
9. (L.O.6) An investment in debt or equity securities may be transferred from one category to another. Assuming the fair value differs from cost at the date of transfer, which of the following will immediately result in reporting an amount on the income statement?

I. Transfer from available-for-sale to trading.
II. Transfer from held-to-maturity to available-for-sale.
III. Transfer from available-for-sale to held-to-maturity.

a. item I only
b. items I and II only
c. items I and III only
d. items II and III only
e. items I, II, and III

Approach and Explanation: Mentally review the accounting requirements for transfers from one investment category to another. Also review the effects of those requirements. Refer to **Illustration 18-5** for a summary of those requirements. (Solution = a.)

QUESTION
10. (L.O.9) A stock dividend received by an investor is accounted for by:

a. crediting the income statement for the market value of the shares received in the dividend.
b. crediting the income statement for the par value of the shares received in the dividend.
c. crediting the investment account for the market value of the shares received.
d. allocating the cost of the original shares to the original investment shares plus the dividend shares.

Explanation: Shares received as a result of a stock dividend or stock split do not constitute revenue to the recipients, because their interest in the issuing corporation is unchanged and because the issuing corporation has not distributed any of its assets. The recipient of such additional shares of stock makes no formal entry. The cost of the original shares purchased now constitutes the total carrying amount of both those shares plus the additional shares received. (Solution = d.)

QUESTION

11.   (L.O.9) Zion Company pays an insurance premium of $4,000 on a $100,000 policy covering the life of the company's president. As a result, the cash surrender value of the policy increases from $16,000 to $16,500 during the period. Which of the following is true regarding the effects of the journal entry to record the premium payment?

      I.   Cash is reduced by $4,000.
      II. Assets are reduced by $3,500.
      III. Stockholders' equity is reduced by $3,500.
      IV. Net income is reduced by $4,000.

    a.   items I and IV only
    b.   items I, II and III only
    c.   items I, II, and IV only
    d.   items I, II, III, and IV
    e.   none of the above

Approach and Explanation: Prepare the journal entry to record the premium payment:

Life Insurance Expense	3,500	
Cash Surrender Value of Life Insurance............................	500	
Cash...		4,000

Analyze the effects of each item in the entry. Expense is increased by $3,500, which reduces net income by $3,500 and, thus, causes a decrease in retained earnings (a component of stockholders' equity). The cash surrender value of life insurance is increased by $500; this item ($16,500) is reported as a long-term investment on the balance sheet. (In practice, some companies report it as an other asset.) Cash (a current asset) is reduced by $4,000. Because one asset increases by $500, and another decreases by $4,000, there is a net decrease in assets of $3,500. (Solution = b.)

CHAPTER 19

REVENUE RECOGNITION

OVERVIEW

The revenue recognition principle provides that revenue is to be recognized when (1) it is realized or realizable and (2) it is earned. This rule sounds simple enough, but the many methods of marketing products and services make it extremely difficult to apply in certain situations. Although a large percentage of entities find it appropriate to recognize revenue at the point of sale (delivery) of a good or service, other entities find it appropriate to use some other basis of revenue recognition which may result in recognizing revenue prior to delivery or at a point in time after delivery. In this chapter, we discuss accounting guidelines for the recognition of revenue.

SUMMARY OF LEARNING OBJECTIVES

1. **Apply the revenue recognition principle.** The revenue recognition principle provides that revenue is recognized when (1) it is realized or realizable and (2) it is earned. Revenues are **realized** when goods and services are exchanged for cash or claims to cash. Revenues are **realizable** when assets received in exchange are readily convertible to known amounts of cash or claims to cash. Revenues are **earned** when the entity has substantially accomplished what it must do to be entitled to the benefits represented by the revenues, that is, when the earning process is complete or virtually complete.

2. **Describe accounting issues involved with revenue recognition at point of sale.** The two conditions for recognizing revenue are usually met by the time a product or merchandise is delivered or services are rendered to customers. Revenues from manufacturing and merchandising activities are commonly recognized at the time of sale. Problems of implementation can arise because of (1) sales with buyback agreements, (2) revenue recognition when right of return exists, and (3) trade loading and channel stuffing.

3. **Apply the percentage-of-completion method for long-term contracts.** To apply the percentage-of-completion method to long-term contracts, one must have some basis for measuring the progress toward completion at particular interim dates. One of the most popular input measures used to determine the progress toward completion is the cost-to-cost basis. Using this basis, the percentage of completion is measured by comparing costs incurred to date with the most recent estimate of the total costs associated with the contract. The percentage that costs incurred to date bear to total estimated costs is applied to the total revenue or the estimated total gross profit on the contract in arriving at the revenue or the gross profit amount to be recognized to date.

4. **Apply the completed-contract method for long-term contracts.** Under this method, revenue and gross profit are recognized only at point of sale, that is, when the contract is completed. Costs of long-term contracts in process and current billings are accumulated, but there are no interim charges or credits to income statement accounts for revenues, costs, and gross profit. The entries to record costs of constructing, progress billings, and collections from customers would be identical to those for the percentage-of-completion method with the significant exclusion of the recognition of revenue and gross profit.

5. **Identify the proper accounting for losses on long-term contracts.** Two types of losses can become evident under long-term contracts: (1) **Loss in current period on a profitable contract:** Under the percentage-of-completion method only, the estimated cost increase requires a current period adjustment of excess gross profit recognized on the project in prior periods. This adjustment is recorded as a loss in the current period because it is a change in accounting estimate. (2) **Loss on an unprofitable contract:** Under both the percentage-of-completion and the completed-contract methods, the entire expected contract loss must be recognized in the current period.

6. **Identify alternative revenue recognition bases before delivery.** Three additional revenue recognition bases are: (1) **The completion of production basis:** Revenue is recognized at the completion of production even though no sale has been made. (2) **The accretion basis:** Accretion is the increase in value resulting from natural growth or aging processes. (3) **The discovery basis:** It is based on the significance of discovery in the earning process and the view that the product's market price can be reasonably estimated. Only the completion of production basis is permitted by GAAP.

7. **Describe the installment method of accounting.** The installment method (sometimes called the installment sales method) recognizes income in the periods of collection rather than in the period of sale. The installment method of accounting is justified on the premise that when there is no reasonable basis for estimating the degree of collectibility, revenue should not be recognized until cash is collected.

8. **Explain the cost recovery method of accounting.** Under the cost recovery method, no profit is recognized until cash payments by the buyer exceed the seller's cost of the merchandise sold. After all costs have been recovered, any additional cash collections are included in income. The income statement for the period of sale reports sales revenue, the cost of goods sold, and the gross profit—both the amount that is recognized during the period and the amount that is deferred. The deferred gross profit is offset against the related receivable on the balance sheet. Subsequent income statements report the gross profit as a separate item of revenue when it is recognized as earned.

9.* **Explain revenue recognition for franchises and consignment sales.** In a franchise arrangement, the initial franchise fee is recorded as revenue when and as the franchisor makes substantial performance of the services it is obligated to perform and collection of the fee is reasonably assured. Continuing franchise fees are recognized as revenue when they are earned and receivable from the franchisee. Revenue is recognized by the consignor when an account sales and the cash are received from the consignee. An account sales is a document that shows the merchandise received by the consignee, merchandise sold, expenses chargeable to the consignment, and the cash remitted.

    *This material is covered in Appendix 19-A in the text.

TIPS ON CHAPTER TOPICS

TIP: All revenues cause an increase in net assets (owners' equity); thus, a revenue item also results in either an increase in assets or a decrease in liabilities. **Revenues** are defined in *SFAC No. 6* as: "Inflows of assets and/or settlements of liabilities from delivering or producing goods, rendering services, or other earning activities that constitute an enterprise's ongoing major or central operations during a period."

TIP: The amount of revenue for a period is generally determined independently of expenses. The **revenue recognition principle** is applied to determine in what period(s) revenue transactions are to be reported. Then the **matching principle** is applied to determine in what period(s) expense transactions are to be reported; expenses are to be recognized in the same period as the revenues to which the expenses contributed.

TIP: To **recognize** means to give expression in the accounts. To recognize a revenue means to record an item as revenue in the accounts; thus, the item will get reported as revenue in the financial statements. Likewise, to recognize an asset means to record an increase in an asset account. **Recognition** is "the process of formally recording or incorporating an item in the accounts and financial statements of an entity" (*SFAC No. 6*, par. 143). "Recognition includes depiction of an item in both words and numbers, with the amount included in the totals of the financial statements" (*SFAC No. 5*, par. 6). For an asset or liability, recognition involves recording not only acquisition or incurrence of the item but also later changes in it, including removal from the financial statements.

TIP: Recognition is **not** the same as realization, although the two are sometimes used interchangeably in accounting literature and practice. **Realization** is "the process of converting noncash resources and rights into money and is most precisely used in accounting and financial reporting to refer to sales of assets for cash or claims to cash" (*SFAC No. 6*, par. 143).

TIP: In accordance with the revenue recognition principle: (a) revenue from selling products is recognized at the date of sale, usually interpreted to mean the date of delivery to customers; (b) revenue from services rendered is recognized when services have been performed and are billable; (c) revenue from permitting others to use enterprise assets such as interest, rent, and royalties, is recognized as time passes or as the assets are used; and, (d) revenue from disposing of assets other than products is recognized at the date of sale.

TIP: Revenue is a gross amount (an amount before costs are deducted); whereas, gain is a net amount (an amount after costs are subtracted). Gains (as contrasted to revenues) commonly result from transactions and other events that do not involve an earning process. For gain recognition, being earned is generally less significant than being realized or realizable. Gains are commonly recognized at the time of sale of an asset, disposition of a liability, or when prices of certain assets change. The following example illustrates how revenue is a gross concept, and gain is a net concept.

A company sells two assets for $1,000 each. The first asset is an inventory item which cost $600. The second asset is a piece of equipment which cost $900 and has been depreciated $300 thus far. The first item would cause the following to be reflected in the income statement:

Sales revenue	$1,000
Cost of goods sold	600
Gross profit	$ 400

The second item would cause the following to be reflected in the "other income" section of a multiple-step income statement:

Gain on sale of equipment $400*
     *$900 cost - $300 accumulated depreciation = $600 carrying value
     $1,000 selling price - $600 carrying value = $400 gain

In the case of the second item, it is not an item held for sale in the main course of business. The proceeds ($1,000) and the related cost (carrying value of $600) are netted off the statement, and only the net amount ($400 gain) appears on the face of the income statement.

TIP: The revenue recognition bases or methods, the criteria for their use, and the reasons for departing from the sale basis when accounting for the sale of a product are summarized in **Illustration 19-2**. Review those methods and be able to explain when and why they are used.

TIP: The term **income** is sometimes used to refer to a gross amount (such as dividend income, rent income, interest income) which makes its usage synonymous with revenue. The term income is also used to refer to a net amount, such as net income for a period. Thus, if an exam question asks for the computation of income to be recognized for the current period for a long-term construction contract using the percentage-of-completion method, it may be unclear whether the question is using "income" to mean "revenue" or if "income" means "gross profit" (revenue net of related costs). If it is a multiple choice question, a computation for both revenue and gross profit may quickly solve the mystery.

TIP: The percentage of completion method is used for long-term construction contracts where revenue is appropriately recognized during production (prior to completion and delivery). Justification for recognition of revenue during the construction period is based on the fact that the ultimate sale and the selling price are assured by the contract. The percentage-of-completion method recognizes revenue, costs, and gross profit as progress is made toward completion on a long-term contract. The progress made during a period may be supplied by engineering estimates or determined by the cost-to-cost method (the latter method is used in most textbook situations). Using the cost-to-cost method, the amounts of revenue and gross profit to be recognized each period are computed using the following formula:

$$\left[\frac{\text{Costs incurred to date}}{\text{Estimate of total costs}} \times \begin{array}{c} \text{Estimated total} \\ \text{revenue (or} \\ \text{gross profit)} \end{array} \right] - \begin{array}{c} \text{Total revenue (or gross} \\ \text{profit) recognized} \\ \text{in prior periods} \end{array} = \begin{array}{c} \text{Current period} \\ \text{revenue (or} \\ \text{gross profit)} \end{array}$$

In this formula, estimated total revenue is determined by the contract price, and estimated total gross profit is determined by the contract price reduced by an estimate of total costs. The estimate of total costs includes costs incurred to date **plus** an estimate of remaining costs to be incurred to complete the contract. Costs incurred to date include costs incurred in prior periods **plus** costs incurred in the current period.

TIP: Regardless of whether the percentage-of-completion method or the completed-contract method is used, the difference between the balance of the Construction in Process account and the balance of the Billings on Construction in Process account is reported as a current liability (if Billings on Construction in Process has the larger balance) or as a current asset (if Construction in Process has the larger balance). The balance of the Billings on Construction in Process account is offset against the balance of the inventory account (Construction in Process) because the inventory amount should not be double counted (i.e., the inventory account was not removed when the Accounts Receivable account was increased at the date of a billing to a customer).

TIP: The **installment method of revenue recognition** emphasizes collection of the selling price rather than the sale. It recognizes income in the periods of collection rather than in the period of sale. The installment method is **not** a generally accepted method; it is to be used only for situations where uncollectible accounts cannot be reasonably estimated at the time of sale.

TIP: When using the **installment method of accounting**, the amount of gross profit to be recognized for a particular period is determined by multiplying the amount of cash collected during the period on installment receivables by the appropriate gross profit percentage(s). A rather difficult exam question may give the amount of gross profit recognized along with the gross profit percentage and require the examinee to solve for the amount of cash collected. For example, if gross profit recognized for 1999 is $90,000 and the gross profit percentage is 30%, cash collections during the period amount to $300,000 ($90,000 + 30% = $300,000).

TIP: Inventory on consignment should be reported as inventory by the consignor, not the consignee.

ILLUSTRATION 19-1
JOURNAL ENTRIES FOR LONG-TERM CONSTRUCTION CONTRACTS (L.O.3,4)

ENTRY	PERCENTAGE-OF-COMPLETION METHOD	COMPLETED-CONTRACT METHOD

To record costs of construction	Construction in Process
	    Materials, Cash, Payables, etc.
		Construction in Process
		    Materials, Cash, Payables, etc.

To record progress billings	Accounts Receivable
	    Billings on Construction in Process
		Accounts Receivable
		    Billings on Construction in Process

To record collections	Cash
	    Accounts Receivable
		Cash
		    Accounts Receivable

To recognize revenue and gross profit	Construction in Process GP** Construction Expenses COSTS Revenue from Long-Term Contracts REV	No Entry.*

To record final approval of the contract	Billings on Construction in Process
	    Construction in Process
		Billings on Const. in Process REV
		    Revenue from Long-Term Contracts REV
		Construction Expenses*** COSTS
		    Construction in Process COSTS

GP = Gross Profit   COSTS = Costs Incurred   REV = Revenue

*A loss on an unprofitable contract is recognized, in full, immediately under either method. A loss would be recorded under the completed-contract method by a debit to Loss from Long-Term Contracts and a credit to Construction in Process for the estimated amount of loss.

**When a loss is estimated, this account (Construction in Proces) gets credited for the estimated amount of loss. The rest of the entry is the same as what is shown for a profitable situation.

***The account Construction Expenses can be titled Construction Costs or Costs of Construction.

TIP: An estimated loss on a long-term construction contract is to be recognized in the period it is determined there will ultimately be a loss on completion of the contract, regardless of the method being used to account for the contract. The justification for recognizing the loss before completion even under the completed-contract method lies with the conservatism constraint and the axiom—anticipate no profits but provide for all losses.

ILLUSTRATION 19-2
REVENUE RECOGNITION BASES OTHER THAN
THE SALE BASIS FOR PRODUCTS (L.O.3,4,6,7,8)

Recognition Basis (or Method of Applying a Basis)	Criteria for Use of Basis	Reason(s) for Departing from Sale Basis
Percentage-of-completion method	Long-term construction of property; dependable estimates of extent of progress and cost to complete; reasonable assurance of collectibility of contract price; expectation that both contractor and buyer can meet obligations; and absence of inherent hazards that make estimates doubtful.	Availability of evidence of ultimate proceeds; better measure of periodic income; avoidance of fluctuations in revenues, expenses, and income; performance is a "continuous sale" and therefore not a departure from the sale basis.
Completed-contract method	Use on short-term contracts, and whenever percentage-of-completion criteria are not met for long-term contracts.	Existence of inherent hazards in the contract beyond the normal, recurring business risks; conditions for using the percentage-of-completion method are absent.
Completion-of-production basis	Immediate marketability at quoted prices; unit interchangeability; difficulty of determining costs; and no significant distribution costs.	Known or determinable revenues; inability to determine costs and thereby defer expense recognition until sale.
Accretion basis	Criteria unspecified because accretion basis is not permitted by authoritative literature.	Possible support for recognizing accretion as revenue includes product marketability at known prices and desirability of recognizing changes in assets.
Discovery basis	Criteria unspecified because discovery basis is not permitted by authoritative literature.	Possible support for recognizing revenue at time natural resources are discovered includes the significance of discovery in the earning process and the view that sales prices can be estimated.
Installment sales method and cost recovery method	Absence of a reasonable basis for estimating degree of collectibility and costs of collection.	Collectibility of the receivable is so uncertain that gross profit (or income) is not recognized until cash is actually received.
Deposit method	Cash received before the sales transaction is completed.	No recognition of revenue and income because there is not sufficient transfer of the risks and rewards of ownership.

Source: Adapted from *Survey of Present Practices in Recognizing Revenues, Expenses, Gains, and Losses*, FASB, 1981, pp. 12 and 13.

EXERCISE 19-1

Purpose: (L.O.3,4) This exercise will allow you to compare the results of using the percentage-of-completion method versus the results of applying the completed-contract method to compute the amount of gross profit to be recognized in each year of a three-year contract.

At the beginning of 1999, Buildalot Construction Company signed a fixed-price contract to construct a sports arena at a price of $26,000,000. Information relating to the costs and billings for this contract is as follows:

	1999	2000	2001
Costs incurred during the period	$ 8,320,000	$11,360,000	$ 3,520,000
Estimated costs to complete, as of December 31	12,480,000	4,320,000	-0-
Billings during the year	3,900,000	15,900,000	6,200,000
Collections during the year	3,120,000	12,000,000	10,880,000

Instructions

(a)   Assuming the completed-contract method is used, compute the gross profit to be recognized in (1) 1999, (2) 2000, and (3) 2001.

(b)   Assuming the percentage-of-completion method is used, compute the gross profit to be recognized in (1) 1999, (2) 2000, and (3) 2001.

(c)   Assuming the percentage-of-completion method is used, show how the details related to this construction contract would be disclosed on the balance sheet at December 31, 2000.

Solution to Exercise 19-1

(a) (1)   1999   -0-
    (2)   2000   -0-
    (3)   2001 $2,800,000*

         *Computations:
         Total revenue $26,000,000
         Total costs incurred   23,200,000**
         Total gross profit $ 2,800,000

              **Costs incurred in 1999 $ 8,320,000
                Costs incurred in 2000   11,360,000
                Costs incurred in 2001   3,520,000
                Total costs incurred $23,200,000

Explanation: When the completed-contract method is used, the recognition of all revenue and related costs (and, therefore, resulting gross profit) is deferred until the period of completion (2001 in this case). The only exception to this guideline is in the case where a loss is expected. A loss should be recognized immediately in the period in which it is determined that a loss will result.

(b) (1) 1999 $2,080,000
    (2) 2000 $ (440,000)
    (3) 2001 $1,160,000

Computations:

1999: Costs incurred to date (12/31/99) $ 8,320,000
       Estimated costs to complete as of 12/31/99   12,480,000
       Estimate of total costs as of 12/31/99 $ 20,800,000

       Total revenue (contract price) $ 26,000,000
       Estimate of total costs   20,800,000
       Estimated total gross profit $ 5,200,000

$$\frac{\$8,320,000}{\$20,800,000} \times \$5,200,000 = \underline{\$2,080,000} \quad \text{Gross profit to be recognized in 1999}$$

2000: Costs incurred to date (12/31/00)($8,320,000 + $11,360,000) $ 19,680,000
       Estimated costs to complete as of 12/31/00   4,320,000
       Estimate of total costs as of 12/31/00 $ 24,000,000

       Total revenue (contract price) $26,000,000
       Estimate of total costs   24,000,000
       Estimated total gross profit $ 2,000,000

$$\frac{\$19,680,000}{\$24,000,000} \times \$2,000,000 - \$2,080,000 = \underline{\$(440,000)} \quad \text{Loss to be recognized in 2000}$$

2001: Costs incurred in 1999 $ 8,320,000
       Costs incurred in 2000   11,360,000
       Costs incurred in 2001   3,520,000
       Total costs incurred   23,200,000

       Total revenue (contract price) $26,000,000
       Total costs incurred   23,200,000
       Total gross profit earned on contract   2,800,000
       Gross profit recognized in 1999   (2,080,000)
       Loss recognized in 2000   440,000
       Gross profit to be recognized in 2001 $ 1,160,000

Approach and Explanation: Gross profit to be recognized in a particular year can be determined by applying the following formula:

$$\left[\frac{\text{Costs incurred to date}}{\text{Estimate of total costs}} \times \begin{matrix}\text{Estimated total} \\ \text{gross profit)}\end{matrix} \right] - \begin{matrix}\text{Total gross} \\ \text{profit recognized} \\ \text{in prior periods}\end{matrix} = \begin{matrix}\text{Current period} \\ \text{gross profit}\end{matrix}$$

In the computation for estimated total gross profit, the current (most up-to-date) estimate of total costs is deducted from total revenue (the contract price). The estimate of total costs is likely to change every year which will cause the estimated total gross profit to change each year. Such is the case in this exercise.

In the second year of the contract, Buildalot's cost estimates increased dramatically, which caused the gross profit recognized to date (1999's gross profit of $2,080,000) to exceed the $1,640,000 total gross profit earned to date ($19,680,000 ÷ $24,000,000 x $2,000,000 = $1,640,000). This excess is recognized as a loss of $440,000 in 2000 to bring the total gross profit recognized by the end of 2000 to $1,640,000.

In the last year of the contract, total costs incurred on the contract are deducted from total revenue on the contract to arrive at total gross profit earned on the contract. The amounts reported on prior income statements as gross profit (loss) are deducted from (added to) this amount to arrive at the gross profit to recognize in the last period.

In the situation at hand, the costs incurred in 2001 are less than what was expected, according to the cost estimates at the end of 2000, which results in more total gross profit than was predicted at the end of 2000.

TIP: Notice that **neither** the amount of billings **nor** the amount of cash collections during the year has an impact on the amount of gross profit to be recognized.

TIP: Notice that a loss was recognized in the second year using the percentage-of-completion method but no loss was recognized using the completed-contract method. The reasons for this is that the loss was an interim loss, not an overall loss on the contract. An interim loss refers to the loss that results when the total gross profit to date (at the end of 2000) is less than the amount of gross profit recognized in prior periods (1999). It is a loss in the current period (2000) on a profitable contract. It results from an increase in estimated costs which requires a current period adjustment of excess gross profit recognized on the contract in prior periods. This adjustment is recorded in the current period because it is a change in accounting estimate. If an overall loss is expected on a contract, it must also be recognized immediately even under the completed-contract method.

(c)   Current assets:

Accounts receivable		$4,680,000
Inventories		
Construction in process	$21,320,000	
Less: Billings on construction in process	19,800,000	
Costs and recognized profit in excess of billings		$1,520,000

Approach and Explanation: Draw T-accounts. Mentally think through the journal entries that would be recorded for the facts given. Post these amounts to the T-accounts on paper.

Accounts Receivable			
1999	3,900,000	1999	3,120,000
2000	15,900,000	2000	12,000,000
12/31/00			
Bal.	4,680,000		

Construction in Process			
1999	8,320,000	2000	440,000
1999	2,080,000		
2000	11,360,000		
12/31/00			
Bal.	21,320,000		

Billings on Construction in Process			
		1999	3,900,000
		2000	15,900,000
		12/31/00	
		Bal.	19,800,000

> **TIP:** Notice that the amounts reflected in the balance sheet for accounts receivable ($4,680,000) and inventories ($1,520,000) when combined with the increase in cash from collections of billings ($15,120,000 collections to date) equals $21,320,000 (the balance in the Construction in Process account) which also equals the percentage of the total contract revenue earned to date ($19,680,000/ $24,000,000 x $26,000,000 = $21,320,000). The balance of the Billings on Construction in Process account is deducted from the balance in the Construction in Process account so as not to double count assets related to accounting for construction contracts. The total amount billed thus far ($19,800,000) is either collected ($15,120,000 has been collected so the Cash account has increased which is not shown here) or uncollected ($4,680,000 balance in Accounts Receivable).

EXERCISE 19-2

Purpose: (L.O.3,4) This exercise will illustrate the computations, journal entries, and balance sheet presentations involved in the use of the completed-contract and percentage-of-completion methods of accounting for long-term construction contracts.

The Nifty Construction Company entered into a long-term contract in 1997. The contract price was $1,600,000, and the company initially estimated the total costs of the project to be $1,150,000. The following data pertains to the three years that the contract was in process:

Year	Costs Incurred During the Year	Estimated Costs at End of the Year to Complete Contract	Billings During the Year	Collections During the Year	Operating Expenses
1997	$224,000	$896,000	$ 200,000	$170,000	$80,000
1998	712,000	264,000	1,000,000	900,000	82,000
1999	344,000	-0-	400,000	430,000	74,000

Instructions

(a) Compute the gross profit to be reported in each of the three years using the completed-contract method.

(b) Compute the gross profit to be reported in each of the three years using the percentage-of-completion method based on the costs incurred to date and the estimated costs to complete the contract. (Also compute the amount of revenue and cost of sales reflected in each gross profit figure.)

(c) Prepare the related journal entries for all three years using the completed-contract method.

(d) Prepare the related journal entries for all three years using the percentage-of-completion method.

(e) Prepare a partial balance sheet at the end of each of the three years assuming (1) the completed-contract method is used and (2) the percentage-of-completion method is used.

> **TIP:** The use of T-accounts is helpful here to determine the balances of accounts at the balance sheet date.

Solution to Exercise 19-2

(a) 1997   -0-
     1998   -0-
     1999 $1,600,000 - ($224,000 + $712,000 + $344,000) = <u>$320,000</u>

(b) **1997** Estimate of total costs = $224,000 + $896,000 = $1,120,000
              Estimate of total gross profit = $1,600,000 - $1,120,000 = $480,000

              Gross profit to be recognized in 1997 = $\frac{\$224,000}{\$1,120,000}$ x $480,000 = <u>$96,000</u>

     1998 Costs incurred to date = $224,000 + $712,000 = $936,000
              Estimate of total costs = $936,000 + $264,000 = $1,200,000
              Estimate of total gross profit = $1,600,000 - $1,200,000 = $400,000
              Gross profit to be recognized in 1998 =
              $\left(\dfrac{\$936,000}{\$1,200,000} \times \$400,000\right)$ - $96,000 = <u>$216,000</u>

     1999 Total costs incurred for project = $224,000 + $712,000 + $344,000
                 = $1,280,000
              Contract price of $1,600,000 minus total costs incurred of $1,280,000
                 equals total gross profit on project of $320,000
              Gross profit to be recognized in 1999 = $320,000 - ($96,000 + $216,000)
                 = <u>$8,000</u>

1997 Revenue for 1997 = $\dfrac{\$224,000}{\$1,120,000}$ x $1,600,000 = $320,000

Costs to match with revenue for 1997 = $224,000

Gross profit for 1997 = $320,000 - $224,000 = $96,000

1998 Revenue for 1998 = $\left(\dfrac{\$936,000}{\$1,200,000} \text{ x } \$1,600,000\right)$ - $320,000 = $928,000

Costs to match with revenue for 1998 = $712,000

Gross profit for 1998 = $928,000 - $712,000 = $216,000

1999 Revenue for 1999 = $1,600,000 - ($320,000 + $928,000) = $352,000

Costs to match with revenue for 1999 = $344,000

Gross profit for 1999 = $352,000 - $344,000 = $8,000

(c) **Journal Entries—Completed Contract Method**

	1997		1998		1999	
Accounts	**Dr.**	**Cr.**	**Dr.**	**Cr.**	**Dr.**	**Cr.**
Const. in Process	224,000		712,000		344,000	
Operating Expenses	80,000		82,000		74,000	
Materials, Cash,						
Payables, Etc.		304,000		794,000		418,000
Accounts Receivable	200,000		1,000,000		400,000	
Billings on Const.						
in Process		200,000		1,000,000		400,000
Cash	170,000		900,000		430,000	
Accounts Rec.		170,000		900,000		430,000
Billings on Const. in						
Process					1,600,000	
Revenue from						
Long-term						
Contracts						1,600,000
Construction Exp.					1,280,000	
Const. in Process						1,280,000

(d)   Journal Entries—Percentage-of-Completion Method

	1997		1998		1999	
Accounts	Dr.	Cr.	Dr.	Cr.	Dr.	Cr.
Const. in Process	224,000		712,000		344,000	
Operating Expenses	80,000		82,000		74,000	
Materials, Cash, Payables, Etc.		304,000		794,000		418,000
Accounts Receivable	200,000		1,000,000		400,000	
Billings on Const. in Process		200,000		1,000,000		400,000
Cash	170,000		900,000		430,000	
Accounts Rec.		170,000		900,000		430,000
Const. Expenses	224,000		712,000		344,000	
Const. in Process	96,000		216,000		8,000	
Revenue from Long-Term Contracts		320,000		928,000		352,000
Billings on Const. in Process					1,600,000	
Const. in Process						1,600,000

(e)   1.   Partial Balance Sheet—Completed-Contract Method

	End of 1997		End of 1998		End of 1999
Current assets:					
Accounts receivable		$30,000		$130,000	$100,000
Inventories					
Construction in process	$224,000				
Less: Billings on const. in process	200,000				
Unbilled contract costs		$24,000			
Current liabilities:					
Billings on const. in process			$1,200,000		
Less: Construction in process			936,000		
Billings in excess of costs and recognized profit				$264,000	

Approach: Draw T-accounts and post journal entries to determine account balances.

2.   **Partial Balance Sheet—Percentage-of-Completion Method**

	End of 1997	End of 1998	End of 1999
Current assets:			
Accounts receivable	$30,000	$130,000	$100,000
Inventories			
Construction in process	$320,000	$1,248,000	
Less: Billings on const. in process	200,000	1,200,000	
Costs and recognized profit in excess of billings	$120,000	$48,000	

Approach: Draw T-accounts and post journal entries to determine account balances.

EXERCISE 19-3

Purpose: (L.O.7,8) This exercise will (1) illustrate the computations involved with the installment method of accounting, (2) examine the classification of the Deferred Gross Profit account and (3) apply the cost recovery method.

Arnie Sagar Company has appropriately used the installment method of accounting since it began business in 1998. The following data were obtained for the years 1998 and 1999:

	1998	1999
Installment sales	$800,000	$900,000
Cost of installment sales	592,000	684,000
Cash collections on sales of 1998	280,000	320,000
Cash collections on sales of 1999	-0-	400,000

Instructions
(a)   Compute the amount of realized gross profit to report for (1) 1998, and (2) 1999.

(b)   Compute the balance in the deferred gross profit accounts on (1) December 31, 1998, and (2) December 31, 1999.

(c)   Explain the classification of the total deferred gross profit on the balance sheet at December 31, 1999.

(d)   Prepare the journal entry to record the repossession of merchandise because of a defaulting customer. Assume that at the date of default in 1999, the balance on the related installment receivable (which originated in 1998) was $14,000 and the fair value of the merchandise was $8,500.

(e)   Assume the cost recovery method is used rather than the installment method. Compute the amount of realized gross profit that would be recognized (1) on the 1998 income statement, and (2) on the 1999 income statement.

Solution to Exercise 19-3

(a)   (1)   Gross Profit Ratio—1998:

Installment sales for 1998	$ 800,000
Cost of installment sales for 1998	(592,000)
Gross profit on installment sales for 1998	$ 208,000

$$\frac{\$208,000 \text{ Gross Profit}}{\$800,000 \text{ Sales}} = \underline{26\%} \text{ Gross profit ratio on 1998 sales}$$

Cash collections in 1998 on sales of 1998	$ 280,000
Gross profit ratio for 1998 sales	26%
Gross profit realized in 1998 on 1998 sales	$ 72,800

   (2)   Gross Profit Ratio—1999:

Installment sales for 1999	$ 900,000
Cost of installment sales for 1999	(684,000)
Gross profit on installment sales for 1999	$ 216,000

$$\frac{\$216,000 \text{ Gross profit}}{\$900,000 \text{ Sales}} = \underline{24\%} \text{ Gross profit ratio on 1999 sales}$$

Cash collections in 1999 on sales of 1999	$ 400,000
Gross profit ratio for 1999 sales	24%
Gross profit realized in 1999 on 1999 sales	$ 96,000

Cash collections in 1999 on sales of 1998	$ 320,000
Gross profit ratio for 1998 sales	26%
Gross profit realized in 1999 on 1998 sales	$ 83,200

Gross profit realized in 1999 on 1999 sales	$ 96,000
Gross profit realized in 1999 on 1998 sales	83,200
Total gross profit realized in 1999	$ 179,200

TIP: Always compute a separate gross profit ratio for each year in which there are installment sales. Clearly label each ratio so it is ready for use in subsequent computations. For any given year, the cash collections during the year on Year 1 installment sales multiplied by the gross profit ratio on Year 1 installment sales will yield the gross profit realized during that given year on Year 1 installment sales. The balance of Installment Accounts Receivable, Year 1, at a balance sheet date, multiplied by the gross profit ratio for Year 1 installment sales will yield the appropriate adjusted balance for the related Deferred Gross Profit, Year 1 account at the same date.

(b)   (1)

Deferred Gross Profit, 1998			
1998	72,800[b]	1998	208,000[a]
		12/31/98 Bal.	135,200

(2)

Deferred Gross Profit, 1998			
1999	83,200[c]	12/31/98 Bal.	135,200
		12/31/99 Bal.	52,000

Deferred Gross Profit, 1999			
1999	96,000[e]	1999	216,000[d]
		12/31/99 Bal.	120,000

[a] Gross profit on 1998 installment sales = $800,000 - $592,000 = $208,000.
[b] Gross profit realized in 1998 on 1998 sales = $280,000 collections x 26% = $72,800.
[c] Gross profit realized in 1999 on 1998 sales = $320,000 collections x 26% = $83,200.
[d] Gross profit on 1999 installment sales = $900,000 - $684,000 = $216,000.
[e] Gross profit realized in 1999 on 1999 sales = $400,000 collections x 24% = $96,000.

> **TIP:** The $52,000 balance in the Deferred Gross Profit, 1998 account at December 31, 1999 can be independently verified by multiplying the balance of Installment Accounts Receivable, 1998 at December 31, 1999 [$800,000 - ($280,000 + $320,000) = $200,000] by the gross profit ratio for 1998 installment sales (26%).

(c) Per the answers to part (b) (2) above, the total deferred gross profit at December 31, 1999 amounts to $172,000 [$52,000 + $120,000 = $172,000]. In *SFAC No. 6*, par. 232-234, the FASB states that "deferred gross profit on installment sales is conceptually an asset valuation—that is, a reduction of an asset." However, in practice, deferred gross profit on installment sales is generally treated as unearned revenue and is classified as a current liability (because the operating cycle is longer than the installment period).

(d)   Approach:

Do Second	Deferred Gross Profit (26% x $14,000)............	3,640	
Do Third	Repossessed Merchandise.............................	8,500	
Plug	Loss on Repossession....................................	1,860	
Do First	Installment Accounts Receivable		14,000

Explanation: The amount of the loss is determined by (1) subtracting the deferred gross profit from the amount of the account receivable to determine the unrecovered cost (or book value) of the merchandise repossessed ($14,000 - $3,640 = $10,360), and (2) subtracting the estimated fair value of the merchandise repossessed from the unrecovered cost to get the amount of the loss on repossession ($10,360 - $8,500 = $1,860). As an alternative, the loss on repossession can be charged to the Allowance for Doubtful Accounts account.

(e)   (1) Using the cost recovery method, no gross profit would be recognized on the 1998 income statement because the $280,000 cash collections did not exceed the $592,000 cost of the merchandise sold.

(2)   Using the cost recovery method of revenue recognition, gross profit of $8,000 would be reported in 1999 due to installment sales made in 1998. No gross profit would be recognized on 1999 sales because cash collections did not exceed the cost of the merchandise sold.

Computations:

Cumulative cash collections on 1998 sales	$ 600,000*
Cost of 1998 installment sales	(592,000)
Gross profit to be recognized in 1999 using cost recovery method	$ 8,000

*$280,000 + $320,000 = $600,000

Explanation: The cost recovery method provides for gross profit to be recognized **only** after all costs of related sales have been recovered. All subsequent cash collections are recognized as profit.

EXERCISE 19-4

Purpose: (L.O.9) This exercise will examine the treatment for an initial franchise fee under three scenarios.

Ma's Best Cookies Inc. charges an initial franchise fee of $110,000. Upon the signing of the agreement, a payment of $50,000 is due; thereafter, three annual payments of $20,000 are required. The credit rating of the franchisee is such that it would have to pay interest at 10% to borrow money.

Instructions

Prepare the entries to record the initial franchise fee on the books of the franchisor under the following assumptions:

(a)   The down payment is not refundable, no future services are required by the franchisor, and collection of the note is reasonably assured.

(b)   The franchisor has substantial services to perform, and the collection of the note is very uncertain.

(c)   The down payment is not refundable, collection of the note is reasonably certain, the franchisor has yet to perform a substantial amount of services, and the down payment represents a fair measure of the services already performed.

Solution to Exercise 19-4

(a)	Cash		50,000	
	Notes Receivable...		60,000	
	Discount on Notes Receivable....................................			10,263
	[$60,000 - ($20,000 x 2.48685*)]			
	Revenue from Franchise Fees			99,737
	($50,000 + $60,000 - $10,263)			
(b)	Cash		50,000	
	Unearned Franchise Fees			50,000
(c)	Cash		50,000	
	Notes Receivable...		60,000	
	Discount on Notes Receivable....................................			10,263
	Revenue from Franchise Fees			50,000
	Unearned Franchise Fees ($20,000 x 2.48685*).........			49,737

*The factor for the present value of an ordinary annuity of 1 for $n = 3$, $i = 10\%$ is 2.48685.

> **TIP:** The amount of revenue recognized and the carrying value of the note receivable recorded by the franchisor upon the receipt of the franchise agreement and the initial franchise fee depend upon several factors, including: (1) whether or not the fee may be refundable, (2) an estimate of the collectibility of the note, (3) a measure of the future services to be performed by the franchisor, and (4) the incremental borrowing rate of the franchisee.

EXERCISE 19-5

Purpose: (L.O.9) This exercise will review computations involved with consignment sales.

On April 15, 1999, Stayfit Company consigned 70 treadmills, costing $600 each, to Higley Company. The cost of shipping the treadmills amounts to $800 and was paid by Stayfit Company. On December 30, 1999, an account sales was received from the consignee, reporting that 35 treadmills had been sold for $700 each. Remittance was made by the consignee for the amount due, after deducting a commission of 6%, advertising of $200, and total delivery costs of $300 on the treadmills sold.

Instructions
(a)   Compute the inventory value of the units unsold in the hands of the consignee.
(b)   Compute the profit for the consignor for the units sold.
(c)   Compute the amount of cash that will be remitted by the consignee.

Solution to Exercise 19-5

(a)   Inventoriable Costs:

	70 units shipped at cost of $600 each	$ 42,000
	Freight to consignee	800
	Total inventoriable cost	$ 42,800
	35 units on hand (1/2 x $42,800)	$ 21,400

(b)   Computation of Consignment Profit:

	Consignment sales (35 x $700)	$ 24,500
	Cost of units sold (1/2 x $42,800)	(21,400)
	Commission charged by consignee (6% x $24,500)	(1,470)
	Advertising costs	(200)
	Delivery costs to customers	(300)
	Profit on consignment sales	$ 1,130

(c)   Remittance of Consignee:

	Consignment sales		$ 24,500
	Less: Commissions	$ 1,470	
	Advertising	200	
	Delivery	300	1,970
	Remittance from consignee		$ 22,530

ANALYSIS OF MULTIPLE-CHOICE TYPE QUESTIONS

QUESTION

1.   (L.O.1) The process of formally recording or incorporating an item in the financial statements of an entity is:
a.   allocation.
b.   articulation.
c.   realization.
d.   recognition.

Approach and Explanation: Write down a brief definition of each term listed. Select the one that matches the description in the stem of the question. **Allocation** is the accounting process of assigning or distributing an amount according to a plan or formula. Allocation is a broad term and includes amortization, which is the accounting process of reducing an amount by periodic payments or writedowns. **Articulation** refers to the interrelation of elements of the financial statements. **Realization** means the process of converting noncash resources and rights into money (such as the sale of assets for cash or claims to cash). **Recognition** is defined in *SFAC No. 6* as the process of formally recording or incorporating an item in the financial statements of an entity. (Solution = d.)

QUESTION

2. (L.O.1) Dot Point, Inc. is a retailer of washers and dryers and offers a three-year service contract on each appliance sold. Although Dot Point sells the appliances on an installment basis, all service contracts are cash sales at the time of purchase by the buyer. Collections received for service contracts should be recorded as:

a.   service revenue.
b.   deferred service revenue.
c.   a reduction in installment accounts receivable.
d.   a direct addition to retained earnings.

Approach and Explanation: Recall the revenue recognition principle and think about how it would apply to this situation. Revenue is to be recognized when it is realized (or realizable) and earned. The service contract revenue is realized at the date the cash is received; however, it is earned over the three-year period to which the contract pertains. Therefore, at the point of collection, the cash should be recorded by a credit to a Deferred (Unearned) Service Revenue account. The revenue will be earned over the three-year period as the company performs the services it promises by the contract. (Solution = b.)

QUESTION

3. (L.O.2) L. Mahoney Corporation sells equipment. On December 31, 1998, Mahoney sold a piece of equipment to C. Bailey for $30,000 with the following terms: 2% cash discount if paid within 30 days, 1% discount if paid between 31 and 60 days of purchase, or payable in full within 90 days if not paid within a discount period. Bailey had the right to return this equipment to Mahoney if Bailey could not resell it before the end of the 90-day payment period, in which case Bailey would no longer be obligated to Mahoney. How much should be included in Mahoney's net sales for 1998 because of the sale of this machine?

a. $30,000
b. $29,700
c. $29,400
d. $0

Explanation: Per the terms of the sale/purchase, Bailey has the right to return the equipment to the seller if Bailey is not able to resell the equipment before expiration of the 90-day payment period. According to *SFAS No. 48*, if an enterprise sells its product but gives the buyer the right to return the product, revenue from the sales transaction is **not** recognized at the time of the sale if the buyer's obligation to pay the seller is contingent upon resale of the product. (Solution = d.)

QUESTION

4. (L.O.3) Designer Homes Construction Company uses the percentage-of-completion method. The costs incurred to date as a proportion of the estimated total costs to be incurred on a project are used as a measure of the extent of progress made toward completion of the project. During 1998, the company entered into a fixed-price contract to construct a mansion for Donald Thrumper for $24,000,000. The following details pertain to that contract:

	At December 31, 1998	At December 31, 1999
Percentage of completion	25%	60%
Estimated total costs of contract	$18,000,000	$20,000,000
Gross profit recognized to date	1,500,000	2,400,000

The amount of construction costs incurred during 1999 was:
a. $2,000,000.
b. $4,500,000.
c. $7,500,000.
d. $12,000,000.

Approach and Explanation: Write down the formula used to compute the gross profit recognized to date at the end of 1999. Look at the components of the fraction.

$$\frac{\text{Costs incurred to date}}{\text{Estimate of total costs}} \times \frac{\text{Estimated total}}{\text{gross profit}} = \frac{\text{Total gross profit}}{\text{earned to date}}$$

According to the facts given, the fraction at December 31, 1999 is equal to 60%. Therefore, the costs incurred by the end of 1999 = 60% x $20,000,000 = $12,000,000. According to the facts given, the fraction for the same formula at the end of 1998 is equal to 25%. Therefore, the costs incurred by the end of 1998 = 25% x $18,000,000 = $4,500,000. The difference between the cumulative costs at the end of 1999 ($12,000,000) and the cumulative costs at the end of 1998 ($4,500,000) equals the costs incurred during 1999 of $7,500,000. (Solution = c.)

QUESTION

5.   (L.O.7,8) A manufacturer of large equipment sells on an installment basis to customers with questionable credit ratings. Which of the following methods of revenue recognition is **least** likely to overstate the amount of gross profit reported?
a.   at the time of completion of the equipment (completion of production method)
b.   at the date of delivery (sale method)
c.   the installment method
d.   the cost recovery method

Explanation: Recognition of income at the time the equipment is completed would be the method **most** likely to overstate gross profit. The recognition of gross profit at the time the equipment is completed or at the date the equipment is delivered would provide for the recognition of profits before any or much of the cash has been received; thus, these methods are not appropriate for situations where there is doubt about the collectibility of the selling price. The use of the installment method would allow for the recognition of profits in proportion to the amount of the revenue collected in cash. The cost recovery method defers the recognition of all gross profit until cash collections of revenue are equal to the cost of the item sold; all remaining cash collections are reported as profit. Therefore, the cost recovery method is **least** likely to overstate the amount of gross profit reported. (Solution = d.)

QUESTION

6.   (L.O.7) Eazy-Pay Sales Company has appropriately used the installment method of accounting since it began operations at the beginning of 1999. The following information pertains to its operations for 1999:

Installment sales	$ 600,000
Cost of installment sales	420,000
Collections on installment sales	240,000
General and administrative expenses	60,000

The amount to be reported on the December 31, 1999 balance sheet as Deferred Gross Profit should be:

a. $360,000.
b. $144,000.
c. $108,000.
d. $72,000.

Explanation: The $360,000 balance of Installment Accounts Receivable, 1999 ($600,000 - $240,000 = $360,000) is multiplied by the 1999 gross profit ratio of 30% ($600,000 - $420,000 = $180,000; $180,000 ÷ $600,000 = 30%) to arrive at deferred gross profit of $108,000 ($360,000 x 30% = $108,000) at the balance sheet date. (Solution = c.)

> **TIP:**   General and administrative expenses have no effect on the computations of realized gross profit or deferred gross profit. They are to be classified as operating expenses on the income statement of the period in which they are incurred.

QUESTION

7.   (L.O.7) Kayla Inc. appropriately uses the installment method of accounting to recognize income in its financial statements. Some pertinent data relating to this method of accounting include:

	1998	1999
Installment sales	$ 300,000	$ 360,000
Cost of sales	180,000	252,000
Gross profit	$ 120,000	$ 108,000
Collections during year:		
On 1998 sales	100,000	100,000
On 1999 sales		120,000

What amount of realized gross profit should be reported on Kayla's income statement for 1999?

a. $108,000
b. $88,000
c. $76,000
d. $66,000
e.   None of the above

Approach and Explanation: (1) Compute the gross profit percentages for 1998 and 1999. (2) Apply the appropriate gross profit percentage to the amount of collections of installment receivables during 1999.

Computations:
(1) $120,000 ÷ $300,000 = 40% gross profit percentage for 1998 installment sales

$108,000 ÷ $360,000 = 30% gross profit percentage for 1999 installment sales

(2)

Collections in 1999 on 1998 installment sales	$ 100,000
Gross profit percentage for 1998 installment sales	40%
Gross profit realized in 1999 on 1998 installment sales	$ 40,000
Collections in 1999 on 1999 installment sales	$ 120,000
Gross profit percentage for 1999 installments sales	30%
Gross profit realized in 1999 on 1999 installment sales	$ 36,000
Gross profit realized in 1999 on 1998 installment sales	$ 40,000
Gross profit realized in 1999 on 1999 installment sales	36,000
Total gross profit realized in 1999	$ 76,000

(Solution = c.)

QUESTION
8.   (L.O.7) Marvel Mart sells large-screen televisions on an installment basis and appropriately uses the installment sales method of accounting. A customer with an account balance of $4,000 refuses to make any more payments and the merchandise is repossessed. The gross profit rate on the original sale is 40%. Marvel estimates that the television can be sold as is for $1,250, or for $1,500 if $100 is spent to refurbish the cabinet. The loss on repossession is:
a. $1,000.
b. $1,150.
c. $1,600.
d. $2,750.

Approach and Explanation: Prepare the journal entry to record the repossession; it is as follows:

Deferred Gross Profit ($4,000 x 40%)..............................	1,600	
Repossessed Merchandise ($1,500 - $100)	1,400	
Loss on Repossession	1,000	
[($4,000 - $1,600) - ($1,500 - $100)]		
Installment Accounts Receivable.............................		4,000

The book value of the receivable is removed from the accounts ($4,000 - $1,600), the repossessed merchandise is recorded at its fair value (or net realizable value of $1,400 in this case), and a loss ($1,000) is recorded for the excess of the receivable's book value ($4,000 - $1,600 = $2,400) over its net realizable value ($1,400) (a measure of fair value). (Solution = a.)

CHAPTER 20

ACCOUNTING FOR INCOME TAXES

OVERVIEW

Most revenue type transactions are **taxable amounts** (they increase taxable income) in some time period, and most expense type transactions are **deductible amounts** (they decrease taxable income) in some time period. Interperiod income tax allocation procedures are required when a revenue or expense item is reported on the tax return in one year but is reported on the income statement in a different time period. Thus, the income tax consequences of revenues and expenses are reflected on the income statement in the **same** year that the revenues and expenses are reported on the financial statements, regardless of when the revenues and expenses appear on the tax return.

SUMMARY OF LEARNING OBJECTIVES

1.   **Identify differences between pretax financial income and taxable income.** Pretax financial income (or income for book purposes) is computed in accordance with generally accepted accounting principles. Taxable income (or income for tax purposes) is computed in accordance with prescribed tax regulations. Because tax regulations and GAAP are different in many ways, pretax financial income and taxable income frequently differ. Differences may exist, for example, in the timing of revenue recognition and the timing of expense recognition. That is, revenues are recognized on the income statement in the period they are earned, but they may be taxable in a different period. Also, expenses are reported on the income statement in the period incurred, but they may be tax deductible in a different period.

2.   **Describe a temporary difference resulting in future taxable amounts.** A credit sale that is recognized as revenue for book purposes in the period it is earned but is deferred and reported as revenue for tax purposes in the period it is collected will result in future taxable amounts. A deferred tax liability is to be recognized for the deferred tax consequences of the revenue and related account receivable already reflected in the financial statements. The recording of the deferred tax liability causes the total income tax expense to exceed the amount of income tax payable for the period in which the credit sale occurs. The future taxable amounts will occur in the periods the related account receivable for book purposes is recovered and the collections are reported as revenue for tax purposes. These future taxable amounts increase taxable income in the later periods in which they occur.

3.   **Describe a temporary difference resulting in future deductible amounts.** An accrued warranty expense that is paid for and is deductible for tax purposes in a period later than the period in which it is recognized for book purposes will result in future deductible amounts. A deferred tax asset is to be recognized for the deferred tax consequences of the warranty expense and related warranty liability already reflected in the financial statements. The recording of the deferred tax asset causes the total income tax expense to be less than the amount of income tax payable for the period in which the warranty expense is recognized for book purposes. The future deductible amounts will occur in the periods the related warranty liability for

book purposes is settled and the expenditures are reported as expense for tax purposes. These future deductible amounts decrease taxable income in the later periods in which they occur.

4. **Explain the purpose of a deferred tax asset valuation allowance.** A deferred tax asset should be reduced by a valuation allowance if, based on all available evidence, it is more likely than not (a level of likelihood that is at least slightly more than 50%) that some portion or all of the deferred tax asset will **not** be realized. All available evidence, both positive and negative, should be carefully considered to determine whether, based on the weight of available evidence, a valuation allowance is needed.

5. **Describe the presentation of income tax expense in the income statement.** The significant components of income tax expense should be disclosed in the income statement or in the notes to the financial statements. The most commonly encountered components are the current tax expense (or current tax benefit) and the deferred tax expense (or deferred tax benefit).

6. **Describe various temporary and permanent differences.** Examples of temporary differences are: (1) revenue or gains that are taxable **after** they are recognized in financial income, (2) expenses or losses that are deductible **after** they are recognized in financial income, (3) revenues or gains that are taxable **before** they are recognized in financial income, and (4) expenses or losses that are deductible **before** they are recognized in financial income. Permanent differences are: (1) items recognized for financial reporting purposes but **not** for tax purposes, and (2) items recognized for tax purposes but **not** for financial reporting purposes.

7. **Explain the effect of various tax rates and tax rate changes on deferred income taxes.** The tax rate that is used to measure deferred tax liabilities and deferred tax assets (called the **applicable tax rate**) is the enacted tax rate(s) expected to apply to taxable income in the years that the related future taxable amounts and future deductible amounts are expected to occur. Presently enacted changes in tax rates that become effective for a particular future year or years must be considered when determining the tax rate to apply to temporary differences reversing in that year or years. Tax rates for the current year are used to tax effect cumulative temporary differences if no changes have been enacted for future years. When a change in the tax rate is enacted into law, its effect on the existing deferred income tax accounts should be recorded immediately; this effect is reported as an adjustment to income tax expense in the period of the rate change.

8. **Apply accounting procedures for a loss carryback and a loss carryforward.** A company may carry a net operating loss back 3 years and receive funds for income taxes paid in those years. The loss must be applied to the earliest year first and then sequentially to the second and third years. Any loss remaining after the 3-year carryback may be carried forward up to 15 years to offset future taxable income. A company may elect to forgo the loss carryback and use the loss carryforward, offsetting future taxable income for up to 15 years. For financial reporting purposes, the benefits of a loss carryback are recognized by a debit to a receivable account and a credit to the income statement in the loss year. The benefits of a loss carryforward are recognized by a debit to Deferred Tax Asset and a credit to the income statement in the loss year; a valuation allowance is established against the deferred tax asset if it is more likely than not that a portion or all of the related tax benefits will not be realized.

9. **Describe the presentation of deferred income taxes in financial statements.** Deferred tax accounts are reported on the balance sheet as assets and liabilities. They should be classified as a **net** current and a **net** noncurrent amount. An individual deferred tax liability or asset is classified as current or noncurrent based on the classification of the related asset or liability for financial reporting purposes. A deferred tax liability or asset that is not related to an asset or liability for financial reporting purposes, including a deferred tax asset related to loss carryforwards, shall be classified according to the expected reversal date of the temporary difference.

10. **Identify special issues related to deferred income taxes.** A number of issues related to deferred income taxes require special treatment: (1) multiple temporary differences, (2) necessity for a valuation allowance, (3) multiple tax rates, (4) pattern of taxable and deductible amounts, (5) alternative minimum tax, and (6) intraperiod tax allocation.

11. **Indicate the basic principles of the asset-liability method.** The basic principles applied in accounting for income taxes at the date of the financial statements are: (1) a current tax liability or asset is recognized for the estimated taxes payable or refundable on the tax return for the current year; (2) a deferred tax liability or asset is recognized for the estimated future tax effects attributable to temporary differences and carryforwards using the applicable tax rate; (3) the measurement of current and deferred tax liabilities and assets is based on provisions of the enacted tax law; and (4) the measurement of deferred tax assets is adjusted, if necessary, by the amount of any tax benefits that, based on available evidence, are not expected to be realized.

12.* **Understand and apply the concepts and procedures of interperiod tax allocation.** Accounting procedures for deferred taxes include calculating taxable income and income tax payable for the current year, computing deferred income taxes at the end of the year, determining deferred tax expense (benefit), making the journal entry to record income taxes, and classifying deferred tax assets and liabilities as current and noncurrent in the financial statements.

 *This material is covered in Appendix 20-A in the text.

13.** **Understand the arguments for and against interperiod tax allocation and the alternative approaches.** Although the predominant view holds that comprehensive tax allocation is appropriate, there are those who support no allocation or partial allocation. Of those who support tax allocation, three different methods of allocation have been proposed: (1) the deferred method, (2) the asset-liability method, and (3) the net-of-tax method.

 **This material is covered in Appendix 20-B of the text.

TIPS ON CHAPTER TOPICS

TIP: The term **pretax financial income (loss)** refers to the difference between revenues earned and expenses incurred (other than income tax expense) on the accrual basis income statement for a given year. The term **taxable income (loss)** refers to the difference between taxable amounts and tax deductible amounts on the tax return for a given year. Pretax financial income appears on the income statement with the caption "Income before income taxes." **Pretax financial income** is often referred to as **income for book purposes**, **accounting income**, or **income for financial reporting purposes**.

TIP: An excess of tax deductible expenses over taxable revenues on an entity's tax return is often called a **net operating loss (NOL)**. The tax law provides that an NOL may be carried back three years and forward fifteen years. In the carryback situation, the NOL is first applied to the **earliest** of the three years prior to the loss year. Any remaining NOL is then carried to the next oldest year and then to the most recent prior year. Any remaining NOL is then carried forward to future years. (Although a corporation can elect to forego the carryback and use only a carryforward, do not assume this election is used in doing homework problems.) The provisions of the tax law must be applied in accounting for the tax benefits of an NOL.

TIP: **Income tax payable for a period** is also the amount of **current tax expense** and is determined by applying the provisions of the tax law to the taxable income (or loss) figure for the period. In the case where an NOL results in a carryback, the entity will have **income tax refundable** (rather than income tax payable) which results in a **current tax benefit**.

TIP: A revenue or an expense amount that appears on the income statement or the tax return in one year but **never** appears on the other report is called a **permanent difference**. Deferred income taxes are **never** recorded for permanent differences because these differences will never reverse (i.e., they will neither cause future taxable nor future deductible amounts). Examples of permanent differences appear in **Illustration 20-1**.

TIP: A **temporary difference** is a difference between the tax basis of an asset or liability and its reported amount (book value or carrying amount) in the financial statements that will result in taxable or deductible amounts in future years when the reported amount of the asset is recovered or the liability is settled. Temporary differences that will result in taxable amounts when the related assets are recovered are often called **taxable temporary differences**; temporary differences that will result in deductible amounts in future years when the related liabilities are settled are often called **deductible temporary differences. Taxable temporary differences give rise to recording deferred tax liabilities; deductible temporary differences give rise to recording deferred tax assets.**

TIP: Most temporary differences are caused by reporting a revenue or an expense in one year for financial reporting purposes and reporting the same revenue or expense in a different year for income tax purposes. Examples of these situations appear in **Illustration 20-2**. Other causes of temporary differences are not addressed in this book.

TIP: **Deferred tax expense (or benefit) for a period results from changes in the deferred tax asset and liability accounts.** A **deferred tax expense** results from an increase in a deferred tax liability or a decrease in a deferred tax asset; a **deferred tax benefit** results from an increase in a deferred tax asset or a decrease in a deferred tax liability. This is true because the other half of the journal entry dealing with a deferred tax account (a balance sheet item) is the income tax expense account (an income statement item). A deferred tax expense **increases** total income tax expense for the period; a deferred tax benefit **reduces** total income tax expense for the period.

TIP: **Total income tax expense (or benefit)** is the sum of **current tax expense (or benefit)** and **deferred tax expense (or benefit)**. Income tax expense is often referred to as provision for income taxes. Hence, there is usually both a current portion and a deferred portion of the income tax provision. The meaning of the word "current" in this text bears **no relationship** to the meaning of the term "current" as used to refer to a balance sheet classification of deferred taxes.

TIP: A temporary difference originating in the current period that causes an increase in a deferred tax liability will also cause a debit (charge) to the provision for deferred income taxes on the income statement; an increase in a deferred tax asset will result in a credit to the provision for deferred taxes.

TIP: Pay close attention to terminology in this chapter and be careful not to confuse the many terms introduced. When describing deferred taxes from a balance sheet perspective, we speak about deferred tax assets and deferred tax liabilities. Whereas, when talking about the effects of deferred taxes on the income statement, we speak about deferred tax expense or deferred tax benefit. There is a correlation, however, because it is changes in deferred tax assets and liabilities on the balance sheet that result in deferred tax expense or benefit on the income statement.

TIP: A corporation often makes estimated tax payments during the year and charges them to an account called Prepaid Income Taxes. The balance of this account is used to offset the balance of the Income Tax Payable account for reporting purposes. The net amount is classified as a current asset if the prepaid account has the larger balance; the net amount is classified as a current liability if the payable account has the larger balance.

TIP: The **effective tax rate** for a period is calculated by dividing total income tax expense on the income statement by income before income taxes on the income statement. The effective tax rate for a period may differ from the statutory tax rate for the same period because of (a) permanent differences, and (b) changes in cumulative temporary differences that have been tax effected at statutory tax rates enacted for future (or prior) periods.

TIP: Deferred tax accounts are **not** to be reported at discounted amounts.

TIP: **Future deductible amounts** are often called **future tax deductible amounts**.

ILLUSTRATION 20-1
EXAMPLES OF PERMANENT DIFFERENCES (L.O.6)

1. **Revenues that are recognized for financial reporting purposes but are never included for tax purposes:**
   a. Interest received on state and municipal obligations.
   b. Proceeds from life insurance carried by the company on key officers or employees.

2. **Expenses that are recognized for financial reporting purposes but are never included for tax purposes:**
   a. Compensation expense associated with certain employee stock options.
   b. Premiums paid for life insurance carried by the company on key officers or employees (company is beneficiary).
   c. Fines and expenses resulting from a violation of law.
   d. Expenses incurred in obtaining tax-exempt income.

3. **Revenues that are recognized for tax purposes but are never included in financial statements:**
   a. No examples exist at the current time.

4. **Expenses or other deductions that are recognized for tax purposes but are never included in financial statements:**
   a. "Percentage depletion" of natural resources in excess of their cost.
   b. The deduction for dividends received from U.S. corporations, generally 70% to 80%.

ILLUSTRATION 20-2
EXAMPLES OF TEMPORARY DIFFERENCES (L.O.6)

1. **Revenues or gains that are taxable after they are included in financial income.** This situation will result in **future taxable amounts**.
    - An example is the use of the accrual method in accounting for installment sales for financial reporting purposes and the use of the installment (cash) method for tax purposes. This situation causes an excess of the reported amount of an asset (receivable) over its tax basis that will result in a taxable amount in a future year(s) when the asset is recovered (when the cash is collected).
    - Other examples include:
        - Contracts which are accounted for under the percentage-of-completion method for financial reporting purposes, but a portion of the related gross profit is deferred for tax purposes.
        - Investments which are accounted for under the equity method for financial reporting purposes and under the cost method for tax purposes.
        - Gain on involuntary conversion of a nonmonetary asset which is recognized for financial reporting purposes but is deferred for tax purposes.
        - Accrued revenues that are reported on the income statement in the period earned but included on the tax return in the period collected.
        - Unrealized holding gain on investment in trading securities.

2. **Expenses or losses that are deductible after they are included in financial income.** This situation will result in **future tax deductible amounts**.
    - An example would be the accrual of an expense or loss contingency (e.g., litigation accrual) in computing pretax financial income. This item is deductible for tax purposes only when it is realized. This situation causes a liability's reported amount to exceed its tax basis (zero) which will result in deductible amounts in a future year(s) when the liability (estimated litigation obligation) is settled.
    - Other examples include:
        - Product warranty liabilities.
        - Estimated liabilities related to discontinued operations or restructurings.
        - Bad debt expense recognized using the allowance method for financial reporting purposes and the direct write-off method used for tax purposes.
        - Unrealized holding loss on investment in trading securities.

ILLUSTRATION 20-2 (Continued)

3. **Revenues or gains that are taxable before they are included in financial income.** This situation will result in **future tax deductible amounts**.
    - An example would be revenue received in advance for rent or subscriptions. For tax purposes, the revenue is taxable in the period the related cash is received, but the revenue is not included in the computation of pretax financial income until the period in which it is earned. This type of case causes the reported amount for a liability (unearned revenue) on the balance sheet to exceed its tax basis (zero) which will result in future tax deductible amounts when the liability is settled.

        > **TIP:** This situation is said to result in future tax deductible amounts because of the future sacrifices required to provide goods or services or to provide refunds to those who cancel their orders.

    - Other examples include:
        - Sales and leasebacks for financial reporting purposes (income deferral) and sales for tax purposes.
        - Prepaid contracts and royalties received in advance.

4. **Expenses or losses that are deductible before they are included in financial income.** This situation will result in **future taxable amounts**.
    - An example is the situation where a depreciable asset is depreciated faster for tax purposes than it is depreciated for financial accounting purposes. This causes the asset's reported value to exceed its tax basis. Amounts received upon the future recovery of the asset's reported value (through use or sale) will exceed its tax basis, and the excess will be taxable when the asset is recovered.
    - Other examples include:
        - Depleted resources and intangibles (such as goodwill and organization costs) which may be amortized faster for tax purposes.
        - Deductible pension funding which exceeds the amount of pension expense.
        - Prepaid expenses that are deducted on the tax return in the period paid but are deducted on the income statement in the period incurred.

**ILLUSTRATION 20-3
RECONCILIATION OF PRETAX FINANCIAL INCOME
TO TAXABLE INCOME (L.O.6)**

Pretax financial income

PERMANENT DIFFERENCES

- − Revenue recognized for books this period, but never recognized for tax purposes
- + Expense recognized for books this period, but never recognized for tax purposes
- + Revenue recognized for tax purposes this period, but never recognized for books.
- − Expense recognized for tax purposes this period, but never recognized for books.

ORIGINATING TEMPORARY DIFFERENCES

- − Revenue recognized for books this period, but recognized later for tax purposes
- + Expense recognized for books this period, but recognized later for tax purposes
- + Revenue recognized for tax purposes this period, but recognized later for books.
- − Expense recognized for tax purposes this period, but recognized later for books.

REVERSING TEMPORARY DIFFERENCES

- − Revenue recognized for books this period, but recognized earlier for tax purposes
- + Expense recognized for books this period, but recognized earlier for tax purposes
- + Revenue recognized for tax purposes this period, but recognized earlier for books.
- − Expense recognized for tax purposes this period, but recognized earlier for books.

= **Taxable income**

TIP: No deferred taxes are to be recognized for permanent differences because they will not have any future tax consequences.

ILLUSTRATION 20-3 (Continued)

TIP: Temporary differences that **originate** in the current period and give rise to **future taxable amounts** are to be **deducted** from pretax financial income in this reconciliation. These differences will result in an increase in **deferred tax liabilities** during the current period for the deferred tax consequences of those future taxable amounts.

TIP: Temporary differences that **originate** in the current period and give rise to **future deductible amounts** are to be **added** to pretax financial income in this reconciliation. These differences will result in an increase in **deferred tax assets** during the current period for the deferred tax consequences of those future deductible amounts.

TIP: Refer to **Illustration 20-1** for examples of permanent differences; refer to **Illustration 20-2** for examples of temporary differences. The four types of examples addressed in those two illustrations appear in the same order there as they are referenced in this illustration. Thus, the first type of permanent difference listed in **Illustration 20-3** corresponds to the first type described in **Illustration 20-1**. Also, the first type of the temporary differences listed in **Illustration 20-3** corresponds to the first type described in **Illustration 20-2**.

TIP: This reconciliation will aid you in solving some homework assignments and exam questions, but it is not relevant to all situations. The temporary differences used in this reconciliation are **only** the ones that originated or reversed during the current year. The reconciliation does **not** use cumulative temporary differences. This reconciliation can be used to solve for taxable income, pretax financial income, or changes in cumulative temporary differences.

CASE 20-1

Purpose: (L.O.6) This case will provide practice in distinguishing between temporary differences and permanent differences. It will also provide practice in distinguishing between taxable type and deductible type temporary differences.

In reviewing the records of a client, you find the items listed below pertain to the current year.

Instructions

For each item in the list, use the appropriate letter to indicate if it is:
   a.   A temporary difference which gives rise to future deductible amounts.
   b.   A temporary difference which gives rise to future taxable amounts.
   c.   A permanent difference.

_____   1. MACRS depreciation was used for tax purposes, and straight-line depreciation was used for accounting purposes for some depreciable assets.

_____   2. The client is a landlord and collected some rents in advance.

_____   3. An installment sale of an investment was accounted for by the accrual method for books and the installment method for tax purposes.

_____   4. Interest was received on an investment in municipal obligations.

_____   5. The costs of guarantees and warranties were estimated and accrued for accounting purposes.

_____   6. Expenses were incurred in obtaining tax-exempt income.

_____   7. Proceeds were received from a life insurance company because of the death of a key officer (the company carries a policy on key officers).

_____   8. For some assets, straight-line depreciation was used for both accounting purposes and tax purposes, but the assets' lives were shorter for tax purposes.

_____   9. The tax return reports a deduction for 70% of the dividends received from U.S. corporations. For accounting purposes, the fair value method was used in accounting for the related investments in available-for-sale securities.

_____   10. Estimated losses on pending lawsuits and claims were accrued for books. These losses will be tax deductible in the year(s) they are realized.

_____   11. Interest and property taxes were incurred during construction of a building. The building is being constructed for the company's own use and is expected to have a service life of 40 years. For tax purposes, the interest and property taxes incurred during construction are capitalized as a part of the basis of the related asset. For tax purposes, the building will be depreciated over 19 years.

_____   12. The company paid a fine for violation of a law.

_____   13. Goodwill is amortized over 20 years for accounting purposes and over 15 years for tax purposes.

_____   14. The company recognized a loss on the income statement due to a temporary decline in the fair value of the trading portfolio of investment in marketable equity securities.

_____   15. "Percentage depletion" of natural resources was in excess of the cost of natural resources.

_____   16. The income statement reports earnings from investments in stock accounted for by the equity method. No dividends were received during the year from the investee. When dividends are received in future years, 70% will be eligible for the dividends received deduction.

_____ 17. The company has a construction division which uses the percentage-of-completion method for books and the completed-contract method for tax purposes.

_____ 18. The company paid $8,000 in premiums for life insurance which it carries on key officers. The cash surrender value of the related policies increased $1,200.

_____ 19. The company has made a formal plan for discontinuing a segment of business. The segment will continue to operate for the first six months of the next year and is expected to produce operating income of $100,000 during those six months. A loss of $500,000 is expected on the disposal of the assets of the segment to be discontinued.

_____ 20. Prepaid advertising expense is deferred and amortized for accounting purposes and deducted as an expense when paid for tax purposes.

_____ 21. The company received a condemnation award from the state for land and a building that it owned which lay in the path of a proposed highway. The award of $500,000 exceeded the property's carrying value (and tax basis) of $220,000. The company used the entire proceeds received to replace the property within two years and, therefore, was able to defer the related gain for tax purposes.

_____ 22. The corporation owns a patent and allows another company to use the rights embodied in the patent in exchange for royalty payments which are collected in advance.

_____ 23. A transaction accounted for as a sale and leaseback for accounting purposes was treated as a sale for tax purposes. A gain resulted from the sale.

_____ 24. The amount funded for the company pension plan this year was less than the amount expensed for financial reporting purposes. Only the amount funded was deductible on this year's tax return.

_____ 25. The company collected subscriptions in advance for a magazine it publishes.

_____ 26. The accrual for postretirement benefits other than pensions was made in accordance with *SFAS No. 106.* This amount will be charged to the tax returns of the years in which amounts are paid for these benefits.

_____ 27. Plant assets were acquired in the current year. The depreciation taken for book purposes exceeded the depreciation reported for tax purposes for the current year.

_____ 28. An accrued revenue was reported on the income statement for the current year; the revenue will be taxable when it is collected.

Solution to Case 20-1

1.   b

2.   a

3.   b   •The use of the accrual method for books causes the entire gross profit from the installment sale to be reflected in the income statement of the period of sale. The use of the installment method for tax purposes causes the gross profit to be allocated over the collection period; the amount of gross profit recognized in a period is proportionate to the amount of sales price collected in the period.

4.   c   •The interest is tax exempt revenue.

5.   a

6.   c

7.   c

8.   b

9.   c

10.   a

11.   b   •Interest and property taxes incurred during construction are also capitalized for financial reporting purposes. *SFAS No. 34* requires that avoidable interest cost during construction be capitalized. Therefore, the interest and property taxes will be amortized to income via the depreciation process. The amortization (depreciation) period is shorter for tax purposes in this particular case, causing a net future taxable amount.

12.   c

13.   b   •When any asset is amortized faster for tax purposes than it is amortized for book purposes, the cumulative temporary difference existing at a balance sheet date will result in **net** future taxable amounts.

14.   a   •This loss will not be deductible for tax purposes until the future period in which the loss is realized (that is, in the period the securities are sold).

15.   c   •Percentage depletion is often referred to as statutory depletion.

16.   b   •The 70% is a permanent difference and 30% of the total difference is a temporary
      &   difference.
      c

17.   b

18.   c   •The amount of the permanent difference is $6,800, which is the amount expensed on the income statement. The $1,200 increase in cash surrender value of life insurance is reflected as an increase in assets on the GAAP basis balance sheet and does not result in either a permanent or temporary difference.

19.   a   •The amount of the temporary difference is $400,000, according to the rules of *APB Opinion No. 30*. The loss accrued for books in the current period is $400,000. The loss cannot be deducted for tax purposes until the period of realization.

20.   b

21.   b   •A gain of $280,000 must be recognized for financial reporting purposes. (*FIN No. 30*); the entire gain is deferred for tax purposes because all proceeds received were reinvested in replacement property within two years of the involuntary conversion of nonmonetary assets to monetary assets.

22.   a   •The royalty receipts are to be included in taxable income in the period they are received.

23.	a	•The gain is generally deferred for accounting purposes but reported currently for tax purposes.
24.	a	
25.	a	•The collections are included in taxable income in the period received. The related revenue is deferred for financial reporting purposes until it is earned.
26.	a	
27.	a	
28.	b	

ILLUSTRATION 20-4
COMPOUND JOURNAL ENTRY TO RECORD INCOME TAXES (L.O.1,2,3,5)

In recording income taxes, the best approach is to perform the following steps in order:

1. **Compute the amount of income tax payable for the current period.** This is always based on the amount of taxable income and the tax rate for the current year. This amount is also referred to as "current tax expense"; it is recorded by a credit to Income Tax Payable. If there is a net operating loss for the current year, then the benefits of a loss carryback are called "current tax benefit" and are recorded by a debit to a receivable account.

2. **Compute the change required in the deferred tax account(s).** To do this, the appropriate balance of the deferred tax account(s) at the balance sheet date must be determined and this may require a scheduling process. The appropriate balance represents the deferred tax consequences of cumulative temporary differences and operating loss carryforwards existing at the balance sheet date. The difference between the ending balance and the beginning balance of a deferred tax account is called "deferred tax expense" or "deferred tax benefit" or "benefits of loss carryforward," whichever is appropriate. It is recorded by a debit or a credit to a deferred tax asset or liability account.

3. **Record income tax expense** which is the total of current tax expense (or benefit) and deferred tax expense (or benefit). In a compound journal entry, it is the "plug" figure required to make the journal entry balance.

> **TIP:** In computing deferred income taxes at a balance sheet date, the amount of cumulative temporary differences must be determined. Information on when those differences originated is **not** needed; some or all of the differences could have originated in prior periods. Information about the individual future years in which these differences are expected to reverse is generally **not** needed because the tax rate is usually the same flat rate year after year. One case in which this information **is** needed is the situation where there are different tax rates enacted for the individual future years in which existing temporary differences are expected to cause taxable and deductible amounts to occur. Thus, if a single tax rate applies to all future years, an aggregate computation for deferred income taxes is appropriate. However, if different tax rates apply to individual future years, a scheduling of future taxable and deductible amounts (due to temporary differences at the balance sheet date) with a separate computation for each future year affected is required.

ILLUSTRATION 20-4 (Continued)

TIP: In determining the future tax consequences of temporary differences (Step 2) when there is a phased-in change in tax rates, it is necessary to prepare a schedule showing in which future years existing temporary differences will result in taxable or deductible amounts. In determining the applicable tax rate, you must make assumptions about whether the entity will report taxable income or losses in the various future years expected to be affected by the reversal of existing temporary differences. Thus, you calculate the taxes payable or refundable in the future, due to existing temporary differences. In making these calculations, you apply the provisions of the tax law and enacted tax rates for the relevant periods. The following guidelines are used to determine the applicable tax rate:

1. If taxable income is expected in the year that a future taxable (or deductible) amount is scheduled, use the enacted rate for the future year to calculate the related deferred tax liability (or asset).

2. If an NOL is expected in the year that a future taxable (or deductible) amount is scheduled, use the enacted rate of the prior year to which the NOL would be carried back or the enacted rate of the future year to which the carryforward would apply, whichever is appropriate to calculate the related deferred tax liability (or asset).

TIP: Single entries (rather than one compound journal entry) can be used to record income taxes. With this approach, you could perform Step 1 above and record the results by either a credit to Income Tax Payable (if there is taxable income for the current period) or a debit to Income Tax Refund Receivable (if there is a loss on the current tax return and a carryback is appropriate). The other half of this first entry is a debit or credit (whichever is needed to make the entry balance) to Income Tax Expense. A second entry would be recorded for the results of Step 2 above. In this second entry, a debit or credit would be recorded to Deferred Tax Asset or Deferred Tax Liability, whatever is needed to properly report deferred taxes on the balance sheet. The other half of this second entry would be either a debit or credit to Income Tax Expense, as appropriate, to make the entry balance. Step 2 is repeated (and another single entry is recorded) if there is more than one reason for having temporary differences. Thus, if one entity has three types of temporary differences, Step 2 is performed three times and there would be a total of four single entries to record income taxes for the period.

CASE 20-2

Purpose: (L.O.2,5,11) This case examines the focus of the liability method and the steps in the annual computation of deferred tax assets and liabilities.

The objectives of accounting for income taxes are to recognize (a) the amount of taxes payable or refundable for the current year, and (b) deferred tax liabilities and assets that arise because of the future tax consequences of events that have been recognized in an enterprise's financial statements or tax returns.

Instructions

(a)   If a revenue item is reported on the income statement in 1999, but is included on the tax return in 2000, explain whether the related income tax effect should be reflected on the income statement in 1999 or 2000, and why.

(b)   Explain whether the liability method of accounting for deferred taxes focuses on the proper valuation of assets and liabilities (balance sheet orientation) or on income determination (income statement orientation).

(c)   List the steps to be included in the annual computation of deferred tax liabilities and assets.

Solution to Case 20-2

(a)   The tax consequences of a transaction or event are to be recognized in the same period that the transaction or event is recognized in the financial statements. This is the essence of the comprehensive income tax allocation approach. Thus, the income tax effect of revenue recognized in 1999 should also be recognized on the income statement in 1999, even though the payment of the resulting tax is deferred until a later year.

(b)   At any given balance sheet date, deferred income taxes are computed by applying the applicable tax rate(s) to future taxable and deductible amounts stemming from temporary differences existing at the balance sheet date. Thus, a deferred tax liability (or asset) is recognized for taxes payable (or a reduction in taxes payable) in future years due to existing temporary differences. The amount of deferred tax expense (or benefit) for the income statement is determined by the change in deferred tax accounts from one balance sheet date to another; thus, deferred income tax expense (or benefit) is a residual figure (commonly called a plug figure). Therefore, the liability method is said to be balance sheet oriented.

(c)   The procedures in the computation of deferred income taxes are as follows:
1.   Identify (a) the types and amounts of existing temporary differences, and (b) the nature and amount of each type of operating loss and tax credit carryforward and the remaining length of the carryforward period.
2.   Measure the total deferred tax liability for taxable temporary differences using the applicable tax rate.

3.   Measure the total deferred tax asset for deductible temporary differences and operating loss carryforwards using the applicable tax rate.
4.   Measure deferred tax assets for each type of tax credit carryforward.
5.   Reduce deferred tax assets by a **valuation allowance** if, based on the weight of available evidence, it is **more likely than not** (a likelihood of more than 50 percent) that some portion or all of the deferred tax assets will **not** be realized. The valuation allowance should be sufficient to reduce the deferred tax assets to the amount that is more likely than not to be realized.

EXERCISE 20-1

Purpose: (L.O.1,2,5,10) This exercise will illustrate how to record current tax expense and deferred tax expense when one taxable temporary difference exists. It will also illustrate the effect of the reversal of the same temporary difference on income tax expense.

Gary Winarski, Inc. has pretax financial income for 1999 of $400,000. There were no deferred taxes at the beginning of 1999. At the end of 1999, temporary differences of $85,000 exist which are expected to result in taxable amounts in 2001. The enacted tax rates are as follows:

Year	Tax Rate
1998	50%
1999-2000	40%
2001 and later	30%

Instructions
(a)   Compute taxable income for 1999 and record income tax payable.
(b)   Compute deferred taxes at December 31, 1999 and record the change in deferred taxes, assuming taxable income is expected in all future years.
(c)   Draft the income tax expense section of the income statement for 1999 (beginning with "Income before income taxes").
(d)   Draft the income tax expense section of the income statement for 2001 assuming taxable income for 2001 is $360,000 (begin with the line "Income before income taxes").

Solution to Exercise 20-1

(a)   Pretax financial income $ 400,000
       Originating temporary difference resulting in future
           taxable amounts   (85,000)
       Taxable income $ 315,000

       Income Tax Expense   126,000
               Income Tax Payable ($315,000 x 40%)   126,000
                   (To record current tax expense)

Approach and Explanation: Use the reconciliation format in **Illustration 20-3** to compute taxable income. Because there was no deferred taxes (and, thus, no temporary differences) existing at the beginning of 1999, all $85,000 of temporary differences existing at the end of 1999 must have originated (came about) during 1999. Because these originating temporary differences will result in future taxable amounts, they cause taxable income to be lower than pretax financial income in 1999.

(b)

Future taxable amounts	$ 85,000
Enacted tax rate for applicable future year	30%
Balance needed for deferred tax liability at December 31, 1999	25,500
Balance of deferred tax liability at January 1, 1999	0
Increase in deferred tax liability during 1999	$ 25,500

Income Tax Expense	25,500	
Deferred Tax Liability		25,500*
(To record the change in deferred taxes)		

     *See computation above.

Explanation: The deferred tax liability at December 31, 1999 is measured by using the tax rate enacted for the future year (2001) in which the underlying temporary difference will result in future taxable amounts.

> **TIP:** Refer to **Illustration 20-4** and the last **TIP** for that illustration. This exercise makes use of the single entry approach to recording income taxes. The entries for parts (a) and (b) of this exercise are often combined for a compound journal entry as follows:
>
> | | | |
> |---|---:|---:|
> | Income Tax Expense.. | 151,500 | |
> | Income Tax Payable .... | | 126,000 |
> | Deferred Tax Liability.................................... | | 25,500 |

(c)

Income before income taxes		$ 400,000
Income tax expense:		
Current tax expense	$ 126,000	
Deferred tax expense	25,500	151,500
Net income		$ 248,500

> **TIP:** Notice that the effective tax rate for 1999 is 37.875% ($151,500 ÷ $400,000 = .37875). This rate is lower than the 40% statutory tax rate for 1999 because $315,000 of the $400,000 is tax effected at 40% and $85,000 of the $400,000 is tax effected at 30%.

(d)

Income before income taxes		$ 275,000[a]
Income tax expense:		
Current tax expense	$ 108,000[b]	
Deferred tax benefit	(25,500)[c]	82,500
Net income		$ 192,500

[a]Pretax financial income $\quad\quad\quad\quad\quad\quad\quad\quad\quad$ $ X
Reversing taxable temporary difference $\quad\quad\quad$ 85,000
Taxable income $\quad\quad\quad\quad\quad\quad\quad\quad\quad\quad$ $ 360,000

$\quad\quad$ Solving for X: $\quad$ X + $85,000 = $360,000
$\quad\quad\quad\quad\quad\quad\quad\quad$ X = $360,000 - $85,000
$\quad\quad\quad\quad\quad\quad\quad\quad$ X = $275,000 = Pretax financial income

[b]Taxable income for 2001 $\quad\quad\quad\quad\quad\quad\quad$ $ 360,000
Enacted tax rate $\quad\quad\quad\quad\quad\quad\quad\quad\quad$ 30%
Income tax payable for 2001 $\quad\quad\quad\quad\quad$ $ 108,000

[c]There is no temporary difference existing at the end of 2001, so the balance in the deferred tax liability account would be eliminated. A decrease in a deferred tax liability results in a deferred tax benefit on the income statement.

TIP: Notice that the effective tax rate for 2001 is 30% ($82,500 ÷ $275,000 = .30), which equals the statutory tax rate for 2001.

EXERCISE 20-2

Purpose: (L.O.1,2,3,5,6) This exercise illustrates how to account for income taxes when there are both permanent and temporary differences involved and a flat tax rate is enacted for all periods affected.

The Monte Neece Corporation has pretax financial income of $200,000 for 1999 (the first year of operations). The difference between revenues and expenses reported on the tax return for 1999 and the income statement for 1999 are as follows:

	Tax Return	Income Statement
Depreciation expense	$ 80,000	$ 62,000
Insurance premiums expense		8,000
Warranty expense	10,000	19,000
Interest revenue from municipal bonds		2,000
Rent revenue	6,200	5,000

The insurance premiums pertain to life insurance on the lives of corporate officers, and the beneficiary is the corporation.

The tax rate for 1999 is 40%, and no new rate has been enacted for future years.

Instructions
(a) $\quad$ Compute taxable income for 1999.
(b) $\quad$ Prepare the journal entry to record income taxes for 1999.
(c) $\quad$ Prepare the portion of the income statement for 1999 that reports income taxes. Begin with the caption "Income before income taxes."

Solution to Exercise 20-2

(a)
Pretax financial income for 1999	$ 200,000
Nondeductible expense—life insurance on officers	8,000
Nontaxable revenue—interest on municipal bonds	(2,000)
Excess depreciation per tax return for 1999	(18,000)
Excess warranty expense per books for 1999	9,000
Excess rent revenue per tax return for 1999	1,200
Taxable income for 1999	$ 198,200

(b)
Income Tax Expense	82,400[e]	
Deferred Tax Asset—Warranties	3,600[d]	
Deferred Tax Asset—Rents	480[c]	
Deferred Tax Liability—Depreciation		7,200[b]
Income Tax Payable		79,280[a]

[a]$198,200 x 40% = $79,280.
[b]$18,000 x 40% = $7,200.
[c]$1,200 x 40% = $480.
[d]$9,000 x 40% = $3,600.
[e]$79,280 + $7,200 - $480 - $3,600 = $82,400.

> **TIP:** Although some people may choose to use only one deferred tax asset account in the above entry, the use of a separate deferred tax account for each type of temporary difference (as illustrated above) is helpful when later classifying deferred taxes on the balance sheet.

(c)
Income before income taxes		$ 200,000
Provision for income taxes:		
Current tax expense	$ 79,280	
Deferred tax expense	3,120*	82,400
Net income		$ 117,600

*Deferred tax expense of $7,200, deferred tax benefit of $480, and deferred tax benefit of $3,600, net to a deferred tax expense of $3,120.

> **TIP:** The amount reported for total income tax expense ($82,400 in this exercise) should agree with the balance of the Income Tax Expense account before closing.

EXERCISE 20-3

Purpose: (L.O.1,2,3,5,7,10) This exercise illustrates the steps involved in computing and recording income taxes when two types of temporary differences exist and there is a phased-in change in tax rates.

T&C Benyon Corporation has the following facts available:
1.   Pretax financial income for Year 1 is $105,000.
2.   Year 1 is the first year of operations.
3.   One temporary difference exists at the end of Year 1 that will result in deductible amounts of: $20,000 in Year 2.
                                                              $30,000 in Year 3.
4.   Another temporary difference exists at the end of Year 1 which will result in taxable amounts of: $11,000 in Year 2.
                                                              $14,000 in Year 3.
5.   Tax rates enacted by the end of Year 1 are: 50% for Year 1.
                                                        40% for Year 2.
                                                        30% for Year 3.
6.   Taxable income is expected in all future years.

Instructions
(a)   Compute taxable income for Year 1.
(b)   Compute the deferred taxes to be reported on the balance sheet at the end of Year 1.
(c)   Prepare the journal entry to record income taxes for Year 1.
(d)   Draft the income tax expense section of the income statement for Year 1.

Solution to Exercise 20-3

(a)   Pretax financial income for Year 1 $ 105,000
       Temporary differences originating:
              Deductible temporary difference   50,000
              Taxable temporary difference   (25,000)
       Taxable income for Year 1 $ 130,000

(b)   At December 31, Year 1, a deferred tax asset of $17,000 and a deferred tax liability of $8,600 should be reflected on the balance sheet. Deferred taxes are computed by a scheduling process as follows:

	Current Year	Future Years		
	Year 1	Year 2	Year 3	Total
Taxable income	$130,000			
Future deductible amounts		($20,000)	($30,000)	($50,000)
Future taxable amounts		11,000	14,000	25,000
Enacted tax rates	50%	40%	30%	
Deferred tax (asset) liability		($8,000)	($9,000)	($17,000)
		4,400	4,200	$ 8,600

(c)   Deferred Tax Asset... 17,000

Income Tax Expense 56,600

        Income Tax Payable.. 65,000

        Deferred Tax Liability 8,600

Computations:

Step 1:   Taxable income $ 130,000

           Tax rate for Year 1   50%

           Income tax payable $ 65,000

Step 2:   See the scheduling in part (b) for determination of the $17,000 ending balance for deferred tax asset and $8,600 ending balance for deferred tax liability.

           The change in deferred taxes is computed as follows:

           Balance of deferred tax asset at end of Year 1 $ 17,000

           Balance of deferred tax asset at beginning of Year 1   0

           Increase in deferred tax asset (which is a deferred tax benefit) $ 17,000

           Balance of deferred tax liability at end of Year 1 $ 8,600

           Balance of deferred tax liability at beginning of Year 1   0

           Increase in deferred tax liability (a deferred tax expense) $ 8,600

Step 3:   Deferred tax benefit $(17,000)

           Deferred tax expense   8,600

           Net deferred tax benefit   (8,400)

           Current tax expense   65,000

           Total income tax expense for Year 1 $ 56,600

> **TIP:**   The three following single entries are equivalent to the one compound journal entry above. Notice the first one records the current tax expense and a current tax obligation of $65,000. The second entry adjusts the deferred tax asset account and records a deferred tax benefit of $17,000; a deferred tax benefit reduces total income tax expense. The third one adjusts the deferred tax liability account and records a deferred tax expense of $8,600; a deferred tax expense increases total income tax expense. These three entries can be used in place of the one compound entry.

Income Tax Expense..	65,000	
Income Tax Payable		65,000
Deferred Tax Asset	17,000	
Income Tax Expense		17,000
Income Tax Expense..	8,600	
Deferred Tax Liability..........................		8,600

(d)   The relevant section of the income statement would appear as follows:

Income before income taxes		$ 105,000
Income tax expense:		
Current tax expense	$ 65,000	
Deferred tax benefit	(8,400)	56,600
Net income		$ 48,400

EXERCISE 20-4

Purpose: (L.O.2,3,5,10) This exercise will review a situation that involves both a deferred tax asset and a deferred tax liability, one with a beginning balance. It also reviews the relationships existing in the reconciliation of pretax financial income and taxable income.

The following facts relate to the Tasty Bits Corporation:
1. Deferred tax liability, January 1, 1999, $80,000.
2. Deferred tax asset, January 1, 1999, $0.
3. Taxable income for 1999, $164,000.
4. There are no permanent differences in 1999.
5. Cumulative temporary difference at December 31, 1999, giving rise to future taxable amounts, $440,000.
6. Cumulative temporary difference at December 31, 1999, giving rise to future deductible amounts, $70,000.
7. Tax rate for all years, 40%.
8. The company is expected to operate profitably in all future years.

Instructions
(a)   Prepare the journal entry to record income tax payable, deferred income taxes, and income tax expense for 1999.
(b)   Draft the income tax expense section of the income statement for 1999, beginning with the line "income before income taxes."

Solution to Exercise 20-4

(a)   Journal entry:

Income Tax Expense	133,600	
Deferred Tax Asset	28,000	
Income Tax Payable ($164,000 x 40%)		65,600
Deferred Tax Liability		96,000

Computations:

	Future Taxable (Deductible)	Tax	Deferred Tax	
Temporary Difference	**Amounts**	**Rate**	**(Asset)**	**Liability**
Taxable type	$ 440,000	40%		$176,000
Deductible type	(70,000)	40%	$(28,000)	
Totals	$ 370,000	40%	$(28,000)	$176,000**

**Because of a flat tax rate, these totals can be reconciled:
    $370,000 x 40% = ($28,000) + $176,000

Deferred tax liability, 12/31/99	$ 176,000
Deferred tax liability, 12/31/98	80,000
Deferred tax expense, 1999	$ 96,000
(net increase required in a deferred tax liability)	
Deferred tax asset, 12/31/99	$ 28,000
Deferred tax asset, 12/31/98	0
Deferred tax expense (benefit), 1999	$ (28,000)
(net increase required in a deferred tax asset)	
Deferred tax expense for 1999	$ 96,000
Deferred tax benefit for 1999	(28,000)
Net deferred tax expense for 1999	68,000
Current tax expense, 1999	65,600
Total income tax expense, 1999	$ 133,600

(b)
Income before income taxes		$ 334,000*
Income tax expense:		
Current tax expense	$ 65,600	
Deferred tax expense	68,000	133,600
Net income		$ 200,400

*Because of the flat tax rate for all years, the amount of cumulative temporary difference existing at the beginning of the year can be calculated by dividing the $80,000 beginning balance in Deferred Tax Liability by 40%, which equals $200,000. This information may now be combined with the other facts given in the exercise to reconcile pretax financial income with taxable income for 1999 as follows:

Pretax financial income	$ X
Net originating temporary difference giving rise to future taxable amounts ($440,000 - $200,000)	(240,000)
Originating temporary difference giving rise to future deductible amounts	70,000
Taxable income	$ 164,000

Solving for X: X - $240,000 + $70,000 = $164,000;
$$X = \$334,000$$

EXERCISE 20-5

Purpose: (L.O.9) This exercise illustrates the application of guidelines for the classification of deferred income taxes.

The Chicone Corporation has several temporary differences existing at December 31, 1999. The following information pertains:
1. The carrying value of plant assets exceeds the tax basis of those assets by $500,000.
2. A long-term pension liability of $700,000 appears on the balance sheet due to the accrual of pension costs. Only the amounts funded have been deducted on the tax returns over the years.
3. For tax purposes, $400,000 of income on contracts has been deferred until 2000.
4. The company recognized a loss of $80,000 in 1999 associated with a discontinued segment of business. The disposal date is scheduled for 2000; thus, an accrued liability for plant closing costs is classified as a current liability.
5. An allowance for doubtful accounts of $220,000 appears on the GAAP basis balance sheet. Uncollectible accounts are tax deductible only when individual accounts are written off. All accounts receivable are classified as current assets.
6. An estimated liability for litigation settlements of $130,000 appears in the long-term liability section of the balance sheet. This liability has a tax basis of zero.

A flat tax rate of 40% is enacted for all years.

Instructions
Compute the deferred tax assets and liabilities to appear on the balance sheet at December 31, 1999. Indicate how they are to be classified.

> **TIP:** Deferred income tax assets and liabilities are to be reported on the balance sheet in a **net** current and a **net** noncurrent amount. Deferred tax liabilities and assets are to be classified as current or noncurrent based on the classification of the related asset or liability for financial reporting. A deferred tax liability or asset that is **not** related to an asset or liability for financial reporting, including deferred tax assets related to carryforwards, should be classified according to the expected reversal date of the temporary difference.

Solution to Exercise 20-5

Temporary Difference	Resulting Deferred Tax (Asset)	Liability	Related Balance Sheet Account	Deferred Tax Classification
1. Excess depreciation for tax purposes.		$200,000	Plant Assets	Noncurrent
2. Excess pension expense for book purposes.	$(280,000)		Pension Liability	Noncurrent
3. Excess contract income for book purposes.		160,000	None	Current
4. Accrual of plant closing costs for books.	(32,000)		Accrued Liability for Plant Closing	Current
5. Accrual of uncollectible accounts for books.	(88,000)		Allowance for Doubtful Accounts	Current
6. Accrual of litigation settlements.	(52,000)		Estimated Obligation for Lawsuits	Noncurrent
	$(452,000)	$360,000		

Summary: The net current amount is a liability of $40,000 [$160,000 - ($32,000 + $88,000) = $40,000]. The net noncurrent amount is an asset of $132,000 ($280,000 - $200,000 + $52,000 = $132,000).

Explanation:

1. $500,000 future taxable amounts x 40% = $200,000 deferred tax liability. There is a related asset on the books, Plant Assets, and its classification is noncurrent. Therefore, the resulting deferred tax liability account is noncurrent.

2. $700,000 future deductible amounts x 40% = $280,000 deferred tax asset. There is a related Pension Liability on the GAAP balance sheet, and its classification is noncurrent. Therefore, the resulting deferred tax asset is noncurrent.

3. $400,000 future taxable amounts x 40% = $160,000 deferred tax liability. There is no asset or liability on the balance sheet that is related to the deferral of contract income for tax purposes. The classification of the deferred taxes is, therefore, dependent on the expected reversal date of the temporary difference. The expected reversal date

(2000) is the year immediately following the balance sheet date; hence, the classification of the deferred tax account is current.

4. $80,000 future deductible amounts x 40% = $32,000 deferred tax asset. There is a related liability on the balance sheet, Accrued Liability for Plant Closing Costs, and its classification is current. Therefore, the resulting deferred tax asset is current.

5. $220,000 future deductible amounts x $40% = $88,000 deferred tax asset. There is a related contra asset account, Allowance for Doubtful Accounts, in the current asset section of the balance sheet. Hence, the related deferred tax account is a current asset.

6. $130,000 future deductible amounts x 40% = $52,000 deferred tax asset. There is a related accrued liability account, Estimated Obligation for Lawsuits, reported as a long-term liability on the balance sheet. The related deferred tax asset is therefore a noncurrent asset.

> **TIP:** A commonly confusing point stems from the fact that the term **current** is used in association with **two totally unrelated amounts** involved with accounting for income taxes. These two amounts are the **current portion of income tax expense on the income statement and the current portion of deferred taxes on the balance sheet**. On the income statement, income tax expense is comprised of both current and deferred portions. On the balance sheet, deferred taxes are classified as either current or noncurrent. A change during the period in both current and noncurrent deferred taxes on the balance sheet results in the deferred portion of income tax expense for the same period on the income statement.

EXERCISE 20-6

Purpose: (L.O.8) This exercise reviews the accounting procedures for an actual net operating loss.

The T. Evans Corporation has had no permanent or temporary differences since it began operations. Information regarding taxable income and taxes paid is as follows:

Year	Taxable Income (Loss)	Tax Rate	Taxes Paid
1	$ 60,000	40%	$ 24,000
2	100,000	40%	40,000
3	80,000	35%	28,000
4	160,000	35%	56,000
5	(400,000)	30%	

The tax rate enacted for Year 6 and subsequent years is 25%.

Instructions
(a) Assuming the NOL (net operating loss) in Year 5 is carried back to the extent possible, prepare the journal entry to record the benefits of the carryback and the journal entry to record the expected benefits of any related NOL carryforward. Assume it is likely that the benefits of any carryforward will be fully realized.

(b) Explain how all of the accounts in the entries above are to be reported in the financial statements for Year 5. Draft the income tax expense section of the income statement for Year 5, beginning with the line "Operating loss before income taxes."

(c) Assuming taxable income is $100,000 (before considering the NOL carryforward) in Year 6, prepare the journal entry to record income taxes. Also, draft the income tax expense section of the income statement for Year 6, beginning with the line "Income before income taxes."

Solution to Exercise 20-6

(a) Income Tax Refund Receivable... 124,000
      Benefits Due to Loss Carryback...................................   124,000
         ($40,000 + $28,000 + $56,000 = $124,000)

   Deferred Tax Asset... 15,000
      Benefits Due to Loss Carryforward.............................   15,000
         ($400,000 - $100,000 - $80,000 - $160,000 = $60,000)
         ($60,000 x 25% = $15,000)

> **TIP:** The expected benefits of an operating loss carryforward are recognized in the year of the loss which gives rise to the carryforward. The tax rate enacted for the future year in which the benefits are expected to be realized is used to calculate the related deferred tax asset.
>
> **TIP:** Benefits Due to Loss Carryback and Benefits Due to Loss Carryforward are both negative components of total income tax expense; therefore, they are credits to the income statement. The Benefits Due to Loss Carryback represent a current tax benefit, and the Benefits Due to Loss Carryforward are a deferred tax benefit.
>
> **TIP:** If it is **more likely than not** that a portion or all of the deferred tax asset will **not** be realized, a valuation allowance should be established by a charge to income tax expense and a credit to an allowance account. For example, in the case above, if one-half of the benefits of the operating loss carryforward were not expected to be realized within the carryforward period, an adjusting entry for $7,500 would be recorded by a debit to Benefits Due to Loss Carryforward and a credit to Allowance to Reduce Deferred Tax Asset to Expected Realizable Value.

(b) The Income Tax Refund Receivable account is to be classified as a current asset on the balance sheet. The Deferred Tax Asset relates to an NOL carryforward so it is to be classified as a current asset **if** the benefits of the carryforward are expected to be realized in the year that immediately follows the balance sheet date. If the benefits are expected in a later year, the Deferred Tax Asset is to be classified as a noncurrent asset (in the Other Assets classification).

The other two accounts are negative components of income tax expense. The income statement would reflect them as follows:

Operating loss before income taxes	$(400,000)
Benefits due to loss carryback	124,000
Benefits due to loss carryforward	15,000
Net loss	$(261,000)

(c) Income Tax Expense 25,000

     Income Tax Payable.. 10,000*

     Deferred Tax Asset ($60,000 x 25%) 15,000

*$100,000 - $60,000 = $40,000 taxable income for Year 6.
$40,000 x 25% = $10,000 income tax payable.

Income before income taxes		$ 100,000
Income tax expense:		
Current tax expense	$ 10,000	
Deferred tax expense	15,000	25,000
Net income		$ 75,000

EXERCISE 20-7

Purpose: (L.O.10) This exercise illustrates how existing depreciable assets can give rise to deductible amounts in some future years and taxable amounts in other future years; the net amount is generally a future taxable amount.

An enterprise acquired a depreciable asset at the beginning of 1999. The asset has a cost of $120,000 and no salvage value. It is being depreciated over six years using the straight-line method for financial reporting purposes and is being depreciated over three years using the straight-line method and one-half year convention for tax purposes. The depreciation schedules for both financial reporting purposes and tax purposes are as follows:

Year	Depreciation for Financial Reporting	Depreciation for Tax Purposes	Difference
1999	$ 20,000	$ 20,000	$ ---
2000	20,000	40,000	(20,000)
2001	20,000	40,000	(20,000)
2002	20,000	20,000	---
2003	20,000	---	20,000
2004	20,000	---	20,000
	$ 120,000	$ 120,000	$ ---

Instructions

(a)   Determine the cumulative temporary difference at the end of each year and describe its impact on future tax returns.

(b)   Show how the future taxable (deductible) amounts would appear on a schedule at the end of 2000.

(c)   Show how the future taxable (deductible) amounts would appear on a schedule at the end of 2001.

(d)   Compute the deferred taxes to be reported on the balance sheet at the end of 2000, assuming a flat tax rate of 40% for all years.

(e)   Compute the deferred taxes to be reported on the balance sheet at the end of 2000, assuming enacted tax rates as follows: 50% for 1999 and 2000, 40% for 2001 and 2002, and 35% for 2003 and 2004.

TIP: Typically, temporary differences of this type accumulate over several years and then eliminate over several subsequent years. **Future** temporary differences for **existing** depreciable assets (in use at the balance sheet date) are considered in determining the future years in which existing temporary differences result in taxable or deductible amounts.

Solution to Exercise 20-7

(a)

Year	Temporary Difference Originating (Reversing)	Cumulative Temporary Difference At End of Year	Effect on Future Tax Returns
1999	$ -0-	$ -0-	None
2000	20,000	20,000	Net future taxable amounts
2001	20,000	40,000	Net future taxable amounts
2002	-0-	40,000	Net future taxable amounts
2003	(20,000)	20,000	Net future taxable amounts
2004	(20,000)	-0-	None
	$ -0-		

(b)

	Future Years				
	2001	2002	2003	2004	Total
Future taxable (deductible) amounts	$(20,000)	$ ---	$20,000	$20,000	$20,000

TIP: At the end of 2000, the cumulative temporary difference of $20,000 will result in a **net future taxable amount**. However, more **originating** differences in 2001 will cause some **deductible** amounts before the temporary difference **reverses** and causes taxable amounts in 2003 and 2004.

(c)

	Future Years			
	2002	**2003**	**2004**	**Total**
Future taxable (deductible) amounts	$ --	$20,000	$20,000	$40,000

(d) Cumulative temporary difference at December 31, 2000,
     giving rise to net future taxable amounts $ 20,000
     Enacted tax rate for future years   40%
     Deferred tax liability at December 31, 2000 $ 8,000

(e) A deferred tax liability of $6,000 at December 31, 2000 would be determined by tax effecting the amounts appearing in the scheduling process in part (b) above. The computations are as follows:

	Future Years				
	2001	**2002**	**2003**	**2004**	**Total**
Future taxable (deductible) amounts	$(20,000)	$ ---	$20,000	$20,000	$20,000
Enacted tax rate	40%	40%	35%	35%	
Deferred tax (asset) liability	$(8,000)	$ ---	$7,000	$7,000	$6,000

Explanation: In most instances, we can compute deferred taxes at a balance sheet by multiplying the cumulative temporary difference by one applicable tax rate as was done in part (d) above. However, if there are phased-in changes in tax rates, individual future tax rates are applied to the taxable (deductible) amounts scheduled for particular years, and the pattern of the future taxable (deductible) amounts (as determined by the scheduling process) has an impact on the computation of deferred taxes.

EXERCISE 20-8

Purpose: (L.O.2,3,5,7) This comprehensive exercise will illustrate how the interperiod allocation of income taxes affects the financial statements.

The following facts pertain to the Michael Hess Corporation:
- There were no deferred taxes on the December 31, 1998 balance sheet.
- Pretax financial income for 1999 is $113,000.
- Revenue of $20,000 reported on the 1999 income statement will be included on the 2000 income tax return.
- Expense of $7,000 reported on the 1999 income statement will be reported on the 2001 income tax return.
- There are no differences between pretax financial income and taxable income for 1999, other than the two items mentioned above.
- Enacted tax rates are as follows as of December 31, 1999:

Year	Rate
1999	50%
2000	40%
2001	30%

- Taxable income is expected in all future years.

Instructions

(a)   Compute the amount of taxable income for the year ending December 31, 1999.

(b)   Compute the amount of income tax payable for the year ending December 31, 1999.

(c)   Describe how each of the two temporary differences will impact future income tax returns.

(d)   Compute the deferred taxes to be reported on the balance sheet at December 31, 1999. Describe how they will affect the income statement for the year ending December 31, 1999.

(e)   Prepare the journal entry(ies) to record income taxes for 1999.

(f)   Describe how the deferred tax accounts will be reported on the balance sheet at December 31, 1999.

(g)   Prepare the section of the 1999 income statement involving income tax expense, beginning with "Income before income taxes."

Solution to Exercise 20-8

(a)

Pretax financial income for 1999	$ 113,000
Temporary difference originating that gives rise to a future taxable amount	(20,000)
Temporary difference originating that gives rise to a future deductible amount	7,000
Taxable income for 1999	$ 100,000

(b)

Taxable income for 1999	$ 100,000
Enacted tax rate for 1999	50%
Income tax payable for 1999	$ 50,000

(c)   The revenue of $20,000 that is being deferred for tax purposes will result in a **taxable amount** (an amount which increases taxable income) on the 2000 income tax return. The expense of $7,000 that is being deferred for tax purposes will result in a **deductible amount** (an amount which reduces taxable income) on the 2001 income tax return.

(d)

	Current Year	Future Years		
	1999	**2000**	**2001**	**Total**
Taxable income	$100,000			
Future taxable (deductible) amounts				
Revenue deferred for tax purposes		$20,000		$20,000
Expense deferred for tax purposes			$(7,000)	$ (7,000)
Enacted tax rate	50%	40%	30%	
Deferred tax liability		$ 8,000		$ 8,000
Deferred tax asset			$(2,100)	$ (2,100)

There is no balance in the Deferred Tax Liability account at the beginning of 1999. Therefore, the journal entry(ies) to record income taxes for 1999 will include an increase in Deferred Tax Liability (credit) of $8,000. This will cause a corresponding increase in Income Tax Expense (debit) of $8,000, which is referred to as **deferred tax expense** of $8,000. There is no balance in the Deferred Tax Asset account at the beginning of 1999. Therefore, the journal entry(ies) to record income taxes for 1999 will include an increase in Deferred Tax Asset (debit) of $2,100. This will cause a corresponding decrease in Income Tax Expense (credit) of $2,100, which is referred to as **deferred tax benefit** of $2,100. The deferred tax expense of $8,000 is combined with the deferred tax benefit of $2,100 on the income statement to produce a net deferred tax expense of $5,900.

> **TIP:**   Notice that the future tax consequences of the $20,000 revenue item being deferred for tax purposes are recognized in the income statement in 1999 (which is the year in which that revenue item appears in the income statement). Those tax consequences are an increase in taxes of $8,000. Also, notice that the future tax consequences of the $7,000 expense item being deferred for tax purposes are recognized in the income statement in 1999 (which is the year in which that expense item appears in the income statement). Those tax consequences are a reduction in taxes of $2,100.

TIP: Examine the definition of "taxable temporary difference," "deferred tax liability," and "deferred tax expense" and how they apply to this situation. Those definitions and applications are as follows:

Taxable temporary difference: *Definition*—a temporary difference that results in taxable amounts in a future year(s) when the related asset or liability is recovered or settled, respectively. *Application*—a revenue item of $20,000 is being recognized for financial reporting purposes in 1999 but is being deferred for tax purposes. Thus, it may be an accrued revenue for book purposes which results in recording an account receivable or accrued receivable. In 2000, this asset (receivable) will be recovered (through collection of the receivable) which will result in reporting the $20,000 revenue item on the future (2000) tax return; that is, a taxable amount of $20,000 will appear on the 2000 tax return. Thus, at December 31, 1999, there is a temporary difference giving rise to a future taxable amount of $20,000.

Deferred tax liability: *Definition*—the deferred tax consequences attributable to taxable type temporary differences. *Application*—the taxable temporary difference of $20,000 existing at December 31, 1999 will cause an increase of $8,000 in income taxes payable in the future when the related taxable amount is reported on the 2000 tax return. Thus, a deferred tax liability of $8,000 is to be reported on the balance sheet at December 31, 1999.

Deferred tax expense: *Definition*—an increase in a deferred tax liability or a reduction in a deferred tax asset during the period. *Application*—the increase of $8,000 during 1999 in a deferred tax liability account on the balance sheet results in a deferred tax expense of $8,000 on the income statement for 1999.

TIP: Examine the definitions of "deductible temporary difference," "deferred tax asset," and "deferred tax benefit" and how they apply to this situation. Those definitions and applications are as follows:

Deductible temporary difference: *Definition*—a temporary difference that results in deductible amounts in a future year(s) when the related asset or liability is recovered or settled, respectively. *Application*—an expense item of $7,000 is being recognized for financial reporting purposes in 1999 but is being deferred for tax purposes. Thus, it may be an accrued expense for book purposes which results in recording an account payable or accrued payable. In 2001, this accrued payable will be settled (by payment of the payable) which will result in reporting the $7,000 expense item on the future (2001) tax return; that is, a deductible amount of $7,000 will appear on the 2001 tax return. Thus, at December 31, 1999, there is a temporary difference giving rise to a future deductible amount of $7,000.

> **Deferred tax asset:** *Definition*—the deferred tax consequences attributable to deductible type temporary differences and loss carryforwards. *Application*—the deductible temporary difference of $7,000 existing at December 31, 1999 will cause a decrease of $2,100 in taxes payable in the future when the related deductible amount is reported on the 2001 tax return. Thus, a deferred tax asset of $2,100 is to be reported on the balance sheet at December 31, 1999.
>
> **Deferred tax benefit:** *Definition*—an increase in a deferred tax asset or a reduction in a deferred tax liability during the period. *Application*—the increase of $2,100 during 1999 in a deferred tax asset account on the balance sheet results in a deferred tax benefit of $2,100 on the income statement for 1999.

(e)   The journal entry to record current tax expense (the amount of income taxes payable) for 1999 as determined by applying the provisions of the enacted tax law to the taxable income for 1999 is as follows:

Income Tax Expense	50,000	
Income Tax Payable ($100,000 x 50%)		50,000

The journal entry to record the increase in deferred tax liability during 1999 is as follows:

Income Tax Expense	8,000	
Deferred Tax Liability		8,000

The journal entry to record the increase in deferred tax asset during 1999 is as follows:

Deferred Tax Asset	2,100	
Income Tax Expense		2,100

> **TIP:** The three entries above are usually combined to form one compound journal entry as follows:
>
> | | | |
> |---|---|---|
> | Income Tax Expense | 55,900 | |
> | Deferred Tax Asset | 2,100 | |
> | Deferred Tax Liability | | 8,000 |
> | Income Tax Payable | | 50,000 |

(f)   The deferred tax accounts on the balance sheet are classified as current or noncurrent, based on the classification of any related asset or liability. Assuming the $20,000 temporary difference has a related accrued receivable on the books classified as a current asset, the resulting $8,000 deferred tax liability will be classified as a current liability. Assuming the $7,000 temporary difference has a related accrued payable on the books classified as a noncurrent liability, the resulting $2,100 deferred tax asset will be classified under "other assets" on the balance sheet. Deferred tax assets and liabilities are netted for reporting purposes **only** where they are both current or both noncurrent classification.

(g)   Income before income taxes $ 113,000
      Income tax expense:
              Current expense $ 50,000
              Deferred expense   5,900
                      Total income tax expense   55,900
          Net income $ 57,100

> **TIP:**   Notice that the effective tax rate for 1999 ($55,900 ÷ $113,000) is not equal to the statutory tax rate for 1999 (50%) because a $20,000 revenue item reflected in the $113,000 is tax effected at 40% in determining the related increase in 1999 income tax expense and a $7,000 expense item reflected in the $113,000 is tax effected at 30% in determining the related reduction in 1999 income tax expense.
>
> **TIP:**   Recall the objectives of the asset-liability method of accounting for income taxes and review the solution above to see how these objectives are met. These objectives are:
> (1)   to recognize the amount of taxes payable (or refundable) for the current year, and
> (2)   to recognize deferred tax liabilities and assets for the **future tax consequences** of events that have been recognized in the financial statements or tax returns.
>
> **TIP:**   Think about what will happen in 2000 when the $20,000 taxable temporary difference is eliminated (reverses). In 2000, the $20,000 will appear as a revenue item on the tax return but not on the income statement for that year. Therefore, there will be no deferred tax liability on the December 31, 2000 balance sheet. The reduction in the deferred tax liability (a debit) in 2000 will result in a deferred tax benefit (a credit) of $8,000 on the 2000 income statement and current tax expense for 2000 will exceed total income tax expense for that year because the tax consequences of the $20,000 revenue item were reflected in the total income tax expense amount in 1999.
>
> **TIP:**   Think about what will happen in 2001 when the $7,000 deductible temporary difference is eliminated (reverses). In 2001, the $7,000 will appear as an expense item (deduction) on the tax return but not on the income statement for that year. Therefore, there will be no deferred tax asset on the December 31, 2001 balance sheet. The reduction in the deferred tax asset (a credit) in 2001 will result in a deferred tax expense (a debit) of $2,100 on the 2001 income statement and current tax expense for that year will be less than total tax expense for 2001 because the tax consequences (a tax savings) of the $7,000 expense item were reflected in the total income tax expense amount in 1999.

ANALYSIS OF MULTIPLE-CHOICE TYPE QUESTIONS

QUESTION
1.   (L.O.2,3,5) Kaminsky Company reported deferred tax expense of $70,000 on its income statement for the year ended December 31, 1999. This could be the result of an increase in a:

	Deferred Tax Asset	Deferred Tax Liability
a.	Yes	Yes
b.	No	No
c.	Yes	No
d.	No	Yes

Approach and Explanation: Think about the journal entry to record deferred tax expense. The entry involves a debit to Income Tax Expense and a credit to a balance sheet account for deferred taxes. Thus, this credit is either an increase in the Deferred Tax Liability account or a decrease in the Deferred Tax Asset account. (Solution = d.)

QUESTION
2.   (L.O.6,7) The Kay Bryan Company has the following cumulative taxable temporary differences:

12/31/99	12/31/98
$ 450,000	$ 320,000

The tax rate enacted for 1999 is 40%, while the tax rate enacted for future years is 30%. Taxable income for 1999 is $800,000 and there are no permanent differences. Kay Bryan's pretax financial income for 1999 is:
a. $350,000.
b. $670,000.
c. $930,000.
d. $1,250,000.

Approach and Explanation: Use the format for the reconciliation of pretax financial income with taxable income (see **Illustration 20-3** and its accompanying **TIP**). Enter the data given. Solve for the unknown. (Solution = c.)

Pretax financial income	$ X
Temporary differences originating this period which will result in future taxable amounts ($450,000 - $320,000)	(130,000)
Taxable income	$ 800,000

Solving for X: X - $130,000 = $800,000
                    X = $930,000

TIP: No tax rates were used in this solution.

QUESTION

3.   (L.O.2,7) Mixner Corporation reported $50,000 in revenues in its 1999 financial statements, of which $22,000 will not be included in the tax return until 2000. The enacted tax rate is 40% for 1999 and 35% for 2000. What amount should Mixner report for deferred income tax liability in its balance sheet at December 31, 1999?

   a. $7,700
   b. $8,800
   c. $9,800
   d. $11,200

Approach and Explanation: At the balance sheet date, December 31, 1999, there is a temporary difference of $22,000. That temporary difference will result in a taxable amount of $22,000 in 2000. The taxes payable on that amount will be $7,700 ($22,000 x 35%). The deferred tax consequences are to be reflected in the financial statements for 1999. The journal entry to record these consequences (assuming no balance of deferred taxes at the beginning of the period) would include a credit to Deferred Tax Liability and a debit to Income Tax Expense for $7,700. Therefore: (1) revenue of $50,000; and (2) a current tax expense of $11,200 ($28,000 x 40%) and a deferred tax expense of $7,700 ($22,000 x 35%) will be reflected on the 1999 income statement. Thus, the tax consequences of the full $50,000 appear on the same income statement as the $50,000 revenue, regardless of when the taxes are to be paid. (Solution = a.)

QUESTION

4.   (L.O.2,5,6) CPA-CPE Corporation prepared the following reconciliation for its first year of operations:

Pretax financial income for 1999	$ 600,000
Tax exempt interest	(50,000)
Originating temporary difference	(150,000)
Taxable income	$ 400,000

The temporary difference will reverse evenly over the next two years at an enacted tax rate of 40%. CPA-CPE's effective tax rate for 1999 is 28%. What amount should be reported in its 1999 income statement for total income tax expense?

   a. $108,000
   b. $112,000
   c. $154,000
   d. $168,000

Explanation: The effective tax rate for 1999 is determined by dividing total income tax expense by income before income taxes for 1999. Thus, total income tax expense for 1999 is 28% x $600,000 = $168,000. (Solution = d.)

QUESTION
5.   (L.O.2,5,6) Refer to the facts of Question 4 above. In CPA-CPE's 1999 income statement, what amount should be reported as the deferred portion of its provision for income taxes?
    a. $80,000 debit
    b. $60,000 debit
    c. $60,000 credit
    d. $56,000 credit
    e. $42,000 debit

Explanation: The temporary difference existing at December 31, 1999 will result in future taxable amounts and thus gives rise to a deferred tax liability of $60,000 ($150,000 cumulative temporary difference x 40%) to be reported on the balance sheet at that date. There was no beginning deferred tax liability (1999 is the first year of operations). Thus, the $60,000 increase in deferred tax liability results in deferred tax expense (debit) of $60,000 on the 1999 income statement. (Solution = b.)

> **TIP:** Recall that "provision for income taxes" is another name for "income tax expense."

QUESTION
6.   (L.O.5) Refer to the facts of Question 4 above. In CPA-CPE's 1999 income statement, what amount should be reported as the current portion of its provision for income taxes?
    a. $108,000
    b. $112,000
    c. $154,000
    d. $168,000

Explanation: The effective tax rate for 1999 is determined by dividing total income tax expense by income before income taxes for 1999. Thus, total income tax expense for 1999 is 28% x $600,000 = $168,000. The deferred portion of the provision is $60,000 [($150,000 cumulative temporary difference x 40%) - $0 beginning balance in Deferred Tax Liability]. Therefore, the current portion of the provision is $108,000 ($168,000 total income tax expense - $60,000 deferred tax expense = $108,000 current tax expense). (Solution = a.)

> **TIP:** The enacted statutory tax rate for 1999 could be computed by dividing the $108,000 current tax expense by $400,000 taxable income to arrive at 27%. However, it is not needed for any solution to questions asked here.

QUESTION
7.   (L.O.2,6) Assuming a 40% statutory tax rate applies to all years involved, which of the following situations will give rise to reporting a deferred tax liability on the balance sheet?

        I.   A revenue is deferred for financial reporting purposes but not for tax purposes.

        II.   A revenue is deferred for tax purposes but not for financial reporting purposes.

        III.   An expense is deferred for financial reporting purposes but not for tax purposes.

        IV.   An expense is deferred for tax purposes but not for financial reporting purposes.

    a.   item II only
    b.   items I and II only
    c.   items II and III only
    d.   items I and IV only

Approach and Explanation: Notice that each situation described involves a difference in the timing of revenue or expense recognition for financial reporting purposes (accounting purposes or book purposes) and tax purposes (tax reporting purposes). Thus, each situation involves a temporary difference. For each, determine if future taxable or deductible amounts will occur. Because a flat tax rate applies to all periods involved, a temporary difference resulting in net future taxable amounts will give rise to reporting a deferred tax liability, and a temporary difference giving rise to net future deductible amounts will result in reporting a deferred tax asset. Items II and III will give rise to future taxable amounts; items I and IV will give rise to future deductible amounts. (Solution = c.)

QUESTION
8.   (L.O.2,5) At the December 31, 1999 balance sheet date, Garth Brooks Corporation reports an accrued receivable for financial reporting purposes but not for tax purposes. When this asset is recovered in 2000, a future taxable amount will occur and:

    a.   pretax financial income will exceed taxable income in 2000.
    b.   Garth will record a decrease in a deferred tax liability in 2000.
    c.   total income tax expense for 2000 will exceed current tax expense for 2000.
    d.   Garth will record an increase in a deferred tax asset in 2000.

Explanation: The receivable stems from a revenue earned but not received; the revenue has been booked for accounting purposes but not for tax purposes. When this asset (receivable) is recovered through collection of the receivable in 2000, it will result in a taxable amount (taxable revenue on the 2000 income tax return). Thus, in 2000, pretax financial income will be less than taxable income because of the elimination (reversal) of the temporary difference. Also in 2000, Garth will record a decrease in the deferred tax liability, resulting in a deferred tax benefit on the 2000 income statement (which causes current tax expense in 2000 to exceed total tax expense for 2000). (Solution = b.)

QUESTION

9.   (L.O.10) A depreciable asset is purchased at the very beginning of 1998 for $150,000. It is to be depreciated by the straight-line method over five years for accounting purposes and over three years for tax purposes. There is no salvage value and the one-half year convention is to be used for tax purposes. There is a 40% tax rate for all years affected. On its December 31, 1999 balance sheet, the company should report a:

a.   current deferred tax liability of $8,000 and a noncurrent deferred tax asset of $14,000.

b.   noncurrent deferred tax asset of $8,000 and a noncurrent deferred tax liability of $14,000.

c.   noncurrent deferred tax liability of $6,000.

d.   noncurrent deferred tax asset of $6,000.

Approach and Explanation: Compare the depreciation schedules for accounting purposes and tax purposes. Determine the cumulative temporary difference existing at December 31, 1999. Compute the related deferred income taxes and determine its classification. The process would be as follows:

Year	Depreciation for Books	Depreciation for Tax Return	Difference
1998	$ 30,000	$ 25,000	$ 5,000
1999	30,000	50,000	(20,000)
2000	30,000	50,000	(20,000)
2001	30,000	25,000	5,000
2002	30,000		30,000
	$ 150,000	$ 150,000	

The cumulative temporary difference at the end of 1999 is $15,000 [$5,000 + ($20,000) = ($15,000) and the brackets are ignored here for purposes of stating the total]. It will result in net future taxable amounts of $15,000 [($20,000) for 2000 + $5,000 for 2001 + $30,000 for = 2002 = $15,000 and the positive amount here indicates a net future taxable amount]. Although a scheduling of the individual future taxable (deductible) amounts can be prepared at this point, a single flat tax rate for all years affected makes it possible to avoid the scheduling and perform an aggregate calculation as follows:

$ 15,000	Net future taxable amounts
40%	Enacted tax rate for future years
$ 6,000	Deferred tax liability at December 31, 1999

The entire $6,000 deferred tax liability is to be classified as a noncurrent liability because there is a related asset (the depreciable asset) on the GAAP basis balance sheet, and that asset appears in a noncurrent classification. Thus, the related deferred tax liability is classified as a long-term (noncurrent) liability. (Solution = c.)

TIP: A scheduling, although unnecessary, could be prepared as follows:

		Future Years		
	2000	**2001**	**2002**	**Total**
Future taxable (deductible) amounts	$(20,000)	$5,000	$30,000	$15,000
Enacted tax rate	40%	40%	40%	
Deferred tax (asset) liability	$(8,000)	$2,000	$12,000	$ 6,000

TIP: You should be able to solve for a similar situation when the tax rates vary for individual future years. For example, if the enacted tax rate for 2001 and 2002 was 35%, the scheduling process would appear as follows at the end of 1999:

		Future Years		
	2000	**2001**	**2002**	**Total**
Future taxable (deductible) amounts	$(20,000)	$5,000	$30,000	$15,000
Enacted tax rate	40%	35%	35%	
Deferred tax (asset) liability	$(8,000)	$1,750	$10,500	$ 4,250

QUESTION

10. (L.O.7) At December 31, 1998 Malcohm Corporation reported a deferred tax liability of $60,000 which was attributable to a taxable type temporary difference of $200,000. The temporary difference is scheduled to reverse in 2002. During 1999, a new tax law increased the corporate tax rate from 30% to 40%. Which of the following entries will correctly account for the effect of this change on deferred taxes?

a.	Retained Earnings	20,000	
	Deferred Tax Liability		20,000
b.	Retained Earnings	6,000	
	Deferred Tax Liability		6,000
c.	Income Tax Expense	6,000	
	Deferred Tax Liability		6,000
d.	Income Tax Expense	20,000	
	Deferred Tax Liability		20,000

Approach and Explanation: Deferred tax liabilities and assets are to be adjusted in the period of enactment for the effect of an enacted change in tax laws or rates. The effect is included in income from continuing operations as a component of income tax expense [$200,000 x (40% - 30%) = $20,000]. (Solution = d.)

QUESTION

11. (L.O.4) Norman Corporation has a deferred tax asset at December 31, 1999 of $50,000 due to the recognition of potential tax benefits of an operating loss carryforward. The enacted tax rates are as follows: 40% for 1996-1998; 35% for 1999; and 30% for 2000 and thereafter. Assuming that management expects that only 50% of the related benefits will actually be realized, a valuation account should be established in the amount of:
   a. $25,000.
   b. $10,000.
   c. $8,750.
   d. $7,500.

Approach and Explanation: Prepare the journal entry to record the necessary valuation account for the portion of the deferred tax asset that more likely than not will not be realized. That entry is as follows:

Benefit Due to Loss Carryforward
   (or Income Tax Expense)... 25,000
      Allowance to Reduce Deferred Tax Asset
         to Expected Realizable Value 25,000

Because only 50% of the benefits are expected to be realized, a valuation account is needed for the 50% (50% x $50,000 = $25,000) that is not expected to be realized. The tax rates are not relevant in this question. The future tax rate (30%) was used to apply to the NOL carryforward amount in computing the $50,000 of potential benefits reflected in the Deferred Tax Asset account. (Solution = a.)

> **TIP:** From the facts given, we can determine that the NOL carryforward amount was $166,666.67 ($50,000 ÷ 30% = $166,666.67).

QUESTION

12. (L.O.3) The Mary Colson Corporation collects rent revenue in advance from tenants. The collection of $50,000 in 1999 is reported as revenue for tax purposes; it will be reported on the income statement in 2000 when it is earned. This situation will:
   a. result in future deductible amounts.
   b. result in reporting a deferred tax liability on the balance sheet at the end of 1999.
   c. cause total income tax expense to be less than income tax payable in 2000.
   d. cause pretax financial income to exceed taxable income in 1999.

Explanation: The collection and reporting of revenue for tax purposes in a period before it is earned and recognized for book purposes will result in future deductible amounts. A deferred tax asset is to be recognized for the deferred tax consequences of the revenue already reflected in the income tax return. In a later period, the unearned revenue per books (a liability) will be settled by delivering goods or services to the customers or by refunding the customers' money; the related outlays are, therefore, tax deductible in the later period in which the revenue is earned. In that later period, pretax financial income will exceed taxable income. Also, in that later period, total income tax expense will exceed income tax payable (current tax expense) by the amount of the decrease in the related Deferred Tax Asset account due to the reversal of the temporary difference. (Solution = a.)

QUESTION

13. (L.O.8) Carrie Freeman Corporation began operations in 1995. There have been no permanent differences or temporary differences to account for since the inception of the business. The following data are available:

Year	Enacted Tax Rate	Taxable Income	Taxes Paid
1995	50%	$100,000	$ 50,000
1996	40%	200,000	80,000
1997	40%	240,000	96,000
1998	30%	300,000	90,000
1999	25%		
2000	20%		

In 1999, Carrie Freeman has an NOL of $300,000. What amount of income tax benefits should be reported on the 1999 income statement due to this NOL?

a. $60,000
b. $75,000
c. $90,000
d. $120,000
e. $130,000

Explanation: The loss is carried back three years and must be applied to the earliest year first and then sequentially to the second and third years. The $300,000 loss is therefore applied as follows:

1996	$200,000 x 40%	=	$ 80,000
1997	100,000 x 40%	=	40,000
	Benefits of NOL carryback		$ 120,000

The future rate (2000 and beyond) would only be used to compute the benefits of an NOL carryforward. An NOL carryforward will result when the NOL is larger than the combined taxable income for the three years involved in the carryback period or when a company elects to forego the carryback procedure and use only the carryforward. The tax rate for the current period (1999) is not used to compute the benefits of an NOL carryback or carryforward. (Solution = d).

CHAPTER 21

ACCOUNTING FOR PENSIONS AND POSTRETIREMENT BENEFITS

OVERVIEW

A pension plan is an arrangement whereby an employer provides benefits to employees after they retire. A defined benefit plan defines the benefits the employees will receive at the time of retirement. The accounting for a defined benefit plan is complex. Pension cost is a function of service cost, interest on the pension liability, return on plan assets, amortization of prior service cost, and recognition of gains and losses. Recognition of a minimum liability and other disclosures are required. The accounting for health care and other benefits provided to retirees is similar to the accounting for pension plans. The topic "other postretirement benefit plans" is also covered in this chapter.

SUMMARY OF LEARNING OBJECTIVES

1. **Distinguish between accounting for the employer's pension plan and accounting for the pension fund.** The company or employer is the organization sponsoring the pension plan. It incurs the cost and makes contributions to the pension fund. The fund or plan is the entity that receives the contributions from the employers, administers the pension assets, and makes the benefit payments to the pension recipients (retired employees). The fund should be a separate legal and accounting entity for which a set of books is maintained and financial statements are prepared.

2. **Identify types of pension plans and their characteristics.** The two most common types of pension arrangements are: (1) **Defined contribution plans:** the employer agrees to contribute to a pension trust a certain sum each period based on a formula. This formula may consider such factors as age, length of employee service, employer's profits, and compensation level. Only the employer's contribution is defined; no promise is made regarding the ultimate benefits paid out to the employees. (2) **Defined benefit plans:** define the benefits that the employee will receive at the time of retirement. The formula typically used provides for the benefits to be a function of the employee's years of service and the employee's compensation level when he or she nears retirement.

3. **Explain alternative measures for valuing the pension obligation.** One measure of the pension obligation bases it only on the benefits vested to the employees. Vested benefits are those that the employee is entitled to receive even if the employee renders no additional services under the plan. The **vested benefits pension obligation** is computed using current salary levels and includes only vested benefits. Another measure of the obligation, called the **accumulated benefit obligation**, bases the computation of the deferred compensation amount on all years of service performed by employees under the plan—both vested and nonvested—using current salary levels. A third measure, called the **projected benefit obligation**, bases the

computation of the deferred compensation amount on both vested and nonvested service using expected future salaries.

4. **Identify the components of pension expense.** Pension expense is a function of the following components: (1) service cost, (2) interest on the pension liability, (3) actual return on plan assets, (4) amortization of unrecognized prior service cost, and (5) gain or loss.

5. **Utilize a work sheet for employer's pension plan entries.** A work sheet unique to pension accounting may be utilized to record both the formal entries and the memo entries to keep track of all the employer's relevant pension plan items and components.

6. **Describe the amortization of unrecognized prior service cost.** Prior service cost is the cost of retroactive benefits granted in a plan amendment. The amount of the prior service cost is computed by an actuary. Amortization of the unrecognized prior service cost is an accounting function performed with the assistance of an actuary. The FASB prefers a "years-of-service" amortization method that is similar to a units-of-production computation. First, the total estimated number of service-years to be worked by all of the participating employees is computed. Second, the unrecognized prior service cost is divided by the total number of service-years to obtain a cost per service-year (the unit cost). And third, the number of service-years consumed each year is multiplied by the cost per service-year to obtain the annual amortization charge. *SFAS No. 87* allows an alternative method of computing amortization of unrecognized prior service cost; employers may use straight-line amortization over the average remaining service life of the employees.

7. **Explain the accounting procedure for recognizing unexpected gains and losses.** In estimating the projected benefit obligation (the liability), actuaries make assumptions about such items as mortality rate, retirement rate, turnover rate, disability rate, and salary amounts. Any change in these actuarial assumptions changes the amount of the projected benefit obligation. These unexpected gains or losses from changes in the projected benefit obligation are liability gains and losses. Liability gains (resulting from unexpected decreases in the liability balance) and liability losses (resulting from unexpected increases) are deferred (unrecognized). The liability gains and losses are combined in the same Unrecognized Net Gain or Loss account used for asset gains and losses and are accumulated from year to year, **off-balance-sheet**, in a memo record account.

8. **Explain the corridor approach to amortizing unrecognized gains and losses.** The Unrecognized Net Gain or Loss account balance is considered too large and must be amortized when it exceeds the arbitrarily selected FASB criterion of 10% of the larger of the beginning balances of the projected benefit obligation or the market-related value of the plan assets. If the balance of the Unrecognized Net Gain or Loss account stays within the upper and lower limits of the corridor, no amortization is required.

9. **Explain the recognition of a minimum liability.** Immediate recognition of a liability (referred to as the minimum liability) is required when the accumulated benefit obligation exceeds the fair value of plan assets. The purpose of this minimum liability requirement is to assure that if a significant plan amendment or actuarial loss occurs, a liability will be recognized at least to the extent of the unfunded portion of the accumulated benefit obligation. The amount of the adjustment required (i.e., the additional pension liability) considers any existing balance of accrued or prepaid pension cost. An existing credit balance in the Prepaid/Accrued Pension Cost account **reduces** the amount of the adjustment; an existing debit balance in the Prepaid/Accrued Pension Cost account **increases** the amount of the adjustment.

10. Describe the reporting requirement for pension plans in financial statements. The current financial statement disclosure requirements for pension plans are as follows: (1) A description of the plan including employee groups covered, type of benefit formula, funding policy, type of assets held, and the nature and effect of significant matters affecting comparability of information for all periods presented. (2) The components of net periodic pension expense for the period. (3) A schedule reconciling the funded status of the plan with amounts reported in the employer's statement of financial position. (4) The weighted-average assumed discount rate and rate of compensation increase used to measure the projected benefit obligation and the weighted-average expected long-term rate of return on plan assets.

11.* Identify the differences between pension plans and postretirement health care benefit plans. Pension plans are generally funded, but health care benefit plans are generally not funded. Pension benefits are generally well-defined and level in amount, but health care benefits are generally uncapped and variable. Pension benefits are payable monthly, but health care benefits are paid as needed and used. Pension plan variables are reasonably predictable, whereas health care plan variables are difficult to predict.

12.* Contrast accounting for pensions to accounting for other postretirement benefits. Many of the basic concepts and much of the accounting terminology and measurement methodology applicable to pensions also apply to other postretirement benefit accounting. Because other postretirement benefit plans are unfunded, large transition obligations occur; these may be recognized immediately in net income as a change in accounting principle or amortized on a straight-line basis over the average remaining service period of employees expected to receive benefits under the plan. However, if the average remaining service period is less than 20 years, the employer may elect to use a 20-year period for amortization. Two significant concepts peculiar to accounting for other postretirement benefits are (a) expected postretirement benefit obligation (EPBO) and (b) accumulated postretirement benefit obligation (APBO). Also, there is no minimum liability reported for other postretirement benefits.

 *This material is covered in Appendix 21-A in the text.

TIPS ON CHAPTER TOPICS

> **TIP:** The **accumulated benefit obligation (ABO)** measures the pension obligation at a balance sheet date using current salary levels. The **projected benefit obligation (PBO)** measures the same obligation using future salary levels. Notice which of these is used in various computations in the chapter and whether a beginning-of-period or end-of-period balance is required for a particular purpose. Such as:
> 1. The **beginning** balance of the PBO is used to compute the interest component of pension expense for the period. (L.O.4)
> 2. The greater of the **beginning** balance of the PBO **or market-related plan asset value** (beginning of period) is used to compute the 10% corridor in determining the need for amortization of the balance of unrecognized net gain or loss. (L.O.8)
> 3. The **ending** balance of the ABO is used to compare with the fair value of plan assets at the end of the period to compute the minimum liability. (L.O.9)
> 4. The **ending** balance of the PBO is used to reconcile the funded status of the plan with amounts reported in the employer's balance sheet. (L.O.10)

TIP: The **actual return on plan assets** is the increase in plan assets from interest, dividends, and realized and unrealized changes in the market value of the plan assets. If the actual return is positive (gain), it is subtracted in the computation of pension expense. The actual return on pension plan assets can be computed by (1) finding the change in the fair value of plan assets, (2) deducting contributions, and (3) adding benefits paid.

TIP: A debit balance in the Prepaid/Accrued Pension Cost account is reported as an asset; whereas, a credit balance is reported as a liability.

TIP: Plan adoptions or amendments often include provisions to increase benefits for employee service provided in prior years. This **prior service cost** is allocated to pension expense in the current and future periods.

TIP: **Gains and losses** result from changes in the market value of plan assets (often called **asset gains and losses**) or from changes in the projected benefit obligation caused by changes in actuarial assumptions (often called **liability gains and losses**). The net gain or loss is amortized by the **corridor approach**; the net gain or loss is amortized when it exceeds 10% of the larger of the beginning balances of the projected benefit obligation or the market-related value of the plan assets.

TIP: Although the balances of the projected benefit obligation, plan assets, unamortized prior service cost, and unamortized net gain or loss do **not** appear on the employer's balance sheet, they have an impact on the determination of amounts that do appear on the employer's income statement and balance sheet and amounts that appear in the notes to those financial statements.

TIP: A pension work sheet includes both formal entries and memo entries. The formal journal entry to record pension expense and the annual contribution to the pension fund is a debit to Pension Expense for the appropriate amount computed, a credit to Cash for the amount funded for the period, and a debit or credit to Prepaid/Accrued Pension Cost for the difference.

TIP: When the accumulated benefit obligation exceeds the fair value of plan assets, a **minimum liability** must be reported for the amount of the excess (i.e., the unfunded accumulated benefit obligation). Therefore, an adjustment is made to record what is called the **additional liability**. The additional liability required considers any existing balance of accrued or prepaid pension cost. If an accrued pension cost exists (i.e., credit balance in the Prepaid/Accrued Pension Cost account), the additional liability equals the excess of the minimum liability over the accrued pension cost balance. If a prepaid pension cost exists (i.e., debit balance in the Prepaid/Accrued Pension Cost account), the additional liability equals the minimum liability amount plus the balance of the prepaid pension cost. The journal entry to record the additional liability includes a debit to Intangible Asset—Deferred Pension Cost and a credit to Additional Pension Liability. When the additional liability exceeds the amount of unrecognized prior service cost, the excess is debited to Excess of Additional Pension Liability Over Unrecognized Prior Service Cost (which is reported as a contra account in stockholders' equity) rather than to the intangible asset account.

ILLUSTRATION 21-1
COMPONENTS OF PENSION EXPENSE (L.O.4)

COMPUTATION OF PENSION EXPENSE:

	SERVICE COST
+	INTEREST ON THE PBO LIABILITY
-	ACTUAL RETURN ON PLAN ASSETS
+	AMORTIZATION OF UNRECOGNIZED PRIOR SERVICE COST
+/-	EFFECTS OF GAINS OR LOSSES
=	PENSION EXPENSE

DEFINITIONS OF COMPONENTS:

Service Cost. The expense caused by the increase in pension benefits payable (the projected benefit obligation) to employees because of their services rendered during the current year. Actuaries compute **service cost** as the present value of the new benefits earned by employees during the year.

Interest on the Liability. Because a pension is a deferred compensation arrangement, there is a time value of money factor. As a result, it is recorded on a discounted basis. **Interest accrues each year on the projected benefit obligation just as it does on any discounted debt.** The accountant receives help from the actuary in selecting the interest rate, called for this purpose the **settlement rate**.

Actual Return on Plan Assets. The return earned by the accumulated pension fund assets in a particular year is relevant in measuring the net cost to the employer of sponsoring an employee pension plan. Therefore, **annual pension expense should be adjusted for interest and dividends that accumulate within the fund as well as increases and decreases in the market value of fund assets**.

Amortization of Unrecognized Prior Service Cost. Pension plan amendments (including initiation of a pension plan) often include provisions to increase benefits (in rare situations to decrease benefits) for employee service provided in prior years. Because plan amendments are granted with the expectation that the employer will realize economic benefits in future periods, **the cost (prior service cost) of providing these retroactive benefits is allocated to pension expense in the future, specifically to the remaining service-years of the affected employees**.

Gain or Loss. Volatility in pension expense can be caused by sudden and large changes in the market value of plan assets and by changes in the projected benefit obligation (which changes when actuarial assumptions are modified or when actual experience differs from expected experience). Two items comprise this gain or loss: (1) the difference between the actual return and the expected return on plan assets and (2) amortization of the unrecognized net gain or loss from previous periods. This computation is complex.

In summary, the components of pension expense and their effect are as follows:
- Service cost (increases pension expense).
- Interest on the liability (increases pension expense).
- Actual return on plan assets (decreases pension expense if positive).
- Amortization of unrecognized prior service cost (generally increases pension expense).
- Gain or loss (decreases or increases pension expense).

ILLUSTRATION 21-1 (Continued)

TIP: Refer to the description of the gain or loss component above. The **expected return on plan assets** is calculated by multiplying the expected rate of return times the market-related asset value at the beginning of the year. If the actual return is higher than the expected return, the unexpected gain is added to pension expense; and when the actual return is lower, the unexpected loss is deducted from pension expense. As a result, the **expected return** is the amount actually used to compute pension expense.

Reread this **TIP** (it contains a confusing aspect) and review the computation for pension expense. Notice that the actual return on plan assets is deducted in the computation of pension expense for the current period. Assume the actual return is $80,000 which includes an unexpected gain of $9,000. Thus, the $80,000 actual return would be deducted and the $9,000 unexpected gain would be added in the pension expense computation; thus, only the $71,000 expected return is reflected in the pension expense balance.

TIP: For the gain or loss component: (1) an unexpected asset gain occurring in the current period (i.e., actual return exceeds expected return) will be added; an unexpected asset loss will be deducted; and, (2) amortization of a net unrecognized net gain from previous periods will be deducted; amortization of a net unrecognized net loss from previous periods will be added in computing pension expense.

TIP: Throughout *SFAS No. 87,* the term "periodic pension cost" is used rather than "pension expense" because part of the cost recognized in a period may be capitalized along with other costs as part of an asset such as inventory. For example, pension cost related to factory workers in a manufacturing company is charged to Factory Labor, which is accounted for as a product cost; thus, it is incorporated in the cost of inventory until the period the related product is sold, at which time it is charged to Cost of Goods Sold. "Pension expense" is used in this chapter as a means of simplification; its use is appropriate when the pension cost relates to employees whose salaries and wages are expensed rather than capitalized (i.e., employees such as sales clerks and most executives).

EXERCISE 21-1

Purpose: (L.O.4) This exercise will enable you to practice computing pension expense.

The following data relate to Kleen Company's pension plan for the year 1999:

Accrued pension cost at January 1, 1999	$ 6,000
Actual and expected return on plan assets	60,000
Benefits paid	40,000
Contributions to plan	105,000
Plan assets at January 1, 1999	684,000
Prior service cost amortization	15,000
Projected benefit obligation at January 1, 1999	850,000
Service cost	90,000
Unrecognized prior service cost at January 1, 1999	160,000
Settlement rate	10%

Instructions
Compute the pension expense for 1999.

Solution to Exercise 21-1

Service cost	$ 90,000
Interest cost ($850,000 x 10%)	85,000
Actual (and expected) return on plan assets	(60,000)
Amortization of unrecognized prior service cost	15,000
Pension expense for 1999	$ 130,000

Approach: Whenever you are to compute pension expense, use the format in **Illustration 21-1**. Select or solve for the data needed.

> **TIP:** Because the actual return on plan assets equals the expected return on plan assets for 1999, there was no difference (unexpected gain or loss) to include in the expense computation.

ILLUSTRATION 21-2
CHANGES IN THE PROJECTED BENEFIT OBLIGATION
AND PLAN ASSETS (L.O.4,5)

	Projected benefit obligation, balance at beginning of the period
+	Service cost for the period
+	Interest for the period on beginning projected benefit obligation balance
-	Benefits paid to employees during the period
+/-	Liability gains and losses due to changes in actuarial assumptions
=	Projected benefit obligation, balance at end of the period

	Plan assets, fair value at beginning of the period
+	Contributions to plan during the period
	Benefits paid to employees during the period
+/-	Actual return on plan assets during the period*
=	Plan assets, fair value at end of the period

*Includes realized earnings such as dividends and interest, realized gains and losses due to sales of plan assets, and unrealized asset gains and losses from changes in the fair value of plan assets.

TIP: It is helpful to know the various reasons for changes in the projected benefit obligation and plan assets over the course of time. For example, if you are given the amounts funded by the employer during the year, the benefits paid from the pension fund during the year, and the net increase in fair value of plans assets for the year, you can solve for the actual return on plan assets for the period.

TIP: Although the balance of the projected benefit obligation and the balance of plan assets are **not** reported on the employer's balance sheet, these balances are used in determining certain amounts that do appear in the financial statements.

TIP: One of the reasons for a change in the balance of the projected benefit obligation is "liability gains and losses due to changes in actuarial assumptions." Liability **gains reduce** the PBO balance, whereas liability **losses increase** the PBO balance.

TIP: One of the reasons for a change in the plan assets' fair value balance is the "actual return on plan assets during the period." This actual return includes unexpected asset gains and losses. Asset **gains increase** the plan assets' fair value balance, whereas asset **losses reduce** the plan assets' fair value balance.

EXERCISE 21-2

Purpose: (L.O.5) This exercise illustrates the mechanics of the pension work sheet.

Instructions

(a)   Using the data in **Exercise 21-1,** prepare a pension work sheet. Insert January 1, 1999 balances and show the journal entry for pension expense for 1999 and the December 31, 1999 balances.

(b)   Prepare a reconciliation schedule.

Preparation of pension work sheet and reconciliation schedule:

TIP: In using the work sheet, the Prepaid/Accrued Pension Cost account balance equals the net of the balances in the memo accounts. If the net of the memo record balances is a **credit**, the reconciling amount in the prepaid/accrued cost column will be a **credit** equal in amount.

TIP: The "Memo Record" columns maintain balances of the **unrecognized (noncapitalized)** pension items.

TIP: The reconciliation schedule reconciles the balances of the off-balance-sheet items with the prepaid/accrued pension cost balance reported in the balance sheet.

Solution to Exercise 21-2

(a)

Kleen Company
PENSION WORK SHEET--1999*

| | General Journal Entries | | | Memo Record | | |
	Annual Pension Expense	Cash	Prepaid/ Accrued Cost	Projected Benefit Obligation	Plan Assets	Unrecognized Prior Service Cost
Balance, January 1, 1999			6,000 Cr.	850,000 Cr.	684,000 Dr.	160,000 Dr.
(1) Service cost	90,000 Dr.			90,000 Cr.		
(2) Interest cost	85,000 Dr.			85,000 Cr.		
(3) Actual return	60,000 Cr.				60,000 Dr.	
(4) Amortization of PSC	15,000 Dr.					15,000 Cr.
(5) Contributions		105,000 Cr.			105,000 Dr.	
(6) Benefits				40,000 Dr.	40,000 Cr.	
Journal entry for 1999	130,000 Dr.	105,000 Cr.	25,000 Cr.			
Balance, December 31, 1999			31,000 Cr.	985,000 Cr.	809,000 Dr.	145,000 Dr.

*The use of this pension entry work sheet is recommended and illustrated by Paul B. W. Miller, "The New Pension Accounting (Part 2)," *Journal of Accountancy* (February 1987), pp. 86-94.

(b) **Reconciliation Schedule--December 31, 1999**

Projected benefit obligation (Credit)	$(985,000)
Plan assets at fair value (Debit)	809,000
Funded status	(176,000)
Unrecognized prior service cost (Debit)	145,000
Prepaid/accrued pension cost (Credit)	$ (31,000)

EXERCISE 21-3

Purpose: (L.O.8) This exercise illustrates the use of the corridor approach to amortizing unrecognized gains and losses.

Beginning-of-the-year present values for Learn Company's projected benefit obligation and beginning-of-the-year market-related values for its pension plan assets are:

	Projected Benefit Obligation	Market-Related Value of Plan Assets
1999	$ 3,200,000	$ 3,600,000
2000	3,700,000	3,900,000
2001	4,300,000	4,200,000
2002	5,000,000	4,800,000

The cumulative unrecognized net gain is $300,000 on January 1, 1999. The unrecognized net gain or loss that occurred during the year is: 1999, $210,000 gain; 2000, $25,000 loss; 2001, $50,000 loss; and 2002, $100,000 gain. The average remaining service life per employee is 12 years in 1999 and 2000, and is 15 years in 2001 and 2002.

Instructions
Set up an appropriate schedule to compute the amount of unrecognized net gain or loss to be amortized to pension expense each year using the corridor approach.

Solution to Exercise 21-3

Corridor Amortization Schedule

Year	Projected Benefit Obligation (1)	Market-Related Value of Plan Assets (1)	10% Corridor (2)	Cumulative Unrecognized Net Gain (1)	Minimum Amortization of Gain
1999	$ 3,200,000	$3,600,000	$360,000	$300,000	$ -0-
2000	3,700,000	3,900,000	390,000	510,000	10,000 (3)
2001	4,300,000	4,200,000	430,000	475,000 (4)	3,000 (5)
2002	5,000,000	4,800,000	500,000	422,000 (6)	- 0-

(1)   All as of the beginning of the year.
(2)   10% of the greater of projected benefit obligation or plan assets' market-related value.
(3)   ($510,000 - $390,000) ÷ 12 = $10,000.
(4) $510,000 - $10,000 net gain amortized - $25,000 loss = $475,000.
(5)   ($475,000 - $430,000) ÷ 15 = $3,000.
(6) $475,000 - $3,000 net gain amortized - $50,000 loss = $422,000.

TIP: Unexpected gains or losses from changes in the balance of the projected benefit obligation due to changes in actuarial assumptions are called "liability gains and losses" by the FASB. These liability gains and losses (liability gains result from unexpected decreases in the liability balance and liability losses result from unexpected increases) are deferred (unrecognized). They are combined in the same Unrecognized Net Gain or Loss account used for asset gains and losses (this is an off-balance-sheet account). (Refer to the "Explanation" in the **Solution for Exercise 21-5** for a description of asset gains and losses.) All unexpected gains and losses are accumulated from year to year, off-balance-sheet, in a memo account.

If the balance of the Unrecognized Net Gain or Loss account stays within the upper and lower limits of the corridor, no amortization is required—the unrecognized net gain or loss balance is carried forward unchanged. If amortization is required, the minimum amortization amount is the excess (beyond the corridor) gain or loss divided by the average remaining service life to expected retirement of all active employees.

EXERCISE 21-4

Purpose: (L.O.4) This exercise requires calculation of actual return on plan assets.

White Company reports the following pension plan data:

Fair value of plan assets, January 1, 1999	$ 3,200,000
Fair value of plan assets, December 31, 1999	3,600,000
Benefits paid during 1999	460,000
Contributions to the plan during 1999	640,000

Instructions
Compute the actual return on plan assets for 1999.

Solution to Exercise 21-4

Plan assets, fair value at beginning of the year	$ 3,200,000
Contributions to plan during the year	640,000
Benefits paid to employees during the year	(460,000)
Actual return on plan assets during the year	+ X
Plan assets, fair value at end of the year	$ 3,600,000

Solving for X: X = $220,000

Approach: Write down the format for reconciling beginning and ending balances of plan assets at fair value (see **Illustration 21-2**). Enter the data given. Solve for the unknown.

EXERCISE 21-5

Purpose: (L.O.4) This exercise requires calculation of the expected return on plan assets and examines its use in determining pension expense.

White Company (from **Exercise 21-4**) also reports:

Market-related asset value, January 1, 1999	$ 3,000,000
Market-related asset value, December 31, 1999	3,300,000
Expected return on plan assets	10%

Instructions

(a) Compute the expected return on plan assets during 1999 and the unexpected gain or loss.

(b) Explain how the actual return and the unexpected gain or loss enter into the calculation of pension expense for 1999.

Solution to Exercise 21-5

(a) 10% x $3,000,000 = $300,000 expected return on plan assets.

Expected return	$ 300,000
Actual return (Exercise 21-4)	220,000
Unexpected loss	$ 80,000

(b) The actual return on plan assets of $220,000 is deducted in the calculation of pension expense because earnings generated by the plan assets reduce the total pension cost to the employer. The unexpected loss of $80,000 is also deducted in the pension expense computation because unexpected gains and losses **are to be deferred** rather than recognized currently. As a result, the expected return of $300,000 is the amount actually used to compute current pension expense. (If the unexpected loss was not deducted, the current period's pension expense would be higher which would reflect recognition of the unexpected loss in the current period.)

Explanation: The expected return on plan assets is determined by multiplying the expected rate of return on plan assets times the beginning-of-the-year market-related asset value. Differences between the expected return and the actual return, often referred to as the unexpected gain or loss, are called "asset gains and losses" by the FASB and are deferred.

TIP: The market-related asset value is used in two calculations: (1) the expected return on plan assets, and (2) the determination of the corridor. In both cases, it is the market-related asset value at the beginning of the year.

TIP: The gain or loss component of pension expense for a period is the sum of (a) the difference between the actual return on plan assets and the expected return on plan assets, and (b) the amortization of the unrecognized net gain or loss from previous periods.

EXERCISE 21-6

Purpose: (L.O.9) This exercise illustrates how to compute and record the minimum pension liability.

Sure Great Company provides this data related to its pension plan:

	1999	**2000**	**2001**
Projected benefit obligation at Dec. 31	$550,000	$700,000	$800,000
Plan assets (at fair value) at Dec. 31	370,000	450,000	640,000
Accumulated benefit obligation at Dec. 31	490,000	610,000	660,000
Pension expense	180,000	240,000	250,000
Contributions	200,000	225,000	230,000
Unrecognized prior service cost at Dec. 31	600,000	550,000	500,000

Prior to 1999, contributions were equal to pension expense.

Instructions

Prepare journal entries to record pension expense, employer's contributions, and the minimum pension liability for 1999, 2000, and 2001.

Solution to Exercise 21-6

1999	Pension Expense...	180,000	
	Prepaid/Accrued Pension Cost..	20,000	
	Cash...		200,000
	Intangible Asset—Deferred Pension Cost.........................	140,000	
	Additional Pension Liability....................................		140,000

Explanation:

Prepaid/accrued pension cost at beginning of year	$ -0-
Pension expense	(180,000)
Contributions	200,000
Prepaid (accrued) pension cost at end of year	$ 20,000

Accumulated benefit obligation at December 31, 1999	$(490,000)
Plan assets (at fair value) at December 31, 1999	370,000
Unfunded accumulated benefit obligation (minimum liability)	(120,000)
Prepaid pension cost at December 31, 1999	(20,000)
Additional liability at December 31, 1999	(140,000)
Additional liability at December 31, 1998	-0-
Additional liability increase required at December 31, 1999	$(140,000)

> **TIP:** The entire additional liability increase required at the end of 1999 is charged to an intangible asset account because the amount of the additional liability to be reported at that date ($140,000) does not exceed the amount of unrecognized prior service cost ($600,000).

2000

Pension Expense...	240,000	
Prepaid/Accrued Pension Cost.............................		15,000
Cash..		225,000

Intangible Asset—Deferred Pension Cost..........................	25,000	
Additional Pension Liability......................................		25,000

Explanation:

Prepaid (accrued) pension cost at beginning of year	$ 20,000
Pension expense	(240,000)
Contributions	225,000
Prepaid (accrued) pension cost at end of year	$ 5,000

Accumulated benefit obligation at December 31, 2000	$(610,000)
Plan assets (at fair value) at December 31, 2000	450,000
Unfunded accumulated benefit obligation (minimum liability)	(160,000)
Prepaid pension cost at December 31, 2000	(5,000)
Additional liability at December 31, 2000	(165,000)
Additional liability at December 31, 1999	140,000
Additional liability increase required at December 31, 2000	$ (25,000)

> **TIP:** The entire additional liability increase required at the end of 2000 ($25,000) is charged to an intangible asset account because the amount of the additional liability to be reported at that date ($165,000) does not exceed the amount of unrecognized prior service cost ($550,000).

2001

Pension Expense...	250,000	
Prepaid/Accrued Pension Cost.............................		20,000
Cash..		230,000

Additional Pension Liability	160,000	
Intangible Asset—Deferred Pension Cost..............		160,000

Explanation:

Prepaid (accrued) pension cost at beginning of year	$ 5,000
Pension expense	(250,000)
Contributions	230,000
Prepaid (accrued) pension cost at end of year	$ (15,000)
Accumulated benefit obligation at December 31, 2001	$(660,000)
Plan assets (at fair value) at December 31, 2001	640,000
Unfunded accumulated benefit obligation (minimum liability)	(20,000)
Accrued pension cost at December 31, 2001	15,000
Additional liability at December 31, 2001	(5,000)
Additional liability at December 31, 2000	165,000
Additional liability reduction required at December 31, 2001	$ 160,000

ILLUSTRATION 21-3
PENSION RECONCILIATION SCHEDULE (L.O.10)

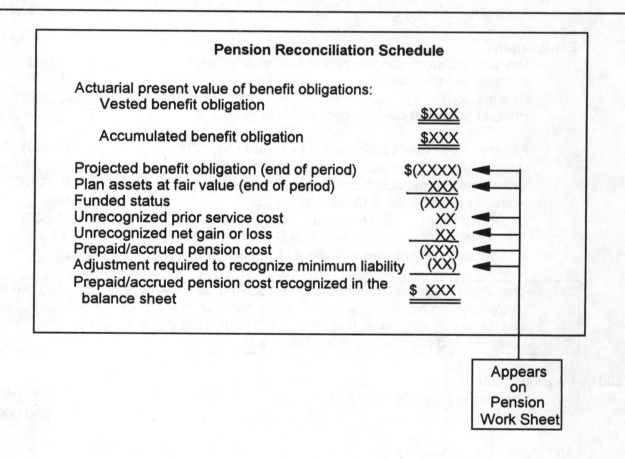

Pension Reconciliation Schedule	
Actuarial present value of benefit obligations:	
Vested benefit obligation	$XXX
Accumulated benefit obligation	$XXX
Projected benefit obligation (end of period)	$(XXXX)
Plan assets at fair value (end of period)	XXX
Funded status	(XXX)
Unrecognized prior service cost	XX
Unrecognized net gain or loss	XX
Prepaid/accrued pension cost	(XXX)
Adjustment required to recognize minimum liability	(XX)
Prepaid/accrued pension cost recognized in the balance sheet	$ XXX

Appears on Pension Work Sheet

EXERCISE 21-7

Purpose: (L.O.10) This exercise illustrates the schedule used to reconcile the funded status of a pension plan with the asset/liability reported on the balance sheet.

Steele Company provided the following data at December 31, 1999:

Accumulated benefit obligation	$ 770,000
Market-related asset value	610,000
Plan assets (at fair value)	590,000
Projected benefit obligation	850,000
Unrecognized net gain	30,000
Unrecognized prior service cost	190,000
Vested benefit obligation	320,000

Instructions
Present the schedule reconciling the funded status with the asset/liability reported on the balance sheet. Assume no prepaid/accrued pension cost existed at the beginning of the year.

Solution to Exercise 21-7

Actuarial present value of benefit obligations:	
Vested benefit obligation	$(320,000)
Accumulated benefit obligation	$(770,000)
Projected benefit obligation	$(850,000)
Plan assets at fair value	590,000
Funded status	(260,000)
Unrecognized prior service cost	190,000
Unrecognized net gain	(30,000)
Accrued pension cost	(100,000)
Adjustment required to recognize minimum liability	(80,000)
Pension liability reported on the balance sheet	$(180,000)

Approach and Explanation: Refer to **Illustration 21-3** for the appropriate format. Recall that the difference between the accumulated benefit obligation and the fair value of the plan assets is the minimum liability reported on the balance sheet.

Accumulated benefit obligation	$(770,000)
Plan assets at fair value	590,000
Minimum pension liability	$(180,000)

EXERCISE 21-8

Purpose: (L.O.12) This exercise is related to postretirement benefits other than pensions.

Handy Company reports the following data related to postretirement benefits for 1999:

APBO at January 1, 1999	$ 480,000
EPBO at January 1, 1999	540,000
Actual return on plan assets in 1999	27,000
Expected return on plan assets in 1999	30,000
Service cost	52,000
Discount rate	10%
Benefits paid	43,000
Contributions (funding)	60,000
Amortization of unrecognized net gain	2,000
Amortization of transition amount	36,000

Instructions

(a)   Compute the amount of postretirement expense for 1999.

(b)   Prepare the journal entry to record postretirement expense and Handy's contribution for 1999.

(c)   Compute the amount of APBO at December 31, 1999.

TIP: EPBO stands for Expected Postretirement Benefit Obligation. EPBO is the actuarial present value of all benefits expected to be paid after retirement to employees and their dependents.

TIP: APBO stands for Accumulated Postretirement Benefit Obligation. APBO is the actuarial present value of future benefits attributed to employees' services rendered to date. The EPBO includes an additional amount related to services to be rendered by employees before they are fully eligible for benefits.

Solution to Exercise 21-8

(a)

Service cost	$ 52,000
Interest cost (10% x $480,000)	48,000
Actual return on plan assets	(27,000)
Unexpected loss ($27,000 - $30,000)	(3,000)
Amortization of unrecognized net gain	(2,000)
Amortization of transition amount	36,000
Postretirement expense—1999	$ 104,000

Explanation: Postretirement expense consists of many of the same components used to compute pension expense.

> **TIP:** Service cost is the portion of the EPBO attributed to employee service during the period.
>
> **TIP:** Interest cost is the discount rate times the APBO at the beginning of the year.
>
> **TIP:** When the expected return is greater than the actual return, there is an unexpected loss. In the computation of postretirement expense, the actual return is deducted and an unexpected loss is also deducted so that the expected return is the amount actually reflected in the current expense; thus, the unexpected loss is deferred. An unexpected gain would be added in the expense computation.
>
> **TIP:** A net gain ultimately reduces the cost to the employer of postretirement benefits; therefore, the amortization of a net gain reduces postretirement expense.
>
> **TIP:** At the beginning of the year of adoption of *SFAS No. 106*, a **transition amount** (obligation or asset) is computed as the difference between (1) the ABPO and (2) the fair value of the plan assets, plus any accrued obligation or less any prepaid cost (asset). Because most plans are unfunded and most employers are accruing postretirement benefit costs for the first time, large transition obligations occur. The amortization of a transition obligation increases postretirement expense.

(b) Postretirement Expense (Computed above) 104,000
        Prepaid/Accrued Cost ($104,000 - $60,000)   44,000
        Cash   60,000

Explanation: The journal entry to record postretirement expense is similar to the entry to record pension expense.

(c)
APBO at January 1, 1999	$ 480,000
Service cost for 1999	52,000
Interest cost for 1999	48,000
Benefits paid in 1999	(43,000)
APBO at December 31, 1999	$ 537,000

Explanation: Examine the APBO column in a postretirement benefits work sheet in your text. Note that service cost and interest cost increase the APBO and benefits paid decrease the APBO.

ANALYSIS OF MULTIPLE-CHOICE TYPE QUESTIONS

QUESTION

1.   (L.O.4) The following information is related to the pension plan of Jay, Inc. for 1999.

Actual return on plan assets	$ 80,000
Amortization of unrecognized net gain	33,000
Amortization of unrecognized prior service cost	60,000
Expected return on plan assets	92,000
Interest on projected benefit obligation	145,000
Service cost	320,000

Pension expense for 1999 is:
a. $400,000.
b. $412,000.
c. $466,000.
d. $478,000.

Explanation: Service cost and interest cost increase pension expense. Remember that the adjustment of actual return on plan assets for an unexpected gain or loss means that the amount of the expected return on plan assets is used to compute the pension expense ($80,000 actual return + $12,000 unexpected loss = $92,000 expected return). The amortization of a net unrecognized gain reduces pension expense. Amortization of unrecognized prior service cost increases pension expense. The computation is:

Service cost	$ 320,000
Interest cost	145,000
Actual return on plan assets	(80,000)
Unexpected loss ($80,000 - $92,000)	(12,000)
Amortization of unrecognized net gain	(33,000)
Amortization of unrecognized prior service cost	60,000
Pension expense for 1999	$ 400,000

(Solution = a.)

QUESTION

2.   (L.O.9) The following pension plan information is for Kent Company at December 31, 1999.

Projected benefit obligation	$ 5,600,000
Accumulated benefit obligation	5,000,000
Plan assets (at fair value)	4,100,000
Market-related asset value	4,300,000
Unrecognized prior service cost	360,000
Pension expense for 1999	2,000,000
Contribution for 1999	1,600,000

Prior to 1999, cumulative pension expense equaled cumulative contributions. The amount to be reported as the total liability for pensions on the December 31, 1999 balance sheet is:

a. $700,000.
b. $900,000.
c. $1,300,000.
d. $1,500,000.

Explanation:

Accumulated benefit obligation	$ 5,000,000
Plan assets (at fair value)	(4,100,000)
Total liability for pensions	$ 900,000

The total liability for pensions in this case is the excess of the accumulated benefit obligation over the fair value of plan assets. The excess is not adjusted for prepaid or accrued pension cost. This is the minimum liability computation. (Solution = b.)

> **TIP:**   In this instance, the minimum liability of $900,000 is in excess of the accrued pension cost balance of $400,000 ($2,000,000 pension expense - $1,600,000 contributions = $400,000 accrued pension cost recorded in 1999; beginning balance of $0 + $400,000 = $400,000 ending balance of accrued pension cost). Thus, an additional liability of $500,000 is required.

QUESTION

3.   (L.O.9) Refer to the data in Question 2. The amount to be reported as Intangible Asset—Deferred Pension Cost on the December 31, 1999 balance sheet is:
a. $300,000.
b. $360,000.
c. $500,000.
d. $900,000.

Explanation: Kent's contribution for 1999 was $400,000 less than the pension expense for 1999, resulting in accrued pension cost of $400,000 ($2,000,000 - $1,600,000) at December 31, 1999. The additional liability to be recorded is the minimum liability of $900,000 ($5,000,000 - $4,100,000) minus the $400,000 liability for accrued pension cost already recorded, which equals $500,000. When the additional liability exceeds the amount of unrecognized prior service cost, the intangible asset account balance is limited to that amount, which in this case is $360,000. The journal entry would be:

Intangible Asset—Deferred Pension Cost..........................	360,000	
Excess of Additional Pension Liability Over		
Unrecognized Prior Service Cost...................................	140,000	
Additional Pension Liability......................................		500,000

(Solution = b.)

> **TIP:** The account charged for $140,000 in this entry is a contra stockholders' equity account.

QUESTION

4.   (L.O.4) The following data are for the pension plan for the employees of Chip Company.

	1/1/98	12/31/98	12/31/99
Market-related asset value	$2,200,000	$2,900,000	$3,100,000
Plan assets (at fair value)	2,300,000	3,000,000	3,300,000
Accumulated benefit obligation	2,500,000	2,600,000	3,400,000
Projected benefit obligation	2,700,000	2,800,000	3,700,000
Unrecognized net loss	-0-	480,000	500,000
Settlement rate (for year)		10%	9%
Expected rate of return (for year)		8%	7%

Chip's contribution was $420,000 in 1999 and benefits paid were $375,000. Chip estimates that the average remaining service life is 15 years. The actual return on plan assets in 1999 is:

a. $155,000.
b. $200,000.
c. $255,000.
d. $300,000.

Approach and Explanation: Recall that the actual return is found by (1) computing the change in plan assets (at fair value), (2) deducting contributions, and (3) adding benefits paid. The calculation is:

Plan assets, 12/31/99	$ 3,300,000
Plan assets, 12/31/98	3,000,000
Increase during 1999	300,000
Deduct contributions	(420,000)
Add benefits paid	375,000
Actual return, 1999	$ 255,000

(Solution = c.)

QUESTION

5.   (L.O.4,7) Refer to the data in Question 4. You know that the actual return on plan assets in 1999 is $255,000. The unexpected gain or loss on plan assets in 1999 is:
   a. $24,000 gain.
   b. $38,000 gain.
   c. $45,000 gain.
   d. $52,000 gain.

Explanation: The expected return is the expected rate of return times the market-related asset value at the beginning of the year. For 1999, the expected return is $203,000 (7% x $2,900,000). Since the actual return is $255,000, there is an unexpected gain of $52,000 ($255,000 - $203,000). (Solution = d.)

QUESTION

6.   (L.O.8) Refer to the data in Question 4. The corridor for amortization of unrecognized net gain or loss in 1999 is:
   a. $280,000.
   b. $290,000.
   c. $300,000.
   d. $370,000.

Explanation: The corridor is 10% of the larger of the beginning balances of the projected benefit obligation ($2,800,000) or the market-related value of the plan assets ($2,900,000). Chip's corridor in 1999 is $290,000 (10% x $2,900,000). (Solution = b.)

> **TIP:**   The cumulative unrecognized net gain or loss is the result of both asset gains and losses and liability gains and losses experienced to date.

QUESTION

7.   (L.O.8) Refer to the data in Question 4. You know that the corridor for 1999 is $290,000. The amount of unrecognized net loss amortized in 1999 is:
   a. $12,667.
   b. $14,000.
   c. $32,000.
   d. $33,333.

Explanation: The amount of unrecognized net loss that is subject to being amortized is the portion of the unrecognized net loss at the beginning of the period that is greater than the corridor. The minimum amortization is computed by dividing the excess over the corridor by the average remaining service life. The amount of net loss in excess of the corridor is $190,000 ($480,000 - $290,000). The net loss amortized in 1999 is $12,667 ($190,000 ÷ 15). (Solution = a.)

QUESTION

8. (L.O.12) The following data relate to the Shield Company postretirement plan for 1999:

APBO at January 1, 1999 (transition amount)	$ 400,000
EPBO at January 1, 1999	500,000
Service cost	95,000
Discount rate	10%
Average remaining service periods to full eligibility	20 years
Average remaining service periods to expected retirement	25 years

The amount of postretirement expense for 1999 is:
   a. $111,000.
   b. $151,000.
   c. $155,000.
   d. $161,000.

Explanation: Postretirement expense includes service cost, interest cost, an adjustment for return on plan assets, and amortization of the transition amount. The interest cost is the discount rate times the APBO at the beginning of the year. There is no actual return or expected return on plan assets for 1999 because there were no plan assets as of the beginning of 1999 (as evidenced by the fact that the transition amount was the same amount as the APBO at the beginning of the period that *SFAS No. 106* was adopted). The transition amount is amortized over the average remaining service periods to expected retirement.

Service cost	$ 95,000
Interest cost (10% x $400,000)	40,000
Amortization of transition amount ($400,000 ÷ 25)	16,000
Postretirement expense for 1999	$ 151,000

(Solution = b.)

QUESTION

9. (L.O.12) The following data relate to the Boyd Company postretirement benefits plan for 1999:

APBO at January 1, 1999	$ 300,000
EPBO at January 1, 1999	400,000
Service cost	82,000
Discount rate	8%
Actual return on plan assets in 1999	13,000
Expected return on plan assets in 1999	17,000

The amount of postretirement expense for 1999 is:
   a. $89,000.
   b. $93,000.
   c. $97,000.
   d. $106,000.

Explanation: Recall that postretirement expense includes service cost, interest cost, an adjustment for return on plan assets, and amortization for the transition amount (if any). The interest cost is the discount rate times the APBO at the beginning of the year. A positive actual return is deducted in the calculation. Because the postretirement expense is credited for an unexpected loss or debited for an unexpected gain on plan assets (the difference between the actual and the expected return), this component is really the expected return. No information was given about a transition amount; it apparently was recognized as a change in accounting principle in the period *SFAS No. 106* was adopted.

Service cost	$ 82,000
Interest cost (8% x $300,000)	24,000
Actual return during 1999	(13,000)
Unexpected loss ($13,000 - $17,000)	(4,000)
Postretirement expense	$ 89,000

(Solution = a.)

CHAPTER 22

ACCOUNTING FOR LEASES

OVERVIEW

Many entities lease assets. Leasing will often offer tax and cash flow advantages when compared to the purchase of these assets. Some leases are pure rentals; others are, in substance, an installment purchase of the asset by the lessee. This chapter will discuss both operating and nonoperating type leases but will focus on the nonoperating type where we must account for substance over form. That is, even though it is legally a rental situation, in substance the transaction is an installment purchase of the asset by the lessee.

SUMMARY OF LEARNING OBJECTIVES

1. **Explain the nature, economic substance, and advantages of lease transactions.** A lease is a contractual agreement between a lessor and a lessee that conveys to the lessee the right to use specific property (real or personal), owned by the lessor, for a specified period of time. In return for this right, the lessee agrees to make periodic cash payments (rents) to the lessor. The advantages of lease transactions are: (1) 100% financing, (2) protection against obsolescence, (3) flexibility, (4) less costly financing, (5) possible tax advantage, and (6) off-balance-sheet financing.

2. **Describe the accounting criteria and procedures for capitalizing leases by the lessee.** A lease is a capital lease if one or more of the following four criteria are met: (1) the lease transfers ownership of the property to the lessee, (2) the lease contains a bargain purchase option; (3) the lease term is equal to 75% or more of the estimated economic life of the leased property; (4) the present value of the minimum lease payments (excluding executory costs) equals or exceeds 90% of the fair value of the leased property. For a capital lease, the lessee records an asset and a liability at the lower of (1) the present value of the minimum lease payments or (2) the fair market value of the leased asset at the inception of the lease. If a lease does not meet the criteria to be classified as a capital lease, it is an operating lease from the lessee's standpoint.

3. **Contrast the operating and capitalization methods of recording leases.** The total charges to operations are the same over the span of time the asset is used by the lessee whether the lease is accounted for as a capital lease or as an operating lease; under the capital lease treatment, the charges are higher in the earlier years and lower in the later years. If an accelerated method of depreciation is used, the differences between the amounts charged to operations under the two methods would be even larger in the earlier and later years. The following occurs if a capital lease instead of an operating lease is employed: (1) an increase in the amount of reported debt (both short-term and long-term), (2) an increase in the amount of total assets (specifically long-lived assets), and (3) a lower net income early in the life of the lease and, therefore, lower retained earnings.

4. **Identify the classifications of leases for the lessor.** From the standpoint of the lessor, all leases may be classified for accounting purposes as follows: (1) operating leases, (2) direct

financing leases, or (3) sales-type leases. The lessor should classify and account for an arrangement as a direct financing lease or a sales-type lease if at the date of the lease agreement one or more of the Group I criteria (which are the same four criteria as listed in learning objective 2 for lessees) are met and both of the following Group II criteria are met. *Group II:* (1) Collectibility of the minimum lease payments is reasonably predictable, and (2) no important uncertainties surround the amount of unreimbursable costs yet to be incurred by the lessor under the lease. All leases that fail to meet the criteria are classified and accounted for by the lessor as operating leases.

5. **Describe the lessor's accounting for direct financing leases.** Leases that are in substance the financing of an asset purchase by a lessee require the lessor to substitute a "lease payments receivable" for the leased asset on the lessor's books. The information necessary to record a direct financing lease is: (1) gross investment ("lease payments receivable"), (2) unearned interest revenue, and (3) net investment. There often is uncertainty on the part of a student as to how to account for a residual value (guaranteed or unguaranteed) when computing gross investment. Gross investment is defined as minimum lease payments plus any unguaranteed residual value. A guaranteed residual value is a component of minimum lease payments. Therefore, a residual value, whether guaranteed or unguaranteed, is included as part of gross investment if it is relevant to the lessor (i.e., if the lessor expects to get the asset back). The lessor often uses the Lease Payments Receivable account to record the gross investment.

6. **Identify special features of lease arrangements that cause unique accounting problems.** The features of lease arrangements that cause unique accounting problems are: (1) residual values, (2) sales-type lease (lessor), (3) bargain purchase option, (4) initial direct costs, (5) current versus noncurrent classification, and (6) disclosures.

7. **Describe the effect of a residual value, guaranteed or unguaranteed, on lease accounting.** Whether an estimated residual value is guaranteed by the lessee or unguaranteed is of both economic and accounting consequence to the lessee. The accounting difference is that the minimum lease payments, the basis for capitalization, includes a guaranteed residual value but excludes any unguaranteed residual value. If the lessee is the party agreeing to guarantee a residual value, the guaranteed residual value affects the lessee's computation of minimum lease payments and, therefore, the amounts capitalized as a leased asset and a lease obligation. In effect, it is an additional lease payment that will be paid in property or cash, or both, at the end of the lease term. An unguaranteed residual value has no effect upon the computation of the minimum lease payments, the lessee's cost of the leased asset, or the lessee's reported amount for the lease obligation.

8. **Describe the lessor's accounting for sales-type leases.** The information needed to record a sales-type lease is as follows: (1) gross investment (also called "lease payments receivable"), (2) unearned interest revenue, (3) sales price of the leased asset, and (4) cost of goods sold. The computations for gross investment and the unearned interest revenue reflect any residual value involved (a guaranteed residual or an unguaranteed residual that will be available to the lessor). When recording sales revenue and cost of goods sold, there is a difference in the accounting for a guaranteed or an unguaranteed residual value. A guaranteed residual value can be considered part of sales revenue because the lessor knows that the entire asset has been sold. There is less certainty that the unguaranteed residual portion of the asset has been "sold;" therefore, sales and cost of goods sold are recognized only for the portion of the asset for which realization is assured. However, the gross profit amount on the sale of the asset is the same whether a guaranteed or unguaranteed residual value is involved.

9. **Describe the disclosure requirements for leases.** The disclosure requirements for the **lessee** are classified as follows: (1) capital leases, (2) operating leases having initial or remaining noncancelable lease terms in excess of one year, (3) all operating leases, and (4) a general description of the lessee's arrangements. The disclosure requirements for the **lessor** are classified as follows: (1) sales-type and direct financing leases, (2) operating leases, and (3) a general description of the lessor's leasing arrangements.

10. **Describe the lessee's accounting for a sale-leaseback transaction.** If the lease meets one of the four criteria for treatment as a capital lease, the seller-lessee accounts for the transaction as a sale and the lease as a capital lease. Any profit or loss experienced by the seller-lessee from the sale of an asset that is leased back under a capital lease should be deferred and amortized over the lease term (or the remaining economic life of the asset if either criteria 1 or 2 of Group I is satisfied) in proportion to the amortization of the leased asset. If none of the capital lease criteria are satisfied, the seller-lessee accounts for the transaction as a sale and the lease as an operating lease. Under an operating lease, a profit or loss on the sale of the asset generally should be deferred and amortized in proportion to the rental payments over the period of time the asset is expected to be used by the lessee.

TIPS ON CHAPTER TOPICS

TIP: For a nonoperating type lease, **always draw a time line** and enter on that diagram all the cash flows associated with the lease which are expected by the party for whom you are accounting. For a lessee, those will be the minimum lease payments. For a lessor, those will be the minimum lease payments plus any unguaranteed residual value to the lessor.

TIP: **Minimum lease payments** include the following:
1. Regular periodic rental payments, excluding executory costs (an annuity).
2. Bargain purchase option (a single sum), if any.
3. Guaranteed residual value (a single sum), if any.
4. Penalty for failure to renew, if any.

TIP: The **cost** (and initial amount of obligation) **for an asset under a capital lease** is determined by the present value of the minimum lease payments (excluding executory costs included therein). However, the amount recorded should not exceed the fair market value of the asset at the inception date. The rate to use in the discounting process is the lessee's incremental borrowing rate or the lessor's implicit rate. The lessor's rate is used when it is known **and** when it is the lower of the two rates.

TIP: The time period to be used for depreciation of an asset under capital lease depends on which criteria the lease meets in determining that it is a capital lease. If there is automatic transfer of title of the asset at the end of the lease term or if there is a bargain purchase option, the asset is expected to be with the lessee for the remainder of its economic life; therefore, to comply with the matching principle, the asset should be depreciated over its remaining useful life. If the lease contract does not provide for the automatic transfer of title and there is no bargain purchase option, the asset will be used by the lessee only for the lease term; therefore, to comply with the matching principle, the asset should be depreciated over the lease term.

TIP: A **bargain purchase option** is defined as an option to purchase at a bargain price. A bargain price is a price substantially below the expected market value of the **asset at** the date the option becomes exercisable. If the option price is 30% of the expected market value, accountants would agree that the price constitutes a bargain. If the option price is 90% of the expected market value, accountants would agree that the price does not constitute a bargain. The range that lies between these two extremes provides room for controversy. A question appearing on a recent CPA examination considered a 50% relationship to constitute a bargain. But what about 70% or 80%? Judgment is required in this area.

TIP: The amount representing gross investment in lease for a lessor is recorded in the lessor's books in the account Lease Payments Receivable; an alternate name for this account is Gross Investment in Lease. Gross investment in lease is defined as minimum lease payments plus unguaranteed residual value, if any. Minimum lease payments include a guaranteed residual value, if any. Thus, both guaranteed residual value (because it is included as part of minimum lease payments) and unguaranteed residual value (because it is added in to compute the gross investment) are included as part of lease payments receivable if a portion of the residual value is guaranteed in the lease agreement and if the unguaranteed portion is relevant to the lessor (that is, if the lessor expects to get the asset back).

TIP: For an **operating** type lease, minimum lease payments are recognized as rental expense by the lessee on a **straight-line basis**, even if not payable on a straight-line basis. Thus, situations involving a lease bonus, scheduled rent increases, or free rent must conform to this guideline. For example: a lessee signs a five-year operating lease and receives ten months of free rent. The cost of the 50 (60 - 10 = 50) rental payments is to be divided by the 60-month lease term to determine the monthly rental expense.

TIP: For an operating lease, rents are recognized as revenue by the lessor on a straight-line basis over the lease term as they are earned. If the cash is not received in the period the revenue is earned, a deferral (or an accrual) type adjustment is required.

ILLUSTRATION 22-1
CLASSIFICATION OF LEASES (L.O.2,4)

CLASSIFICATION OF LEASES BY THE LESSEE

From the standpoint of the lessee, all leases may be classified for accounting purposes as follows:
- (a)   Operating leases.
- (b)   Capital leases.

If at the inception of a noncancelable lease agreement the lease meets **one or more** of the following four criteria, the lessee shall classify and account for the arrangement as a **capital lease**:
1.   The lease transfers ownership of the property to the lessee.
2.   The lease contains a bargain purchase option.
3.   The lease term is equal to 75% or more of the estimated economic life of the leased property.
4.   The present value of the minimum lease payments (excluding executory costs) equals or exceeds 90% of the fair value of the leased property.

CLASSIFICATION OF LEASES BY THE LESSOR

From the standpoint of the **lessor**, all leases may be classified for accounting purposes as follows:
- (a)   Operating leases.
- (b)   Direct financing leases.
- (c)   Sales-type leases.

If at the inception of a lease agreement the lessor is party to a lease that meets **one or more** of the following Group I criteria (1, 2, 3, and 4) and **both** of the following Group II criteria (1 and 2), the lessor shall classify and account for the arrangement as a **direct financing lease** or as a **sales-type lease**. (If the lessor's net investment at inception equals the asset's carrying value, the lease is a direct financing lease; if the net investment is unequal to the asset's carrying value, the lease is a sales-type lease.)

GROUP I
1.   The lease transfers ownership of the property to the lessee.
2.   The lease contains a bargain purchase option.
3.   The lease term is equal to 75% or more of the estimated economic life of the leased property.
4.   The present value of the minimum lease payments (excluding executory costs) equals or exceeds 90% of the fair value of the leased property.

GROUP II
1.   Collectibility of the payments required from the lessee is reasonably predictable.
2.   No important uncertainties surround the amount of unreimbursable costs yet to be incurred by the lessor under the lease (i.e., lessor's performance is substantially complete and future costs are reasonably predictable).

ILLUSTRATION 22-1 (Continued)

> **TIP:** Note that the Group I criteria are identical to the criteria that must be met for a lease to be classified as a capital lease by a lessee.
>
> **TIP:** In certain cases, the lessee may capitalize the lease while the lessor does not. This situation results because the lease meets one or more Group I criteria, but the lease does not meet both Group II criteria; thus, the lease meets the qualifications required for capitalization by the lessee but the lease does not meet the qualifications required for capitalization by the lessor. Therefore, both parties will report the leased asset on their balance sheets, and both parties will record depreciation each period for financial reporting purposes. They must agree who is to take depreciation for tax purposes because the IRS will not allow both parties to report depreciation on the leased asset.

ILLUSTRATION 22-2
STEPS IN EVALUATING AND ACCOUNTING
FOR A LEASE SITUATION FOR A LESSEE (L.O.2,7)

STEP 1:   **Examine the facts regarding the lease agreement.**
Determine if the lease meets the criteria to capitalize the lease (the criteria are listed in **Illustration 22-1**). If so, perform the rest of the steps below; if not, account for the lease as an operating lease.

STEP 2:   **Draw the time line.**

STEP 3:   **Compute the present value of the minimum lease payments.**
- The minimum lease payments include:
  - (a)   periodic rental payments
  - (b)   bargain purchase option, if any
  - (c)   guaranteed residual value, if any residual value is guaranteed by the lessee
- Use the lessee's incremental borrowing rate or the lessor's implicit rate, whichever is lower. (The lessor's rate must be known for it to be used.)

STEP 4:   **Determine the cost of the asset under capital lease.**
- The cost is the **lower** of the present value of the minimum lease payments (Step 3) or the asset's fair value.
- If the fair value is the lower, a new effective interest rate must be determined. That new rate is the interest rate which sets the minimum lease payments equivalent to the fair value of the asset, giving effect to the time value of money.

ILLUSTRATION 22-2 (Continued)

STEP 5:   **Prepare the lessee's amortization schedule.**
            The beginning obligation balance is the amount determined in Step 4. (The
            interest rate for Step 5 is the rate used in Step 3, unless that rate was replaced
            in Step 4.)

STEP 6:   **Prepare journal entries to record the transactions related to the lease on
            the lessee's books.**

ILLUSTRATION 22-3
STEPS IN EVALUATING AND ACCOUNTING
FOR A LEASE SITUATION FOR A LESSOR (L.O.5,7,8)

STEP 1:   **Examine the facts regarding the lease agreement.**
            Determine if the lease meets the criteria for the lessor to capitalize the lease
            (the criteria are listed in **Illustration 22-1**). If so, perform the rest of the steps
            below; if not, account for the lease as an operating lease.

STEP 2:   **Determine the periodic rental payments required by the lessor to yield the
            desired rate of return on the investment if that payment is not given data.**
            • The future cash flows to the lessor from the leased asset are to allow the
              lessor to recover the asset's fair value or its cost.
            • The present value of any single sum expected by the lessor at the end of
              the lease term (bargain purchase option or guaranteed residual value or
              unguaranteed residual value) is deducted from the asset's fair value (or
              cost) to arrive at the present value of the periodic rents. The amount of a
              single rent is determined by solving for Rent in the following formula:

                   Present Value of an Annuity = Rent (Present Value Factor)

STEP 3:   **Draw the time line.**

STEP 4:   **Compute the net investment at inception.**
            • Net investment is the present value of the minimum lease payments plus
              the present value of any unguaranteed residual value that will be
              available to the lessor.
            • Use the lessor's implicit rate in the discounting process.

ILLUSTRATION 22-3 (Continued)

STEP 5:   **Prepare the lessor's amortization schedule.**
The beginning net investment (computed in Step 4) is the starting point for this schedule. Use the lessor's implicit rate to compute interest revenue.

STEP 6:   **Prepare the journal entries to record the transactions related to the lease on the lessor's books.**

EXERCISE 22-1

Purpose: (L.O.2,5) This exercise illustrates how a lessee and a lessor are to account for a lease when the contract allows for automatic transfer of title to the leased asset at the end of the lease term.

The following facts pertain to a lease between Sun Bank Leasing and JMJ Schmitt Printers for an electronic laser printer:

1. The lease is for a five-year term, beginning January 1, 1999. The remaining economic life of the asset is five years.
2. The lessor's implicit rate is 10%; the lessee's incremental borrowing rate is 10%.
3. The fair value of the leased asset is $100,000. The lessor's cost is $100,000.
4. The annual rent payments are $25,981.62; the first one is due on January 1, 1999. This amount includes $2,000.00 for executory costs.
5. The title to the asset automatically transfers to the lessee at the end of the lease term. The asset is expected to have a fair value of $5,000 at that date.
6. Both the lessee and the lessor use the calendar year for their accounting periods.

Instructions

(a)   Describe the type of lease from the viewpoint of the: (1) lessee and (2) lessor.
(b)   Prepare an amortization schedule for use by the lessee and the lessor. Explain why they could both use the same schedule in this situation. Also, draw a time line for the lessor.
(c)   Prepare the journal entry to record the inception of the lease on the lessee's books.
(d)   Prepare the journal entry to record the inception of the lease on the lessor's books.
(e)   Indicate the amount(s) to appear in the lessee's December 31, 2000 balance sheet for this lease. Also indicate the portion that will appear in the current liability section, and the portion that will appear in the long-term liability classification. Explain how to determine these amounts.

(f)   Indicate the amount to appear in the lessor's December 31, 2000 balance sheet for net investment in lease. Also indicate the portion that will appear in the current asset section, and the portion that will appear in the long-term investment section of the balance sheet. Also show the gross investment and unearned interest components of each net investment figure. Explain how to determine these amounts.

Solution to Exercise 22-1

(a)   The lease is a capital lease for the lessee because the title to the leased asset automatically transfers to the lessee at the end of the lease term. (The lease also meets two other criteria required by the lessee for capitalization.) Assuming that uncollectible lease payments are reasonably estimable and there are no important uncertainties surrounding future unreimbursable costs to be incurred by the lessor with respect to the lease, the lessor has a nonoperating type lease because of the automatic transfer of the title of the leased asset at the end of the lease term. The lessor has a direct financing type lease because the net investment at inception equals the lessor's carrying value.

Computations:
$25,981.62 - $2,000.00 executory costs = $23,981.62
$23,981.62 x present value factor for an annuity due for $n = 5$, $i = 10\%$ = net investment
$23,981.62 x 4.16986 = $100,000.00 net investment

(b)   **AMORTIZATION SCHEDULE**

Date	Rent Excluding Executory Costs	10% Interest	Reduction of Present Value	Present Value Balance
1/1/99				$ 100,000.00
1/1/99	$ 23,981.62*	$ -0-	$ 23,981.62	76,018.38
1/1/00	23,981.62	7,601.84	16,379.78	59,638.60
1/1/01	23,981.62	5,963.86	18,017.76	41,620.84
1/1/02	23,981.62	4,162.08	19,819.54	21,801.30
1/1/03	23,981.62	2,180.32**	21,801.30	-0-
	$ 119,908.10	$19,908.10	$ 100,000.00	

*$25,981.62 - $2,000.00 = $23,981.62
**Includes rounding error of $.19.

The lessor and the lessee can use the same amortization schedule in this situation because they are using the same interest rate to account for the lease, and the lessor has no unguaranteed residual value for which to account. For these same reasons, both parties have the same time line for the lease which is depicted as follows:

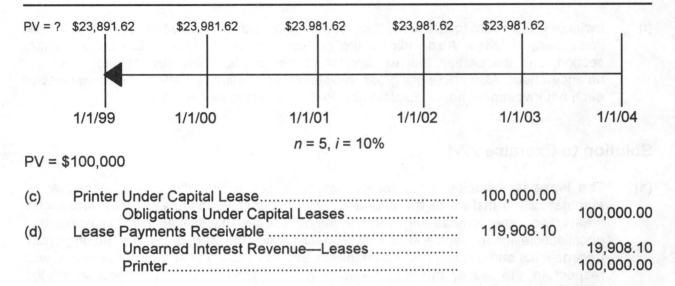

PV = ? $23,891.62 $23,981.62 $23.981.62 $23,981.62 $23,981.62

1/1/99   1/1/00   1/1/01   1/1/02   1/1/03   1/1/04

$n = 5, i = 10\%$

PV = $100,000

(c)	Printer Under Capital Lease..	100,000.00	
	Obligations Under Capital Leases...........................		100,000.00
(d)	Lease Payments Receivable	119,908.10	
	Unearned Interest Revenue—Leases		19,908.10
	Printer...		100,000.00

(e) The asset Printer Under Capital Lease for $100,000 will appear in the property, plant, and equipment section of the lessee's balance sheet. Accumulated depreciation of $38,000 would also appear in that section. In computing the periodic depreciation, the residual value is deducted from the asset's cost because the lessee expects to recover $5,000 from disposal of the asset after the end of the lease term when the title to the asset automatically transfers to the lessee. Thus, ($100,000 - $5,000) ÷ 5 years = $19,000 per year. The present value of the obligation under capital lease at December 31, 2000 is $65,602.46 ($59,638.60 + $5,963.86 = $65,602.46). The present value amount will be reported on the lessee's balance sheet at this date as follows:

Current liabilities
    Interest payable $ 5,963.86
    Obligations under capital leases   18,017.76
Long-term liabilities
    Obligations under capital leases   41,620.84

To determine these amounts, look at the amortization schedule. Find the date on the schedule that is the balance sheet date (December 31, 2000). If the balance sheet date is not on the schedule (as is the case here), locate the date that most recently precedes the balance sheet date. That date is January 1, 2000 in this exercise. Find the balance on that payment line (which is $59,638.60) and add any interest that has accrued since that date (i.e., $59,638.60 x 10% = $5,963.86). The total is the present value of the remaining minimum lease payments at the balance sheet date. The liability due to the accrued interest expense belongs in the current liability classification. The portion of the principal that is to be shown in current liabilities is the amount on the **next** payment line (1/1/01) of the amortization schedule in the "Reduction of Present Value" column ($18,017.76); the portion of the principal that is noncurrent is on that same (1/1/01) line in the "Present Value Balance" column ($41,620.84).

(f) The net investment in lease at December 31, 2000 is $65,602.46 ($59,638.60 + $5,963.86 = $65,602.46). This will appear on the lessor's December 31, 2000 balance sheet as follows:

Current assets

Lease payments receivable	$ 23,981.62
Unearned interest revenue—leases	-0-
Net investment in lease	$ 23,981.62

Long-term investments

Lease payments receivable	$ 47,963.24
Unearned interest revenue—leases	(6,342.40)
Net investment in lease	$ 41,620.84

TIP: To check on the accuracy of the current and noncurrent portions, add the two portions together; that total ($23,981.62 + $41,620.84 = $65,602.46) should equal the present value of the lease at the balance sheet date ($65,602.46). It does in this case.

To determine the amounts to appear in the current asset section, refer to the amortization schedule. Look for the balance sheet date or the date that most recently precedes the balance sheet date. The rent on the following line is the amount of gross investment to be classified as a current asset. The interest portion of that rent that is yet unearned at the balance sheet date is to be deducted to arrive at net investment. In the exercise at hand, none of the $5,963.86 interest due on 1/1/01 is unearned at 12/31/00 because it was all earned during 2000; therefore $0 unearned interest revenue is reflected in the current asset section. The rents (and other receipts) appearing on all subsequent lines ($23,981.62 + $23,981.62 = $47,963.24) are to be reflected as gross investment in a noncurrent asset classification. The interest portion of each of those rents ($4,162.08 + $2,180.32 = $6,342.40) is to be deducted as unearned interest revenue to arrive at the noncurrent portion of net investment.

EXERCISE 22-2

Purpose: (L.O.2,5) This exercise is a comprehensive illustration of the accounting procedures for a lease where the leased asset will revert back to the lessor at the end of the lease term and still have some value. This exercise illustrates (1) how the lessor determines the amount of the periodic lease payment, (2) the lessor's computations for recording the transactions associated with the lease, (4) the meaning of the terms "gross investment" and "net investment," (5) the lessee's computations for recording the transactions associated with the lease, (6) the journal entries on the lessor's books, and (7) the journal entries on the lessee's books.

On January 1, Year 1, Leaseco has a piece of equipment with a cost of $80,000 and a fair value of $80,000. On that date, Leaseco leases the asset to Rentco for a five-year term at an implicit rate of 10%. The annual lease payment is due at the beginning of each year, and the first payment is to be collected at the inception date. The leased asset will revert back to

Leaseco at the end of the lease term; its market value at that date is estimated to be $7,000. Both Leaseco and Rentco have a calendar-year reporting period. Rentco is aware of the lessor's implicit rate; Rentco's incremental borrowing rate is 12%. Leaseco can reasonably estimate uncollectible lease payments and has no important uncertainties regarding future unreimbursable costs associated with this lease.

Instructions

Assuming the lease is a capital lease to the lessee and a direct financing lease to the lessor:
(a)   Compute the amount of the annual lease payment (excluding executory costs) to be collected by the lessor.
(b)   Draw the time line for the lessor.
(c)   For the lessor, compute the (1) gross investment in lease at inception, and (2) net investment in lease at inception.
(d)   Compute the amount of interest revenue to be reported by the lessor for: (1) Year 1, (2) Year 2, and (3) Year 5.
(e)   Prepare the amortization schedule for the lessor.
(f)   Compute the cost of the lessee's asset under capital lease.
(g)   Draw the time line for the lessee.
(h)   Compute the amount of interest expense to be reported by the lessee for (1) Year 1, (2) Year 2, and (3) Year 5.
(i)   Prepare the amortization schedule for the lessee.
(j)   Explain why the lessee's amortization schedule is different than the lessor's amortization schedule. Under what circumstances would the two parties be able to use the same amortization schedule?
(k)   Prepare all of the journal entries for the lessor's books for Years 1 and 2, assuming reversing entries are used.
(l)   Prepare all of the journal entries for the lessee's books for Years 1 and 2, assuming reversing entries are used.
(m)   Compare and contrast the journal entries for the lessee [part (l)] with the journal entries for the lessor [part (k)].

Solution to Exercise 22-2

(a)

Total amount to be recovered	$80,000.00
Present value of unguaranteed residual ($7,000 x .62092[1])	(4,346.44)
Present value of annual payments	75,653.56
Factor for present value of an annuity due of 1 for $n = 5$, $i = 10$	÷ 4.16986
Annual rent required	**$18,142.95**

[1].62092 is the factor for present value of 1 for $n = 5$, $i = 10\%$.

> **TIP:**   In this case, the asset's fair value (or cost) is to be recovered through annual payments by the lessee and through the asset's market value ($7,000.00) at the end of the lease. Today's cash equivalent of $7,000.00 due in five years is less than $7,000.00, due to the time value of money.

(b)

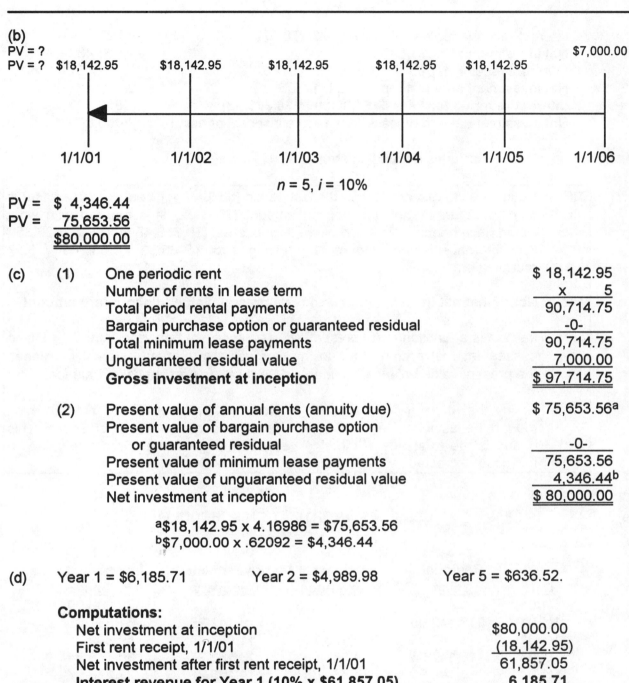

PV = ?
PV = ? $18,142.95 $18,142.95 $18,142.95 $18,142.95 $18,142.95 $7,000.00

1/1/01   1/1/02   1/1/03   1/1/04   1/1/05   1/1/06

$n = 5, i = 10\%$

PV = $ 4,346.44
PV =   75,653.56
       $80,000.00

(c)   **(1)**   One periodic rent $ 18,142.95
                   Number of rents in lease term   x   5
                   Total period rental payments   90,714.75
                   Bargain purchase option or guaranteed residual   -0-
                   Total minimum lease payments   90,714.75
                   Unguaranteed residual value   7,000.00
                   Gross investment at inception $ 97,714.75

          (2)   Present value of annual rents (annuity due) $ 75,653.56[a]
                   Present value of bargain purchase option
                       or guaranteed residual   -0-
                   Present value of minimum lease payments   75,653.56
                   Present value of unguaranteed residual value   4,346.44[b]
                   Net investment at inception $ 80,000.00

                   [a]$18,142.95 x 4.16986 = $75,653.56
                   [b]$7,000.00 x .62092 = $4,346.44

(d)   Year 1 = $6,185.71   Year 2 = $4,989.98   Year 5 = $636.52.

Computations:
    Net investment at inception $80,000.00
    First rent receipt, 1/1/01   (18,142.95)
    Net investment after first rent receipt, 1/1/01   61,857.05
    Interest revenue for Year 1 (10% x $61,857.05)   6,185.71
    Net investment at 12/31/01   68,042.76
    Second rent receipt, 1/1/02   (18,142.95)
    Net investment after second rent receipt, 1/1/02   49,899.81
    Interest revenue Year 2 (10% x $49,899.81)   4,989.98
    Net investment at 12/31/02   54,889.79
    Third rent receipt, 1/1/03   (18,142.95)
    Net investment after third rent receipt, 1/1/03   36,746.84
    Interest revenue for Year 3 (10% x $36,746.84)   3,674.68
    Net investment at 12/31/03   40,421.52
    Fourth rent receipt, 1/1/04   (18,142.95)
    Net investment after fourth rent receipt, 1/1/04   22,278.57

Interest revenue for Year 4 (10% x $22,278.57)	2,227.86
Net investment at 12/31/04	24,506.43
Fifth rent receipt, 1/1/05	(18,142.95)
Net investment after last rent receipt, 1/1/05	6,363.48
Interest revenue for Year 5 ($7,000.00 - $6,363.48)	**636.52[a]**
Net investment at end of lease term before disposal of asset	$ 7,000.00

[a]Includes a rounding error of $0.17.

TIP: Notice the interest amount for the last period ($636.52 for Year 5, in this case) is a "plug" figure. When the derived amount ($636.52) is compared with what would have been a calculated amount for interest ($6,363.48 x 10% = $636.35), the difference is the amount of rounding error ($636.52 - $636.35 = $.17 rounding error).

TIP: Notice that **net investment in lease is a present value (discounted) amount**.

TIP: Interest is a function of (a) present value balance, (b) rate, and (c) time. As time passes, interest accrues (due to the time value of money). Interest **increases** the present value balance; payments **decrease** the present value balance.

TIP: Notice that there is interest to be earned by the lessor during Year 5, even though the last lease payment is to be received at the beginning of Year 5. This is due to the existence of the single sum (the unguaranteed residual value, in this case) expected by the lessor at the end of the lease term.

(e)   **LESSOR'S AMORTIZATION SCHEDULE**

Date	Receipts Residual Value	10% Interest Revenue	Net Investment Recovery	Net Investment Balance
1/1/01				$80,000.00
1/1/01	$18,142.95		$18,142.95	61,857.05
1/1/02	18,142.95	$ 6,185.71	11,957.24	49,899.81
1/1/03	18,142.95	4,989.98	13,152.97	36,746.84
1/1/04	18,142.95	3,674.68	14,468.27	22,278.57
1/1/05	18,142.95	2,227.86	15,915.09	6,363.48
12/31/05	7,000.00	636.52*	6,363.48	-0-
	$97,714.75	$17,714.75	$80,000.00	

*Includes a rounding error of $0.17.

TIP: The interest included in a rent is the interest for the period that occurs **prior** to the due date of the rent. Thus, the interest shown on the 1/1/03 line on the amortization schedule is the interest charged for the calendar year of Year 2.

TIP: The amounts on the amortization schedule were derived by the computations performed in part (d) above. However, the components are arranged a little differently on the amortization schedule.

TIP: There is no interest included in the first rent receipt because the first rent is to be received on the inception date (hence, the rents constitute an annuity due). There is no passage of time between the inception date and the first rent receipt date; therefore, no interest is earned.

TIP: The rounding error is always to be plugged in the interest column on the last line of the amortization schedule. If all computations are performed correctly and are rounded to the nearest cent, the rounding error will be small—usually less than $10.00. Therefore, a rounding error larger than this will generally indicate that there are errors in the schedule. There may be math errors or more serious procedural errors.

TIP: All items that appear on the time line in part (b) are to appear in the "Receipts" column of the amortization schedule.

TIP: The total of the "Net Investment Recovery" column is equal to the beginning figure in the "Net Investment Balance" column.

TIP: The total of the "Receipts" column is the initial gross investment in lease amount [see solution to part (c)].

TIP: Notice how the net investment amount at December 31, Year 1, as derived from the appropriate numbers on the amortization schedule, can be proved by an independent present value calculation as of that date.

Computations:
From the amortization schedule:

Net investment balance at 1/1/01	$ 61,857.05
Interest for Year 1	6,185.71
Net investment balance at 12/31/01	$ 68,042.76

Present value computations:
Present value of an annuity due of 1, $n = 4$, $i = 10\% = 3.48685$
Present value of 1, $n = 4$, $i = 10\% = .68301$

$18,142.95 x 3.48685	$ 63,261.75
$7,000.00 x .68301	x 4,781.07
Present value at end of Year 1	$ 68,042.82

The 6 cents difference between $68,042.76 and $68,042.82 is due to rounding errors.

(f)   Annual rent payment $ 18,142.95
      Present value of an annuity due of 1, *n* = 5, *i* = 10   x 4.16986
      Present value of annual rents   75,653.56
      Present value of bargain purchase option or guaranteed residual   -0-
      Present value of minimum lease payments $ 75,653.56

> **TIP:**   The lessee's cost of asset under capital lease is the lower of the asset's fair value or the present value of the minimum lease payments. The interest rate to be used in determining the present value of the minimum lease payments is the lessee's incremental borrowing rate or the lessor's implicit rate, whichever is lower. (The lessor's rate cannot possibly be used if it is unknown.)
>
> **TIP:**   When the leased asset is to revert back to the lessor at the end of the lease term rather than remain with the lessee, and the lessee does not guarantee a residual value, the lessee does not find the residual value of any relevance; hence, under these circumstances, the lessee does **not** use the residual value for any of its accounting.

(g)

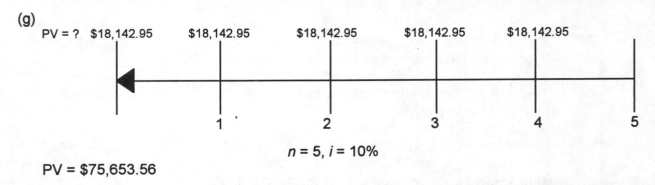

PV = ? $18,142.95 $18,142.95 $18,142.95 $18,142.95 $18,142.95

           1   2   3   4   5

                              n = 5, *i* = 10%

PV = $75,653.56

> **TIP:**   The lessee's time line differs from the lessor's time line in this case because the lessor has an unguaranteed residual value that is not relevant to the lessee.

(h)   Year 1 = $5,751.06   Year 2 = $4,511.87   Year 5 = $0.

Computations:

Present value of obligation at inception	$ 75,653.56
First rent payment, 1/1/01	(18,142.95)
Present value of obligation after first rent payment, 1/1/01	57,510.61
Interest expense for Year 1 (10% x $57,510.61)	**5,751.06**
Present value of obligation at 12/31/01	63,261.67
Second rent payment, 1/1/02	(18,142.95)
Present value of obligation after second rent payment, 1/1/02	45,118.72
Interest expense for Year 2 (10% x $45,118.72)	**4,511.87**
Present value of obligation at 12/31/02	49,630.59
Third rent payment, 1/1/03	(18,142.95)
Present value of obligation after third rent payment, 1/1/03	31,487.64
Interest expense for Year 3 (10% x $31,487.64)	3,148.76
Present value of obligation at 12/31/03	34,636.40
Fourth rent payment, 1/1/04	(18,142.95)
Present value of obligation after fourth rent payment, 1/1/04	16,493.45

Interest expense for Year 4 ($18,142.95 - $16,493.45)	1,649.50[a]
Present value of obligation at 12/31/04	18,142.95
Fifth rent payment, 1/1/05	(18,142.95)
Present value after last rent payment, 1/1/05	-0-
Interest expense for Year 5 (10% x $0)	-0-
Present value at end of lease term	$ -0-

[a]$18,142.95 - $16,493.45 = $1,649.50 interest including rounding error.
$16,493.45 x 10% = $1,649.35 interest if there was no rounding error.
$1,649.50 - $1,649.35 = $.15 rounding error.

> **TIP:** In this situation, there is no interest expense for the last year of the lease because the obligation is to be fully paid as of the beginning of the fifth year.

(i)

LESSEE'S AMORTIZATION SCHEDULE

Date	Payments	10% Interest Expense	Reduction of Obligation	Obligation Balance
1/1/01				$75,653.56
1/1/01	$18,142.95		$18,142.95	57,510.61
1/1/02	18,142.95	$ 5,751.06	12,391.89	45,118.72
1/1/03	18,142.95	4,511.87	13,631.08	31,487.64
1/1/04	18,142.95	3.148.76	14,994.19	16,493.45
1/1/05	18,142.95	1,649.50[a]	16,493.45	-0-
	$90,714.75	$15,061.19	$75,653.56	

[a]Includes rounding error of $.15.

> **TIP:** The total of the "Payments" column minus the total of the "Interest Expense" column equals the total of the "Reduction of Obligation" column, and the total of the "Reduction of Obligation" column equals the obligation's present value at inception (the beginning amount for the schedule).

(j) Even though the lessee and the lessor both use the same interest rate in this scenario, the lessee's amortization schedule differs from the lessor's because the $7,000 unguaranteed residual value must be accounted for by the lessor but not by the lessee. The lessor and the lessee can use the same amortization schedule when they use the same interest rate and when there is one of the following: (1) an automatic transfer of title, or (2) a bargain purchase option, or (3) a residual value guaranteed by the lessee to the lessor, or (4) an unguaranteed residual value for the lessor of zero.

(k)

1/1/01 Lease Payments Receivable	97,714.75	
Equipment		80,000.00
Unearned Interest Revenue—Leases		17,714.75
Cash	18,142.95	
Lease Payments Receivable		18,142.95

12/31/01	Unearned Interest Revenue—Leases...............	6,185.71	
	Interest Revenue—Leases........................		6,185.71

1/1/02   There are no adjustments appropriate for reversal.

1/1/02	Cash..	18,142.95	
	Lease Payments Receivable.....................		18,142.95

12/31/02	Unearned Interest Revenue—Leases...............	4,989.98	
	Interest Revenue—Leases........................		4,989.98

(l) 1/1/01

Leased Equipment Under Capital Leases.........	75,653.56	
Obligations Under Capital Leases..............		75,653.56
Obligations Under Capital Leases....................	18,142.95	
Cash..		18,142.95

12/31/01

Interest Expense.......................................	5,751.06	
Interest Payable....................................		5,751.06
Depreciation Expense.................................	15,130.71	
Accumulated Depreciation........................		15,130.71
($75,653.56 ÷ 5 years = $15,130.71)		

1/1/02

Interest Payable...	5,751.06	
Interest Expense....................................		5,751.06
Interest Expense.......................................	5,751.06	
Obligations Under Capital Leases....................	12,391.89	
Cash..		18,142.95

12/31/02

Interest Expense.......................................	4,511.87	
Interest Payable.....................................		4,511.87
Depreciation Expense.....................................	15,130.71	
Accumulated Depreciation..........................		15,130.71

(m) (1) At the inception date, the lessor records the **gross** amounts to be received in a receivable account (Lease Payments Receivable); whereas the lessee records the **present value** of amounts to be paid in a payable account (Obligations Under Capital Leases). Because receivables and payables are to be reported at present value, the lessor has to set up a contra receivable account (Unearned Interest Revenue—Leases) to reduce the carrying value of its receivable to the present value of all future cash flows associated with the lease.

(2) The lessor accounts for interest as a **deferral** situation, but the lessee accounts for interest as an **accrual** situation. Therefore, the lessor records interest only at the end of an accounting period; this recording is accomplished by an adjusting entry. The lessee records interest when a cash payment is made **and** at the end

of an accounting period (by an adjusting entry) because the accounting period ends at a date other than a rent payment date. The lessor's adjusting entry to record the recognition of interest earned is never reversed; the lessee's adjusting entry to accrue interest can be reversed.

(3)   The lessor's entry to record a rental receipt is the same each period. (Debit Cash and credit Lease Payments Receivable for the entire rent receipt.) The lessee's entry to record a rental payment is different each period because the amount of the payment attributable to interest versus the amount going to reduce the obligation balance differs for each payment.

(4)   Both the lessor and the lessee account for interest, **but** only the lessee accounts for depreciation in this scenario.

EXERCISE 22-3

Purpose: (L.O.8) This exercise will provide an example of: (1) the accounting procedures for a lessor with a sales-type lease, (2) lease periods that do not coincide with accounting periods, and (3) a lease with a purchase option.

The following facts relate to a lease made by the Wandie Warmus Company to the Harker Marina Corporation.

Inception of lease	May 1, 1999
Annual payment due at beginning of each lease year, first one is due on May 1, 1999	$10,000
Lease term	5 years
Remaining economic life of asset	7 years
Residual value at end of lease term	$8,000
Purchase option at end of lease term	$2,000
Lessor's cost	$40,000
Lessor's implicit rate	10%
Annual accounting period	Calendar year

Instructions

(a)   Prepare the amortization schedule and draw the time line for the lessor.
(b)   Answer the following questions from the viewpoint of the lessor:
   (1)   What is the gross investment at inception?
   (2)   What is the net investment at inception?
   (3)   What amount of gross profit should be reported on the income statement for 1999?
   (4)   What amount of gross profit should be reported on the income statement for 2000?
   (5)   What amount should be reported as interest revenue on the income statement for 1999?
   (6)   What amount should be reported as interest revenue on the income statement for 2000?

(c)   Prepare the following journal entries for the lessor:
(1)   Inception of the lease on May 1, 1999.
(2)   Rent receipt on May 1, 1999.
(3)   Adjusting entry at December 31, 1999.
(4)   Rent receipt on May 1, 2000.
(5)   Adjusting entry at December 31, 2000.
(d)   If the lessee has an incremental borrowing rate of 10%, can the lessee use the same amortization schedule as the lessor in this situation?
(e)   Explain how the entry in part (c)(1) would be different for the lessor if there was no purchase option and the estimated residual value to the lessor (unguaranteed) at the end of the lease term was $2,000. Also, explain whether the lessee could use the same amortization schedule as the lessor in this latter instance.

Solution to Exercise 22-3

(a)   AMORTIZATION SCHEDULE FOR LESSOR

Date	Rents Plus BPO[a]	10% Interest	Reduction of Present Value	Present Value Balance
5/1/99				$42,940.44
5/1/99	$10,000.00		$10,000.00	32,940.44
5/1/00	10,000.00	$3,294.04	6,705.96	26,234.48
5/1/01	10,000.00	2,623.45	7,376.55	18,857.93
5/1/02	10,000.00	1,885.79	8,114.21	10,743.72
5/1/03	10,000.00	1,074.37	8,925.63	1,818.09
4/30/04	2,000.00	181.91*	1,818.09	-0-
	$52,000.00	$9,059.56	$42,940.44	

[a]BPO is an abbreviation for "bargain purchase option." The option to purchase is deemed to constitute a bargain purchase option because the option price is only 25% ($2,000 ÷ $8,000 = 25%) of the estimated market value of the asset at the date the option is exercisable.

*Includes a rounding error of $0.10.

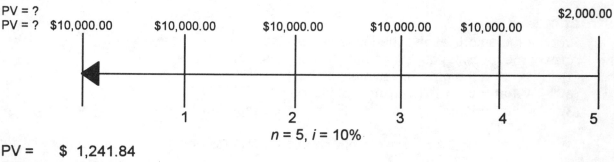

PV = ?
PV = ? $10,000.00 $10,000.00 $10,000.00 $10,000.00 $10,000.00 $2,000.00

1   2   3   4   5
$n = 5, i = 10\%$

PV = $ 1,241.84
PV =   41,698.60
        $42,940.44

(b) (1)

Total rents: 5 x $10,000	$ 50,000.00
Bargain purchase option	2,000.00
Minimum lease payments	52,000.00
Unguaranteed residual value	-0-
Gross investment at inception	$ 52,000.00

(2)

Present value of rents ($10,000 x 4.16986[a])	$ 41,698.60
Present value of BPO ($2,000 x .62092[b])	1,241.84
Present value of minimum lease payments	42,940.44
Present value of unguaranteed residual value	-0-
Net investment at inception	$ 42,940.44

[a]Factor for present value of an annuity due for n=5, i=10%.
[b]Factor for present value of a single sum for n=5, i=10%.

(3)

Sales price	$ 42,940.44[a]
Cost of goods sold	40,000.00[b]
Gross profit to be recognized during 1999	$ 2,940.44

[a]The sale price is equal to the present value of the minimum lease payments:

Present value of rents ($10,000 x 4.16986)	$41,698.60
Present value of BPO ($2,000 x .62092)	1,241.84
Present value of minimum lease payments	$42,940.44

[b]Cost of goods sold is equal to the lessor's carrying value less the present value of any unguaranteed residual value for the lessor:

Carrying value	$40,000.00
Present value of unguaranteed residual value	-0-
Cost of goods sold	$40,000.00

(4) None. All of the gross profit attributable to a sales-type lease is to be recognized in the year in which the inception of the lease occurs. In this case, that year is 1999.

TIP: Do not confuse this situation with that of a sale-leaseback transaction in which the profit (gain) on the sale of an asset (that is leased back to the seller) is generally deferred and amortized.

---

(5) $3,294.04 x 8/12 = $2,196.03 interest for 1999

There are eight months between May 1, 1999 and December 31, 1999. The interest for those eight months are reflected on the 5/1/00 payment line of the amortization schedule. The $3,294.04 interest showing on that 5/1/00 payment line is for the twelve-month period preceding 5/1/00. The interest for the last eight months of 1999 is therefore 8/12 x $3,294.04.

(6) $3,294.04 x 4/12 $ 1,098.01
$2,623.45 x 8/12   1,748.97
Interest for 1997 $ 2,846.98

> **TIP:** The amortization schedule is **always** prepared using the interest dates (which are dictated by the lease periods). The interest amount appearing on a given payment line is then apportioned to the appropriate accounting period(s). In examining the amortization schedule in part (a), the interest appearing on the 5/1/00 line is the interest for 5/1/99 through 4/30/00. Thus, 8/12 of it belongs on the 1999 income statement and 4/12 of it is reported on the 2000 income statement. Likewise, the $2,623.45 appearing on the 5/1/01 payment line reflects the interest for 5/1/00 through 4/30/01. Thus, 8/12 of it is reported on the 2000 income statement.

(c)   (1)   5/1/99

Lease Payments Receivable	52,000.00	
Cost of Goods Sold	40,000.00	
Unearned Interest Revenue—Leases		9,059.56
Inventory		40,000.00
Sales Revenue		42,940.44

     (2)   5/1/99

Cash	10,000.00	
Lease Payments Receivable		10,000.00

     (3)   12/31/99

Unearned Interest Revenue—Leases	2,196.03	
Interest Revenue		2,196.03
($3,294.04 x 8/12 = $2,196.03)		

     (4)   5/1/00

Cash	10,000.00	
Lease Payments Receivable		10,000.00

     (5)   12/31/00

Unearned Interest Revenue—Leases	2,846.98	
Interest Revenue		2,846.98
($3,294.04 x 4/12 = $1,098.01)		
($2,623.45 x 8/12 = $1,748.97)		
($1,098.01 + $1,748.97 = $2,846.98)		

(d)   Yes. The lessee will record the asset under capital lease and the obligation under capital lease at $42,940.44. The lessee's amortization schedule will appear exactly like the lessor's amortization schedule.

> **TIP:** The lessee will depreciate the entire $42,940.44 cost of the asset under capital lease over the useful life of the asset to the lessee, which is 7 years. Due to the existence of the bargain purchase option, the lessee is expected to use the asset for its entire remaining economic life. Thus, the matching principle will dictate that the asset's cost be allocated over the 7 years.

(e)   If there was no bargain purchase option, but there was a $2,000.00 unguaranteed residual value relevant to the lessor, the lessor's journal entry at inception would be:

Lease Payments Receivable	52,000.00	
Cost of Goods Sold	38,758.16[a]	
Unearned Interest Revenue—Leases		9,059.56[b]
Inventory		40,000.00
Sales Revenue		41,698.60[c]

[a]Carrying value of the asset	$40,000.00
Present value of unguaranteed residual value	(1,241.84)[1]
Cost of goods sold	$38,758.16

[1]$2,000.00 x .62092 = $1,241.84

[b]Gross investment in lease	$52,000.00
Net investment in lease	42,940.44[2]
Unearned interest revenue	$ 9,059.56

[2]Present value of minimum lease payments	$41,698.60
Present value of unguaranteed residual	1,241.84
Net investment in lease	$42,940.44

[c]Present value of rents	$41,698.60[3]
Present value of BPO or GRV	-0-
Present value of minimum lease payments	$41,698.60

[3]$10,000.00 x 4.16986 = $41,698.60

The entry differs from part (c) (1) in that both Sales Revenue and Cost of Goods Sold are reduced by the cash equivalent value of the $2,000.00 unguaranteed residual value to be received in five years. In this instance, a portion of the asset ($2,000.00) is considered **not** to be sold to the lessee; the remainder of the asset is treated as a sale.

The lessor's amortization schedule would be the same as it appears now in part (a), except that the column heading "Rents Plus BPO" would be changed to "Rents Plus Residual Value;" however, the lessee's amortization schedule would differ, even if both parties are using a 10% interest rate.

The lessor's amortization schedule would include accounting for the $2,000.00 unguaranteed residual value. The lessee's schedule would not include any accounting for the $2,000.00 unguaranteed residual value to the lessor. The lessee's schedule would begin with $41,698.60, rather than $42,940.44.

ILLUSTRATION 22-4
USE OF RESIDUAL VALUE IN NONOPERATING LEASE SITUATIONS (L.O.7)

Residual value is the estimated value of an asset at some given future point in time. Residual value may be estimated at the end of the lease term or at the end of the asset's useful life, depending on which, if either, is relevant to the party for whom you are accounting.

The residual value at the end of the lease term is used by the lessor in determining the amount to charge the lessee as the periodic rent if either of the following is true:
- The asset will revert back to the lessor at the end of the lease and the residual value is guaranteed.
- The asset will revert back to the lessor at the end of the lease and the residual value is unguaranteed.

The residual value at the end of the lease term is used by the lessor in determining the gross investment and the net investment in the lease if either of the following is true:
- The asset will revert back to the lessor at the end of the lease and the residual value is guaranteed.
- The asset will revert back to the lessor at the end of the lease and the residual value is unguaranteed.

The residual value at the end of the lease term is used by the lessee in determining the cost of the asset under capital lease **only** if the following is true:
- The asset will revert back to the lessor at the end of the lease and the residual value is guaranteed by the lessee.

The residual value at the end of the lease term (or at the end of the asset's life) is used by the lessee in determining the periodic depreciation if either of the following is true:
- The asset will revert back to the lessor at the end of the lease and the residual value is guaranteed by the lessee. (Use the residual value at the end of the lease term.)
- The asset will transfer to the lessee at the end of the lease term either through an automatic transfer clause or a bargain purchase option. (Use the residual at the end of the asset's life.)

CASE 22-1

Purpose: (L.O.7) This case will review the lessee's and lessor's accounting procedures for a lease with a guaranteed residual value.

Instructions

Refer to the facts of **Exercise 22-3** above. Assume there is no purchase option at the end of the lease term. Further, assume the asset reverts back to the lessor at the end of five years and the lessee guarantees the lessor a residual value of $2,000 at that date.

(a)   Explain how the lessor's accounting procedures for a lease with a $2,000 guaranteed residual value will differ from the procedures for a lease containing a $2,000 bargain purchase option.

(b)   Explain how the lessee's accounting procedures for a lease requiring the lessee to guarantee a residual value of $2,000 will differ from the procedures for a lease containing a $2,000 bargain purchase option.

Solution to Case 22-1

(a)   From the lessor's standpoint, there is no difference in the computations, time line, or journal entries if the $2,000 is a guaranteed residual value rather than a bargain purchase option. Thus, the **Solution to Exercise 22-3**, parts (a) through (c) would also hold for the $2,000 guaranteed residual value (refer to that solution, and every place you see "bargain purchase option" or "BPO" simply change that phrase to "guaranteed residual value" or "GRV").

(b)   From the lessee's standpoint, the time line, journal entries, and most of the computations are the same for a lease containing a guaranteed residual value as those pertaining to a lease that contains a bargain purchase option. The major difference lies in the computation of depreciation:

- If the lease contains a bargain purchase option, the cost of the asset under capital lease (reduced by any residual value available to the lessee at the end of the asset's economic life) is depreciated over the remaining economic life of the asset.
- If the lease contains a guaranteed residual value, the cost of the asset under capital lease reduced by the guaranteed residual value is depreciated over the lease term.

Thus, using the data from **Exercise 22-3**, and assuming the lessee uses a 10% interest rate to account for the lease and the straight-line depreciation method, depreciation calculations for the lessee would be as follows:

Assuming a bargain purchase option of $2,000:

$$\frac{\$42,940.44 - 0^a}{7 \text{ years}} = \$6,134.35 \text{ depreciation per year for 7 years}$$

[a]Assumes a zero residual value at the end of seven years.

Assuming a guaranteed residual value of $2,000:

$$\frac{\$42,940.44 \ - \ \$2,000.00}{5 \ \text{years}} = \$8,188.09 \ \text{depreciation per year for 5 years}$$

> **TIP:** When the $2,000 is assumed to be a guaranteed residual value and the lessee uses the same interest rate as the lessor, the lessee's amortization schedule is the same as the lessor's amortization schedule.

EXERCISE 22-4

Purpose: (L.O.9) This exercise will illustrate how to classify receivables and payables related to leases on the balance sheet.

The following amortization schedule is properly being used by a lessee and a lessor. The lease contains a bargain purchase option (BPO). Both the lessee and the lessor have a calendar-year reporting period.

Date	Rent Plus BPO	10% Interest	Reduction of Present Value	Present Value Balance
5/1/99				$ 42,940.44
5/1/99	$ 10,000.00		$ 10,000.00	32,940.44
5/1/00	10,000.00	$3,294.04	6,705.96	26,234.48
5/1/01	10,000.00	2,623.45	7,376.55	18,857.93
5/1/02	10,000.00	1,885.79	8,114.21	10,743.72
5/1/03	10,000.00	1,074.37	8,925.63	1,818.09
4/30/04	2,000.00	181.91	1,818.09	-0-
	$ 52,000.00	$9,059.56	$ 42,940.44	

Instructions
Fill in the blanks that follow. Show computations.

(1)   The amount of gross investment to be reported in the current asset section of the lessor's balance sheet at December 31, 2000 is $_____.

(2)   The amount of net investment to be reported in the current asset section of the lessor's balance sheet at December 31, 2000 is $_____.

(3)   The amount to be reported in the current liability section of the lessee's balance sheet at December 31, 2000 by the caption "Interest Payable" is $_____.

(4)   The amount to be reported in the current liability section of the lessee's balance sheet at December 31, 2000 by the caption "Obligations Under Capital Leases" is $_____.

(5)   The amount to be reported in the long-term liability section of the lessee's balance sheet at December 31, 2000 by the caption "Obligations Under Capital Leases" is $_____.

Solution to Exercise 22-4

(1) $10,000.00 gross investment in current assets at December 31, 2000.

The most recent payment prior to the balance sheet date (December 31, 2000) was May 1, 2000. The payment line following that line shows a receipt of $10,000 is due on May 1, 2001, which is within one year of the balance sheet date.

(2)   Gross investment classified in current assets $10,000.00
Unearned interest revenue classified in current assets (874.48)[a]
Net investment in current assets at December 31, 2000 $ 9,125.52

[a]$2,623.45 x 4/12 = $874.48

The interest portion of the rent payment due to be received on May 1, 2001 is $2,623.45. That interest is for the twelve months that precedes May 1, 2001. Thus, at December 31, 2000, four months of that interest remains unearned.

> TIP: The net investment reflected in noncurrent assets (in the long-term investments classification) on the lessor's December 31, 2000 balance sheet would be determined as follows:
>
> Gross investment classified in noncurrent assets $22,000.00[a]
> Unearned interest revenue classified in noncurrent assets (3,142.07)[b]
> Net investment in noncurrent assets at 12/31/00 $18,857.93
>
> [a]Rents due 5/1/02 and 5/1/03 and BPO = $10,000 + $10,000 + $2,000.00 = $22,000.00
> [b]Interest portion of rents due 5/1/02 and 5/1/03 and interest portion of BPO = $1,885.79 + $1,074.37 + $181.91 = $3,142.07.

(3)   Balance of obligation at May 1, 2000 $ 26,234.48
Interest rate 10%
Interest for twelve months, 5/1/00 to 4/30/01 2,623.45
Fraction of year from 5/1/00 to 12/31/00 x   8/12
Interest for 5/1/00 to 12/31/00,
    which is a current liability at 12/31/00 $ 1,748.97

(4)   Current portion of Obligations under Capital Leases at 12/31/00 $ 7,376.55

The payment line that follows the balance sheet date (12/31/00) is 5/1/01. The principal portion of the rent payment due on that date ($7,376.55) represents the current portion of the lessee's obligation under capital lease [excluding any accrued interest computed in part (3)] at 12/31/00.

> **TIP:** The interest portion of a rent payment is for a span of time, so it gets apportioned (allocated) between accounting periods; however, the principal portion of a rent payment falls in only one period and does **not** get allocated. Thus, the interest of $2,623.45 on the 5/1/01 payment line is to be expensed 8/12 in 2000 and 4/12 in 2001. The entire $7,376.55 principal payment appearing on the 5/1/01 rent line becomes due at a point in time and does not get apportioned.
>
> **TIP:** In published financial statements, the amount of accrued interest payable [solution to part (3)] is often combined with the current portion of the remaining principal [solution to part (4)] and reported as a single line item in current liabilities.

(5)   Noncurrent portion of Obligations Under Capital Leases at 12/31/00 $18,857.93
(This figure is the present value balance on the 5/1/01 rent line.)

EXERCISE 22-5

Purpose: (L.O.2,5) This exercise will review the accounting procedures for an operating lease for both the lessee and the lessor.

On January 1, 1999, Clarence Avery Corp. leased office space to Mexico Service Corp. The following data apply:

1.   The lease is appropriately classified as an operating lease by both the lessee and the lessor.
2.   The lease term is for 5 years.
3.   The rent payment is $50,000 for 1999 and is scheduled to increase by $10,000 each year.
4.   Rent payments are due each January 1 and the first one is paid on January 1, 1999.
5.   The lessee paid a $5,000 bonus payment on January 1, 1999 to obtain the lease.
6.   The lessor's cost of the asset is $900,000. The lessor uses the straight-line depreciation method and estimates the asset has a service life of 25 years with no residual value.
7.   The lessor paid an $8,000 finder's fee to a leasing agent for their service.
8.   Annual insurance and property taxes on the property amount to $7,200 and are borne by the lessor.

Instructions
(a)   Compute the rental expense for the lessee for (1) 1999 and (2) 2000.
(b)   Compute the lessor's operating profit (loss) on the leased asset for (1) 1999 and (2) 2000.

Solution to Exercise 22-5

(a) (1) $71,000
     (2) $71,000

Computations:

Average rental	$ 70,000[a]
Amortization of lease bonus	1,000[b]
Rent expense per year	$ 71,000

[a]Rental for 1999	$ 50,000
Rental for 2000	60,000
Rental for 2001	70,000
Rental for 2002	80,000
Rental for 2003	90,000
Total rents	$ 350,000

$350,000 ÷ 5 years = $70,000 per year

[b]$5,000 bonus ÷ 5 years = $1,000 per year

Explanation: For an operating lease, minimum lease payments are recognized as rental expense on a straight-line basis, even if not payable on a straight-line basis. Thus, the lease bonus and scheduled rent increases are amortized to rent expense by the lessee over the lease term on a straight-line basis.

(b) (1) $26,200
     (2) $26,200

Computations:

Average rental		$ 70,000[a]
Amortization of lease bonus		1,000[b]
Rental revenue		$ 71,000
Less: Depreciation	$ 36,000[c]	
Amortization of initial direct costs	1,600[d]	
Executory costs—taxes and insurance	7,200	44,800
Operating profit on leased asset		$ 26,200

[a]Same calculation as in part (a) above.
[b]Same calculation as in part (a) above.
[c]($900,000 - 0) ÷ 25 years = $36,000 depreciation per year
[d]$8,000 ÷ 5 years = $1,600 amortization per year

Explanation: For an operating lease, each rental receipt by the lessor is recorded as rental revenue. The amount of revenue recognized in each accounting period is a level amount (straight-line basis) regardless of the lease provisions, unless another systematic and rational basis is more representative of the time pattern in which the benefit is derived from the leased asset. Thus, the lease bonus and scheduled rent increases are amortized to rent revenue by the lessor over the lease term on a straight-line basis. The leased asset is depreciated in the normal manner. Costs paid to independent third parties such as appraisal fees, finder's fees, and other initial direct costs of the lease are amortized over the life of the lease. Executory costs (taxes, insurance, etc.) are charged to expense in the period to which they pertain.

ANALYSIS OF MULTIPLE-CHOICE TYPE QUESTIONS

QUESTION

1.   (L.O.2) Max Wells Company leases equipment from Bill Kennedy Corp. under an agreement which meets the criteria to be a capital lease for Max Wells. The ten-year lease requires payment of $34,000 at the beginning of each year, including $5,000 per year for maintenance, insurance, and taxes. The incremental borrowing rate for the lessee is 15%; the lessor's implicit rate is 12% and is known by the lessee. The present value of an annuity due of 1 for ten years at 15% is 5.77158. The present value of an annuity due of 1 for ten years at 12% is 6.32825. According to the accounting guidelines for leases, the lessee should record the leased asset at:

   a.   ($29,000) (5.77158) = $167,376.
   b.   ($29,000) (6.32825) = $183,519.
   c.   ($34,000) (5.77158) = $196,234.
   d.   ($34,000) (6.32825) = $215,161.

Approach and Explanation: Think through the steps involved in accounting for a lease for a lessee (see **Illustration 22-2**). Compute the present value of the minimum lease payments (excluding executory costs). Use the lessee's incremental borrowing rate to do the discounting process, unless the lessor's implicit rate is known and is lower. In this scenario, the $5,000 executory costs must be deducted from the $34,000 to arrive at a $29,000 rent excluding executory costs. The lessor's implicit rate of 12% is known by the lessee and is lower than 15%; therefore, the 12% is to be used to compute the present value of the minimum lease payments. That present value figure is determined by multiplying the rent (excluding executory costs) by the factor for present value of an annuity due of 1 for n = 10, i = 12%. There is no indication that the asset's fair value may be lower than the computed present value amount; therefore, the asset is to be recorded at the present value figure. (Solution = b.)

QUESTION

2. (L.O.2) Danzler Corporation is a lessee with a capital lease. The asset is recorded at $180,000 and has an economic life of 8 years. The lease term is 5 years. The asset is expected to have a market value of $60,000 at the end of 5 years, and a market value of $20,000 at the end of 8 years. The lease agreement provides for the automatic transfer of title of the asset to the lessee at the end of the lease term. What depreciable base and what service life should the lessee use to compute depreciation for the first year of the lease?

	Depreciable Base	Service Life
a.	$180,000 - $20,000	5 years
b.	$180,000 - $20,000	8 years
c.	$180,000 - $60,000	5 years
d.	$180,000 - $60,000	8 years

Approach and Explanation: Determine what will provide the best matching of costs with revenues. Because of the automatic transfer of title, the lessee is expected to hold and use the asset for eight years. The benefits to be consumed over the eight years are determined by the difference between the asset's recorded cost ($180,000) and its expected value at the end of its useful life to the lessee ($20,000). (Solution = b.)

QUESTION

3. (L.O.2,5,7) Three different lease situations are described below:

1. Lessee's incremental borrowing rate is 12%.
   Lessor's implicit rate is 12%.
   Asset will revert to the lessor at the end of the lease term when the
      asset is expected to have a fair value of $60,000.

2. Lessee's incremental borrowing rate is 12%.
   Lessor's implicit rate is 12%.
   Lease requires lessee to guarantee a residual value of $30,000 to
      the lessor.

3. Lessee's incremental borrowing rate is 12%.
   Lessor's implicit rate is 14%.
   Lease contains a bargain purchase option of $20,000.

In which of the above cases will the lessor and the lessee have the same amortization schedule?
   a. 1 and 2 only.
   b. 2 and 3 only.
   c. 1 and 3 only.
   d. 1, 2, and 3.
   e. None of the above.

Approach and Explanation: The lessee and lessor can use the same amortization schedule when both of the following two conditions exist: (1) the lessee and the lessor both use the same interest rate to account for the lease, and (2) the lessor does **not** have an unguaranteed residual value to account for. The lessee and the lessor have the same rate in case 1 and case 2. The lessee and the lessor will **not** use the same rate in case 3 because the lessee is to use the lower of the two rates, which in this case is **not** the lessor's implicit rate. Therefore, in case 3, the two parties cannot use the same amortization schedule. In case 1, the asset reverts to the lessor at the end of the lease term when the asset has a fair value of $60,000 which constitutes an unguaranteed residual value that will have to be reflected in the lessor's amortization schedule but will not affect the lessee's amortization schedule. Therefore, the two parties cannot use the same amortization schedule for case 1. Thus, case 2 is the only scenario listed in the question in which the two parties can use the same amortization schedule. (Solution = e.)

QUESTION

4.   (L.O.2,9) On December 31, 1998, Ryan Corporation leased a yacht from Sean Company for an eight-year period expiring December 30, 2006. Equal annual payments of $80,000 are due on December 31 of each year, beginning with December 31, 1998. The lease is properly classified as a capital lease on Ryan's books. The present value at December 31, 1998 of the eight lease payments over the lease term discounted at 10% is $469,474. Assuming all payments are made on time, the amount that should be reported by Ryan Corporation as the total obligation under capital leases on its December 31, 1999 balance sheet is:

a. $348,421.
b. $400,063.
c. $436,421.
d. $480,000.
e.   none of the above.

Approach and Explanation: Compute the information for the first three lines on the lessee's amortization schedule. The schedule will appear as follows: (Solution = a.)

Date	Rent	Interest	Principal	Balance
12/31/98				$469,474.00
12/31/98	$80,000.00	0	$80,000.00	389,474.00
12/31/99	80,000.00	$38,947.40	41,052.60	348,421.40

QUESTION

5.   (L.O.2,4) The following facts pertain to a single lease:

1.   A lease provides that the asset will revert back to the lessor at the end of its 7-year term.

2.   The present value of the minimum lease payments is equal to $54,000 and the fair value of the asset at the inception date is $60,000.

3.   The remaining economic life of the leased asset is estimated to be 10 years.

4.   Uncollectible lease payments are subject to a reasonable estimation.

5.   The lessor guarantees the asset against obsolescence.

6.   The fair value of the asset exceeds its cost on the lessor's books.

How should the lease be classified on the books of the lessee and lessor, respectively?

	Lessee	Lessor
a.	Capital	Sales-type
b.	Capital	Operating
c.	Operating	Sales-type
d.	Operating	Operating

Approach and Explanation: Review the facts and determine how the lease should be classified on the books of the lessee. Repeat the process to determine how the lease should be classified on the books of the lessor. Refer to **Illustration 22-1**. The lease meets criterion 4 in Group I. Thus, it is a capital lease from the standpoint of the lessee because it meets at least one criterion in Group I. Because the lease does **not** meet **both** of the criteria in Group II, it is an operating lease from the standpoint of the lessor.

The significance of the facts given is as follows:

1.   The asset will be returned to the lessor at the end of the lease; therefore, the lease does not meet criterion 1 or 2 of Group I.

2.   The present value of the minimum lease payments ($54,000) is equal to 90% of the asset's fair value ($60,000) at the inception date; hence, the lease agreement meets criterion 4 in Group I.

3.   The term of the lease is 7 years, which is only 70% of the remaining economic life of the asset; hence, criterion 3 of Group I is not met.

4.   The lessor can reasonably estimate any uncollectible lease payments; therefore, criterion 1 of Group II is met by the lessor.

5.   The lessor guarantees the asset against obsolescence. This means that the costs of meeting this promise are indeterminable, which further means that an important uncertainty exists surrounding the amount of unreimbursable costs yet to be incurred by the lessor under the lease. Thus, criterion 2 of Group II is not met.

6. The fair value of the asset (which usually establishes the lessor's initial amount of net investment in lease) exceeds the lessor's carrying value for the asset. This means that the lease would be a sales-type lease on the books of the lessor **if** the lease met one criterion from Group I and both criterion from Group II. (Solution = b.)

QUESTION

6. (L.O.5) A lessor has a direct financing type lease. The end of the lessor's accounting period does not coincide with a lease payment date. At the end of the lessor's accounting period, the journal entry to record interest earned since the last rental payment date would be:

a.	Cash	XX	
	Interest Revenue		XX
b.	Interest Receivable	XX	
	Interest Revenue		XX
c.	Unearned Interest Revenue	XX	
	Interest Revenue		XX
d.	Interest Expense	XX	
	Interest Payable		XX

Explanation: A lessor accounts for interest as a deferral situation. Thus, at the date of inception, the lessor includes all the amounts ever to be received from the lease (gross investment) in the Lease Payments Receivable account. These amounts include interest to be earned over the term of the lease; hence, a contra account called Unearned Interest Revenue is established in order to reduce the carrying value of the receivable down to the present value of the components of gross investment (that present value amount is called net investment). As interest is earned, it is transferred from the Unearned Interest Revenue account to an earned interest account (Interest Revenue). A confusing aspect of lease accounting often results from the fact that the lessee uses an accrual approach to accounting for interest. Thus, the lessee initially records only the present value of the lease obligation in the Obligations Under Capital Leases account. Thus, at a balance sheet date, an adjusting entry on the lessee's books will include a debit to Interest Expense and a credit to Interest Payable. (Solution = c.)

QUESTION

7. (L.O.7) At the inception of a capital lease, a residual value guaranteed by a lessee should be included as part of minimum lease payments on the books of the:

	Lessee	**Lessor**
a.	Yes	Yes
b.	Yes	No
c.	No	Yes
d.	No	No

Approach and Explanation: List the components of minimum lease payments. They are: (a) regular periodic rental payments (excluding executory costs), (b) bargain purchase option, (c) guaranteed residual value, and (d) penalty for failure to renew. If the lessor has a guaranteed residual value, it is included in the lessor's computation of minimum lease payments, regardless of whether the lessee or a third party is the guarantor. The lessee includes a guaranteed residual value in its computation of minimum lease payments only if the lessee is the one providing the guarantee. (Solution = a.)

QUESTION

8.   (L.O.8) A lessor with a sales-type lease involving an unguaranteed residual value available to the lessor at the end of the lease term will report sales revenue in the period of inception of the lease at which of the following amounts?
- a.   the minimum lease payments plus the unguaranteed residual value
- b.   the present value of the minimum lease payments
- c.   the cost of the asset to the lessor, less the present value of any unguaranteed residual value
- d.   the present value of the minimum lease payments plus the present value of the unguaranteed residual value

Explanation: The unguaranteed residual value is viewed as pertaining to a portion of the asset that is not yet sold. Therefore, the sales revenue figure is the present value (today's cash equivalent) of all future cash flows expected to be received by the lessor for the leased asset **except** for the unguaranteed residual value. Therefore, sales revenue is computed by determining the present value of the minimum lease payments. Answer section "a" describes the gross investment calculation, answer selection "c" describes the lessor's cost of goods sold computation, and answer selection "d" describes the lessor's net investment in lease amount. (Solution = b.)

QUESTION

9.   (L.O.8) A lease has an 8-year term, and the related asset has a remaining economic life of 10 years. The lease is appropriately classified as a sales-type lease on the books of the lessor. The gross profit related to this lease should be:
- a.   recognized wholly in the period of the inception of the lease.
- b.   amortized evenly over 8 years.
- c.   amortized evenly over 10 years.
- d.   amortized over 8 years using the effective interest method of amortization.

Explanation: The gross profit related to a sales-type lease is recognized wholly in the period in which the lease's inception date occurs. The lessor's journal entry at the date of inception includes a credit to Sales Revenue (for the present value of the minimum lease payments) and a debit to Cost of Goods Sold (for the asset's carrying value less the present value of any unguaranteed residual value). When these two amounts are reported on the income statement, the resulting difference is the amount of gross profit earned on the lease. (Solution = a.)

QUESTION
10. (L.O.10) Trim Corporation sold a greenhouse to Laventhall Company for $800,000 and realized a gain of $300,000. The buyer immediately leased the asset back to the seller under a capital lease arrangement for the remainder of the asset's economic life of ten years. The lessee uses the straight-line depreciation method. The profit on the sale of the greenhouse should be:
   a. recognized in full in the year of sale.
   b. deferred and amortized over the term of the lease.
   c. deferred and recognized in full at the end of the lease term.
   d. credited directly to retained earnings.

Explanation: Any profit or loss experienced by the seller-lessee from the sale of the assets that are leased back under a capital lease should be deferred and amortized over the lease term (or the asset's economic life if criterion 1 or 2 is satisfied) in proportion to the amortization of the leased assets. At a balance sheet date, the balance of the deferred gain is reported as an asset valuation allowance. (Solution = b.)

QUESTION
11. (L.O.5) Tom Hanks Leasing Co. has an operating lease. Rents are a constant amount each year. Rent payments collected in 1999 that pertain to use of the leased asset in 2000 should be reported as:
   a. rent revenue in 1999.
   b. accrued rent on the December 31, 1999 balance sheet.
   c. unearned rent on the December 31, 1999 balance sheet.
   d. rent receivable on the December 31, 1999 balance sheet.

Explanation: Rent revenue received in advance represents a liability at the December 31, 1999 balance sheet date. Revenue received in advance is often called unearned rent revenue or deferred rent revenue. (Solution = c.)

CHAPTER 23

ACCOUNTING CHANGES AND ERROR ANALYSIS

OVERVIEW

In order to have **comparability** of financial statements for successive periods for an entity, the accountant must be consistent in the application of generally accepted accounting principles (**quality of consistency**). However, sometimes there is justification for a change. The accountant must then meet the requirements of **full disclosure** in reporting the change. Accounting changes are discussed in this chapter.

The accountant may be consistent in the application of accounting practices but may make some type of error (such as a math mistake or misapplication of generally accepted accounting principles). When the error is discovered, the effects must be properly reported. Error analysis is also discussed in this chapter.

SUMMARY OF LEARNING OBJECTIVES

1.   **Identify the types of accounting changes.** The three different types of accounting changes are: (1) **Change in accounting principle:** a change from one generally accepted accounting principle to another generally accepted accounting principle. (2) **Change in accounting estimate:** a change that occurs as the result of new events or additional information or as more experience is acquired. (3) **Change in reporting entity:** a change from reporting as one type of entity to another type of entity.

2.   **Describe the accounting for a change in accounting principle.** A change in accounting principle involves a change from one generally accepted accounting principle to another generally accepted accounting principle. A change in accounting principle is not considered to result from the adoption of a new principle in recognition of events that have occurred for the first time or that were previously immaterial. If the accounting principle previously followed was not acceptable, or if the old principle was applied incorrectly, a change to a generally accepted accounting principle (or to the correct application of the accounting principle) is considered a correction of an error rather than an accounting change.

3.   **Understand how to account for cumulative-effective type accounting changes.** Most changes in accounting principles are to be reported currently (that is, receive current treatment). This means that the cumulative effect of the change (net of tax) is to be shown near the bottom of the current year's income statement (after extraordinary items, if any) and that pro-forma net income and earnings per share amounts are to be reported for all prior periods presented.

4. **Understand how to account for retroactive type accounting changes.** A number of accounting principle changes are to be reported retroactively (that is, receive retroactive treatment). This means prior years' financial statements are to be recast on a basis consistent with the newly adopted principle, and any part of the effect attributable to years prior to those presented is to be treated as an adjustment (net of tax) of the earliest retained earnings balance presented.

5. **Understand how to account for a change to LIFO.** In changing to the LIFO method of inventory pricing, the base year inventory for all subsequent LIFO calculations is the opening inventory in the year the method is adopted. There is generally no calculation of the effect of the change on prior years' income because it is just too impractical to do so.

6. **Describe the accounting for a change in accounting estimate.** A change in accounting estimate must be handled prospectively; that is, accounted for in (a) the period of change if the change affects that period only or (b) the period of change and future periods if the change affects both. Thus, no changes should be made in previously reported results. Opening balances are not adjusted, and no attempt is made to "catch up" for prior periods. Financial statements of prior periods are not restated, and pro-forma amounts for prior periods are not reported.

7. **Identify and account for a change in a reporting entity.** An accounting change that results in financial statements that are actually the statements of a different entity should be reported by restating the financial statements of all prior periods presented to show the financial information for the new reporting entity for all periods.

8. **Describe the accounting for a correction of an error.** As soon as it is discovered, an error must be corrected by a proper entry in the accounts and reported in the financial statements. The profession requires that a correction of an error in previously issued financial statements be treated as a prior period adjustment, be recorded in the year in which the error was discovered, and be reported in the financial statements as an adjustment (net of tax) to the beginning balance of retained earnings. If comparative statements are presented, the prior period statements affected should be restated to correct for the error. The disclosures need not be repeated in the financial statements of subsequent periods.

9. **Identify economic motives for changing accounting principles (methods).** Managers might have varying profit motives depending on economic times and whom they seek to impress. Some of the reasons of changing accounting methods are: (1) political costs, (2) capital structure, (3) bonus payments, and (4) smoothing of earnings.

10. **Analyze the effect of errors.** Three types of errors can occur: (1) *Balance sheet error:* affects only the asset, liability, or stockholders' equity accounts. (2) *Income statement error:* affects only the nominal accounts in the income statement. (3) *Balance sheet and income statement error:* involves both balance sheet and income statement accounts. Errors affecting both balance sheet and income statement accounts are classified into two types: (a) *Counter-balancing errors:* will be offset in the period that immediately follows the period in which the error first occurred. (b) *Noncounterbalancing errors:* are **not** offset in the accounting period that immediately follows the period in which the error first occurred; they take longer than two periods to correct themselves.

TIPS ON CHAPTER TOPICS

TIP: There are actually only two basic types of **accounting changes.** They are: (1) change in accounting principle, and (2) change in accounting estimate. A change in the reporting entity is a special type of a change in accounting principle (because prior period financial statements are to be restated). A correction of an error in previously issued financial statements is not an accounting change; it is a prior period adjustment.

TIP: A **change in accounting principle** occurs when there is a change from one generally acceptable accounting principle to another generally accepted accounting principle or a change in applying an acceptable accounting principle. In this context, an accounting method or policy constitutes an accounting principle. Therefore, a change from one generally acceptable inventory pricing method to another generally accepted inventory pricing method is a change in an accounting principle. A change from an accounting method that is **not** generally accepted to a method that is GAAP is not an accounting change—it is a correction of an error.

TIP: The term **accounting principle** includes not only accounting principles and practices but also the methods of applying them. Thus, a switch from the aggregate basis to the individual basis for determining the lower-of-cost-or-market valuation of inventory constitutes a change in accounting principle.

TIP: A **change in accounting estimate** occurs when an entity has a change from one good faith estimate to another good faith estimate. Accounting estimates change as new events occur, as more experience is acquired, or as additional information is obtained. A change in estimate results from new information or subsequent developments and **not** from oversights or misuse of facts.

TIP: A change from one generally accepted depreciation method to another generally accepted depreciation method is a change in an accounting principle. Students commonly misidentify this situation as a change in estimate because depreciation is an estimate of the cost of benefits consumed during a period. A change in depreciation method is a change in an accounting principle because it is a change in the method of computing an estimate. On the other hand, a change in the estimated service life or a change in the estimated residual value of a depreciable asset constitutes a change in accounting estimate.

TIP: **Errors** include mathematical mistakes, oversights, misapplications of accounting principles, and misuse of facts.

TIP: Generally, a change in an accounting principle is to be accounted for currently. However, *APB Opinion No. 20* lists some special cases of a change in accounting principle which are to be handled retroactively; these are identified in the next **TIP.** A change in accounting estimate is to be accounted for prospectively. Refer to **Illustration 23-1** for a summary of the relevant reporting requirements.

TIP: Accounting changes that require retroactive treatment include:

(1)   A change from LIFO to any other generally acceptable inventory pricing method.

(2)   A change in the method of accounting for long-term construction contracts.

(3)   A change to or from the "full cost" method which is used in the extractive industries.

(4)   A change in the reporting entity.

(5)   A change specifically covered by another professional pronouncement that specifies the use of the retroactive method for that change.

TIP: Any of the following will constitute a change in the reporting entity:

(1)   Presenting consolidated or combined statements in place of statements of individual companies.

(2)   Changing specific subsidiaries comprising a group for which consolidated financial statements are presented.

(3)   Changing the companies included in combined financial statements.

(4)   Accounting for a pooling of interests.

(5)   A change in the fair value, equity, or consolidation method of accounting for subsidiaries and investments.

TIP: In recording a change in accounting principle, the Retained Earnings account is used when retroactive treatment is appropriate; whereas, the Cumulative Effect of a Change in Accounting Principle account is used when current treatment is required. It is **never** appropriate to use both Retained Earnings and Cumulative Effect of a Change in Accounting Principle in the same entry to record the total effect on prior periods of a change in accounting principle. To do so would be to apply two mutually exclusive treatments to one change.

TIP: Several items in this chapter are to be reported net of the related income tax effect. The quickest way to compute an amount net of tax is to apply a net-of-tax rate to the amount. The net-of-tax rate is determined by deducting the tax rate from 100%.

TIP: Most errors are **counterbalancing**. Therefore, if a counterbalancing error causes an understatement of net income in one period, the same error will cause an overstatement of net income in the immediately following period by the same amount. This type of error will effect two income statements and one balance sheet (the balance sheet at the end of the period in which the error occurred). The balance sheet at the end of the following period will not be affected as the error will have "offset" itself or counterbalanced by that date.

TIP: Errors that are not counterbalancing will affect two or more income statements and two or more balance sheets. The error will "wash out" at some point in time, although it may take many years to do so. Conceivably, some may not "reverse" until a particular asset is disposed of, maybe at the point where a business ceases to exist. In the context of error analysis, the terms "offset," "reverse," "self-correct," and "wash out" are synonymous.

TIP: If an error causes an **understatement** in revenue, it will cause an **understatement** of net income for that same year; however, if an error causes an **understatement** of expense, it will cause an **overstatement** of net income for that same year.

> **TIP:** All the error situations discussed in this chapter maintain balance in the basic accounting equation (often called the balance sheet equation). Thus, when you analyze the effects of these errors, always make sure your analysis maintains balance in the balance sheet equation (A = L + OE).
>
> **TIP:** Most of the errors illustrated in this chapter are the result of using the cash basis of accounting rather than the accrual basis of accounting.
>
> **TIP:** If an entity has an error correction, a change in accounting principle, and a change in an accounting estimate all in the same period, the items should be handled in the order in which they are mentioned in this sentence.

ILLUSTRATION 23-1
SUMMARY OF REPORTING REQUIREMENTS
FOR ACCOUNTING CHANGES (L.O.3,4,6)

TREATMENT	WHEN TO USE	MANNER OF REPORTING
Current	Change in accounting principle—general (non-special) case. Example: Change in depreciation method such as from double-declining-balance to straight-line. Change from FIFO to average cost method for inventory pricing. Change from average cost method to FIFO for inventory pricing.	1. A catch-up adjustment is recorded using an account called Cumulative Effect of Change in Accounting Principle. 2. The balance of the Cumulative Effect of Change in Accounting Principle account (which represents the cumulative effect on prior periods of the retroactive application of the new method) is a line item on the income statement (after extraordinary items) and is shown net of the tax effect. 3. No formal restatement of financial statements for prior periods is made. 4. Pro-forma figures (for income before extraordinary items, net income, and the related two EPS amounts) to reflect retroactive application of the new method are to be shown supplementary for all periods presented. 5. The effect of the change on the year of change is to be disclosed in the notes. (The effect on the year of change means the effect on income before cumulative effect of the year of change.)

ILLUSTRATION 23-1 (Continued)

TREATMENT	WHEN TO USE	MANNER OF REPORTING
Retroactive	Change in accounting principle—special case. Examples: Change from LIFO to any other pricing method such as change from LIFO to FIFO or change from LIFO to average cost. Change in method used to account for long-term construction contracts such as change from completed-contract to percentage-of-completion or vice versa. Change in the reporting entity.	1. A catch-up adjustment is recorded using the Retained Earnings account. 2. "Adjustment Due to Effect of Accounting Change on Prior Periods" is a line item on the statement of retained earnings. It is an adjustment to the beginning balance of retained earnings and is shown net of the related tax effect. The beginning balance in this case is often captioned "Retained earnings balance beginning of period, as previously reported." 3. Financial statements of prior periods presented are formally restated (recast). 4. No supplementary pro-forma figures are presented because of the formal restatement procedures applied. 5. The effect of the change on each year presented is to be disclosed in the notes.
Prospective	Change in accounting estimate. Examples: Change in the estimated service life of a fixed asset. Change in the estimated residual value of a fixed asset. Change in the percentage used for estimate of bad debts. Change in accounting principle necessitated by a change in estimate.	1. Usually, no catch-up adjustment for the change itself is appropriate. 2. The effect of the change on prior periods will be reflected in the amount of a revenue or expense reported in the income statement for the current period or for the current and future periods, as appropriate. 3. No restatement of financial statements for prior periods is made. 4. No supplementary pro-forma figures are to be reported. 5. Generally, the effect of the change on the year of change is to be disclosed in the notes.

TIP: A change in accounting principle receiving current treatment is often referred to in examination questions as a "cumulative-effect type accounting change."

ILLUSTRATION 23-1 (Continued)

TIP:	The computations for the first two treatments (current and retroactive) are the same because they both involve "retroactive application" of a new accounting method. The computations involve determining the effect of the change on the balance of retained earnings as of the beginning of the period of change. The two treatments differ, however, in the account used to record the cumulative effect of the change on prior periods' income and in the manner of reporting that total effect on prior periods. The first treatment (current) includes the effect of the change on prior periods in the income statement of the current year (year of change) and does **not** restate prior period statements. The second treatment (retroactive) takes the effect of the change on prior periods directly to the Retained Earnings account (rather than running it through the current income statement) and **does** restate prior period statements presented.
TIP:	The term "pro-forma" means "as if" or "based on assumptions." In the context of accounting changes, pro-forma presentations are shown as **supplementary** information on the face of the income statement, in a separate schedule, or in the notes to the financial statements. Think of the supplementary use of pro-forma amounts as a shortened version of restatement. They show what income before extraordinary items, net income, and the related EPS amounts would have been **IF** the new accounting method had been used in all periods. Pro-forma amounts are shown **only** for a change in accounting principle receiving current treatment (that is, a change in accounting principle—nonspecial case).
TIP:	A change in an accounting estimate that necessitates a change in an accounting principle is to be accounted for as a change in accounting estimate. This situation is often referred to as a change in accounting estimate that is recognized in whole or in part by a change in accounting principle. The reason for using the prospective treatment in this case is that the effect of the change in principle cannot be separated from the effect of the change in estimate. An example is the change from the policy of deferring and amortizing preproduction costs to the policy of expensing such costs because the estimate of the periods benefited has changed and any future benefits now appear doubtful.
TIP:	The **restatement of financial statements** for a prior period involves making revisions within the previously prepared statements before they are republished in comparative statements. When restatement is appropriate, the accountant will restate only those prior periods that are being published again for readers' use. For example, assume a company used LIFO from the company's inception in 1993 through 1998. In 1999, the company changes to FIFO. This change is to receive retroactive treatment. Thus, if at the end of 1999, the company presents income statements for 1997 and 1998 along with 1999 (comparative statements), the income statements previously published for 1997 and 1998 would be restated (that is, changed or revised) to reflect the individual amounts that would have been reported in the body of the statements in the prior years if the new method (FIFO) had been used. The effect on the periods prior to the first year being republished (1993 through 1996 are the years prior to 1997 which is the earliest year being presented in the set of comparative reports) would be shown as an adjustment to the balance of Retained Earnings at the beginning of 1997 on the statement of retained earnings for 1997 in the comparative statements of retained earnings. Thus, computations related to this change involve data from six prior years (1993 through 1998), but only two prior years (1997 and 1998) are formally restated because they are the only years being presented in comparative financial statements. Restated financial statements reflect "as if" type amounts in the body of the statements.

ILLUSTRATION 23-1 (Continued)

This formal restatement procedure differs from showing supplementary pro-forma amounts for a change in accounting principle when the current treatment is applied. With the current treatment, prior period statements are republished just as they appeared when they were first published in a prior period. Supplementary pro-forma amounts are shown for key figures (such as net income and earnings per share) to inform the reader what those key figures would have been if all of the financial statements had been restated to reflect the use of a newly adopted accounting principle. These pro-forma amounts are often on the face of the income statements at the bottom. To obtain these supplementary pro-forma amounts, the accountant must perform the same calculations that would be performed for a restatement situation, but the calculations are only performed on a work paper if formal restatement is not applicable.

CASE 23-1

Purpose: (L.O.1 thru 8) This case will provide examples of changes in accounting principles, changes in accounting estimates, and changes from nongenerally accepted methods to accepted methods (error corrections). It will also identify the proper accounting treatment for each.

The following is a list of changes.

Instructions
For each item in the list:
(a)   Use the appropriate number to indicate if it is:
      1.   A change in accounting principle—not a special case.
      2.   A change in accounting principle—special case.
      3.   A change in accounting estimate.
      4.   An error correction.
      5.   None of the above.
(b)   Use the appropriate letter to indicate if it is to receive:
      C.   Current treatment.
      R.   Retroactive treatment.
      P.   Prospective treatment.
      N.   None of the above.

(a)   (b)

_____ _____   1. Change in the estimate for obsolescence of inventory.

_____ _____   2. Change in the composition of companies included in the consolidated financial statements.

_____ _____   3. Change from completed-contract to percentage-of-completion method in accounting for long-term construction contracts.

_____ _____   4. Change from straight-line to double-declining-balance depreciation method for all assets held.

_____ _____   5. Change from sum-of-the-years'-digits depreciation method to straight-line method for all assets held.

_____ _____   6. Change to straight-line depreciation method for all new assets acquired; 150% declining-balance method will continue to be used for all assets acquired in prior years.

_____ _____   7. Change from double-declining-balance method to straight-line depreciation method; this change was not planned when the asset was acquired and the accelerated method was adopted.

_____ _____   8. Change in the estimated residual value for a fixed asset.

_____ _____   9. Change from the FIFO cost method to the average cost method for inventory pricing.

_____ _____   10. Change from LIFO to the average cost inventory pricing method.

_____ _____   11. Change from FIFO to LIFO inventory cost method.

_____ _____   12. Change from LIFO to FIFO for inventory pricing.

_____ _____   13. Change to or from the full cost method as used in the extractive industries.

_____ _____   14. Change from the cash basis to the accrual basis of accounting.

_____ _____   15. Change from the direct write-off method to the allowance method to account for bad debts where bad debts have always been (and continue to be) a material amount.

_____ _____   16. Change from the direct write-off method to the allowance method to account for uncollectible accounts where bad debts have just become a material amount in the current period.

(a) (b)

_____ _____ 17. Change from direct costing to full absorption costing for a manufacturing company.

_____ _____ 18. Change from pay-as-you-go to accrual basis in accounting for pension costs.

_____ _____ 19. Change from the installment basis to the accrual basis in accounting for installment sales where uncollectible accounts have always been subject to a reasonable estimation.

_____ _____ 20. Change from not amortizing recorded goodwill to amortizing purchased goodwill.

_____ _____ 21. Change from expensing interest incurred during the construction of a new plant to capitalizing interest incurred during construction.

_____ _____ 22. Change in the interest rate used to compute pension expense.

_____ _____ 23. Change from capitalizing R & D costs to expensing R & D costs in the period incurred.

_____ _____ 24. Adoption of a new accounting method because this is the first time a new type of transaction has occurred.

_____ _____ 25. Change from double-declining-balance method to straight-line depreciation method at the midpoint of the asset's life; this change was planned at the time the asset was acquired (and the accelerated depreciation method was adopted) to fully depreciate the cost over the estimated life of the asset.

Solution to Case 23-1

Answers		Explanation and/or Comment
(a)	(b)	
3	P	1.
2	R	2. This situation is a change in the reporting entity which is a special case of a change in accounting principle.
2	R	3.
1	C	4.
1	C	5.

Answers			Explanation and/or Comment
(a)	(b)		
5	N	6.	Only footnote disclosure is required. New method is used only for new assets.
1	C	7.	Assume the change is for all assets held.
3	P	8.	
1	C	9.	
2	R	10.	
1	C	11.	The cumulative effect on prior periods and the supplementary pro-forma amounts are generally not determinable; disclose that fact.
2	R	12.	
2	R	13.	
4	R	14.	The cash basis of accounting is not GAAP.
4	R	15.	The direct write-off method is not GAAP where bad debts are material.
5	N	16.	Treat like an initial adoption. The initial adoption of an accounting principle is not a change; neither is the adoption or modification of a method due to a substantive change in the kinds of transactions or events being recorded.
4	R	17.	Direct costing is not GAAP. (The direct costing method is often called variable costing method.) The prime costing and direct costing methods are not generally accepted accounting methods because they treat some elements of manufacturing costs as period costs rather than as product costs. Only the full absorption costing method is GAAP; it assigns all manufacturing costs to inventory.
4	R	18.	The pay-as-you-go approach is not GAAP.
4	R	19.	The installment basis is not GAAP unless you cannot reasonably estimate uncollectibles.
4	R	20.	*APB Opinion No. 17* requires the amortization of recorded goodwill.
4	R	21.	*SFAS No. 34* requires the capitalization of interest incurred during construction.
3	P	22.	Assume both old and new rates are good faith estimates.
4	R	23.	In general, *SFAS No. 2* requires that R & D costs be expensed in the period incurred.
5	N	24.	The initial adoption of a method is not an accounting change.
5	N	25.	This is not an accounting change; rather, the method used is a hybrid or combination method.

Explanation and Approach: First determine the nature of the change. Then determine how to treat that change. Notice how the answer to part (a) automatically determines the solution to part (b). A change in an accounting principle—nonspecial case is to be treated currently (it is a cumulative-effect type change). A change in an accounting principle—special case and a correction of an error are both treated retroactively. A change in an accounting estimate is accounted for prospectively. Therefore, an answer of 1 to (a) means a response of C for part (b), an answer of 2 or 4 to (a) means a response of R for part (b), and an answer of 3 for part (a) calls for an answer of P for part (b).

ILLUSTRATION 23-2
HOW TO COMPUTE AND RECORD THE EFFECTS OF
A CHANGE IN ACCOUNTING PRINCIPLE (L.O.3,4)

A. Compute the effect of a change in accounting method (principle) on income of periods prior to the change and record it as follows:
1. Determine the effect of the change on retained earnings as of the beginning of the period of change as follows:
    (a) Identify the revenue and/or expense item(s) and amounts that were affected in the prior periods by use of the old method.
    (b) Compute what the amount of those revenue and/or expense item(s) would have been in the prior periods if the new method was used in all periods. Also consider the effect on the amount of taxes reported.
    (c) Compare the amounts in (a) above with those in (b) above. The net difference is the effect of the change on income of prior periods (net of tax effect).
2. Record the effect of the change on prior periods as follows:
    (a) Determine if the adjustment for the effect on prior periods is a debit or a credit.
        (1) If use of the new method would have resulted in higher net incomes in prior years, the adjustment needed is a credit.
        (2) If use of the new method would have resulted in lower net incomes in prior years, the adjustment needed is a debit.
    (b) Determine if the adjustment is to be made directly to retained earnings or to go through the current income statement.
        (1) If the change is a special case of a change in accounting principle, it is to receive retroactive treatment; thus, the adjustment goes directly to the Retained Earnings account.
        (2) If the change in accounting principle is **not** a special case, it is to receive current treatment; thus, the adjustment goes through the income statement of the period of change. (Use the Cumulative Effect of Change in Accounting Principle account).
    (c) Record the rest of the entry so that asset and liability account balances are restated to balances that would have existed at the beginning of the period of change had the new method been used in all prior periods.

B. Compute the effect of a change in accounting method on the income of the **current** period (period of change) and report it as follows:
1. Identify the amount of revenue and/or expense on the income statement for the current period computed as a result of the use of the new method.
2. Compute what the amount of the particular revenue and/or expense item would be in the current period if the old method was used.
3. Compare the amount(s) in "1" above with the amount(s) in "2" above. The net difference is the effect on the period of change.

> **TIP:** The effect on the period of change does **not** include the cumulative effect on prior periods.

4. Disclose the effect on the period of change (net of tax effect) in the notes to the financial statements of the period of change.

EXERCISE 23-1

Purpose: (L.O.3) This exercise will illustrate the following for a change in accounting principle: (1) computation of effect on prior periods, (2) computation of effect on the period of change, and (3) computation of pro-forma amounts.

The Water Lab Corp. used the sum-of-the-years'-digits method for the first three years for both book and tax purposes to compute depreciation for its equipment. During the fourth year, the company changed to the straight-line method for book purposes for all assets held. The following facts pertain:

Cost of equipment	$70,000
Date acquired	January 1, Year 1
Estimated service life	10 years
Residual value	$15,000
Tax rate	40%
Number of shares of stock outstanding	10,000

Instructions

(a)   Compute the cumulative effect on periods prior to the year of change.
(b)   Prepare the journal entry to record the accounting change.
(c)   Compute the depreciation expense for Year 4 and prepare the appropriate adjusting entry.
(d)   Compute the effect of the change on the year of change. Indicate the direction of change (increase or decrease in net income).
(e)   Compute the book value of the equipment to be reported on the balance sheet at the end of Year 4.
(f)   Compute the pro-forma net income figures for Years 1-4, assuming the following amounts were reported prior to the change:

Net income—Year 1	$50,000
Net income—Year 2	55,000
Net income—Year 3	60,000
Income before cumulative effect—Year 4	68,000

(g)   Explain all of the relevant reporting and disclosure requirements.

Solution to Exercise 23-1

(a)

	Depreciation Using OLD (SYD) Method	Depreciation Using NEW (Straight-line) Method
Year 1	$10,000[a]	$ 5,500[d]
Year 2	9,000[b]	5,500
Year 3	8,000[c]	5,500
	$27,000	$16,500

Depreciation expense was	$27,000	for Years 1-3 using old method.
Depreciation would have been	16,500	for Years 1-3 using new method.
Difference is	$10,500	cumulative effect on prior periods.
Net-of-tax rate	x 60%	(100% - 40% tax rate)
Cumulative effect, net of tax	$ 6,300	

a
$$\frac{10}{\dfrac{10\ (10\ +\ 1)}{2}} \times (\$70,000 - \$15,000) = \$10,000$$

b
$$\frac{9}{\dfrac{10\ (10\ +\ 1)}{2}} \times (\$70,000 - \$15,000) = \$9,000$$

c
$$\frac{8}{\dfrac{10\ (10\ +\ 1)}{2}} \times (\$70,000 - \$15,000) = \$8,000$$

d
$$\frac{\$70,000\ -\ \$15,000}{10\ \text{years}} = \$5,500$$

TIP: Take a few minutes to refresh your memory by reviewing the guidelines for computing depreciation using various methods. A quick review of the material in Chapter 11 of your *Self-Study Problems/Solutions Book I* will enhance your recall of that subject and will improve your success rate on exam questions over this chapter.

TIP: Refer to the guidelines in **Illustration 23-2** in performing the relevant computations required in this exercise.

Explanation: The current year (year of change) is Year 4. Therefore, the prior years affected are Years 1, 2, and 3. The total amount that was reported as depreciation in the prior years (as determined by using the old depreciation method) is compared to what would have been reported as depreciation in those same years if the new method had been used for all periods. The difference is the total effect on the prior periods' income before taxes ($10,500) which is commonly called the cumulative effect on prior periods. The net-of-tax answer for the cumulative effect ($6,300) is determined by multiplying the cumulative effect by the 60% net-of-tax rate (100% minus the 40% tax rate).

(b) Accumulated Depreciation... 10,500
    Cumulative Effect of Change in Accounting Principle—
       Depreciation 6,300
    Deferred Tax Liability (40% x $10,500)................................... 4,200

Explanation: The new method (straight-line) would have yielded less depreciation expense and more net income if it had been used in prior periods; therefore, the adjustment to record the cumulative effect on periods prior to the change is a credit. The adjustment is run through the current income statement (rather than directly to retained earnings) because the change described is a change in accounting principle, general case.

The rest of the journal entry restates balances for a contra asset account and a liability account to balances that would have existed at the beginning of the year of change (Year 4) if the new method had been used in all prior periods. At the end of Year 3, accumulated depreciation would have been less by $10,500 if the straight-line method had been used since the acquisition date of the asset. Use of an accelerated depreciation method for tax purposes would have resulted in a temporary difference that would have given rise to future taxable amounts of $10,500 and a deferred tax liability at the end of Year 3 of $4,200 ($10,500 x 40% = $4,200).

> **TIP:** The old method is assumed to be continued for tax purposes.

(c)   Straight-line depreciation: $\frac{\$70,000 - \$15,000}{10 \text{ years}}$ = $\underline{\$5,500}$ Depreciation for Year 4

Depreciation Expense...	5,500	
Accumulated Depreciation...		5,500

> **TIP:** Do not confuse this computation with the procedures employed for a change in accounting estimate. This computation for depreciation ignores what was actually depreciated in prior periods because the journal entry in part (b) restated the accounts to balances that would have existed if the new method had been used in all prior periods.

(d)

Depreciation Year 4 using new method	$5,500
Depreciation Year 4 using old method	7,000*
Increase in income before income taxes, Year 4	1,500
Net-of-tax rate	60%
Increase in income Year 4, net of tax	$ 900

*7/55 ($70,000 - $15,000) = $7,000

> **TIP:** The effect on the year of change refers to the effect on "income before cumulative effect" in the year of change. The cumulative effect on prior periods is **not** a component of this computation.
>
> **TIP:** A decrease in expense results in an increase in net income.

(e)

Cost of equipment	$70,000
Accumulated depreciation, end of Year 4	(22,000)*
Book value, end of Year 4	$48,000

*This balance is best determined by reconstructing the entries that would be reflected in the Accumulated Depreciation account as follows:

Accumulated Depreciation		
Adjustment for cumulative effect of change in method 10,500	Depreciation for Year 1	10,000
	Depreciation for Year 2	9,000
	Depreciation for Year 3	8,000
	Depreciation for Year 4	5,500
	Balance, end of Year 4	22,000

TIP: Notice that because the journal entry in part (b) has put the books on a basis as if the new method (straight-line) had been used in all periods, the balance of Accumulated Depreciation at the end of Year 4 is four years worth of $5,500 (straight-line depreciation for one year).

(f)

	Year 1	Year 2	Year 3	Year 4
Depreciation reported	$10,000	$ 9,000	$ 8,000	$ 5,500
Depreciation using new method	5,500	5,500	5,500	5,500
Increase in income before taxes	4,500	3,500	2,500	0
Net-of-tax rate (100% - 40%)	60%	60%	60%	---
Increase in net income	2,700	2,100	1,500	---
Net income reported	50,000	55,000	60,000	---
Income before cumulative effect	---	---	---	68,000
Pro-forma net income	$52,700	$57,100	$61,500	$68,000

TIP: Supplementary pro-forma amounts are to be reported for all periods presented, which includes the current period. The pro-forma net income for the year of change is equal to income before cumulative effect for that period.

(g)   The reporting and disclosure requirements for this change in accounting principle (nonspecial case) can be summarized as follows:

1.   The cumulative effect of the change on periods prior to the year of change is to be reported net of tax as a separate line item on the income statement in the year of change. It is the last line on the income statement before the net income figure. That net-of-tax amount is $6,300 in this situation.

2.   If prior period financial statements are included for comparative purposes, those statements are to be republished without restatement. Supplementary pro-forma amounts for key items are to be included on the face of the income statements for all periods presented. Those key items are:
   a.   Income before extraordinary items.
   b.   Net income.
   c.   EPS on income before extraordinary items.
   d.   EPS on net income.

3.   A footnote (note to the financial statements) should include the following:
a.   Nature of the change.
b.   Justification for the change.
c.   Effect on the year of change (increase of $900 net of tax, in this case).
d.   Reference to the effect on prior periods included in the income statement ($6,300 credit, in this case).

The footnote could be written as follows:

In Year 4, depreciation of equipment is computed by use of the straight-line method. In prior years, beginning in Year 1, depreciation of equipment was computed by the sum-of-the-years'-digits method. The new method of depreciation was adopted to provide a better matching of expenses with revenues and has been applied retroactively to equipment acquisitions of prior years to determine the cumulative effect. The effect of the change in Year 4 was to increase income before cumulative effect by $900 (or $.09 per share). The adjustment necessary for retroactive application of the new method, amounting to $6,300, is included in income of Year 4. The pro-forma amounts shown on the income statement have been adjusted for the effect of retroactive application on depreciation and related income taxes.

> **TIP:** The wording of this footnote is often a source of confusion for students. The footnote says "The new method...has been applied retroactively..." and "...retroactive application of the new method..." This does **not** mean the change was given retroactive treatment. The new method is applied retroactively just to compute the necessary adjustments to the Accumulated Depreciation and Deferred Tax Liability accounts and to compute the "catch-up" adjustment required; that "catch-up" adjustment, however, is shown in the current income statement rather than taken directly to retained earnings.

> **TIP:** In comparative statements published in Year 4, Water Lab would show the following amounts for depreciation expense:
>
> | | Year 4 | Year 3 | Year 2 | Year 1 |
> |---|---|---|---|---|
> | Depreciation expense | $5,500 | $8,000 | $9,000 | $10,000 |
>
> The prior years are **not** restated, so they reflect use of the old method. The current year's depreciation figure reflects use of the new method. (Restatement would have resulted in using the new method—$5,500 depreciation per year—for reporting depreciation for all years presented).

EXERCISE 23-2

Purpose: (L.O.4) This exercise provides an example of the accounting procedures for a special case of a change in accounting principle.

The Buildaway Construction Company enters into long-term construction contracts. The following data relate to gross profit figures determined first, by use of the completed-contract method, and second, by use of the percentage-of-completion method for Years 1 through 3:

	Completed-Contract	Percentage-of-Completion
Year 1	$ 40,000	$ 140,000
Year 2	160,000	280,000
Year 3	270,000	350,000

The company used the completed-contract method in Years 1 and 2 for both book purposes and tax purposes. In Year 3, the company changed to the percentage-of-completion method for book purposes only. The tax rate is 40% for all years.

Instructions

(a) Compute the effect of the change on periods prior to the change.
(b) Prepare the journal entry to record the accounting change.
(c) Compute the effect of the change on the year of change.
(d) Explain whether financial statements of prior years are to be restated.

Solution to Exercise 23-2

(a)

Total gross profit for Years 1 and 2 using the old method	$200,000[1]
Total gross profit for Years 1 and 2 using the new method	420,000[2]
Cumulative (total) effect on prior periods	220,000
Net-of-tax rate	60%
Cumulative effect on prior periods, net of tax	$132,000

[1]$40,000 Year 1 + $160,000 Year 2 = $200,000
[2]$140,000 Year 1 + $280,000 Year 2 = $420,000

(b)

Construction in Process	220,000	
Deferred Tax Liability ($220,000 x 40%)		88,000
Retained Earnings		132,000

TIP: This is a special case of a change in accounting principle; therefore, it is to receive retroactive treatment.

TIP: Follow the guidelines in **Illustration 23-2** in performing the computations and selecting the accounts involved in this journal entry.

> **TIP:** The new method would have resulted in reporting higher net incomes if it had been used in prior periods; thus, the adjustment required to record the cumulative effect is a credit. Retroactive treatment is appropriate in this case; hence, the Retained Earnings account is used rather than an income statement account.

(c)

Gross profit for Year 3 using the new method	$ 350,000
Gross profit for Year 3 using the old method	270,000
Increase in income before income taxes for Year 3	80,000
Net-of-tax rate	60%
Increase in net income for Year 3	$ 48,000

(d) Yes, the financial statements are to be restated for all prior years presented. A change in the method employed to account for long-term construction contracts constitutes a special case of a change in accounting principle; therefore, it is to receive retroactive treatment. Retroactive treatment means: (1) restate the financial statements for all prior periods presented, and (2) record the total (cumulative) effect on prior periods as an adjustment directly to the Retained Earnings account; thus, the amount is reported as an adjustment to the beginning balance of retained earnings (as previously reported) on the statement of retained earnings for the period of change.

ILLUSTRATION 23-3
ACCOUNTING FOR A CHANGE IN ESTIMATE FOR A PLANT ASSET (L.O.6)

Whenever there is a change in the estimate of service life or salvage value for a depreciable asset, the following format will aid in the computation of depreciation.

	Original Cost
-	Accumulated Depreciation[a]
=	Book Value
+	Additional Expenditures Capitalized, If Any[b]
=	Revised Book Value
-	Current Estimate of Residual Value
=	Remaining Depreciable Cost to be Allocated Over Remaining Life of Asset

[a]Total depreciation taken prior to beginning of the year of change.

[b]Sometimes an extension of life is obtained by a major overhaul or other expenditure capitalized subsequent to the acquisition of the original asset.

> **TIP:** If a change in estimate occurs during 1999, it does not matter whether the change occurs at the beginning or at the end of the year because the entry for depreciation is not made until the end of the year; that entry should reflect the change as if it occurred at the very beginning of the year of change.

EXERCISE 23-3

Purpose: (L.O.6) This exercise will illustrate the proper accounting procedures for a change in an accounting estimate.

Mitzer Corporation acquired a plant asset costing $300,000 at the beginning of Year 1. After depreciating it for four years using the straight-line method, a ten-year service life and an expected residual value of $30,000, Mitzer estimated the asset would be useful for a total of twelve years and have a residual value of $20,000. The tax rate is 40% for all years.

Instructions

(a) Compute the depreciation expense to report for Year 5. Prepare the appropriate journal entry to record it.

(b) Prepare the journal entry, if any, to record the accounting change. Also, explain the type of treatment to give this situation.

(c) Compute the effect of the change on the year of change. Explain where it is to be reported.

Solution to Exercise 23-3

(a) **Approach:** Apply the format outlined in **Illustration 23-3** to compute depreciation where there has been a change in the estimate of service life and/or the estimate of salvage value for plant assets.

Original cost	$ 300,000
Accumulated depreciation	(108,000)*
Book value, beginning Year 5	192,000
Additional costs capitalized	-0-
Revised book value	192,000
Current estimate of residual value	(20,000)
Remaining depreciable cost	172,000
Divide by the remaining life	÷ 8**
Depreciation per year for Year 5 and subsequent years	$ 21,500

$$*\frac{\$300,000 - \$30,000}{10 \text{ years}} = \$27,000 \text{ per year using old estimates}$$

$27,000 x 4 years = $108,000

**12 years total - 4 years gone = 8 years remaining

Entry:

Depreciation Expense...	21,500	
Accumulated Depreciation......................................		21,500

TIP:	An accounting change is always made as of the beginning of the year of change, even though it is not recorded until the end of the period of change.

(b) **No entry.** There is no journal entry to record this change because a change in estimate is to receive prospective treatment. Therefore, there is no computation of the total effect on prior periods; there is no entry for the effect on prior periods. The total effect on the past is, in this case, spread over the current (Year 5) and future periods (Years 6 through 12).

(c)
Depreciation to be reported for Year 5 (part a)	$ 21,500
Depreciation for Year 5 if old estimate were used	27,000
Increase in income before income taxes for Year 5	5,500
Net-of-tax rate	60%
Increase in net income for Year 5	$ 3,300

The $3,300 effect on the current year is to be disclosed in the footnotes.

ILLUSTRATION 23-4
COMMON RELATIONSHIPS AND ASSUMPTIONS
INHERENT IN ERROR SITUATIONS (L.O.8)

1. An accrued expense that is **not** recorded at the end of one period is assumed to have been paid (and recorded as expense) in the following period.

2. An accrued revenue that is **not** recorded at the end of one period is assumed to have been received (and recorded as revenue) in the following period.

3. A prepaid expense that is omitted in Year 1 is assumed to have been recorded as expense in Year 1 when the cash was disbursed. Unless otherwise indicated, it is assumed to have become an expired cost in Year 2 (although not correctly recorded as such, due to the omission of the prepaid item at the end of Year 1).

4. An unearned revenue that is omitted in Year 1 is assumed to have been recorded as revenue in Year 1 when the cash was received. Unless otherwise indicated, it is assumed to have become earned in Year 2 (although not correctly recorded as such, due to the omission of the unearned item at the end of Year 1).

5. The ending inventory of one period is the beginning inventory of the following period.

6. If purchases of inventory which are made near the end of Year 1 are not recorded and the merchandise is also omitted from the ending inventory for Year 1, there is no net effect on net income of Year 1 or Year 2.

ILLUSTRATION 23-5
GUIDE FOR PREPARING CORRECTING ENTRIES FOR ERRORS (L.O.8)

SHORT METHOD

Step 1: Adjust any current revenue and/or expense (or gain or loss) account affected by the error.

Step 2: Adjust any asset and/or liability account to its proper balance, if needed.

Step 3: Adjust revenue and/or expense items of prior periods by an entry to retained earnings.

> **OR**

LONG METHOD

Step 1: Reconstruct the erroneous entry that was actually made (sometimes no entry was made).

Step 2: Reconstruct the entry that should have been made. Analyze it to determine the effects (what was understated, overstated, etc.). Remember: A = L + OE.

Step 3: Make a correcting entry to bring accounts to the balances that should be shown at a current point in time. You can do so by "reversing" the entry that was made and by recording the entry that should have been made and by doing three additional steps:

Step 3(a): If any revenue or expense accounts of prior periods are involved, cross them out and replace them with Retained Earnings.

Step 3(b): Clean up the entry by combining like items.

Step 3(c): Make an adjusting entry for the current year, if necessary.

EXERCISE 23-4

Purpose: (L.O.8) This exercise will provide examples of errors, their effects on net income, and their effects on the balance sheet.

The Kennedy Corporation discovered errors during a recent audit. The company has a calendar-year reporting period. The errors are as follows:

Error 1 Accrued interest on notes payable of $3,500 was omitted at the end of 1998.

Error 2 Prepaid insurance expense of $1,800 was overlooked at the end of 1998. (The premium paid in advance relates to coverage in 1999.)

Error 3 Accrued interest on investments of $5,100 was understated at the end of 1998.

Error 4 Unearned rent revenue of $4,500 was understated at the end of 1998.

Error 5 A truck with a cost of $10,000, a service life of four years, and a residual value of $4,000 was expensed when it was purchased at the beginning of 1998.

Error 6 Amortization of patent, $700, was omitted in 1998.

Instructions

(a) Assuming net income of $50,000 was reported for 1998, and net income of $72,000 was reported for 1999 (before discovery of the errors), compute the correct net income figures for 1998 and 1999.

(b) For each error, describe the following:
1. Effect on net income for 1998.
2. Effect on the elements of the basic accounting equation at December 31, 1998.
3. Effect on net income for 1999.
4. Effect on the elements of the basic accounting equation at December 31, 1999.

(c) Prepare the correcting entry for each error, assuming the errors are discovered at the end of 1999 before closing.

Solution to Exercise 23-4

(a)

	1998	1999
Net income as previously reported	$ 50,000	$ 72,000
Failure to accrue interest expense in 1998	(3,500)	3,500
Failure to defer insurance expense in 1998	1,800	(1,800)
Failure to accrue interest revenue in 1998	5,100	(5,100)
Failure to defer rent revenue in 1998	(4,500)	4,500
Failure to capitalize truck in 1998 and depreciate	8,500	(1,500)
Failure to amortize a patent in 1998	(700)	0
Net income, as corrected	$ 56,700	$ 71,600

> **TIP:** To correct a net income figure that is understated, add the amount in error; to correct a net income figure that is overstated, deduct the amount in error.

(b) and (c) The solution and explanation for each error is presented below:

> **TIP:** Notice how the analysis of the effects of each error maintains balance in the basic accounting equation (A = L + OE).

> **TIP:** When you are asked to describe the effects of an error, you are to describe the effects on all periods affected, assuming the error is allowed to run its course. Do not assume the error is corrected. To assume correction would mean there are no effects remaining.

Approach to part (b): Reconstruct what was done. Compare that with what should have been done. The effects of the error should then be readily determinable.

Approach to part (c): Follow the three easy steps in the "short method" in **Illustration 23-5** to prepare the correcting entries. Refer to the Explanation to part (b) of the Solution to analyze what corrections are needed.

ERROR 1

(b) **Effects of Error 1:** Failure to accrue interest expense in 1998:
1. Net income for 1998 is overstated (because interest expense is understated).
2. Liabilities are understated, and owners' equity is overstated at 12/31/98.
3. Net income for 1999 is understated (because interest expense is overstated).
4. There is no effect on the balance sheet at 12/31/99.

> **TIP:** All income statement accounts are closed to owners' equity; therefore, if net income is affected in the year that an error originates, owners' equity is misstated in the same direction and by the same amount as net income.

Explanation:

What Was Done			*What Should Have Been Done*		
12/31/98	No Entry		Interest Expense	3,500	
			Int. Payable		3,500
During	Int. Expense	3,500	Interest Payable	3,500	
1999	Cash	3,500	Cash		3,500

An adjusting entry to record an accrued interest expense of $3,500 was omitted in 1998. The interest would, therefore, have been paid and recorded as an expense in 1999. The disbursement in 1999 should have been recorded as a reduction in a liability, but the liability was never reflected on the books.

> **TIP:** This is an example of a counterbalancing error. Therefore, two successive income statements and the balance sheet in between them are affected. The balance sheet at the end of the second period is unaffected because by that time the error has counterbalanced (or washed out).

(c) **Correcting entry for Error 1 at 12/31/99 before closing:**

Retained Earnings	3,500	
Interest Expense		3,500

Error 1: Explanation for entry:
Step 1: Interest Expense in 1999 will be overstated unless a correcting entry is made; Interest Expense for 1999 is reduced by a credit.
Step 2: No assets or liabilities are affected at 12/31/99.
Step 3: Interest Expense for 1998 was understated. The Interest Expense for 1998 cannot be debited because all income statement amounts for 1998 have been closed to Retained Earnings. Therefore, debit Retained Earnings to correct for the error.

ERROR 2

(b)   **Effects of Error 2:** Failure to defer insurance expense in 1998:
1.   Net income for 1998 is understated (because insurance expense is overstated).
2.   Assets are understated, and owners' equity is understated at 12/31/98.
3.   Net income for 1999 is overstated (because insurance expense is understated).
4.   There is no effect on the balance sheet at 12/31/99.

Explanation:

What Was Done		*What Should Have Been Done*	
12/31/98	No Entry	Prepaid Insurance 1,800	
		Ins. Expense	1,800
12/31/99	No Entry	Insurance Expense 1,800	
		Prepaid Ins.	1,800

In 1998, insurance premiums for 1999 were paid in advance. The payment must have been recorded by a charge to expense. An adjusting entry at the end of 1998 to record the deferral of a portion of the expense to a future period (1999) was omitted. The omission of that adjustment caused the failure to record any expense in 1999, even though some benefits were consumed in 1999.

(c)   **Correcting entry for Error 2 at 12/31/99 before closing:**

Insurance Expense	1,800	
Retained Earnings..		1,800

Error 2: Explanation for entry:
Step 1:   Insurance Expense in 1999 will be understated unless a correcting entry is made; Insurance Expense for 1999 is increased by a debit.
Step 2:   No assets or liabilities are affected at 12/31/99.
Step 3:   Insurance Expense for 1998 was overstated. The Insurance Expense account for 1998 cannot be credited because all income statement amounts for 1998 have been closed to Retained Earnings. Therefore, credit Retained Earnings to correct for the error.

ERROR 3

(b)   **Effects of Error 3:** Failure to accrue interest revenue in 1998:
1.   Net income for 1998 is understated (because interest revenue is understated).
2.   Assets are understated, and owners' equity is understated at 12/31/98.
3.   Net income for 1999 is overstated (because interest revenue is overstated).
4.   There is no effect on the balance sheet at 12/31/99.

Explanation:

What Was Done			*What Should Have Been Done*	
12/31/98	No entry		Interest Receivable 5,100	
			Int. Revenue	5,100
During	Cash	5,100	Cash	5,100
1999	Int. Revenue	5,100	Int. Receivable	5,100

An adjusting entry to record accrued revenue of $5,100 was omitted in 1998. Therefore, the interest would have been received and recorded as a revenue in 1999. The receipt in 1999 should have been recorded as a reduction in a receivable, but the receivable was never reflected on the books.

(c)   **Correcting entry for Error 3 at 12/31/99 before closing:**

Interest Revenue...	5,100	
Retained Earnings...		5,100

Error 3: Explanation for entry:

Step 1:   Interest Revenue in 1999 will be overstated unless a correcting entry is made; Interest Revenue for 1999 is reduced by a debit.

Step 2:   No assets or liabilities are affected at 12/31/99.

Step 3:   The Interest Revenue account for 1998 cannot be credited because all income statement amounts for 1998 have been closed to Retained Earnings. Therefore, credit Retained Earnings to correct for the error.

ERROR 4

(b)   **Effects of Error 4:** Failure to defer rent revenue in 1998:

1.   Net income for 1998 is overstated (because rent revenue is overstated).
2.   Liabilities are understated and owners' equity is overstated at 12/31/98.
3.   Net income for 1999 is understated (because rent revenue is understated).
4.   There is no effect on the balance sheet at 12/31/99.

Explanation:

What Was Done		*What Should Have Been Done*		
12/31/98	No Entry.	Rent Revenue	4,500	
		Unearned Rent Revenue		4,500
12/31/99	No Entry.	Unearned Rent Revenue	4,500	
		Rent Revenue		4,500

In 1998, rental receipts were collected in advance. The receipt must have been recorded by a credit to revenue. An adjusting entry at the end of 1998 to record the deferral of a portion of the revenue to a future period (1999) was omitted. The assumption is that the revenue was earned in 1999 or there would have been a description of another error.

(c)   **Correcting entry for Error 4 at 12/31/99 before closing:**

Retained Earnings	4,500	
Rent Revenue		4,500

Error 4: Explanation for entry:

Step 1:   Rent Revenue in 1999 will be understated unless a correcting entry is made; Rent Revenue is increased by a credit.

Step 2:   No assets or liabilities are affected at 12/31/99.

Step 3:   Rent Revenue for 1998 was overstated. The Rent Revenue account for 1998 cannot be debited because all income statement accounts for 1998 have been closed to Retained Earnings. Therefore, debit Retained Earnings in the correcting entry.

ERROR 5

(b)   **Effects of Error 5:** Failure to capitalize a fixed asset in 1998 and depreciate:

1.   Net income for 1998 is understated by $8,500.
2.   Assets are understated by $8,500, and owners' equity is understated by $8,500 at 12/31/98.
3.   Net income for 1999 is overstated by $1,500.
4.   Assets are understated by $7,000, and owners' equity is understated by $7,000 at 12/31/99.

Explanation:

What Was Done			*What Should Have Been Done*		
Beginning of 1998	Truck Exp. 10,000		Truck	10,000	
	Cash	10,000	Cash		10,000
12/31/98	No Entry.		Depreciation Exp. 1,500		
			Accumulated Dep.		1,500
			[($10,000 - $4,000) ÷ 4 = $1,500]		
12/31/99	No Entry.		Depreciation Exp. 1,500		
			Accumulated Dep.		1,500

The acquisition of a truck in 1998 was incorrectly recorded as an expense of $10,000. The truck should have been depreciated by charging $1,500 to expense over each of four years, beginning with 1998. This means that the income statements for 1998, 1999, 2000, and 2001 will be affected by the error if it is not detected and corrected. The balance sheet at the end of each of those four years will also be in error. This error will turnaround or offset in the period of the disposal of the truck (a gain will be overstated in that period and only then will the error self-correct on the balance sheet).

Effects: Truck Expense is overstated by $10,000 in 1998 and Depreciation Expense is understated by $1,500 in each year the truck is held. Therefore: Net income for 1998 is understated by $8,500; owners' equity at 12/31/98 is understated by $8,500; assets at 12/31/98 are understated by $8,500; net income for 1999 is overstated by $1,500; owners' equity at 12/31/99 is understated by $7,000; assets at 12/31/99 are understated by $7,000.

(c)   **Correcting entry for Error 5 at 12/31/99 before closing:**

Truck..	10,000	
Depreciation Expense...	1,500	
Accumulated Depreciation......................................		3,000
Retained Earnings...		8,500

Error 5: Explanation for entry:

Step 1: Depreciation Expense in 1999 will be understated unless a correcting entry is made; Depreciation Expense of $1,500 is recorded by a debit.

Step 2: The asset Truck will be understated at 12/31/99 by the cost of $10,000 unless a correcting entry is made. Likewise, Accumulated Depreciation will be understated by two years worth of depreciation unless a correcting entry is made. Therefore, debit Truck for $10,000 and credit Accumulated Depreciation for $3,000.

Step 3: Truck Expense for 1998 was overstated by $10,000 and Depreciation Expense for 1998 was understated by $1,500. All income amounts for 1998 have been closed to Retained Earnings. Therefore, credit Retained Earnings for $8,500 (i.e., the amount by which Retained Earnings is understated at the beginning of the year in which the error is corrected).

ERROR 6

(b)   **Effects of Error 6:** Failure to amortize an intangible asset in 1998:

1.   Net income for 1998 is overstated by $700 (because patent amortization is understated).
2.   Assets are overstated by $700 and owners' equity is overstated by $700 at 12/31/98.
3.   Net income for 1999 is not affected
4.   Assets are overstated by $700 and owners' equity is overstated by $700 at 12/31/99.

Explanation:

What Was Done		*What Should Have Been Done*		
12/31/98	No Entry.	Patent Amortization Expense	700	
		Patent		700

The failure to record amortization of a patent is **not** a counterbalancing error. This error will self-correct when the patent is fully amortized (it will be amortized one year after it should have been fully amortized) or when the patent is disposed of (through sale or writeoff). There is no mention of a similar omission in 1999 so the assumption is that the 1999 amortization was recorded properly. Therefore, this error will affect the income statement of 1998 and the income statement of the period of disposal (or of the last period amortized) and every balance sheet prepared between these two periods.

(c)   **Correcting entry for Error 6 at 12/31/99 before closing:**

Retained Earnings	700	
Patent		700

Error 6: Explanation for entry:

Step 1:   Amortization Expense for 1999 is apparently recorded correctly.

Step 2:   The asset Patent will be overstated at 12/31/99 unless a correcting entry is made. Therefore, credit Patent.

Step 3:   Amortization Expense for 1998 was understated. The Patent Amortization Expense account for 1998 cannot be debited because all income statement amounts have been closed to Retained Earnings. Therefore, debit Retained Earnings.

> **TIP:** Very often students have a more detailed approach to correcting entries. The following pairs of entries are alternate answers to some of the correcting entries presented above. Both entries in each pair must be included to be equivalent to the entries shown above.

Error 2:	Prepaid Insurance..	1,800	
	Retained Earnings...........................		1,800
	Insurance Expense......................................	1,800	
	Prepaid Insurance...........................		1,800
Error 4:	Retained Earnings.......................................	4,500	
	Unearned Rent Revenue..................		4,500
	Unearned Rent Revenue............................	4,500	
	Rent Revenue..................................		4,500
Error 5:	Truck.	10,000	
	Accumulated Depreciation...............		1,500
	Retained Earnings...........................		8,500
	Depreciation Expense.................................	1,500	
	Accumulated Depreciation...............		1,500

EXERCISE 23-5

Purpose: (L.O.8) This exercise will illustrate the effects of various errors involving purchases and ending inventory.

Surf & Turf Sports Equipment Company sells sporting goods. By taking a physical count and pricing its inventory using the FIFO cost method, inventory was determined to be $430,000 and $572,000 at December 31, 1998, and December 31, 1999, respectively. Net income was reported to be $200,000 and $218,000 for 1998 and 1999, respectively. The following errors occurred with regard to accounting for inventory transactions:

Error 1: Purchases of $30,000 made near the end of 1998 were shipped f.o.b. shipping point by the vendor on December 29, 1998; they were not received by Surf & Turf until January 3, 1999. These purchases were omitted from the physical count at December 31, 1998, and were not recorded as purchases until January 3, 1999.

Error 2: Merchandise costing $21,000 was on the premises but was overlooked during the physical inventory count at December 31, 1998.

Error 3: Merchandise costing $32,000 was double counted during the physical inventory count at December 31, 1999.

Error 4: Sales made near the end of 1999 were shipped f.o.b. destination by Surf & Turf on December 28, 1999; they were not received by the customers until January 4, 2000. These items, costing $17,000, were omitted from the inventory sheets of the physical count taken on December 31, 1999, and were treated as sales for $28,500 in 1999.

Instructions
Compute the correct net income amounts for 1998 and 1999.

Solution to Exercise 23-5

	1998	**1999**
Net income as previously reported	$200,000	$218,000
Both purchases and ending inventory for 1998 understated	---	---
Ending inventory for 1998 understated	21,000	(21,000)
Ending inventory for 1999 overstated	---	(32,000)
Sales for 1999 overstated	---	(28,500)
Ending inventory for 1999 understated	---	17,000
	$221,000	$153,500

Explanation: Analyses of effects of errors on cost of goods sold:

Error 1:

	1998	1999
Beginning inventory	No effect	Under $30,000
+ Net cost of purchases	Under $30,000	Over $30,000
= Goods available for sale	Under $30,000	No effect
- Ending inventory	Under $30,000	No effect
= Cost of goods sold expense	No effect	No effect

Error 2:

	1998	1999
Beginning inventory	No effect	Under $21,000
+ Net cost of purchases	No effect	No effect
= Goods available for sale	No effect	Under $21,000
- Ending inventory	Under $21,000	No effect
= Cost of goods sold expense	Over $21,000	Under $21,000

Error 3:

	1998	1999	2000
Beginning inventory	No effect	No effect	Over $32,000
+ Net cost of purchases	No effect	No effect	No effect
= Goods available for sale	No effect	No effect	Over $32,000
- Ending inventory	No effect	Over $32,000	No effect
= Cost of goods sold expense	No effect	Under $32,000	Over $32,000

Error 4:

	1998	1999	2000
Beginning inventory	No effect	No effect	Under $17,000
+ Net cost of purchases	No effect	No effect	No effect
= Goods available for sale	No effect	No effect	Under $17,000
- Ending inventory	No effect	Under $17,000	No effect
= Cost of goods sold expense	No effect	Over $17,000	Under $17,000
Also:			
Sales revenue	No effect	Over $28,500	Under $28,500

TIP: If you do not clearly recall how the shipping terms (f.o.b. shipping point and f.o.b. destination) effect inventory valuation, you can find that information in Chapter 8 of your *Self-Study Problems/Solutions Book I.* It would be wise to review that material.

TIP: An error involving purchases and/or ending inventory and/or beginning inventory should be analyzed in terms of its effect on components of the cost of goods sold computation in order to then determine its effect on net income. That computation is:

Beginning inventory
+ Net cost of purchases
= Goods available for sale
- Ending inventory
= Cost of goods sold

TIP: The ending inventory for Year 1 is the beginning inventory for Year 2. Thus, when the ending inventory for Year 1 is overstated, it will cause an overstatement in the net income for Year 1 and an understatement in net income for Year 2. This error will cause retained earnings at the end of Year 1 to be overstated because net income for Year 1 (which is overstated) is closed into retained earnings. The balance of retained earnings at the end of Year 2 will be unaffected by this error because the net income for Year 2 (which is understated by the same amount as the overstatement in retained earnings at the end of Year 1) is closed into retained earnings; the error at this point counterbalances. Working capital at the end of Year 1 is overstated (because inventory is a current asset), but working capital at the end of Year 2 is unaffected because the inventory figure at the end of Year 2 is determined by a physical inventory counting and pricing procedure. No new error in this process is assumed unless otherwise indicated.

TIP: An understatement in ending inventory of Year 1 will cause an understatement in net income for Year 1 and overstatement in net income for Year 2. Thus, retained earnings and working capital at the end of Year 1 are understated. However, assuming no more errors are committed at the end of Year 2, retained earnings and working capital are not affected at the end of Year 2.

TIP: If purchases for Year 1 are understated by the same amount as an understatement in inventory at the end of Year 1, there is no net effect on net income of Year 1 and no net effect on net income of Year 2. The balance sheet at the end of Year 1, however, has errors because assets (inventories) are understated and liabilities (accounts payable) are understated.

TIP: When more than one error affects the net income amount for one year, analyze each error **separately** and write down its effects before you attempt to summarize all the effects on one given year.

TIP: When analyzing an error situation involving inventory, assume a periodic inventory system is in use unless otherwise indicated.

EXERCISE 23-6

Purpose: (L.O.8) This exercise will allow you to practice analyzing the effects of errors on income determination.

The Avery Corporation computed net income of $22,000 and $30,000 for Years 1 and 2, respectively. The following errors were later discovered:

Error 1:   Depreciation on computers was omitted in Year 1, $900.
Error 2:   Deferred expenses were understated at the end of Year 1, $400.
Error 3:   Accrued revenues were omitted at the end of Year 1, $600.
Error 4:   Deferred revenues were understated at the end of Year 1, $980.
Error 5:   Accrued expenses were overlooked at the end of Year 1, $650.

Instructions
Compute the corrected net income figures for Year 1 and Year 2.

Solution to Exercise 23-6

	Year 1	Year 2
Net income as previously reported	$22,000	$30,000
Depreciation omitted—Year 1	(900)	---
Deferred expenses understated—Year 1	400	(400)
Accrued revenues understated—Year 1	600	(600)
Deferred revenues understated—Year 1	(980)	980
Accrued expenses understated—Year 1	(650)	650
Corrected net income	$20,470	$30,630

> **TIP:**   The benefits from the prepaid expense (error 2) are assumed to be consumed in Year 2 and the unearned revenue (error 4) is assumed to be earned in Year 2 because there is no mention of similar errors existing at the end of Year 2.

ANALYSIS OF MULTIPLE-CHOICE TYPE QUESTIONS

QUESTION

1.   (L.O.3) A manufacturing company changes from the FIFO cost method to the average cost inventory pricing method for all inventories held. Which of the following should be reported?

	Cumulative effect of a change in accounting principle	Pro-forma effects of retroactive application
a.	Yes	Yes
b.	Yes	No
c.	No	No
d.	No	Yes

Approach and Explanation: Determine the type of accounting change that has occurred. It is a change in accounting principle—general case. Determine the method of treatment to be accorded that type of change. The current treatment is applied to a change in principle that is not on the list of special cases. The current treatment calls for reporting the cumulative effect of the change on prior periods in the income statement of the year of change. Because this method does not restore comparability of the statements for successive periods (the financial statements of prior periods are not formally restated), supplementary information is to be disclosed that shows the pro-forma effects of applying the new method to all periods presented. (Solution = a.)

QUESTION

2.   (L.O.4) During 1999, a construction company changed from the completed-contract method to the percentage-of-completion method for accounting purposes but not for tax purposes. Gross-profit figures under both methods for the history of the company appear below:

	Completed-Contract	Percentage-of-Completion
1997	$ 190,000	$ 320,000
1998	250,000	380,000
1999	280,000	410,000
	$ 720,000	$ 1,110,000

Assuming an income tax rate of 40% for all years, the affect of this accounting change on prior periods should be reported by a credit of:

a. $156,000 on the 1999 income statement.
b. $234,000 on the 1999 income statement.
c. $156,000 on the 1999 statement of retained earnings.
d. $234,000 on the 1999 statement of retained earnings.

Approach and Explanation: Identify the type of accounting change and the method of treatment. It is a change in accounting principle—special case. It is to get retroactive treatment. Therefore, the total effect on prior periods (net of tax) is to be recorded as an adjustment to the beginning balance of retained earnings and reported on the statement of retained earnings. Identify the prior years and the effect of the change on those prior years. (Solution = c.)

	Old Method	New Method	Difference
1997	$ 190,000	$ 320,000	$ 130,000
1998	250,000	380,000	130,000
	$ 440,000	$ 700,000	260,000
Net-of-tax rate			60%
Effect net of tax			$ 156,000

QUESTION

3.　　(L.O.2,8) A change from a nongenerally accepted accounting principle to a generally accepted accounting principle should be accounted for:

　　a.　currently.
　　b.　retroactively.
　　c.　prospectively.
　　d.　as an initial adoption.

Explanation: A change from a non-GAAP method to one that is GAAP constitutes an error correction. The correction of an error is not an accounting change; it is a prior period adjustment. Prior period adjustments are to receive retroactive treatment. (Solution = b.)

QUESTION

4.　　(L.O.3) The Mercer Mayer Corporation purchased a computer system on January 1, 1997 for $210,000. The company used the straight-line method and no salvage value to depreciate the asset for the first two years of its estimated six-year life. In 1999, Mercer Mayer changed to the sum-of-the-years'-digits depreciation method for this asset. The following facts pertain:

	1997	1998	1999
Straight-line	$35,000	$35,000	$35,000
Sum-of-the-years'-digits	60,000	50,000	40,000

Mercer Mayer is subject to a 40% tax rate. In the journal entry to record the accounting change, the account Cumulative Effect of Change in Accounting Principle will be:

　　a.　credited for $24,000.
　　b.　debited for $24,000.
　　c.　credited for $27,000.
　　d.　debited for $27,000.
　　e.　none of the above.

Approach and Explanation: Follow the procedures described in **Illustration 23-2** to compute the cumulative effect of the change in accounting principle, net of the related tax effect.

Depreciation was	$ 70,000[a] for 1997 and 1998 using old method
Depreciation would have been	110,000[b] for 1997 and 1998 using new method
Difference is	40,000 cumulative effect on prior periods
Net-of-tax rate	60%
Cumulative effect, net of tax	$ 24,000

[a]$35,000 for 1997 + $35,000 for 1998 = $70,000 total for prior periods.
[b]$60,000 for 1997 + $50,000 for 1998 = $110,000 total for prior periods.

The new method would have resulted in lower net incomes if it had been used in prior years; hence, the "catch-up" adjustment needed is a debit. (Solution = b.)

QUESTION

5.   (L.O.3) Refer to the facts in Question 4 above. The amount that Mercer Mayer should report for depreciation expense on its 1999 income statement is:

   a. $40,000.
   b. $35,000.
   c. $24,000.
   d. $21,000.
   e.   none of the above.

Approach and Explanation: Calculate the depreciation for 1999 (the year of change) using the new method (sum-of-the-years'-digits method) as if the new method had been used in all prior periods. The computation is:

$$\frac{4}{21^a} \times (\$210,000 - 0) = \$40,000 \text{ depreciation for 1999 using SYD method.}$$

$$\frac{^a6(6 + 1)}{2} = 21 \qquad\qquad\qquad\qquad (\text{Solution} = a.)$$

> **TIP:**   The journal entry to record the change in accounting principle will adjust balance sheet account balances to what they would have been had the new principle (method) been used in all prior periods. Therefore, the calculation of depreciation expense for 1999 ignores the depreciation that was taken in prior periods and reflects the amount that would have been appropriate for the current year if the new method had been used for all periods.

QUESTION

6.   (L.O.3) Refer to the facts of Question 4 above. If Mercer Mayer prepares comparative financial statements in 1999, the income statement for 1998 included therein will reflect depreciation expense of:

   a. $50,000.
   b. $40,000.
   c. $35,000.
   d. $30,000.

Explanation: A change from one generally acceptable depreciation method to another generally acceptable depreciation method constitutes a change in accounting principle that is to receive current treatment. Therefore, financial statements for prior periods are **not** to be restated if they are republished for comparative purposes. The depreciation expense for 1998 will appear in 1999 comparative reports as it originally appeared when the 1998 income statement was prepared in 1998. Therefore, it will be the amount computed under the straight-line method of $35,000. (Solution = c.)

QUESTION

7.   (L.O.6) A change in accounting estimate should be accounted for:
   a.   as an adjustment to the beginning balance of retained earnings.
   b.   by restating the relevant amounts in the financial statements of prior periods.
   c.   in the period of change or in the period of change and future periods, if the change affects both.
   d.   by reporting pro-forma amounts for all periods presented.

Approach and Explanation: Think about the treatment to be accorded a change in accounting estimate before you read the answer selections. A change in accounting estimate receives prospective treatment; therefore, it is accounted for in the current period or in the current and future periods, whichever is applicable. (Solution = c.)

QUESTION

8.   (L.O.7) Which of the following is an example of a change in reporting entity?
   a.   creation of a new business unit
   b.   purchase of a new subsidiary
   c.   disposition of a subsidiary
   d.   changing specific subsidiaries that constitute the group of companies for which consolidated financial statements are presented

Approach and Explanation: Mentally review the list of items that constitute a change in reporting entity and the items that do not result in a change in reporting entity.

Examples of a change in reporting entity are:
   1.   Presenting consolidated or combined statements in place of statements of individual companies.
   2.   Changing specific subsidiaries that constitute the group of companies for which consolidated financial statements are presented.
   3.   Changing the companies included in combined financial statements.
   4.   Accounting for a pooling of interests.
   5.   A change in the fair value, equity, or consolidation method of accounting for subsidiaries and investments.

A change in the reporting entity does **not** result from creation, cessation, purchase, or disposition of a subsidiary or other business unit. (Solution = d.)

QUESTION

9.   (L.O.8) Merchandise inventory was overstated at December 31, 1998. How would this error affect earnings for 1998, earnings for 1999, working capital at December 31, 1998, and owners' equity at December 31, 1998?

	Earnings 1998	Earnings 1999	Working Capital 12/31/98	Owners' Equity 12/31/98
a.	Overstate	Understate	Overstate	Overstate
b.	Understate	Overstate	Understate	Understate
c.	Overstate	No effect	No effect	Overstate
d.	Overstate	Understate	Understate	Understate

Approach and Explanation: This is a counterbalancing error. The overstatement of 1998 ending inventory will cause net income of 1998 to be overstated (because of the understatement of cost of goods sold) and net income of 1999 to be understated. The overstatement of 1998 net income will cause owners' equity to be overstated. Inventory is a current asset. Therefore, working capital at December 31, 1998 will be overstated. (Solution = a.)

> **TIP:** **Earnings** is synonymous with **net income.**

QUESTION

10. (L.O.8) Accrued interest expense of $7,500 was omitted at December 31, 1998. Accrued interest expense of $10,000 was omitted at December 31, 1999. The net effect of these errors on net income for 1999 is:
    a. overstatement of $10,000.
    b. understatement of $2,500.
    c. understatement of $7,500.
    d. overstatement of $2,500.
    e. none of the above.

Approach and Explanation: Handle each error separately. Fully describe the effects of each error. Write these effects down. Then summarize the effects. (If necessary, draft the entries that were made and the entries that should have been made to analyze the effects on interest expense.) (Solution = d.)

Error 1:	Interest expense for 1998 is understated by $7,500.
	Net income for 1998 is overstated by $7,500.
	Interest expense for 1999 is overstated by $7,500.
	Net income for 1999 is understated by $7,500.
Error 2:	Interest expense for 1999 is understated by $10,000.
	Net income for 1999 is overstated by $10,000.
	Interest expense for 2000 is overstated by $10,000.
	Net income for 2000 is understated by $10,000.

Net effects on 1999 net income:

Understatement	$ 7,500
Overstatement	10,000
Net overstatement	$ 2,500

CHAPTER 24

STATEMENT OF CASH FLOWS

OVERVIEW

A business enterprise that provides a set of financial statements that reports both financial position and results of operations is also required to provide a statement of cash flows for each period for which results of operations are provided. The primary purpose of a statement of cash flows is to provide relevant information about the cash receipts and cash payments of an enterprise during a time period. The information provided in a statement of cash flows, if used with related disclosures and information in the other financial statements, should help investors, creditors, and others to (a) assess the enterprise's ability to generate positive future net cash flows; (b) assess the enterprise's ability to meet its obligations, its ability to pay dividends, and its needs for external financing; (c) assess the reasons for differences between net income and associated cash receipts and payments; and (d) assess the effects on an enterprise's financial position of both its cash and noncash investing and financing transactions during the period.

SUMMARY OF LEARNING OBJECTIVES

1. **Describe the purpose of the statement of cash flows.** The primary purpose of the statement of cash flows is to provide information about cash receipts and cash payments of an entity during a period. A secondary objective is to report the entity's operating, investing, and financing activities during the period.

2. **Identify the major classifications of cash flows.** The cash flows are classified as: (1) Operating activities—all transactions and events that are not defined as investing or financing activities; generally the cash effects of transactions and other events that enter into the determination of net income. (2) Investing activities—lending money and collecting on those loans, and acquiring and disposing of investments, plant assets, and intangible assets. (3) Financing activities—obtaining cash from creditors and repaying loans, issuing and reacquiring capital stock, and paying cash dividends.

3. **Differentiate between net income and net cash flows from operating activities.** Net income on an accrual basis must be adjusted to determine net cash flow from operating activities because some expenses and losses do not cause cash outflows and some revenues and gains do not provide cash inflows. Also, some gains and losses relate to transactions that are classified as investing or financing activities.

4. **Contrast the direct and indirect methods of calculating net cash flow from operating activities.** Under the direct approach, major classes of operating cash receipts and cash disbursements are calculated and reported. Presentation of the direct approach of reporting net cash flow from operating activities takes the form of a condensed cash basis income statement.

The indirect method adds back to net income the noncash expenses and losses and subtracts the noncash revenues and gains.

5. **Determine net cash flows from investing and financing activities.** Once the net cash flow from operating activities is computed, the next step is to determine whether any other changes in balance sheet accounts caused an increase or decrease in cash. Net cash flows from investing and financing activities can generally be determined by examining the changes in noncurrent balance sheet accounts.

6. **Prepare a statement of cash flows.** Preparing the statement of cash flows involves three major steps: (1) Determine the change in cash. This is the difference between the beginning and the ending cash balance shown on the comparative balance sheets. (2) Determine the net cash flow from operating activities. This procedure is complex; it involves analyzing not only the current year's income statement but also the comparative balance sheets and the selected transaction data. (3) Determine cash flows from investing and financing activities. Changes in all balance sheet accounts other than Cash must be analyzed to determine the effects on cash.

7. **Identify sources of information for a statement of cash flows.** The information to prepare the statement usually comes from three sources: (1) Comparative balance sheets—information in these statements indicate the amount of the changes in assets, liabilities, and equities during the period. (2) Current income statement—information in this statement is used in determining the cash provided by operations during the period. (3) Selected transaction data—this information from the general ledger provides additional detail needed to determine how cash was provided or used during the period.

8. **Identify special problems in preparing a statement of cash flows.** The special problems are: (1) adjustments similar to depreciation, (2) accounts receivable (net), (3) other working capital changes, (4) net losses, (5) gains, (6) stock options, (7) postretirement benefit costs, (8) extraordinary items, and (9) significant noncash transactions.

9. **Explain the use of a work sheet in preparing a statement of cash flows.** When numerous adjustments are necessary or other complicating factors are present, a work sheet is often used to assemble and classify the data that will appear on the statement of cash flows. The work sheet is merely a device that aids in the preparation of the statement; its use is optional.

10.* **Understand the purpose and use of the T-account approach to determining the net change in cash.** The purpose of the T-account approach is to determine and explain the net change in cash through the various changes that have occurred in the noncash accounts using the Cash T-account as a summarizing account.

   *This material is covered in Appendix 24-A in the text.

TIPS ON CHAPTER TOPICS

TIP: Homework and examination problems related to the subject of the statement of cash flows very often involve comparative balance sheet data. Although sometimes the older year's information is listed first so that the data is in chronological order, it is a common practice to list the current year's data first. Before beginning to work a problem, carefully note the order of the data so that you properly interpret the changes in accounts as being increases or decreases. These comparative balance sheets are often accompanied by additional information. If no addition information is given about an account, but the account balance has changed, assume that (1) only one transaction is responsible for the change in the balance, and (2) the most common transaction occurred to change that particular account balance.

TIP: In studying this chapter on the statement of cash flows and preparing homework assignments, you will encounter transactions for which you may not recall the proper accounting procedures. One of the challenging aspects about this chapter is that it draws on your knowledge of **all** of the chapters that precede it. Use this opportunity to look up the items you don't recall and refresh your memory. The procedures you review in this manner will likely be easier to recall the next time you need to use them.

TIP: In determining if a cash transaction is an operating activity, investing activity, or financing activity, it is usually helpful to reconstruct the journal entry used to record the transaction. The following observations are also helpful:
1. The journal entry to record a transaction that is an investing activity which results in a cash flow will generally involve: (1) Cash and (2) an asset account other than Cash, such as Investment (short-term or long-term), Land, Building, Equipment, Patent, Franchise, etc.
2. The journal entry to record a transaction that is a financing activity which results in a cash flow will generally involve: (1) Cash and (2) a liability account or an owners' equity account such as Bonds Payable, Notes Payable, Dividends Payable, Common Stock, Paid-in Capital in Excess of Par, Treasury Stock, etc.
3. The journal entry to record a transaction that is an operating activity which results in a cash flow will generally involve: (1) Cash and (2) a revenue account or an expense account; or, a prepaid expense account or an unearned revenue account; or, a receivable account or a payable account.

TIP: The statement of cash flows emphasizes reporting gross cash receipts and payments. Thus, if long-term debt is issued for $2,000,000 and payments of $300,000 on long-term debt occur during the same period, it is **not** permissible to just show the net inflow of $1,700,000. Rather, the inflow of $2,000,000 and the outflow of $300,000 must be separately shown in the financing activity section of the statement of cash flows. Similarly, if acquisitions and disposals of plant assets occur in the same period, the gross cash effects must be reported; they are not to be netted.

> **TIP:** Generally, gross cash receipts and gross cash payments must be separately disclosed. However, for certain items, the turnover is quick, the amounts are large, and the maturities are short. Only net changes need be reported for these items. Examples include cash receipts and payments pertaining to (a) investments (other than cash equivalents); (b) loans receivable; and (c) debt, providing the original maturity of the asset or liability is three months or less. For this purpose, amounts due on demand are considered to have maturities of three months or less.

> **TIP:** **Cash** includes not only currency on hand but demand deposits with banks or other financial institutions. **Cash equivalents** are short-term highly liquid investments that are both (a) readily convertible to known amounts of cash, and (b) so near their maturity that they present insignificant risk of changes in value because of changes in interest rates. Generally, only investments with original maturities of three months or less qualify under that definition. Examples of items commonly considered to be cash equivalents are Treasury bills, commercial paper, and money market funds. Cash equivalents may be combined with cash for presentation on the balance sheet and for reporting cash flows on the statement of cash flows.

> **TIP:** When a homework or exam problem requires use of the indirect method but does not give the net income figure, the amount of net income (or net loss) can usually be derived by analyzing the changes that took place in the balance of retained earnings.

> **TIP:** Cash flows associated with the acquisition and disposition of investments in **trading securities** are classified as **operating activities**. Cash flows related to the acquisition and disposition of investments in **available-for-sale securities** are classified as **investing activities**.

ILLUSTRATION 24-1
OPERATING, INVESTING, AND FINANCING ACTIVITIES (L.O.2)

DEFINITIONS:

Investing Activities: include (a) making and collecting loans; (b) acquiring and disposing of debt and equity instruments of other entities; and (c) acquiring and disposing of property, plant, and equipment and other productive assets.

Financing Activities: include (a) obtaining resources from owners and providing them with a return on and a return of their investment; (b) borrowing money and repaying the amounts borrowed, or otherwise settling the obligation; and (c) obtaining and paying for other resources obtained from creditors.

Operating Activities: include all transactions and other events that are not defined as investing or financing activities. Operating activities generally involve producing and delivering goods and providing services. Cash flows from operating activities are generally the cash effects of transactions and other events that enter into the determination of net income.

ILLUSTRATION 24-1 (Continued)

EXAMPLES:

Investing Activities:
　Cash inflows:
　　From sale of property, plant, and equipment and other productive assets.
　　From sale of debt or equity securities of other entities or return of investments in those instruments.
　　From collection of principal on loans to other entities or sale of loans made to others.
　Cash outflows:
　　To purchase property, plant, and equipment.[a]
　　To purchase debt or equity securities of other entities.
　　To make loans to other entities.

Financing Activities:
　Cash inflows:
　　From sale of equity securities (company's own stock).
　　From issuance of nontrade debt (bonds and notes).
　Cash outflows:
　　To pay dividends to stockholders.
　　To reacquire capital stock.
　　To pay non-trade debt (both short-term and long-term).

Operating Activities:
　Cash inflows:
　　From sales of goods or services (includes cash sales and collections on account).
　　From returns on loans (interest received) and on equity securities (dividends received).
　　From other transactions, such as: Amounts received to settle lawsuits, refunds from suppliers, and some insurance settlements (such as business interruption claims).
　Cash outflows:
　　To suppliers for inventory and other goods and services (includes cash purchases and payments on account).
　　To employees for services.
　　To government for taxes.
　　To lenders for interest.
　　To others for items such as: Payments to settle lawsuits, refunds to customers, and contributions to charities.

[a]The cash outflows included in this category are payments at the time of purchase or soon before or after purchase to acquire property, plant, and equipment and other productive assets. Generally, only advance payments, the down payment, or other amounts paid at the time of purchase or soon before or after purchase of property, plant, and equipment and other productive assets are investing cash outflows. **Incurring directly related debt to the seller is a financing transaction and subsequent payments of principal on that debt thus are financing cash outflows.**

CASE 24-1

Purpose: (L.O.2) This case will help you to classify transactions as being an operating activity, an investing activity, or a financing activity.

There are four situations described below:
1. A company purchased a machine priced at $100,000 by issuing a check for $100,000.
2. A company purchased a machine priced at $100,000 by giving a down payment of $20,000 and by issuing a note payable to the seller for $80,000. During the same year, the company made principal payments of $12,000 on the note and interest payments of $7,000.
3. A company purchased a machine for $100,000. Of that amount, $80,000 was obtained by borrowing from a local bank. During the same year, principal payments of $12,000 and interest payments of $7,000 were made to the bank on this loan.
4. A company acquired a machine by a capital lease agreement. The present value of the minimum lease payments at the inception date was $100,000. The first lease payment of $2,000 was made at the inception date. During the year, additional lease payments of $24,000 were made which included interest of $15,000.

Instructions

For each situation above, explain how it would be reflected in a statement of cash flows. That is, indicate if it is reported in the operating, investing, or financing section of the statement of cash flows or in the schedule of noncash investing and financing activities. Also, indicate the amount reported and if it is a cash inflow or outflow.

Solution to Case 24-1

1. Investing outflow of $100,000

2. Investing outflow of $20,000
    Financing outflow of $12,000
    Operating outflow of $7,000

    The schedule of noncash investing and financing activities would include the acquisition of machinery by issuance of note payable for $80,000.

3. Financing inflow of $80,000
    Investing outflow of $100,000
    Financing outflow of $12,000
    Operating outflow of $7,000

4. Financing outflow of $11,000 ($2,000 + $24,000 - $15,000)
    Operating outflow of $15,000

    The schedule of noncash investing and financing activities would include the acquisition of machinery by capital lease for $100,000.

Approach: Refer to **Illustration 24-1** for a description of the three classifications of activities.

> **TIP:** Note that all interest payments are classified as operating outflows. Also, note that in situations #2 and #4, all payments of principal on seller-financed debt are classified as financing outflows.

ILLUSTRATION 24-2
CONVERSION FROM ACCRUAL BASIS TO CASH BASIS (L.O.3,4)

	ACCRUAL BASIS		CASH BASIS
	Revenues Earned		Cash Received from Operations
-	Expenses Incurred	-	Cash Paid for Operations
=	Net Income	=	Net Cash Provided by Operating Activities

DIRECT METHOD

To Compute Net Cash Provided by Operating Activities:

	Cash Received From Customers
+	Interest and Dividends Received
+	Other Operating Cash Receipts
-	Cash Paid for Operating Expenses and Merchandise Inventory
-	Interest Paid
-	Income Taxes Paid
-	Other Operating Cash Payments
=	Net Cash Provided by Operating Activities

Explanation: The major classes of cash receipts and cash payments from operating activities (for which selected computations are shown below) are listed and summarized on the face of the statement of cash flows when the direct method is used.

To Convert Revenues Earned to Cash Received:

	Revenues Earned
-	Increase in Accounts Receivable
+	Increase in Unearned Revenues
=	Cash Received from Customers

Explanation: An increase in accounts receivable from one balance sheet date to the next indicates that revenues earned exceed cash collections from customers; hence, subtract the increase in accounts receivable from sales revenue to obtain the amount of cash received from customers. (A decrease in receivables would indicate cash collections exceed revenues earned and would be added to revenues earned to compute cash collections.) An increase in unearned revenues indicates that cash collections from customers exceed revenues earned; hence, add the increase in unearned revenues to revenues earned to obtain the amount of cash received from customers.

ILLUSTRATION 24-2 (Continued)

OR

	Revenues Earned
+	Beginning Accounts Receivable
-	Ending Accounts Receivable
-	Beginning Unearned Revenues
+	<u>Ending Unearned Revenues</u>
=	Cash Received from Customers

Explanation: The balance of accounts receivable at the beginning of the period represents revenues earned in a prior period that are collected in the current period; ending accounts receivable stem from revenues earned in the current period that are not yet collected. Beginning unearned revenues represent cash collections in a prior period (not the current period) that are for revenues earned in the current period. Ending unearned revenues come from collections during the current period that are not recognized as earned revenues.

To Convert Cost of Goods Sold to Cash Paid:

	Cost of Goods Sold Expense
+	<u>Increase in Inventory</u>
=	Purchases
-	<u>Increase in Accounts Payable</u>
=	Cash Paid for Merchandise Inventory

Explanation: An increase in inventory means purchases for the period exceed cost of goods sold. An increase in accounts payable indicates purchases exceed cash payments for merchandise. (Decreases indicate opposite relationships.)

OR

	Cost of Goods Sold Expense
-	Beginning Inventory
+	<u>Ending Inventory</u>
=	Purchases
+	Beginning Accounts Payable (for purchases of merchandise)
-	Ending Accounts Payable (for <u>purchases of merchandise)</u>
=	Cash Paid for Merchandise Inventory

Explanation: Beginning inventory represents items purchased in a prior period that were consumed (sold) in the current year. Ending inventory represents items purchased in the current period that are not reported in the cost of goods sold expense (because they are on hand at the balance sheet date). Beginning accounts payable come from purchases of a prior period (as opposed to purchases of the current period) that require cash payment during the current period. The ending accounts payable balance stems from purchases in the current period that are not paid for in the current period.

To Convert Operating Expenses to Cash Paid:

	Operating Expenses Incurred (**Excluding** Depreciation and Bad Debt Expense)
+	Increase in Prepaid Expenses
-	<u>Increase in Accrued Payables</u>
=	Cash Paid for Operating Expenses

Explanation: An increase in a prepaid expense indicates expenses incurred are less than cash payments for those items. Therefore, the increase in the prepaid is added to the expense total to obtain the amount of related cash payments. An increase in accrued payables indicates the expense total exceeds the cash payments for these items; hence, the increase in accrued payables is deducted from the expense balance to arrive at cash payments.

ILLUSTRATION 24-2 (Continued)

OR

Operating Expenses Incurred
   (**Excluding** Depreciation and
   Bad Debt Expense)
- Beginning Prepaid Expenses
+ Ending Prepaid Expenses
+ Beginning Accrued Payables
- Ending Accrued Payables
= Cash Paid for Operating
   Expenses

Explanation: Beginning prepaid expenses represent amounts recognized as expense in the current period for which cash payments are not made in the current period. (The cash payments occurred in a prior period.) Ending prepaids stem from cash payments in the current period for expenses not recognized in the current period. (The expense recognition is being deferred to a future period.) Beginning accrued payables come from expenses recognized in a prior period (not the current year) that require cash payments during the current period. Ending accrued payables stem from expenses recognized during the current year that have not yet been paid.

To Convert Interest Expense to Interest Paid:

   Interest Expense
- Increase in Interest Payable
- Amortization of Discount on Debt
+ Amortization of Premium on Debt
= Interest Paid

Explanation: An increase in an accrued payable indicates that expense exceeds the related cash payments. (A decrease in an accrued payable would indicate the opposite relationship—that expense is less than cash payments.) The amortization of discount on a debt increases total interest expense but does not cause a cash outlay; the amortization of premium on a debt instrument decreases total interest expense but does not reduce the cash outlay required for the interest.

OR

   Interest Expense
+ Beginning Interest Payable
- Ending Interest Payable
- Amortization of Discount on Debt
+ Amortization of Premium on Debt
= Interest Paid

Explanation: The balance of Interest Payable at the beginning of the period comes from interest expense accrued in a prior period. Therefore, that amount requires a cash outlay in the current period that relates to an expense of a prior period. The ending balance of Interest Payable comes from interest accrued in the current period. Therefore, this amount is part of the total interest expense for the current period but it is not part of the cash paid for interest this period. The amortization of discount on a debt instrument increases total interest expense but does not cause a cash outlay; the amortization of premium on a debt instrument decreases total interest expense but does not decrease the corresponding cash outflow.

ILLUSTRATION 24-2 (Continued)

**To Convert Income Tax Expense
to Income Taxes Paid:**

    Income Tax Expense
+   Increase in Prepaid Income Taxes
-   Increase in Income Tax Payable
+   Increase in Deferred Tax Asset
-   <u>Increase in Deferred Tax Liability</u>
=   Income Taxes Paid

Explanation: An increase in Prepaid Income Taxes and/or an increase in Deferred Tax Asset indicates that the amount of income tax expense is less than the amount paid for income taxes during the period. An increase in Income Tax Payable and/or an increase in Deferred Tax Liability indicates that the amount of income tax expense exceeds the amount paid for income taxes during the period.

OR

    Income Tax Expense
-   Beginning Prepaid Income Taxes
+   Ending Prepaid Income Taxes
+   Beginning Income Tax Payable
-   Ending Income Tax Payable
-   Beginning Deferred Tax Asset
+   Ending Deferred Tax Asset
+   Beginning Deferred Tax Liability
-   <u>Ending Deferred Tax Liability</u>
=   Income Taxes Paid

Explanation: A beginning prepaid income tax amount represents taxes recognized as expense in the current period for which a cash payment was made in a prior period. An ending prepaid income tax amount stems from cash payments in the current period for taxes to be expensed in a future period (rather than in the current period). A beginning income tax payable balance stems from income tax expense recognized in a prior period (not the current period) that requires cash payments during the current period. An ending balance in Income Tax Payable stems from income taxes recognized as expense in the current period that have not yet been paid. The treatment of the balance of Deferred Tax Asset is the same as for Prepaid Income Taxes, and the treatment of the balance of Deferred Tax Liability is the same as for Income Tax Payable.

TIP: For all of the items above, a **decrease** in an account balance will be handled in a manner **opposite** of the way an **increase** is to be treated.

ILLUSTRATION 24-2 (Continued)

INDIRECT METHOD

To Compute Net Cash Provided
by Operating Activities:
 Net income
Add noncash charges (such as depreciation
 expense and amortization of intangibles)
Add losses due to writedown of assets
Add losses on sale of assets, settlement of
 debt, and discontinued operations
Add (deduct) decrease (increase) in net
 accounts receivable
Add (deduct) decrease (increase) in accrued
 receivables
Add (deduct) decrease (increase) in
 inventory
Add (deduct) decrease (increase) in prepaid
 expenses
Add (deduct) decrease (increase) in deferred
 tax assets
Add (deduct) increase (decrease) in accounts
 payable
Add (deduct) increase (decrease) in accrued
 payables
Add (deduct) increase (decrease) in unearned
 revenues
Add (deduct) increase (decrease) in deferred
 tax liabilities
Add (deduct) increase (decrease) in accrued
 pension liability
Deduct noncash credits (such as amortization
 of premium on bonds payable and income
 recognized under equity method in excess
 of dividends received)
Deduct noncash gains (such as unrealized
 holding gain on investment in trading
 securities)
Deduct gains on sale of assets, settlement of
 of debt, and discontinued operations
 Net cash provided by operating activities

Explanation: Noncash charges (such as depreciation and amortization) and losses due to writedown of assets are **added** to net income because they are expense or loss items that do not require an outlay of cash. Losses (or gains) from the sale of assets, settlement of debt, and discontinued operations are **added** to (or deducted from) net income because they relate to transactions for which the related cash flows are to be classified as investing or financing activities. An increase in receivables indicates that revenues earned **exceed** cash inflows; therefore, net income **exceeds** net cash provided by operating activities. An increase in inventory or prepaid expenses indicates that expenses are **less** than cash outflows; hence, net income is **more** than net cash provided by operating activities. Increases in accounts receivable, accrued receivables, inventory, and prepaid expenses must therefore be **deducted** from net income to obtain the amount of cash generated by operations. On the other hand, an increase in accounts payable or accrued payables indicates that expenses incurred **exceed** the amount of cash paid for merchandise inventory and operating expenses. An increase in unearned revenues indicates that revenue earned is **less** than the cash received and net income is **less** than net cash generated by operations. Therefore, increases in accounts payable, accrued payables, and unearned revenues must be **added** to net income to compute the amount of cash generated by operations. Noncash credits (such as the recognition of income using the equity method) are **deducted** from net income because they increase net income without having a corresponding cash inflow.

ILLUSTRATION 24-2 (Continued)

SUMMARY OF TREATMENT FOR ACCRUALS AND DEFERRALS

The treatment of increases during the period for deferred revenues, deferred expenses, accrued expenses, and accrued revenues can be summarized for both the direct method and the indirect method as follows:

	Direct Method		Indirect Method
	Revenues	Expenses	Net Income
Increase in Unearned Revenues	+		+
Increase in Prepaid Expenses		+	-
Increase in Payables		-	+
Increase in Receivables			
	Cash Received From Operations	Cash Paid For Operations	Net Cash Provided by Operating Activities

TIP: In examining the summary above, notice the mathematical signs are the **same** for both the direct method and indirect method for handling a change in unearned revenues or a change in receivables. The reasons for this are (1) changes in unearned revenues and receivables are items which explain the difference between revenues earned during a period and cash received from operations; and (2) revenues earned are a **positive** component of net income, and cash received from operations is a **positive** component of net cash provided by operating activities.

Also notice that the mathematical signs are **different** for the direct method and the indirect method for handling a change in prepaid expenses and payables. The reasons for this are (1) changes in prepaid expenses and payables are items which explain the difference between expenses incurred during a period and cash paid for operations; and (2) expenses incurred are a **negative** component of net income, and cash paid out for operations is a **negative** component of net cash provided by operating activities.

TIP: "Cash provided by operating activities" (or "cash provided by operations") is another name for "net income on a cash basis."

EXERCISE 24-1

Purpose: (L.O.6) This exercise will provide you with an opportunity to prepare a statement of cash flows without a check figure.

The following selected transactions and events and account balances pertain to Feudens, Inc.

Selected Transactions and Events for 1999

1.	Reported net income for 1999	$ 52,000
2.	Purchased plant assets	18,000
3.	Reclassified mortgage note payable to current portion of mortgage note payable	22,000
4.	Appropriated retained earnings for future expansion	40,000
5.	Paid long-term note payable	10,500
6.	Recorded depreciation on plant assets	9,200
7.	Amortized discount on long-term note payable	140
8.	Issued common stock (par $12,000) for cash	24,000
9.	Declared and paid cash dividends	8,500
10.	Issued short-term nontrade note payable	4,500
11.	Converted bonds with a par value of $20,000 and a book value of $20,200 to common stock with a market value of $25,000 and par value of $10,000. The book value method was used so no gain or loss was recognized.	

Selected Account Balances:		12/31/99	12/31/98	Increase (Decrease)
12.	Accounts Receivable (net)	$ 14,000	$ 17,500	$ (3,500)
13.	Inventory	34,000	29,000	5,000
14.	Allowance for Inventory Obsolescence	1,900	1,700	200
15.	Accounts Payable	16,000	15,200	800
16.	Accrued Interest Payable	320	400	(80)
17.	Patents	12,500	14,000	(1,500)
18.	Deferred Tax Liability (noncurrent)	5,600	4,900	700
19.	Investment in Land	69,000	40,000	29,000
20.	Current Portion of Mtg. Note Payable	22,000	28,000	(6,000)
21.	Plant Assets	96,000	84,000	12,000
22.	Accumulated Depreciation—Plant Assets	39,200	32,000	7,200
23.	Loss on Sale of Plant Assets	1,700		1,700
24.	Cash	?	7,000	?

Instructions

Prepare a statement of cash flows using the indirect method to present net cash provided by operating activities. Prepare a separate schedule for noncash financing and investing activities.

TIP: You are not given information regarding the ending balance of the Cash account. You must compute the change in the cash balance by successfully identifying the inflows and outflows of cash due to operating, investing, and financing activities.

Solution to Exercise 24-1

Feudens, Inc.
STATEMENT OF CASH FLOWS
For the Year Ending December 31, 1999

Cash flows from operating activities:
Net income $ 52,000
Adjustments to reconcile net income to net cash provided
  by operating activities:

Depreciation	$ 9,200	
Amortization of discount on note payable	140	
Decrease in net accounts receivable	3,500	
Increase in inventory (net)	(4,800)	
Increase in accounts payable	800	
Decrease in accrued interest payable	(80)	
Amortization of patents	1,500	
Increase in deferred tax liability	700	
Loss on sale of plant assets	1,700	12,660
Net cash provided by operating activities		64,660

Cash flows from investing activities:

Purchase of plant assets	(18,000)	
Purchase of land as an investment	(29,000)	
Sale of plant assets	2,300	
Net cash used by investing activities		(44,700)

Cash flows from financing activities:

Issuance of short-term debt	4,500	
Payments on mortgage payable	(28,000)	
Payments to settle long-term debt	(10,500)	
Issuance of common stock	24,000	
Payment of cash dividend	(8,500)	
Net cash used by financing activities		(18,500)

Net increase in cash	1,460
Cash balance at beginning of period	7,000
Cash balance at end of period	$ 8,460

Schedule of Noncash Investing and Financing Activities
Issuance of common stock upon conversion of bonds payable $ 20,200

Approach: Take each fact given and think about where it is reflected on a statement of cash flows. Using abbreviations, write in the margin beside each fact a brief description of what to do with the item. Set up the format for the statement of cash flows by placing the major headings for the three activity classifications approximately where they go. Leave space to fill in the details later (allow about one-fourth of the page for investing activities, about one-fourth of the page for financing activities, and approximately one-half of the page for the operating activities section). Then take each fact in order and process it by placing it where it belongs on the statement.

1.   Reconstruct the journal entries for the selected transactions and events and the most likely transactions that caused the selected account balances to change. Examine each entry to identify if there is an inflow of cash (debit to Cash), or an outflow of cash (credit to Cash), or no effect on cash.
2.   Write down the definitions for investing activities, financing activities, and operating activities. Analyze each transaction to see if it fits one of these definitions.
3.   Identify the items requiring adjustments to net income to convert net income to net cash provided by operating activities by identifying the reconstructed journal entries that involve an income statement account and a balance sheet account **other than** Cash. Often, these are entries that involve accruals or deferrals of revenues or expenses.
4.   Assume purchases and sales of items are for cash unless otherwise indicated.

Explanation:

1.   Net income is the starting point for determining the amount of net cash provided by operating activities. Net income is a summary of all revenues earned, all expenses incurred, and all gains and losses recognized for a period. Most revenues earned during the year result in a cash inflow during the same year, but some cash and revenue flows do not correspond. Most expenses incurred during the year result in a cash outflow during the same year, but some cash and expense flows do not correspond.

2.   The journal entry to record the purchase of the plant asset is reconstructed as follows:

         Plant Assets 18,000
             Cash   18,000

Cash decreases by $18,000 (a cash outflow). The acquisition of property, plant and equipment is an investing activity. This transaction is to be reported as an investing outflow.

3.   The journal entry to reclassify long-term mortgage note payable to current portion of mortgage note payable is reconstructed as follows:

         Long-Term Mortgage Note Payable 22,000
             Current Portion of Mortgage Note Payable.......... 22,000

Cash is not affected. The exchange of one liability for another is a noncash financing activity that is to be disclosed. This item is not a true exchange of one liability for another but some accountants treat it as such because it is similar to one. Therefore, with regard to the reporting requirements for a statement of cash flows, this reclassification is either to be included in the supplementary schedule of noncash investing and financing activities or ignored. For the solution to this exercise, the transaction will be ignored.

4.   The journal entry to appropriate retained earnings for future expansion is reconstructed as follows:

         Retained Earnings—Unappropriated........................... 40,000
             Appropriation of Retained Earnings
                 for Future Expansion   40,000

Cash is not affected. This transaction changes two retained earnings accounts, but it does not represent an investing or financing activity. This transaction is ignored when reporting the statement of cash flows.

5. The journal entry to record the payment of the long-term note payable is reconstructed as follows:

Long-Term Note Payable	10,500	
Cash		10,500

    There is a cash outflow of $10,500. The payment of amounts borrowed is a financing activity. This transaction is to be shown as a financing outflow.

6. The journal entry to record the depreciation on plant assets is reconstructed as follows:

Depreciation Expense	9,200	
Accumulated Depreciation		9,200

    Cash is not affected. This transaction is neither an investing nor a financing activity. Depreciation expense reduces net income. Using the indirect method, depreciation expense must be added to net income to compute the net cash provided by operating activities.

7. The journal entry to record the amortization of discount on long-term note payable is reconstructed as follows:

Interest Expense	140	
Discount on Long-Term Note Payable		140

    Cash is not affected. This transaction is neither an investing nor a financing activity. Amortization of discount on debt reduces net income because it increases interest expense. Using the indirect method, this noncash charge to income must be added back to net income to compute the net cash provided by operating activities.

    > **TIP:** The treatment would be the same if the note was short-term rather than long-term.

8. The journal entry to record the issuance of stock for cash is reconstructed as follows:

Cash	24,000	
Common Stock		12,000
Paid-in Capital in Excess of Par		12,000

    Cash increases by $24,000 (a cash inflow). Obtaining resources from owners is a financing activity. This transaction is to be reported as a financing inflow on the statement of cash flows.

    > **TIP:** Notice that this transaction is reported by a single line item on the statement of cash flows even though it caused two stockholder equity accounts to change.

9.   The journal entries to record the declaration and payment of cash dividends are reconstructed as follows:

Retained Earnings	8,500	
Dividends Payable		8,500
Dividends Payable	8,500	
Cash		8,500

Cash decreases by $8,500. Providing owners with a return on their investment constitutes a financing activity. The declaration of dividends has no effect on cash. The payment of a previously declared dividend reduces cash. The payment of cash dividends is to be reported as a financing outflow.

10.   The journal entry to record the issuance of a short-term nontrade note payable is reconstructed as follows (assume the note was issued for cash):

Cash	4,500	
Short-Term Note Payable		4,500

Cash increases by $4,500. Borrowing money is a financing activity. This transaction is to be reported as a financing inflow.

> **TIP:**   The treatment would be the same for the issuance of a long-term nontrade note payable.
>
> **TIP:**   In the case where a trade note payable is issued, the assumption would be that it was issued for merchandise rather than cash. Therefore, the increase in a trade note payable would indicate that purchases exceed cash outlays for merchandise, and net income is less than net cash provided by operating activities. Thus, the issuance of a trade note payable (short-term or long-term) would be shown as an addition to net income when using the indirect method for the statement of cash flows.

11.   The journal entry to record the conversion of bonds payable to common stock is reconstructed as follows:

Bonds Payable	20,000	
Premium on Bonds Payable	200	
Common Stock		10,000
Paid-in Capital in Excess of Par		10,200

Cash is not affected. The issuance of stock is a financing activity and so is the settlement of debt. This transaction is to be reported in the schedule of noncash financing and investing activities.

12.   A decrease in net accounts receivable results from cash collections from customers or from the recording of bad debts expense or from a combination of the two. Ignoring the estimate for bad debt expense for the period, a decrease in net accounts receivable indicates that cash collections from customers exceed credit sales; therefore, the amount of decrease is added to net income in reconciling net income to net cash provided by operating activities. In examining the journal entry to record bad debt

expense, we find the entry reduces net income (because of the debit to Bad Debt Expense) but does not affect Cash. (The credit is to Allowance for Doubtful Accounts.) It is a noncash charge to income. Therefore, regardless of the reason(s) for a decrease in net accounts receivable, the decrease is added to net income to compute the net cash provided by operating activities.

13.   An increase in Inventory occurs when purchases of inventory for the period exceed withdrawals. Assume all purchases are for cash. The amount of withdrawals is reflected in net income as cost of goods sold. Therefore, the $5,000 increase in Inventory is deducted from net income to arrive at net cash provided by operations.

14.   The Allowance for Inventory Obsolescence account increased due to the write down of inventory. The entry to record obsolescence is reconstructed as follows:

Loss Due to Obsolescence	200	
Allowance for Inventory Obsolescence...............		200

Cash is not affected, but net income decreases. This noncash charge to income must be added back when computing the net cash provided by operating activities.

> **TIP:**   The net change in inventory is a $4,800 increase ($5,000 - $200 = $4,800).

15.   The increase in Accounts Payable results when cash payments are less than the cost of goods and services acquired on credit. Assuming the goods and services have been consumed and charged to income, expenses are more than the cash payments for operating items. Therefore, the increase in the Accounts Payable account is added to net income to compute the net cash provided by operating activities.

16.   The decrease in Accrued Interest Payable results from an excess of cash payments for interest during the period over the amount of interest expense charged to income for the same period. The amount of expense is reflected in the net income figure; whereas, the amount of cash payments is to be reflected in the amount of net cash provided by operations. Therefore, the amount of decrease in the payable account is deducted from net income in computing net cash provided by operating activities.

17.   The most common reason for the Patents account to decrease is the periodic amortization of patents. The journal entry to record that amortization is reconstructed as follows:

Patent Amortization Expense.....................................	1,500	
Patents		1,500

Cash is not affected. This transaction is neither a financing nor an investing activity. The amortization expense reduces net income without a corresponding outlay of cash. Using the indirect method, the amortization expense is added to net income to arrive at net cash provided by operating activities.

18.   Anytime there is a change in the balance of a deferred income tax account, the other half of the entry to record that change involves the Income Tax Expense account. Therefore, the adjustment to record the increase in the Deferred Tax Liability account is reconstructed as follows:

Income Tax Expense...	700	
Deferred Tax Liability...		700

Cash is not affected. This transaction does not involve an investing or financing activity. The recording of a deferred income tax liability reduces net income without a corresponding outlay of cash. Therefore, it is added to net income to arrive at net cash provided by operating activities.

> **TIP:** The analysis and the results are the same, regardless of whether a deferred income tax account is classified as current or noncurrent.

19. The most common reason for an increase in an investment account is the acquisition of an investment. The acquisition is assumed to be by cash payment since there is no indication otherwise. The journal entry to record the acquisition of a new plot of land for an investment is as follows:

Investment in Land...	29,000	
Cash		29,000

There is a cash outflow of $29,000. The purchase of an investment represents an investing activity. Therefore, this transaction is to be reported as an investing outflow.

20. The Current Portion of Mortgage Note Payable account decreased $6,000, even though $22,000 was reclassified from the long-term classification.

> **TIP:** Whenever the change in an account balance is due to more than one transaction or event, it is wise to draw a T-account. Enter the information that relates to the data given; solve for any other transactions causing a change in the account balance. Assume the most common transaction occurred to cause any unexplained change in the account balance.

The T-account for the Current Portion of Mortgage Note Payable for Feudens would appear as follows:

Current Portion of Mortgage Note Payable

Unexplained transaction during 1999	28,000	Jan. 1, 1999 Balance	28,000
		Reclassified during 1999	22,000
		Dec. 31, 1999 Balance	22,000

The most common reason for a debit to a debt account is a payment. The journal entry to record the payment is reconstructed as follows:

Current Portion of Mortgage Note Payable	28,000	
Cash		28,000

There is an outflow of cash. Repayment of money borrowed is a financing activity. Therefore, the payment is reported as a financing outflow of $28,000.

> **TIP:** This is a discriminating point in this exercise; it is the most difficult transaction in this problem for students to detect and treat properly.

21.   (and 22. and 23.) The T-accounts for Plant Assets, Accumulated Depreciation—Plant Assets, and Loss on Sale of Plant Assets would appear as follows:

Plant Assets				
Jan. 1, 1999 Balance	84,000	Unexplained transaction		
Acquisitions during 1999	18,000	during 1999		6,000
Dec. 31, 1999 Balance	96,000			

Accumulated Depreciation--Plant Assets				
Unexplained transaction		Jan. 1, 1999 Balance		32,000
during 1999	2,000	Depreciation for 1999		9,200
		Dec. 31, 1999 Balance		39,200

Loss on Sale of Plant Assets		
Sale of assets during 1999	1,700	

The $18,000 purchase of plant assets was analyzed in Item No. 2 above and the $9,200 charge for depreciation was analyzed in Item No. 6 above.

The most common reason for a credit to the Plant Assets account is the disposal of a plant asset. That transaction also explains the $2,000 reduction in the Accumulated Depreciation—Plant Assets account and the recording of a $1,700 loss. Thus, it appears that an asset with a cost of $6,000 and a book value of $4,000 ($6,000 - $2,000 = $4,000) was sold at a loss of $1,700. This means the cash proceeds amounted to $2,300 ($4,000 book value - $1,700 loss = $2,300 proceeds). The journal entry to record the disposal is reconstructed as follows:

Cash	2,300	
Loss on Sale of Plant Assets......................................	1,700	
Accumulated Depreciation—Plant Assets	2,000	
Plant Assets..		6,000

There is an inflow of $2,300 cash due to an investing activity. Under the indirect method, the loss of $1,700 must be added back to net income because it is a noncash charge (debit) on the income statement; it reduced net income but it had no effect on cash.

> **TIP:** This is a discriminating point in this exercise; it is the second most difficult transaction for students to detect and treat properly in this problem.
>
> **TIP:** Plant Assets (or Property, Plant, and Equipment) is a classification of accounts, not one account. There is a separate account in the ledger for each plant asset. For simplicity of analysis in this chapter, however, we often treat these items as being in one account.

24.   The last step is to subtotal each of the three activity classifications. Inflows are shown as positive amounts; outflows are shown as negative amounts. An excess of inflows over outflows in a category results in a net inflow; an excess of outflows over inflows is

captioned as a net outflow. The subtotals of the three activities are then summarized to determine the net change in cash during the year. That change is used to reconcile the beginning and ending cash balances. In this exercise, only the beginning cash balance is known; the ending cash balance is derived from combining the beginning balance with the net change in cash.

EXERCISE 24-2

Purpose: (L.O.6) This exercise will provide examples of transactions and their treatment on a statement of cash flows using the indirect method.

CODE FOR FORMAT OF STATEMENT OF CASH FLOWS FOR USE WITH EXERCISE 24-2
(Read Instructions for use below)

Code Items	Format of the Statement
	Cash flows from operating activities:
	Net income (loss).
A	Add noncash expenses (charges), losses, and changes in certain accounts needed to convert income to a cash basis.
D	Deduct noncash revenue (credits), gains, and changes in certain accounts needed to convert income to a cash basis.
	Net cash provided (used by operating activities).
	Cash flows from investing activities:
II	Add amount for an **investing** activity that produced a cash **inflow**.
IO	Deduct amount for an **investing** activity that resulted in a cash **outflow**.
	Net cash provided (used) by investing activities.
	Cash flows from financing activities:
FI	Add amount for a **financing** activity that produced a cash **inflow**.
FO	Deduct amount for a **financing** activity that produced a cash **outflow**.
	Net cash provided (used) by financing activities.
	Net increase (decrease) in cash and cash equivalents.
	Cash and cash equivalents at beginning of year.
	Cash and cash equivalents at end of year.
NI	Use this code for a transaction which is an operating activity and a component of net income that has the same effect (positive or negative) on cash as it has on the net income calculation.
NC	Use this code for a noncash financing and/or investing activity to be reported on a separate schedule.
C	Use this code to refer to a transaction which only affects cash and cash equivalents.
X	Use this code for a transaction or event which is not reported or otherwise reflected on the statement of cash flows.

Instructions

For each of the following transactions and events, indicate how it should be reported in a statement of cash flows using the indirect approach. Use the code from the format above for short-hand notations for your responses. Include the appropriate dollar amount with each code. A transaction or event may require more than one code for a complete answer.

_____ $_____ 1. Borrow $50,000 by issuance of a short-term note payable.

_____ $_____
_____ $_____ 2. Sell land used in operations: Selling price, $15,000; cost, $3,500.

_____ $_____
_____ $_____ 3. Exchange long-term mortgage note receivable for stock in another company: Carrying value of receivable, $38,000; fair value of the stock, $36,000. The shares of stock are to be classified as available-for-sale securities.

_____ $_____ 4. Repay short-term nontrade note payable, $5,100.

_____ $_____ 5. Declare and distribute 10% stock dividend: Par value, $10,000; market value, $18,000.

_____ $_____ 6. Pay administrative salaries for the current period, $56,000.

_____ $_____ 7. Accrue interest expense, $1,500.

_____ $_____ 8. Accrue rent revenue, $1,800.

_____ $_____ 9. Collect magazine subscription revenue in advance, $9,000.

_____ $_____
_____ $_____ 10. Recognize revenue of $5,000 from investment using the equity method of accounting. Collect $1,800 dividends from that investee.

_____ $_____ 11. Receive subscription contracts for common stock: Par value, $10,000; subscription price, $24,000.

_____ $_____ 12. Collect $6,000 down payment on stock subscriptions in item #11 above.

_____ $_____ 13. Issue common stock upon the exercise of noncompensatory stock options: Option price, $25,000; par, $10,000.

_____ $_____ 14. Acquire machine by exchange of treasury stock: Par value, $10,000; cost of treasury stock, $18,000; market value of stock, $22,000.

_____ $_____ 15. Acquire machinery by issuance of long-term note payable to the seller: Face amount of note, $50,000; stated interest rate 2%; fair value of machinery, $40,000.

_____ $_____ 16. Amortize premium on bonds payable, $200.

_____ $_____ 17. Record increase in deferred income tax asset, $1,000.

_____ $_____ 18. Use $1,000 cash to purchase a 90-day certificate of deposit.

_____ $_____ 19. Record bad debt expense of $7,000.

_____ $_____
_____ $_____ 20. Settle long-term debt by transfer of a noncurrent investment: Carrying value of debt, $77,000; fair value of assets, $70,000; book vaue of assets, $70,000.

_____ $_____ 21. Amortize deferred service revenue of $600.

_____ $_____
_____ $_____ 22. Sell a plant asset for $1,000: Cost, $7,000; accumulated depreciation, $4,000.

_____ $_____
_____ $_____
_____ $_____ 23. Exchange old truck for new truck and give boot of $11,000: Cost of old truck, $10,000; book value of old truck, $3,000; fair value of old truck, $2,200; list price of new truck, $14,500.

_____ $_____ 24. Recognize temporary decline of $7,000 in fair value of investment in equity securities classified as trading securities.

_____ $_____ 25. Sell merchandise for $400 cash.

_____ $_____ 26. Pay advertising fees of $1,600 for the current period.

_____ $_____ 27. Pay interest charges of $5,000.

_____ $_____ 28. Appropriate $10,000 of retained earnings for future plant expansion.

_____ $_____ 29. Purchase treasury stock: Cost, $7,500; par, $3,000; original issuance price, $7,000; cost method is used.

_____ $_____ 30. Repay short-term trade note payable, $5,700.

_____ $_____
_____ $_____ 31. Acquire a machine by a capital lease: Present value of minimum lease payments at inception, $75,000; first annual payment made at inception, $10,000.

_____ $_____
_____ $_____ 32. Extinguish long-term debt prior to maturity by cash payment of $78,000: Carrying value of debt, $88,000, tax rate is 40%.

Solution to Exercise 24-2

1.	FI	$50,000	17.	D	$1,000
2.	II	$15,000; & D $11,500	18.	C	$1,000
3.	NC	$36,000; & A $2,000	19.	A	$7,000
4.	FO	$5,100	20.	NC	$70,000; & D $7,000
5.	X	$18,000	21.	D	$600
6.	NI	$56,000	22.	II	$1,000; & A $2,000
7.	A	$1,500	23.	IO	$11,000; & A $800;
8.	D	$1,800			& NC $2,200
9.	A	$9,000	24.	A	$7,000
10.	D	$5,000; & A $1,800	25.	NI	$400
11.	X	$24,000 (or possibly	26.	NI	$1,600
		NC $24,000)	27.	NI	$5,000
12.	FI	$6,000	28.	X	$10,000
13.	FI	$25,000	29.	FO	$7,500
14.	NC	$22,000	30.	D	$5,700
15.	NC	$40,000	31.	NC	$75,000; & FO $10,000
16.	D	$200	32.	FO	$78,000; & D $10,000

Approach:

1. Reconstruct the journal entry for each transaction. Examine each entry to identify if there is an inflow of cash, an outflow of cash, or no effect on cash. Assume purchases and sales of items are for cash, unless otherwise indicated.

> **TIP:** The journal entry to record a transaction that is an investing activity which results in a cash flow will involve: (1) Cash and (2) an asset account other than Cash, such as Investment (short-term or long-term), Land, Building, Equipment, Patent, Franchise, etc.

> **TIP:** The journal entry to record a transaction that is a financing activity which results in a cash flow will involve: (1) Cash and (2) a liability account or an owners' equity account such as Bonds Payable, Notes Payable, Dividends Payable, Common Stock, Paid-in Capital in Excess of Par, Treasury Stock, etc.

2. Write down the definitions for investing activities and financing activities (see below). Analyze each transaction to see if it fits one of these definitions:

   a) **Investing activities**: include (1) making and collecting loans; (2) acquiring and disposing of investments in debt and equity instruments; and (3) acquiring and disposing of property, plant, and equipment.

   b) **Financing activities:** include (1) obtaining capital from owners and providing them with a return on and a return of their investment; (2) borrowing money and repaying the amounts borrowed, or otherwise settling the obligation; and (3) obtaining and paying for other resources obtained from creditors.

3.   Identify the items requiring adjustments to net income to convert net income to net cash provided by operating activities by identifying the reconstructed journal entries that involve (a) an income statement account and a balance sheet account other than Cash (for example the entry to record depreciation), or (b) the Cash account and a noncash asset or liability account that relates to operating activity (accounts receivable, inventory, accounts payable, etc.) or (c) a gain or loss that has no cash effect or a gain or loss stemming from a transaction that is classified as an investing or financing activity.

4.   Identify the items which are noncash financing and investing activities by identifying transactions which fit the definitions of investing activities and/or the definition of financing activities but do not affect Cash.

Explanation: The journal entries to record each transaction are reconstructed and analyzed below:

1.   Cash 50,000
           Short-term Note Payable (Nontrade)   50,000

      There is an inflow of cash due to a financing activity.

2.   Cash 15,000
           Land   3,500
           Gain on Sale of Land   11,500

      The cash proceeds from the sale of any asset are to be reflected as a cash inflow. Proceeds of $15,000 from the sale of a plant asset should be reported as an investing inflow. The proceeds of $15,000 represents a recovery of the asset's book value of $3,500 and a gain of $11,500. The gain of $11,500 is also a component of net income. When using the indirect method, the gain must be deducted from net income in reconciling net income with net cash from operating activities so that the $11,500 is not double counted.

3.   Available-for-Sale Securities 36,000
      Loss on Disposal of Investment 2,000
           Investment in Mortgage Note Receivable   38,000

      Cash is not affected. This exchange of one noncash asset for another noncash asset is an investing activity that must be disclosed. Regardless of whether this is a similar or dissimilar exchange of nonmonetary assets, a loss on the disposal of the receivable should be recognized on the income statement. That loss is added to net income when the indirect method is used for the statement of cash flows.

4.   Short-term Note Payable (Nontrade) 5,100
           Cash   5,100

      There is an outflow of cash due to a financing activity.

5. Retained Earnings 18,000
       Common Stock Dividend Distributable 10,000
       Paid-in Capital in Excess of Par 8,000

   Common Stock Dividend Distributable 10,000
       Common Stock 10,000

   Cash is not affected. There is no financing or investing or operating activity. This transaction is ignored in reporting the statement of cash flows. Other accounting requirements call for disclosure of this item because it changes stockholders' equity.

6. Salaries Expense 56,000
       Cash 56,000

   There is a $56,000 decrease in cash due to an operating outflow. There is a reduction of $56,000 reflected in the net income figure due to the expense recognition. When the indirect method is used, no adjustment is needed because this transaction reduced both net income and cash.

7. Interest Expense 1,500
       Interest Payable 1,500

   Net income is reduced but cash is not. This item is added to net income when the indirect method is used.

8. Rent Receivable 1,800
       Rent Revenue 1,800

   Net income is increased but cash is not. This item must be deducted from net income when the indirect method is used.

9. Cash 9,000
       Unearned Subscription Revenue 9,000

   Cash is increased because of collections from customers; this is an operating activity. The inflow is not reflected in net income so the $9,000 increase in unearned revenue is added to net income when the indirect method is used.

10. Investment in Affiliate 5,000
        Revenue from Investment 5,000

    Cash 1,800
        Investment in Affiliate 1,800

    There is a cash flow of $1,800; it is an operating inflow because all dividends received are operating inflows. The first entry increases revenue (and net income) but does not affect cash. The second entry increases cash but does not effect net income. Using the indirect method, the $5,000 credit to income which is not accompanied by a corresponding cash inflow is deducted from net income and the $1,800 cash receipt for dividends is added to net income. Thus, the net $3,200 undistributed earnings of investee is deducted from net income.

11. Stock Subscriptions Receivable... 24,000
         Common Stock Subscribed...   10,000
         Paid-in Capital in Excess of Par....................................   14,000

Cash is not affected. Some people argue that this is a noncash financing activity to be disclosed; others say it can be ignored when reporting the statement of cash flows.

12. Cash 6,000
         Stock Subscriptions Receivable   6,000

There is an inflow of cash from owners; it is a financing inflow.

> **TIP:** Recall that Stock Subscriptions Receivable is a contra stockholders' equity account.

13. Cash 25,000
         Common Stock...   10,000
         Paid-in Capital in Excess of Par....................................   15,000

There is an increase in cash as a result of a financing activity (the company is obtaining resources from owners).

14. Machinery 22,000
         Treasury Stock...   18,000
         Paid-in Capital from Treasury Stock.............................   4,000

Cash is not affected. This is a significant investing activity (acquisition of equipment) and financing activity (disposal of treasury stock) that must be disclosed outside the body of the statement of cash flows.

15. Machinery 40,000
     Discount on Note Payable 10,000
         Long-term Note Payable   50,000

A note payable is issued at an unreasonably low interest rate for a noncash asset; it is to be recorded at the fair value of the asset received. Thus, a discount is established. Cash is not affected. This is a significant investing and financing activity that must be disclosed in the footnotes or in a schedule of noncash investing and financing activities.

16. Premium on Bonds Payable 200
         Interest Expense   200

There is an increase in net income without any corresponding cash inflow. Therefore, this credit to income is deducted from net income in the reconciliation of net income to net cash flow from operating activities.

17. Deferred Tax Asset... 1,000
         Income Tax Expense.. 1,000

This entry causes net income to increase, but it does not affect cash. The increase in the deferred tax asset is deducted from net income when the indirect method is used.

18. Certificate of Deposit—90 Day.. 1,000
         Cash... 1,000

There is a decrease in cash and an increase in cash equivalents. Therefore, there is no change in the total of cash and cash equivalents.

19. Bad Debt Expense.. 7,000
         Allowance for Doubtful Accounts................................... 7,000

Net income decreases but cash does not. This noncash charge to income is added to net income when using the indirect method.

20. Long-term Debt... 77,000
         Long-term Investment... 70,000
         Gain on Settlement of Debt.. 7,000

Cash is not affected. This is a transaction that is a noncash financing and investing activity to be separately disclosed. When using the indirect method, the gain must be deducted from net income because the gain is a credit to net income that relates to a (noncash) financing activity.

21. Unearned Service Revenue.. 600
         Service Revenue... 600

There is an increase in net income, but no corresponding cash inflow. The $600 must be deducted from net income when using the indirect method.

22. Cash 1,000
     Accumulated Depreciation.. 4,000
     Loss on Disposal of Plant Asset 2,000
         Plant Asset... 7,000

There is a cash inflow of $1,000 related to an investing activity. When using the indirect method, the loss of $2,000 must be added back to net income because it is an effect of a transaction (sale of plant asset) that is an investing activity. That activity resulted in a cash inflow, not an outflow.

23. Truck ($11,000 + $2,200) 13,200
     Accumulated Depreciation ($10,000 - $3,000).......................... 7,000
     Loss on Disposal of Truck ($3,000 - $2,200) 800
         Truck 10,000
         Cash.. 11,000

There is an $11,000 cash outflow related to an investing activity (acquisition of property, plant and equipment). This exchange of similar productive assets results in a loss of $800 which must be added back to net income using the indirect method. The exchange of one noncash asset (book value of $2,200 after the write-down for impairment) for another must be disclosed as a noncash investing activity.

24.   Unrealized Holding Gain or Loss—Income 7,000
          Securities Fair Value Adjustment (Trading)   7,000

There is a noncash charge to income. It is added to net income under the use of the indirect method.

> **TIP:** If the securities were classified as available-for-sale, there would be no impact on the statement of cash flows because the change in the fair value adjustment account for the available-for-sale category is **not** reported as a component of net income.

25.   Cash 400
          Sales Revenue   400

There is an inflow of cash due to an operating activity. The effect on cash is the same as the effect on net income.

26.   Advertising Expense 1,600
          Cash   1,600

There is an outflow of cash due to an operating activity. The effect on cash is the same as the effect on net income.

27.   Interest Expense 5,000
          Cash   5,000

There is a cash outflow due to an operating activity. The effect on cash is the same as the effect of net income.

28.   Retained Earnings 10,000
          Retained Earnings Appropriated for Plant Expansion   10,000

Cash is not affected. There is no investing, financing, or operating activity. Therefore, there is no disclosure of this item in connection with the reporting requirements for a statement of cash flows.

29.   Treasury Stock 7,500
          Cash   7,500

There is an outflow of cash for a financing activity (return of investment to owner).

30.   Short-term Note Payable (Trade)...   5,700
          Cash..   5,700

The payment of a trade note is an operating activity. The outflow is not reflected in net income. The $5,700 decrease in the trade note payable is, therefore, deducted from net income to compute net cash flow from operating activities.

31.   Machine Under Capital Lease..   75,000
          Obligation Under Capital Lease...   75,000

       Obligation Under Capital Lease..   10,000
          Cash..   10,000

The inception of the lease is a transaction that qualifies as a noncash investing and financing activity that requires disclosure. The first lease payment results in a cash outflow due to a financing activity.

32.   Long-term Debt...   88,000
          Cash..   78,000
          Gain on Extinguishment of Debt (Extraordinary)   10,000

       Gain on Extinguishment of Debt (Extraordinary).......................   4,000
          Cash ($10,000 x 40%)..   4,000

The payment of $78,000 to the creditor results in an outflow of cash for a financing activity. The extraordinary gain of $10,000 must be reported net of tax on the income statement. However, all income taxes paid are to be classified on the statement of cash flows as operating cash outflows. Therefore, the **gross** gain of $10,000 must be deducted from net income when the indirect method is used for the statement of cash flows. The $78,000 payment to the creditor is shown as a financing outflow. The $4,000 payment of taxes is reflected in the net cash flow from operating activities figure because a net gain of $6,000 is part of net income and the gross gain of $10,000 is deducted in the reconciliation of net income to net cash flow from operating activities.

> **TIP:**   Transactions resulting in extraordinary gains and losses can be rather difficult to handle on the statement of cash flows.

ILLUSTRATION 24-3
HOW TO PREPARE A STATEMENT OF CASH FLOWS—INDIRECT METHOD

I.   **Gather the materials needed** which include information from or about the following:
    A.   Comparative balance sheets.
    B.   Income statement.
    C.   Statement of retained earnings (or statement of stockholders' equity).
    D.   Details of certain transactions and/or account balances.

II. **Compute and present the net cash inflow (or outflow) from operations** by converting the net income figure from the accrual basis to a cash basis:
    A.   **Add back charges reflected in net income which did not require a cash outlay,** such as:
        1.   Depreciation expense.
        2.   Amortization of intangible assets.
        3.   Amortization of discount on bonds payable.

    B.   **Add back losses reflected in net income which did not require a cash outlay,** such as:
        1.   Loss due to obsolescence of inventory.
        2.   Loss due to write-off of patent.
        3.   Unrealized holding loss on investment in trading securities.

    C.   **Add back losses reflected in net income which arose from** transactions and events that are **investing or financing activities** such as:
        1.   Loss on sale of plant assets.
        2.   Loss on settlement of debt.
        3.   Loss on sale of investment.
        4.   Loss on discontinued operations.

    D.   **Add decreases in certain assets accounts** which resulted from transactions of an operating nature that cause a difference between accrual basis income and cash basis income, such as:
        1.   Decrease in net accounts receivable.
        2.   Decrease in accrued receivables.
        3.   Decrease in inventories.
        4.   Decrease in prepaid expenses.
        5.   Decrease in deferred tax assets.

    E.   **Add increases in certain liability accounts** which resulted from transactions of an operating nature that cause a difference between accrual basis income and cash basis income, such as:
        1.   Increase in accounts payable.
        2.   Increase in accrued payables.
        3.   Increase in unearned revenues.
        4.   Increase in deferred tax liabilities.
        5.   Increase in accrued pension liability.

    F.   **Deduct credits reflected in net income which did not have a corresponding cash inflow,** such as:
        1.   Amortization of premium on bonds payable.
        2.   Recognition of investment income using the equity method in excess of cash dividends received.

    G.   **Deduct gains reflected in net income which did not have a corresponding cash inflow,** such as:
        1.   Unrealized holding gain on investment in trading securities.

    H.   **Deduct gains** reflected in net income **which arose from** transactions and events that are **investing or financing activities,** such as:
        1.   Gain on sale of plant assets.
        2.   Gain on settlement of debt.
        3.   Gain on sale of investment.
        4.   Gain on discontinued operations.

ILLUSTRATION 24-3 (Continued)

I.   **Deduct increases in certain asset accounts** which resulted from transactions of an operating nature that cause a difference between accrual basis income and cash basis income, such as:
   1.   Increase in net accounts receivable.
   2.   Increase in accrued receivables.
   3.   Increase in inventories.
   4.   Increase in prepaid expenses.
   5.   Increase in deferred tax assets.

J.   **Deduct decreases in certain liability accounts** which resulted from transactions of an operating nature that cause a difference between accrual basis income and cash basis income, such as:
   1.   Decrease in accounts payable.
   2.   Decrease in accrued payables.
   3.   Decrease in unearned revenues.
   4.   Decrease in deferred tax liabilities.
   5.   Decrease in accrued pension liability.

III.   **List cash inflows and outflows from investing activities and summarize the effect on cash. List inflows (sources) as positive amounts and list outflows (uses) as negative amounts.**

A.   Transactions and events involving investing activities can usually be found by analyzing the reasons for changes in the noncash asset accounts that do **not** relate to transactions that are operating activities. Examples of such accounts include:
   1.   Most of the noncurrent asset accounts (except deferred tax assets), such as:
      a.   Long-term investments.
      b.   Investments in available-for-sale securities and held-to-maturity securities.
      c.   Property, plant and equipment.
      d.   Intangible assets.
   2.   A few current assets accounts, such as:
      a.   Short-term investments (including available-for-sale securities but excluding trading securities).
      b.   Short-term nontrade receivables.

B.   An increase in one of the accounts listed in "A." above is usually due to a transaction or event which is an investing activity that results in an outflow of cash.
   1.   Examples of such transactions include purchase of plant assets and purchase of investments (including investments in available-for-sale securities and held-to-maturity securities).
   2.   An example of an increase in one of the accounts listed in "A." above which is **not** due to an investing activity is the case where investment income is recognized using the equity method (See "II. F." above).

C.   A decrease in one of the accounts listed in "A." above is usually due to a transaction or event which is an investing activity that results in an inflow of cash.
   1.   Examples of such transactions include sale of plant assets and sale of investments (including available-for-sale securities and held-to-maturity securities).
   2.   An example of a decrease in one of the accounts listed in "A." above which is **not** due to an investing activity is the amortization of a patent.

ILLUSTRATION 24-3 (Continued)

IV.   **List cash inflows and outflows from financing activities and summarize the effect on cash. List inflows (sources) as positive amounts and list outflows (uses) as negative amounts.**

A.   Transactions and events involving financing activities can usually be found by analyzing the reasons for changes in all of the liability and owners' equity accounts that do **not** relate to transactions that are operating activities. Examples of such accounts include:
1.   Most of the noncurrent liability accounts (except deferred tax liabilities) such as:
a.   Bonds payable.
b.   Long-term notes payable.
2.   A few current liability accounts, such as:
a.   Short-term note payable (nontrade).
b.   Current portion of long-term debt.
c.   Cash dividends payable.
3.   Stockholder equity accounts, such as:
a.   Capital stock.
b.   Additional paid-in capital (paid-in capital in excess of par).
c.   Retained earnings.
d.   Treasury stock.

B.   A credit to one of the accounts listed in "A." above is usually due to a transaction or event which is a financing activity that results in an inflow of cash.
1.   Examples of such transactions include the issuance of bonds payable and the sale of treasury stock.
2.   An example of a credit to one of the accounts listed in "A." above which is **not** due to a financing activity is the amortization of a discount on bonds payable.

C.   A debit to one of the accounts listed in "A." above is usually due to a transaction or event which is a financing activity that results in an outflow of cash.
1.   Examples of such transactions include the payment of long-term debt, the declaration and payment of cash dividends, and the purchase of treasury stock.
2.   An example of a debit to one of the accounts listed in "A." above which is **not** due to a financing activity is the amortization of a premium on bonds payable.

V.   **List the investing and financing activities not involving cash receipts or payments in a separate schedule.** Examples include:
A.   Conversion of debt to equity.
B.   Acquisition of noncash assets by issuance of debt instruments (including capital lease obligations).
C.   Exchanges of noncash assets (such as exchanges of nonmonetary assets).
D.   Exchange of liabilities (such as refinancing of long-term debt).
E.   Settlement of debt by conveying noncash assets.
F.   Conversion of preferred stock to common stock.
G.   Acquisition of noncash assets by issuing equity securities.

VI.   **Show the net change in cash for the period.**

VII.   **Reconcile beginning and ending cash balances.**

VIII.   **Do NOT report or disclose the following in a statement of cash flows or its supplementary disclosures:**
A.   Declaration and distribution of a stock dividend or stock split.
B.   Write-off of fully depreciated assets.
C.   Appropriation of retained earnings.
D.   Other noncash transactions which are not investing or financing activities.

ANALYSIS OF MULTIPLE-CHOICE TYPE QUESTIONS

QUESTION

1. (L.O.6) Donnegan Company reported salaries expense of $95,000 for 1999. The following data were extracted from the company's financial records:

	12/31/98	12/31/99
Prepaid Salaries	$ 20,000	$ 23,000
Salaries Payable	70,000	85,000

   On a statement of cash flows for 1999, using the direct method, cash payments for salaries should be:
   a. $77,000.
   b. $83,000.
   c. $107,000.
   d. $113,000.

Approach and Explanation: Think of the relationship between salaries expense and cash payments for salaries when there is (1) an increase in prepaid salaries, and (2) an increase in salaries payable. Convert the expense amount to a cash paid figure.

Salaries expense	$ 95,000	
Increase in prepaid salaries	3,000	
Increase in salaries payable	(15,000)	
Cash payments for salaries	$ 83,000	(Solution = b.)

QUESTION

2. (L.O.8) A change in accounts receivable is used to convert sales revenue to cash receipts from customers when the direct method is used. A change in accounts receivable is also used to convert net income to net cash from operating activities when the indirect method is used. Do you use a change in gross accounts receivable or net accounts receivable?

	Direct	Indirect
a.	Gross	Gross
b.	Net	Net
c.	Net	Gross
d.	Gross	Net

Explanation: The change in net accounts receivable includes the change in the Accounts Receivable account and the change in the Allowance for Doubtful Accounts account. The Accounts Receivable account changes because of credit sales, write-offs of individual accounts, cash collections, and the reinstatement of accounts previously written off. The allowance account changes because of the recognition of bad debts expense, write-offs of individual accounts, and the reinstatement of accounts previously written off.

When the direct method is used, only the change in gross receivables is used to convert sales revenue to cash collections from customers because the bad debts expense has no impact on this calculation. When the indirect method is used, the change in net receivables is used to convert net income to net cash provided by operating activities because it reflects the bad debts expense (which does not require a cash outlay) as well as the difference between the accrual basis revenue amount and the cash collections from customers. (Solution = d.)

QUESTION
3. (L.O.5,6) Which of the following would be classified as a financing activity on a statement of cash flows?
    a. declaration and distribution of a stock dividend
    b. deposit to a bond sinking fund
    c. sale of a loan receivable
    d. payment of interest to a creditor

Approach and Explanation: Write down the definitions for investing, financing, and operating activities. Take each of the transactions and see if it meets the definition for a financing activity. Declaration and distribution of stock dividend does not meet any of the definitions. It is an example of an item that is not reported anywhere on a statement of cash flows or in supplementary disclosures related to that statement. Although the journal entry to record the deposit to a bond sinking fund results in an increase in the fund, which is often classified as a long-term investment, most accountants emphasize the purpose of the deposit, which is to ultimately pay for amounts borrowed; thus, it is usually classified as a financing activity. The sale of a loan receivable is clearly an investing activity, and the payment of interest to a creditor is an operating activity. (Solution = b.)

QUESTION
4. (L.O.6) Net cash flow from operating activities for 1999 for Graham Corporation was $75,000. The following items are reported on the financial statements for 1999:

Depreciation and amortization	5,000
Cash dividends paid on common stock	3,000
Increase in accrued receivables	6,000

Based only on the information above, Graham's net income for 1999 was:
    a. $64,000.
    b. $66,000.
    c. $74,000.
    d. $76,000.
    e. none of the above.

Approach and Explanation: Write down the format for the reconciliation of net income to net cash flow from operating activities. Fill in the information given. Solve for the unknown.

Net income	$ X
Depreciation and amortization	5,000
Increase in accrued receivables	(6,000)
Net cash flow from operating activities	$ 75,000

Solving for X, net income = $76,000.

Cash dividends paid on common stock have no effect on this computation because cash dividends paid are not a component of net income, and they are not an operating activity. They are a financing activity. (Solution = d.)

QUESTION

5. (L.O.8) When the indirect method is used for a statement of cash flows, should the gross amount or net-of-tax amount of an extraordinary gain be added to or deducted from net income in computing cash provided by operating activities?
   a. Gross amount of an extraordinary gain should be added to net income.
   b. Gross amount of an extraordinary gain should be deducted from net income.
   c. Net-of-tax amount of an extraordinary gain should be added to net income.
   d. Net-of-tax amount of an extraordinary gain should be deducted from net income.

Explanation: All income taxes paid are to be classified as operating cash outflows. No income taxes are to be allocated to investing and financing transactions. Assume an extraordinary gain from an investing activity is tax effected at 40%:

Cash received	$ 50,000
Gain	10,000
Taxes paid	4,000

By deducting the gross gain of $10,000 from net income, which includes the net gain of $6,000, an outflow of $4,000 (due to income taxes paid) is reflected in the operating activity section of the statement of cash flows. The $50,000 would be classified as an inflow in the investing activity section. (Solution = b.)

QUESTION

6. (L.O.6) In a statement of cash flows, using the indirect method, which of the following are subtracted from net income to determine net cash provided by operating activities?
   I. Amortization of premium on bonds payable.
   II. Loss on sale of equipment.
   III. Depreciation expense.
   a. I only
   b. II only
   c. I and II
   d. I and III
   e. II and III
   f. I, II and III

Approach and Explanation: Think about how each item (1) affects net income and (2) affects cash. Then reason what is needed to reconcile net income to net cash provided by operating activities. The amortization of premium on bonds payable increases net income (because it reduces interest expense), but does not affect cash; thus it is deducted from net income in the reconciliation of net income to net cash provided by operating activities. The loss on sale of equipment reduces net income but does not affect cash; hence, it is added to net income in the reconciliation under discussion. Depreciation expense reduces net income but does not affect cash; thus, it is added to net income in this reconciliation. (Solution = a.)

QUESTION
7.   (L.O.6) The following information was taken from the 1999 financial statements of Jenny Gardner Corporation:

Inventory, January 1, 1999	$ 30,000
Inventory, December 31, 1999	40,000
Accounts payable, January 1, 1999	25,000
Accounts payable, December 31, 1999	40,000
Sales	200,000
Cost of goods sold	150,000

If the direct method is used in the 1999 statement of cash flows, what amount should Jenny Gardner report as cash payments for goods to be sold?
a. $175,000
b. $165,000
c. $155,000
d. $145,000
e. $125,000

Approach and Explanation: Draw T-accounts. Enter the information given.

Cost of Goods Sold	Inventory	Accounts Payable
150,000	Beg. Bal. 30,000 | 150,000 CGS End. Bal. 40,000	25,000 Beg. Bal. 40,000 End. Bal.

Assume all purchases of inventory are on account. Solve for the amount of purchases. Then solve for the amount of cash payments for goods to be sold (assuming all accounts payable arise from purchases of inventory).

Cost of Goods Sold	Inventory	Accounts Payable
150,000	Beg. Bal. 30,000 | 150,000 CGS Purchases 160,000 End. Bal. 40,000	Cash Payments 145,000 | 25,000 Beg. Bal. 160,000 Purchases 40,000 End. Bal.

(Solution = d.)

QUESTION

8.   (L.O.6) The following information was taken from the 1999 financial statements of Greg Nelson Corporation:

Income tax payable, January 1, 1999	$ 50,000
Income tax payable, December 31, 1999	40,000
Deferred tax liability, January 1, 1999	15,000
Deferred tax liability, December 31, 1999	30,000
Income tax expense	200,000

If the direct method is used in the 1999 statement of cash flows, what amount should Greg Nelson report as cash payments for income taxes?

   a. $225,000
   b. $210,000
   c. $205,000
   d. $195,000
   e. $190,000
   f. $175,000

Approach and Explanation: Draw T-accounts. Enter the information given and solve for the missing amounts.

Income Tax Expense		
Curr. Tax Exp.[2]	185,000	
Def. Tax Exp.[1]	15,000	
End. Bal.	200,000	

Income Tax Payable			
		50,000	Beg. Bal.
Taxes Pd.[3] 195,000		185,000	Cur. Tax Exp.[2]
		40,000	End. Bal.

Deferred Tax Liability		
	15,000	Beg. Bal.
		Def. Tax
	15,000	Expense[1]
	30,000	End. Bal.

[1]$30,000	Deferred tax liability, 12/31/99	
(15,000)	Deferred tax liability, 1/1/99	
$15,000	Deferred tax expense for 1999	
[2]$200,000	Total income tax expense for 1999	
(15,000)	Deferred tax expense for 1999	
$185,000	Current tax expense for 1999	
[3]$ 50,000	Income taxes payable, 1/1/99	
185,000	Current tax expense for 1999	
235,000		
(40,000)	Income taxes payable, 12/31/99	
$195,000	Income taxes paid in 1999	(Solution = d.)

TIP:	The use of T-accounts is a good solutions approach because it requires only that you recall the normal balance of relevant accounts and the transactions that affect certain accounts. Picturing the accounts helps you to readily determine the amounts of any debits or credits that affected an account. Another approach that requires more analysis of the relationship of accounts appears as follows:	
	Income tax expense for 1999	$ 200,000
	Increase in deferred tax liability (deferred tax expense)	(15,000)
	Current tax expense for 1999	185,000
	Decrease in income taxes payable	10,000
	Income taxes paid during 1999	$ 195,000

QUESTION

9.   (L.O.6) The following information was taken from the 1999 financial statements of the Laurel Banning Corporation:

Bonds payable, January 1, 1999	$ 100,000
Bonds payable, December 31, 1999	400,000

During 1999
- Bonds payable with a face amount of $40,000 were issued in exchange for equipment.
- A $90,000 payment was made to retire bonds payable with a face amount of $100,000.

In its statement of cash flows for the year ended December 31, 1999, what amount should Laurel Banning report as proceeds from issuance of bonds payable?

a. $300,000
b. $360,000
c. $160,000
d. $340,000
e. $170,000
f. $240,000

Approach and Explanation: Draw a T-account for Bonds Payable. Enter the data given and solve for the unknown.

Bonds Payable			
Retired	100,000	100,000	Bal., Jan. 1, 1999
		40,000	Issued for equipment
		360,000	Issued for cash
		400,000	Bal., Dec. 31, 1999

(Solution = b.)

QUESTION

10.   (L.O.6) During 1999, Jackson Montgomery Corporation had the following activities related to its financial operations:

1. Purchased equipment for cash which was borrowed from a bank.
2. Acquired treasury stock for cash.
3. Declared a cash dividend payable in 2000.
4. Appropriated retained earnings for possible loss from lawsuit.
5. Purchased a 2-month U.S. Treasury bill.
6. Acquired a 5-year certificate of deposit from a bank.
7. Made interest payments on bonds payable.
8. Converted preferred stock to common stock.
9. Received dividends from an investment in stock of another corporation.

In a statement of cash flows, how many of the above transactions are reported as a cash **outflow** from investing activities?

a.   one
b.   two
c.   three
d.   four
e.   five
f.   six

Approach and Explanation: Identify each item as being reported as one of the following:

- A cash inflow from operating activities.
- A cash outflow from operating activities.
- A cash inflow from investing activities.
- A cash outflow from investing activities.
- A cash inflow from financing activities.
- A cash outflow from financing activities.
- An investing or financing activity not affecting cash.

Refer to the definitions in **Illustration 24-1** if you need to do so. Count the number that you identify to be reported as a cash outflow from investing activities.

Item 1:   The purchase of equipment for cash is an investing outflow. The borrowing of cash from a bank is a financing inflow.

Item 2:   The acquisition of treasury stock for cash is a financing outflow.

Item 3:   The declaration of a cash dividend is a transaction not affecting cash and does not get reported on a statement of cash flows. The subsequent payment of the cash dividend will be a financing outflow.

Item 4:   The appropriation of retained earnings is a transaction not affecting cash; it is not reported on a statement of cash flows.

Item 5:   The purchase of a 2-month U.S. Treasury Bill is a transaction where cash is exchanged for a cash equivalent. It is not reported on a statement of cash flows.

Item 6:   The acquisition of a 5-year certificate of deposit is an investing outflow.

Item 7:   Interest payments are an operating outflow.

Item 8: The conversion of preferred stock to common stock is a financing activity that does not affect cash; this transaction is to be disclosed in the supplemental schedule of noncash investing and financing activities.

Item 9: The receipt of dividends (and interest) are cash inflows from operating activities.

Transactions 1 and 6 are reported as cash outflows from investing activities. (Solution = b.)

QUESTION

11. (L.O.6) Refer to the facts of Question 10 above. In a statement of cash flows, how many of the transactions are reported as a cash **outflow** from financing activities?
    a. one
    b. two
    c. three
    d. four
    e. five
    f. six

Approach and Explanation: Refer to the Approach and Explanation for Question 10 above. Only Item 2 is reported as a cash outflow from financing activities. (Solution = a.)

QUESTION

12. (L.O.6) The following facts are available for the Barbara Pace Company:

Sales revenue for 1999	$ 450,000
Accounts receivable, January 1, 1999	35,000
Accounts receivable, December 31, 1999	29,000
Allowance for doubtful accounts, January 1, 1999	5,000
Allowance for doubtful accounts, December 31, 1999	3,500
Bad debt expense for 1999	42,000
Write-off of accounts receivable during 1999	43,500

    The amount of cash collections from customers during 1999 was:
    a. $498,000.
    b. $496,500.
    c. $487,500.
    d. $412,500.
    e. none of the above.

Explanation: The computation for cash collections is as follows:

Sales revenue	$ 450,000
Decrease in accounts receivable	6,000
Write-off of accounts receivable	(43,500)
Cash collections from customers	$ 412,500

(Solution = d.)

TIP: An alternative solution is as follows:

Sales revenue	$ 450,000
Decrease in accounts receivable	6,000
Decrease in allowance for doubtful accounts	(1,500)
Bad debt expense	(42,000)
Cash collections from customers	$ 412,500

TIP: Another way of solving for the above is as follows:

Sales revenue	$ 450,000
Decrease in net accounts receivable	4,500[a]
Bad debt expense	(42,000)
Cash collections from customers	$ 412,500

[a]$35,000 - $5,000   = $30,000 Beginning net receivables
  $29,000 - $3,500   = $25,500 Ending net receivables
  $30,000 - $25,500 = $4,500 Decrease in net receivables

TIP: You may also solve for the cash collections by drawing T-accounts for Sales Revenue, Accounts Receivable, Allowance for Doubtful Accounts, and Bad Debt Expense. Enter the information given and solve for the missing amount. The T-accounts would appear as follows:

Sales Revenue

	450,000
	450,000

Accounts Receivable

Beg. Bal.	35,000		
Sales	450,000	43,500	Write-offs
		412,500	Cash collections
End. Bal.	29,000		

Allowance for Doubtful Accounts

		5,000	Beg. Bal.
Write-offs	43,500	42,000	Bad Debt Expense
		3,500	End. Bal.

Bad Debt Expense

42,000	
42,000	

TIP: Assume all sales were on account. Even if some sales were cash sales, the answer will be the same for total cash collections.

CHAPTER 25

FULL DISCLOSURE IN FINANCIAL REPORTING

OVERVIEW

Financial statements often contain information for which more detail and/or explanation is desired by the users of the statements. Additional detail may be provided in the notes to the statements. Explanation of management's view may be included in the MD&A (management's discussion and analysis) section of the annual report. These and other subjects related to full disclosure in financial reporting are discussed in this chapter.

SUMMARY OF LEARNING OBJECTIVES

1. **Review the full disclosure principle and describe problems of implementation.** The full disclosure principle calls for financial reporting of any financial facts significant enough to influence the judgment of an informed reader. Implementing the full disclosure principle is difficult, because the cost of disclosure can be substantial and the benefits difficult to assess. Disclosure requirements have increased because of (1) the growing complexity of the business environment, (2) the necessity for timely information, and (3) the use of accounting as a control and monitoring device.

2. **Explain the use of notes in financial statement preparation.** Notes are the accountant's means of amplifying or explaining the items presented in the main body of the statements. Information pertinent to specific financial statement items can be explained in qualitative terms, and supplementary data of a quantitative nature can be provided to expand the information in the notes. Common note disclosures relate to such items as the following: accounting policies; inventories; property, plant, and equipment; credit claims; and contingencies and commitments.

3. **Describe the disclosure requirements for major segments of a business.** If only the consolidated figures are available to the analyst, much information regarding the composition of these figures is hidden in aggregated figures. There is no way to tell from the consolidated data the extent to which the differing product lines contribute to the company's profitability, risk, and growth potential. As a result, segment information is required by the profession in certain situations.

4. **Describe the accounting problems associated with interim reporting.** Interim reports cover periods of less than one year. Two viewpoints exist regarding interim reports. One view (discrete view) holds that each interim period should be treated as a separate accounting period. Another view (integral view) is that the interim report is an integral part of the annual report and that deferrals and accruals should take into consideration what will happen for the entire year.

    In general, the same accounting principles used for annual reports should be employed for interim reports. A number of unique reporting problems develop related to the following items: (1) advertising and similar costs, (2) expenses subject to year-end adjustment, (3) income taxes, (4) extraordinary items, (5) accounting changes, (6) earnings per share, and (7) seasonality.

5. **Identify the major disclosures found in the auditor's report.** If the auditor is satisfied that the financial statements present the financial position, results of operations, and cash flows fairly in accordance with generally accepted accounting principles, an unqualified opinion is expressed. A qualified opinion contains an exception to the standard opinion; ordinarily the exception is not of sufficient magnitude to invalidate the financial statements as a whole.

    An adverse opinion is required in any auditor's report in which the exceptions to fair presentation are so material that a qualified opinion is not justified. A disclaimer of an opinion is appropriate when the auditor has gathered so little information on the financial statements that no opinion can be expressed.

6. **Understand management's responsibilities for financial statements.** Management's discussion and analysis section covers three financial aspects of an enterprise's business: liquidity, capital resources, and results of operations. Management has primary responsibility for the financial statements and this responsibility is often indicated in a letter to stockholders in the annual report.

7. **Identify issues related to financial forecasts and projections.** The SEC has indicated that companies are permitted (not required) to include profit forecasts in reports filed with that agency. To encourage management to disclose this type of information, the SEC has issued a "safe harbor" rule. The safe harbor rule provides protection to an enterprise that presents an erroneous forecast as long as the projection was prepared on a reasonable basis and was disclosed in good faith. However, the safe harbor rule has not worked well in practice.

8. **Describe the profession's response to fraudulent financial reporting.** Fraudulent financial reporting is intentional or reckless conduct, whether act or omission, that results in materially misleading financial statements. Fraudulent financial reporting usually occurs because of poor internal control, management's poor attitude toward ethics, and so on. The profession is hard at work attempting to find solutions, and has issued a number of auditing standards that address part of the problem.

9.* **Understand and account for changing prices.** The two most widely used approaches to show the effects of changing prices are (1) constant dollar accounting and (2) current cost accounting. Constant dollar accounting restates financial statement items into dollars that have equal purchasing power. Current cost is the cost of replacing the identical asset owned. Companies now are encouraged to disclose supplemental price-level-adjusted information and are not discouraged from experimenting with different forms of disclosure. Many companies include a discussion of inflation in the management's discussion and analysis section of the annual report.

    *This material is covered in Appendix 25-A in the text.

10.** **Understand the approach to financial statement analysis.** Basic financial statement analysis involves examining relationships between items on the financial statements (ratio and percentage analysis) and identifying trends in these relationships (comparative analysis). Analysis is used to predict the future, but it is limited because the data used are from the past. Also, ratio analysis identifies strengths and weaknesses of a company but it may not reveal why they exist. Although single ratios are helpful, they are not conclusive; they must be compared with industry averages, previous periods, planned amounts, and the like for maximum usefulness.

11.** **Identify major analytic ratios and describe their calculations.** Ratios are classified as liquidity ratios, activity ratios, profitability ratios, and coverage ratios: (1) **Liquidity ratio analysis** measures the short-run ability of the enterprise to pay its currently maturing obligations. (2) **Activity ratio analysis** measures how effectively the enterprise is using its assets. (3) **Profitability ratio analysis** measures the degree of success or failure of an enterprise to generate revenues adequate to cover its costs of operation and provide a return to the owners. (4) **Coverage ratio analysis** measures the degree of protection afforded long-term creditors and investors.

12.** **Explain the limitations of ratio analysis.** One important limitation of ratios is that they are based on historical cost data, which can lead to distortions in measuring performance. Also, where estimated items (such as depreciation and amortization) are significant, income ratios lose some of their credibility. In addition, difficult problems of comparability develop when changes in accounting principles and procedures occur. Finally, it must be recognized that a substantial amount of important information is not included in a company's financial statements.

13.** **Describe techniques of comparative analysis.** Companies present comparative data, which generally includes two years of balance sheet information and three years of income statement information. In addition, many companies include in their annual reports 5- to 10-year summaries of pertinent data that permit the reader to examine and analyze trends.

14.** **Describe techniques of percentage analysis.** Percentage analysis consists of reducing a series of related amounts to a series of percentages of a given base. Two approaches are often used. The first, called horizontal analysis, indicates the proportionate change in financial statement items over a period of time; such analysis is most helpful in evaluating trends. Vertical analysis (common-size analysis) is proportional expression of each item on the financial statements in a given period to a base amount. It analyzes the composition of each of the financial statements from different years (a) to detect trends not evident from the comparison of absolute amounts and (b) to make intercompany comparisons of different sized enterprises.

   **This material is covered in Appendix 25-B in the text.

TIPS ON CHAPTER TOPICS

TIP: The initial note to the financial statements should be a **summary of significant accounting policies.** This disclosure should identify principles applied by the entity that are: (a) selections from existing alternatives, (b) principles peculiar to a particular industry, or (c) unusual or innovative applications. This disclosure may precede the notes to the financial statements.

TIP: **Notes to the financial statements** are sometimes called **footnotes.** They are an integral part of the financial statements.

TIP: **Related party transactions** require separate disclosure because transactions involving related parties cannot be presumed to be carried out on an arms'-length basis because the requisite conditions of competitive, free-market dealings may not exist. The substance rather than the form of these transactions should be reflected in the financial statements.

TIP: In general, the same accounting principles used for annual reports should be employed for interim reports. **An interim period is an integral part of an annual period.** Therefore, expectations for the annual report must be reflected in an interim report. Accruals, deferrals, and allocations are to be utilized.

TIP: Income taxes for an interim period are to be computed using an **estimated annual effective tax rate.** The estimated annual effective tax rate is to be applied to the year-to-date "ordinary" income at the end of each interim period to compute the year-to-date tax. The interim period tax related to "ordinary" income shall be the difference between the amount so computed and the amounts reported for previous interim periods of the fiscal year.

TIP: For interim reporting purposes, extraordinary items are to be reported in the interim period in which they occur rather than arbitrarily allocated over multiple periods.

TIP: The types of information included in the MD&A (management's discussion and analysis) section of the financial statements are not subject to FASB standards.

TIP: In preparing an audit report, the auditor follows these reporting standards:
1. The report shall state whether the financial statements are presented in accordance with generally accepted accounting principles.
2. The report shall identify those circumstances in which such principles have not been consistently observed in the current period in relation to the preceding period.
3. Informative disclosures in the financial statements are to be regarded as reasonably adequate, unless otherwise stated in the report.
4. The report shall contain either an expression of opinion regarding the financial statements taken as a whole or an assertion to the effect that an opinion cannot be expressed. When an overall opinion cannot be expressed, the reasons why should be stated. In all cases where an auditor's name is associated with financial statements, the report should contain a clear-cut indication of the character of the auditor's examination, if any, and the degree of responsibility being taken.

TIP: A **financial forecast** and a **financial projection** are both prospective financial statements that present, to the best of the responsible party's knowledge and belief, an entity's financial position, results of operations, and cash flows for a future time. The difference between a financial forecast and a financial projection is that a forecast attempts to provide information on what is expected to happen; whereas, a projection may provide information on what is not necessarily expected to happen, but might take place.

TIP: The MD&A section of the financial statements must provide information concerning the effects of inflation and changing prices if material to financial statement trends.

The following **TIPS** relate to the material covered in Appendix 25-A in the text:

TIP: **Inflation** or **increase in the general price level** occurs when the average prices of goods and services in the economy increase, thereby decreasing the purchasing power of the dollar. A specific price level change refers to a change in the price of a particular good or service in the economy. Not all prices move in the same direction or at the same rate as the general price level, the CPI-U (Consumer Price Index for all Urban Consumers).

TIP: **Constant dollar accounting** restates financial statement items into dollars that have equal purchasing power. It is **not** a departure from the historical cost principle; it is a change in the measuring unit from a unit of money to a unit of purchasing power.

TIP: By use of the CPI-U index at various dates, we are able to compare dollars expressed in terms of one price level with dollars expressed in terms of another price level. To put the dollars of different years all on the basis of the purchasing power of a selected year, use the formula:

Dollars You are Changing FROM x a TO/FROM Ratio = Dollars You are Changing TO

The TO/FROM ratio is:
$$\frac{\text{Index of the Year You Are Changing TO}}{\text{Index of the Year You Are Changing FROM}}$$

For Example: Assuming index figures of 103 for 1981 and 170 for 1999, the cost of a building purchased in 1981 for $275,000 can be expressed in terms of the purchasing power of the 1999 dollar by multiplying $275,000 by 170/103. We find that the equivalent amount of 1999 dollars is $453,883. (Due to the high rate of inflation over the 18 years, it takes many more 1999 dollars to equal the purchasing power of the 1981 dollars.)

TIP: **Monetary items** are contractual claims to receive or pay a fixed amount of cash. **Monetary assets** include cash, accounts and notes receivable, and investments that pay a fixed rate of interest and will be repaid at a fixed amount in the future. **Monetary liabilities** include accounts and notes payable; accruals, such as wages and interest payable; and long-term obligations payable in a fixed sum. All assets and liabilities not classified as monetary items are classified as nonmonetary for constant dollar accounting purposes. **Nonmonetary items** are items whose prices, in terms of the monetary unit, change in proportion to changes in the general price level. Examples of nonmonetary assets are inventories; property, plant, and equipment; and intangible assets. Most liabilities are monetary items, while components of stockholders' equity are usually nonmonetary. Warranty obligation and unearned revenue are nonmonetary liabilities.

TIP: A debtor gains in a period of inflation because he borrows a specified sum when the price level is at one stage, and then repays the same specified sum at a later date with dollars of less purchasing power. For instance, a debtor borrows $10,000 in Year 1 and repays the $10,000 in Year 5 with "cheaper" dollars (dollars of less purchasing power) than the ones borrowed.

TIP: The price of a specific item may be affected not only by general inflation, but also by individual market forces. A popular means to measure the change in a specific price is current cost. **Current cost** is the cost of replacing the identical asset owned; if the asset is a plant asset, current cost is the cost of acquiring the same service potential as embodied by the asset owned. Current cost may be approximated by reference to current catalogue prices or by applying a specific index to the book value of the asset. The use of the current cost basis of accounting is a departure from the historical cost principle.

TIP: **Purchasing power gains and losses** arise from holding **monetary** items during a period of changing prices. During a period of inflation, purchasing power gains will result from holding monetary liabilities, and purchasing power losses will result from holding monetary assets. (The opposite relationships will occur in a period of deflation.) Purchasing power gains and losses are measured and reported when a **constant dollar basis of accounting** is used.

TIP: **Holding gains and losses** arise from holding **nonmonetary** items during a period of changing prices. A holding gain will occur when there is an increase in the current cost of a nonmonetary item held; whereas, a holding loss will occur when there is a decrease in its current cost. Holding gains and losses are quantified (measured) and disclosed only when a **current cost basis of accounting** is employed.

TIP: Monetary items are automatically stated in terms of the purchasing power of the balance sheet date on which they appear. Therefore, on a constant dollar balance sheet where all items are to be reported in terms of the end-of-year CPI-U index, the monetary items on the current balance sheet will not need to be adjusted (restated). However, items on a balance sheet for a prior year will have to be "rolled forward" (adjusted) for reporting of a comparative balance sheet on a constant dollar basis.

TIP: If there is an excess of monetary assets over monetary liabilities, the entity is said to be in a **positive monetary position** and will suffer net purchasing power losses in a period of inflation. An excess of monetary liabilities over monetary assets is referred to as a **negative monetary position**, and such a situation will lead to experiencing net purchasing power gains in a period of inflation.

The following **TIPS** relate to the material covered in Appendix 25-B:

TIP: The significance of a single absolute dollar amount reported in the general purpose financial statements for an entity is difficult to assess. To determine the meaningfulness of one amount, we must consider the significance of the amount when compared with other relevant amounts. Various techniques can be used to perform this analysis of financial statement data. Ratios developed for a particular company may be compared to industry averages to judge the solvency, strength, earning power, and growth potential of the company.

TIP: A **ratio** is an expression of the relationship of one item (or group of items) to a second item (or group of items). It is determined by dividing the first item (amount) by the second item (amount).

TIP: If A is $100,000 and B is $25,000, the ratio of A to B can be expressed in several ways, such as the following:

A:B	A/B
4:1	4.00
4 to 1	$4.00
4 times	400%

The way in which the ratio is expressed depends on the particular ratio. If it is the current ratio or acid-test ratio, it would likely be expressed as a proportion (4:1 or 4 to 1) or as a rate (4 times). If it is the debt to stockholders' equity ratio, it would likely be expressed as a percentage (400%).

TIP: The average number of days required to collect an account receivable (365 days divided by the receivables turnover) is not very meaningful until it is compared with the company's credit terms.

TIP: When you are analyzing comparative data, carefully notice which information is for prior years and which is for the current year. On a comparative balance sheet, the current year data is typically placed in the first (inside) column. In some situations, however, the reverse may be found.

TIP: The numerator of the current ratio includes total current assets; the numerator of the acid-test ratio includes only cash, marketable securities (short-term), and net receivables.

TIP: The denominator of a turnover ratio (such as for receivables, inventory, or total assets) always involves an **average** balance. That average can be determined by adding the balance at the end of the period to the balance at the beginning of the period and dividing by 2. However, if seasonal variances are significant, the annual average should be determined by adding together the balances at the end of each month and dividing by 12.

TIP: If the return on common stockholders' equity is greater than the return on assets, the interest rate on the debt is less than the average return on total assets; hence, the entity is favorably trading on the equity. However, if the cost of debt exceeds the return on total assets, the return on common stockholders' equity will be less than the return on total assets; hence, the entity will be unfavorably trading on the equity.

TIP: A given piece of financial information which is reported on the financial statements may not be significant to a reader if the only information available is a given dollar amount. When an item for the current year is compared with the same item for the same company of the prior year (to determine the direction, dollar amount, and percent of change) or with other items on the same statement for the same year (to develop component percentages which may be compared to industry averages), the resulting relationship(s) may be more useful in determining the meaningfulness of the information being reported.

TIP: Although the average collection period for accounts receivable is to be computed by dividing 365 days by the receivables turnover ratio, 360 days is often used. Likewise, the average number of days' sales included in inventory is often determined by dividing 360 (rather than 365) days by the inventory turnover.

TIP: One problem with the asset turnover ratio is that it places a premium on using old assets because their book value is low (the lower the denominator of the ratio, the higher the ratio is). Another problem with the asset turnover ratio is that it is affected by the depreciation method employed by the company—the more accelerated the depreciation is, the higher the asset turnover will be.

TIP: The profit margin on sales ratio, combined with the asset turnover ratio, offers an interplay that leads to a rate of return on total assets.

$$\text{Profit margin on sales} = \frac{\text{Net income}}{\text{Net sales}} \qquad \text{Asset Turnover} = \frac{\text{Net sales}}{\text{Average total assets}}$$

Rate of return on assets = Profit margin on sales x Asset turnover

$$\text{Rate of return on assets} = \frac{\text{Net income}}{\text{Net sales}} \times \frac{\text{Net sales}}{\text{Average total assets}}$$

$$\text{Rate of return on assets} = \frac{\text{Net income}}{\text{Average total assets}}$$

The profit margin on sales does not answer the question of how profitable an enterprise was for a given period of time. Only by determining how many times the assets turned over during a period of time is it possible to ascertain the amount of net income earned on the total assets. Many enterprises have a small profit margin on sales and a high turnover (grocery and discount stores); whereas, other enterprises have a relatively high profit margin but a low inventory turnover (jewelry and furniture stores).

TIP: To compute the book value per share of common stock when there is preferred stock also outstanding, use the following steps:

Step 1: **Compute the total book value of preferred stock** by multiplying the book value per share of preferred stock by the number of preferred shares outstanding. The book value per share of preferred is one of the following (listed in order of preference):
   a.   Liquidation value of preferred plus dividends in arrears.
   b.   Call or redemption price of preferred plus dividends in arrears.
   c.   Par value of preferred plus dividends in arrears.

Step 2: **Compute the total book value of common stock** by deducting the total book value of preferred stock from total stockholders' equity.

Step 3: **Compute the book value per share of common stock** by dividing the total book value of common stock by the number of common stock shares outstanding.

TIP: Financial statements can be analyzed in percentage terms by using one of two basic approaches: horizontal analysis or vertical analysis.

TIP: **Horizontal analysis** involves the expression of dollar amounts of financial statement items in percentage terms of the dollar amounts for the same items in a prior year. There may be two or more years involved in the analysis. **Trend analysis** is a type of horizontal analysis that is prepared for more than two years.

TIP: In horizontal analysis, a base year (usually the earliest year being analyzed) is selected. Each dollar item on the statements is then divided by the dollar amount reported in the base year for the same item. For instance, if sales were $33,000 in Year 1, $46,000 in Year 2, and $50,000 in Year 3, horizontal analysis would yield percentages of 100% for Year 1, 139% for Year 2, and 152% for Year 3. The trend for sales is more clearly determined when expressed in percentage terms.

TIP: In **vertical analysis** (or the development of **common-size financial statements**), the relative importance of various items on a single financial statement is indicated by the relationships of these various items to some key figure on the same statement.

TIP: The key figure used for vertical analysis on the income statement is generally net sales, so every other item in the same statement for the same year is expressed in percentage terms of that key figure. This is accomplished by **dividing** every dollar item reported on the income statement by the dollar amount of net sales for the year to obtain the percentages.

TIP: The key figure (the 100% figure) used for vertical analysis of the balance sheet is generally the company's total assets. Each item on the balance sheet is then described as a percentage of the total asset figure.

CASE 25-1

Purpose: (L.O.1 thru 8) This exercise will review the meaning or significance of a number of terms used in this chapter.

Instructions
Select the letter of the item that most directly relates to the numbered statements. Use the letter of the item to identify your response.

A. Summary of significant accounting policies.
B. Related party transactions.
C. Reporting of segment information.
D. Social responsibility disclosures.
E. Errors.
F. Fraudulent financial reporting.
G. Full disclosure principle.
H. Illegal acts.
I. Interim reports.
J. Notes to the financial statements.
K. Auditor's report.
L. Irregularities.
M. Management's discussion and analysis.
N. Financial forecast.
O. Financial projection.

_____ 1. Calls for financial reporting of any financial facts significant enough to influence the judgment of an informed reader.

_____ 2. Information that is an integral part of the financial statements and serves as a means of amplifying or explaining the items presented in the body of the statements.

_____ 3. Disclosure of the accounting methods employed in the preparation of the financial statements.

_____ 4. A business enterprise engages in transactions in which one of the transacting parties has the ability to influence significantly the policies of the other, or in which a nontransacting party has the ability to influence the policies of the two transacting parties.

_____ 5. Unintentional mistakes.

_____ 6. Intentional distortions of financial statements.

_____ 7. Violations of laws and regulations, such as bribes and kickbacks.

_____ 8. Information related to revenues, operating profit or loss, and identifiable assets of different product lines of an entity.

_____ 9. Reports that cover periods of less than one year.

_____ 10. Section of an annual report that covers three financial aspects of an enterprise's business—liquidity, capital resources, and results of operations.

_____ 11. Information related to environmental issues and the reporting entity.

_____ 12. A report that states whether or not the financial statements are presented in accordance with generally accepted accounting principles.

_____ 13. Prospective financial statements based on a company's assumptions reflecting conditions it expects would exist in the future, given one or more hypothetical assumptions.

_____ 14. Prospective financial statements based on a company's assumptions reflecting conditions it expects will exist in the future and the course of action it expects to take.

_____ 15. Intentional or reckless conduct, whether act or omission, that results in materially misleading financial statements.

Solution to Case 25-1

1.	G	6.	L	11.	D
2.	J	7.	H	12.	K
3.	A	8.	C	13.	O
4.	B	9.	I	14.	N
5.	E	10.	M	15.	F

CASE 25-2

Purpose: (L.O.3) This case will review the tests applied in determining the reportable segments of an entity.

Diversified Galore Inc. has several reportable industry segments that account for 80% of its operations.

Instructions

(1) Explain the term "operating segment" as it applies to an entity diversified in its operations.

(2) Explain when the information about two or more operating segments may be aggregated.

(3) Explain what criteria are to be used to determine Diversified's reportable segments.

(4) Indicate what information is to be disclosed for each operating segment.

Solution to Case 25-2

(1)   An **operating segment** is a component of an enterprise:
   (a)   That engages in business activities from which it earns revenues and incurs expenses.
   (b)   Whose operating results are regularly reviewed by the company's chief operating decision maker to assess segment performance and allocate resources to the segment.
   (c)   For which discrete financial information is available that is generated by or based on the internal financial reporting system.

(2)   Information about two or more operating segments may be aggregated only if the segments have the same basic charactertistics in each of the following areas:
   (a)   The nature of the products and services provided.
   (b)   The nature of the production process.
   (c)   The type or class of customer.
   (d)   The methods of product or service distribution.
   (e)   If applicable, the nature of the regulatory environment.

(3)   After the company decides on the segments for possible disclosure, a quantitative materiality test is made to determine whether the segment is significant enough to warrant actual disclosure. An operating segment is regarded as significant and therefore identified as a reportable segment if it satisfies **one or more** of the following quantitative thresholds.
   - Its **revenue** (including both sales to external customers and intersegment sales or transfers) is 10% or more of the combined revenue of all the enterprise's operating segments.
   - The absolute amount of its **profit or loss** is 10% or more of the greater, in absolute amount, of
      (a)   the combined operating profit of all operating segments that did not incur a loss, or
      (b)   the combined loss of all operating segments that did report a loss.
   - Its **identifiable assets** are 10% or more of the combined assets of all operating segments.

In applying these tests, two additional factors must be considered. First, segment data must explain a significant portion of the company's business. Specifically, the segmented results must equal or exceed 75% of the combined sales to unaffiliated customers for the entire enterprise. This test prevents a company from providing limited information on only a few segments and lumping all the rest into one category.

Second, the profession recognizes that reporting too many segments may overwhelm users with detailed information. The FASB decided that 10 is a reasonable upper limit for the number of segments that a company should be required to disclose.

(4)   The FASB now requires that an enterprise report:
 (a)   **General information about its operating segments.** This includes factors that management considers most significant in determining the company's operating segments, and the types of products and services from which each operating segment derives its revenues.
 (b)   **Segment profit and loss related information.** Specifically, the following information about each operating segment must be reported if the amounts are included in the determination of segment profit or loss:
 • Revenues from transactions with external customers.
 • Revenues from transactions with other operating segments of the same enterprise.
 • Interest revenue.
 • Interest expense.
 • Depreciation, depletion, and amortization expense.
 • Unusual items.
 • Equity in the net income of investees accounted for by the equity method.
 • Income tax expense or benefit.
 • Extraordinary items.
 • Significant noncash items other than depreciation, depletion, and amortization expense.
 (c)   **Segment assets.** An enterprise must report each operating segment's total assets.
 (d)   **Reconciliation.** An enterprise must provide a reconciliation of the total of the segments' revenues to total revenues, a reconciliation of the total of the operating segments' profits and losses to its income before income taxes, and a reconciliation of the total of the operating segments' assets to total assets.
 (e)   **Information about products and services and geographic areas.** For each operating segment that has not been determined based on geography, the enterprise must report (unless it is impracticable) [(a) in the enterprise's country of domicile and (b) in each other country if material]: (1) revenues from external customers, (2) long-lived assets, and (3) expenditures during the period for long-lived assets.
 (f)   **Major customers.** If 10 percent or more of the revenues is derived from a single customer, the enterprise must disclose the total amount of revenues from each such customer by segment.

CASE 25-3

Purpose: (L.O.4) This case will review the reporting requirements for interim financial statements.

Bon Jon Surf Shop is located in Daytona Beach, Florida. It sells surf boards, beach wear, and other related merchandise. Some shareholders have requested management to distribute quarterly financial statements to shareholders.

Instructions
(a)   Discuss the accounting principles that should be employed for interim reports.
(b)   Indicate whether or not it is a requirement to include a statement of cash flows in an interim report. Also list the minimum data to be disclosed in an interim report.

Solution to Case 25-3

(a) **The profession indicates that, in general, the same accounting principles used for annual reports should be employed for interim reports.** Revenues should be recognized in interim periods on the same basis as they are for annual periods. Also, costs directly associated with revenues (product costs), such as materials, factory labor and related fringe benefits, and manufacturing overhead should be treated in the same manner for interim reports as for annual reports.

Companies generally should use the same inventory pricing methods (FIFO, LIFO, etc.) for interim reports that they use for annual reports. However, the following exceptions are appropriate at interim reporting periods:
1. Companies may use the gross profit method at interim dates to estimate inventory and cost of goods sold, but disclosure of the method and adjustments to reconcile with annual inventory are necessary.
2. When LIFO inventories are liquidated at an interim date and are expected to be replaced by year end, cost of goods sold should include the expected cost of replacing the liquidated LIFO base and not give effect to the interim liquidation.
3. The use of lower of cost or market may result in inventory losses which should not be deferred beyond the interim period in which the decline occurs. Recoveries of these losses in subsequent periods should be recognized as gains, but only to the extent of losses recognized in previous interim periods of the same fiscal year. Temporary market declines should not be recognized at the interim date since no loss is expected to be incurred in the fiscal year.
4. Planned variances under a standard cost system which are expected to be absorbed by year end ordinarily should be deferred.

Costs and expenses other than product costs, often referred to as period costs, are frequently charged to the interim period as incurred. But they may be allocated among interim periods on the basis of an estimate of time expired, benefit received, or activity associated with the periods. Considerable latitude is exercised in accounting for these costs in interim periods, and many believe more definitive guidelines are needed.

(b) The profession encourages but does not require companies to publish a balance sheet and a statement of cash flows in interim reports. When this information is not presented, significant changes in such items as liquid assets, net working capital, long-term liabilities, and stockholders' equity should be disclosed.

Regarding disclosure, the following interim data should be reported as a minimum:
1. Sales or gross revenues, provision for income taxes, extraordinary items, cumulative effect of a change in accounting principle, and net income.
2. Primary and fully diluted earnings per share where appropriate.
3. Seasonal revenue, cost, or expenses.
4. Significant changes in estimates or provisions for income taxes.
5. Disposal of a segment of a business and extraordinary, unusual, or infrequently occurring items.
6. Contingent items.
7. Changes in accounting principles or estimates.
8. Significant changes in financial position.

EXERCISE 25-1

Purpose: (L.O.9) This exercise will allow you to practice restating amounts originating in different periods to equivalent units of purchasing power. It will provide you with a chance to examine amounts on financial statements that follow conventional financial accounting standards and compare them to amounts on statements that have been adjusted for changes in the general price level.

A machine with an estimated five-year life was purchased by the Callerman Company at the end of Year 1 for $10,000 (when the price level index was 100). It was used in the business until the end of Year 4, when it was sold for $6,200. The straight-line depreciation method was used and no residual value was assumed. Price level information is as follows:

End of Year	Price Level Index
1	100
2	120
3	144
4	173

Instructions

Complete the following blanks that refer to presentations of the machine and the related accumulated depreciation on balance sheets at the end of Years 1 through 3, the depreciation expense on the income statements for Years 1 through 4, and the gain or loss on disposal in the income statement for Year 4.

TIP: Since the asset was purchased at the end of Year 1, no depreciation expense is taken for Year 1.

			Conventional Statements	Constant Dollar Statements
1.	a.	Machine, balance sheet, end of Year 1.	$_____	$_____
	b.	Accumulated Depreciation, balance sheet, end of Year 1.	$_____	$_____
2.	a.	Depreciation Expense, income statement, for Year 2.	$_____	$_____
	b.	Machine, balance sheet, end of Year 2.	$_____	$_____
	c.	Accumulated Depreciation, balance sheet, end of Year 2.	$_____	$_____
3.	a.	Depreciation Expense, income statement, for Year 3.	$_____	$_____
	b.	Machine, balance sheet, end of Year 3.	$_____	$_____
	c.	Accumulated Depreciation, balance sheet, end of Year 3.	$_____	$_____
4.	a.	Depreciation Expense, income statement, for Year 4.	$_____	$_____
	b.	Gain or Loss on Disposal, income statement, for Year 4.	$_____	$_____

SOLUTION TO EXERCISE 25-1

Conventional Statements	Constant Dollar Statements

1. a. $10,000 $10,000 x 100/100   = $10,000

    b.   -0-   -0-

2. a. $10,000 ÷ 5   = $ 2,000 $ 2,000 x 120/100   = $ 2,400

    b. $10,000 $10,000 x 120/100   = $12,000

    c. $ 2,000 $ 2,000 x 120/100   = $ 2,400

3. a. $10,000 ÷ 5   = $ 2,000 $ 2,000 x 144/100   = $ 2,880

    b. $10,000 $10,000 x 144/100   = $14,400

    c. $2,000 x 2   = $ 4,000 $ 4,000 x 144/100   = $ 5,760

4. a. $10,000 ÷ 5   = $ 2,000 $ 2,000 x 173/100   = $ 3,460

    b. $10,000 - 6,000 = $ 4,000 book value $10,000 x 173/100 = $17,300

                                    $ 6,000 x 173/100   = $10,380

        $6,200 - 4,000 = $ 2,200 gain $17,300 - $10,380 = $ 6,920 book value

                                    $ 6,200 - $ 6,920   = $ 720 loss

EXERCISE 25-2

Purpose: (L.O.9) This exercise illustrates the restatement of various items for presentation on constant dollar financial statements.

Presented below are assumed selected price indices for specific dates or periods:

Dec. 31, 1971	100	June 30, 1998	204
Feb. 15, 1972	106	Dec. 31, 1998	215
Mar. 21, 1972	108	Average 1998	210
May 1, 1987	169	June 19, 1999	220
Sept. 23, 1991	190	Dec. 31, 1999	240
Dec. 31, 1994	197	Average 1999	233

1.   Sales made during 1999.
2.   Investments in common stock (purchased Sept. 23, 1991).
3.   Accounts payable (balance Dec. 31, 1999).
4.   Bonds payable (issued Dec. 31, 1994, maturing Dec. 31, 2011).
5.   Purchases made during 1999.
6.   Interest expense on bonds issued December 31, 1994 (incurred evenly through 1999).
7.   Allowance for doubtful accounts (balance Dec. 31, 1999).
8.   Cash (on hand Dec. 31, 1999).
9.   Equipment (purchased Mar. 21, 1972).
10. Common stock, $100 par (issued Dec. 31, 1971).
11. Land (acquired Feb. 15, 1972).
12. Preferred stock, 6% (issued Sept. 23, 1991).
13. Accounts receivable (balance Dec. 31, 1999).
14. Inventory (LIFO, accumulated throughout 1998).
15. Depreciation expense for 1999 (on equipment purchased May 1, 1987).

Instructions

Given the dates and respective price indices above, indicate what the numerator and the denominator would have to be to adjust items 1-15 above for price level changes for presentation in a December 31, 1999 constant dollar balance sheet and the related constant dollar income statement for the year then ended. All constant dollar information is to be expressed in terms of the purchasing power of the dollar at that balance sheet date.

Solution to Exercise 25-2

1. 240/233	4. 240/240	7. 240/240	10. 240/100	13. 240/240
2. 240/190	5. 240/233	8. 240/240	11. 240/106	14. 240/210
3. 240/240	6. 240/233	9. 240/108	12. 240/190	15. 240/169

Approach and Explanation:
1.   Identify each item as (1) a monetary asset or liability, (2) a nonmonetary asset or liability, or (3) not an asset or a liability. (Review the definitions for "monetary items" and "nonmonetary items" on page 25-5.)
    a.   The denominator for a monetary item is the price index at the current balance sheet date because all monetary items are automatically expressed in terms of the purchasing power of the dollar at the balance sheet date.
    b.   The denominator for a nonmonetary asset or liability or stockholders' equity item is the index existing at the date the asset or liability or stockholders' equity item was recorded on the books.
    c.   The denominator for an income statement item is the average index for the period, assuming the revenue or expense was earned or incurred evenly throughout the period, or the index existing at the date the particular transaction occurred.
2.   The numerator for all items is the purchasing power of the dollar at the balance sheet date because the instructions for this constant dollar statement require it.

ILLUSTRATION 25-1
RATIOS: FORMULAS FOR COMPUTATIONS AND PURPOSES (L.O.11)

Ratio	Formula for Computation	Purpose and/or Comments
I. Liquidity		
1. Current ratio	Current assets / Current liabilities	This ratio is an indication of a company's ability to meet its current liabilities with the cash flow that will result from its current assets. It is often called the working capital ratio. The higher the ratio, the greater the short-term solvency.
2. Quick or acid-test ratio	Cash, marketable securities, and receivables / Current liabilities	"Quick" assets are cash, marketable securities, and net receivables. The acid-test ratio (sometimes called the quick ratio) is a more severe test of short-run solvency than the current ratio. A large amount of inventory will cause an entity's acid-test ratio to be significantly less than its current ratio.
3. Current cash debt ratio	Net cash provided by operating activities / Average current liabilities	This ratio measures the company's ability to pay off its current liabilities out of its operations for a given year.
II. Activity		
4. Receivables turnover	Net sales / Average trade receivables (net)	Theoretically, the numerator should include only net credit sales. Unless seasonal factors are significant, average trade receivables outstanding can be computed from the beginning and ending balance of net trade receivables. This ratio is another figure frequently used to measure the quality of the receivables and the efficiency and safety of a company's credit-granting activity. The higher the turnover, the shorter the time period necessary to collect the average account receivable. The receivables turnover is transformed to an average collection period by dividing 365 days by the receivables turnover.
5. Inventory turnover	Cost of goods sold / Average inventory	The inventory turnover ratio measures how quickly inventory is sold. Dividing 365 days by the inventory turnover indicates the average number of days it takes to sell inventory (or average number of days' sales for which inventory is on hand). This ratio is an indication of the efficiency of management in dealing with inventories. The greater the inventory turnover, the more liquid it is, and the lower the costs of storage, property taxes, maintenance costs, and so forth. The lower the turnover, the greater the chance of loss through obsolescence.

ILLUSTRATION 25-1 (Continued)

Ratio	Formula for Computation	Purpose and/or Comments
6. Asset turnover	Net sales / Average total assets	This ratio supposedly indicates how efficiently the company utilizes its assets. If the asset turnover ratio is high, the implication is that the company is using its assets effectively to generate sales. If the turnover is low, the company either needs to use its assets more efficiently or dispose of them.
III. Profitability		
7. Profit margin on sales	Net income / Net sales	The ratio measures the profit on each sales dollar received. It provides some indication of the buffer available in case of higher costs or lower sales in the future.
8. Rate of return on assets	Net income / Average total assets	Some analysts modify this ratio by adding interest charges, net of tax effect, to the numerator because interest is a cost of securing additional assets and, therefore, should not be considered as a deduction in arriving at the amount of return on total assets.
9. Rate of return on common stock equity	Net income minus preferred dividends / Average common stockholders' equity	If this ratio is greater than the rate of return on total assets ratio, the company is using creditor sources and is favorably trading on the equity. Trading on the equity increases the company's financial risk, but it enhances residual earnings whenever the rate of return on assets exceeds the cost of debt capital.
10. Earnings per share	Net income minus preferred dividends / Weighted shares outstanding	The EPS figure is one of the most important ratios used by investment analysts, yet it is one of the most deceptive. A dual presentation is required for a complex capital structure.
11. Price earnings ratio	Market price of stock / Earnings per share	The P/E ratio is an oft-quoted statistic used by analysts in discussing the investment possibility of a given enterprise. The higher the market's perception of the company's growth potential, the higher the P/E ratio is likely to be.
12. Payout ratio	Cash dividends / Net income minus preferred dividends	Growth companies are characterized by low payout ratios because they reinvest most of their earnings. Another closely related ratio that is often used is the dividend yield—the cash dividend per share divided by the market price of the stock.

ILLUSTRATION 25-1 (Continued)

Ratio	Formula for Computation	Purpose and/or Comments
IV. Coverage		
13. Debt to total assets	$\dfrac{\text{Debt}}{\text{Total assets or equities}}$	This ratio provides creditors with some idea of the corporation's ability to withstand losses without impairing the interests of creditors. From a creditor's point of view, a low ratio of debt to total assets is desirable; the lower the ratio, the more "buffer" there is available to creditors before the corporation becomes insolvent. There are other similar ratios that are used for the same purpose, such as the ratio of debt to stockholders' equity or the ratio of stockholders' equity to the sum of debt and stockholders' equity. These ratios have a very definite effect on the company's ability to obtain additional financing.
14. Times interest earned	$\dfrac{\text{Income before interest charges and taxes}}{\text{Interest charges}}$	This ratio stresses the importance of a company being able to cover all interest charges. If a company pays preferred dividends, the number of times the preferred dividends were earned is computed by dividing the net income for the year by the annual preferred dividend requirement.
15. Cash debt coverage ratio	$\dfrac{\text{Net cash provided by operating activities}}{\text{Average total liabilities}}$	This ratio measures a company's ability to repay its total liabilities in a given year out of its operating cash flow.
16. Book value per share of common stock	$\dfrac{\text{Common stockholders' equity}}{\text{Outstanding shares}}$	Book value per common share of stock is the amount each common share would receive if the company were liquidated on the basis of amounts reported on the balance sheet. The figure loses much of its relevance if the valuations on the balance sheet do not approximate fair market value of the assets. When more than one class of stock is outstanding, stockholders' equity must be allocated among the various classes of stock and then expressed on a per share basis within each class.

EXERCISE 25-3

Purpose: (L.O.11) This exercise will give you practice in developing key ratios.

The balance sheets at December 31, 1998 and December 31, 1999 and the income statement for 1999 for the Robert E. Busch, Jr. Corporation are presented below:

Robert E. Busch, Jr. Corporation
COMPARATIVE BALANCE SHEET
December 31, 1998 and 1999

	December 31 1998	December 31 1999
Assets		
Cash	$ 50,000	$ 40,000
Marketable securities	20,000	35,000
Accounts receivable (net)	60,000	85,000
Inventory	150,000	170,000
Plant and equipment (net)	500,000	470,000
Total assets	$ 780,000	$ 800,000
Liabilities and Stockholders' Equity		
Accounts payable	$ 130,000	$ 95,000
Accrued liabilities	10,000	8,000
6% Bonds payable	100,000	100,000
Common stock, $10 par	300,000	300,000
Retained earnings	240,000	297,000
Total liabilities and stockholders' equity	$ 780,000	$ 800,000

Robert E. Busch, Jr. Corporation
INCOME STATEMENT
For the Year Ending December 31, 1999

Net sales		$ 900,000
Cost of goods sold		
Inventory, January 1, 1999	$ 150,000	
Purchases, net	570,000	
Goods available for sale	720,000	
Inventory, December 31, 1999	170,000	550,000
Gross profit		350,000
Operating expenses		
Depreciation	30,000	
Other	194,000	224,000
Income from operations		126,000
Bond interest expense		6,000
Income before taxes		120,000
Provision for income taxes		48,000
Net income		$ 72,000
Earnings per share		$ 2.40

Additional information: Dividends of $.50 per share were paid in 1999 to common stockholders. All sales during 1999 were on credit. The market value per share of common stock was $30 at December 31, 1999. Cash provided by operating activities during 1999 was $20,000.

Instructions

(a)   Fill in the blanks below with the appropriate amounts to develop ratios for the Robert E. Busch Jr. Corporation. (You do not have to compute the ratios, but a full solution is provided if you choose to do so.)

1.   The current ratio at the end of 1999 would be computed by dividing:
     $_____ by $_____.

2.   The acid-test ratio at the end of 1999 would be computed by dividing:
     $_____ by $_____.

3.   The ratio of debt to total assets at the end of 1999 would be computed by dividing: $_____ by $_____.

4.   The rate of return on common stockholders' equity for 1999 would be computed by dividing: $_____ by $_____.

5.   The debt to stockholders' equity ratio at the end of 1999 would be computed by dividing: $_____ by $_____.

6.   The asset turnover ratio for 1999 would be computed by dividing:
     $_____ by $_____.

7.   The number of times bond interest earned ratio for 1999 would be computed by dividing: $_____ by $_____.

8.   The profit margin on sales for 1999 would be computed by dividing:
     $_____ by $_____.

9.   The rate of return on assets for 1999 would be computed by dividing:
     $_____ by $_____.

10. The payout ratio for 1999 would be computed by dividing:
     $_____ by $_____.

11. The book value per common share at December 31, 1999 would be computed by dividing: $_____ by _____.

12. The cash debt coverage ratio would be computed by dividing:
     $_____ by _____.

13. The receivables turnover for 1999 would be determined by dividing:
    $_____ by $_____.
    The average number of days required to collect from a customer for a credit sale would be determined by dividing _____ by _____.

14. The inventory turnover for 1999 would be determined by dividing:
    $_____ by $_____.
    The average number of days sales included in inventory would be computed by dividing _____ by _____.

15. Earnings per share for 1999 would be determined by dividing:
    $_____ by _____.

16. The price earnings ratio at the end of 1999 would be computed by dividing:
    $_____ by $_____.

(b)   Which of the ratios in Part (a) above would be used to evaluate the company's financial strength and future solvency? Indicate your answers by use of the appropriate numbers.

(c)   Which of the ratios in Part (a) above would be used to evaluate the company's earning power and growth potential? Indicate your answers by use of the appropriate numbers.

Solution to Exercise 25-3

(a)
1.	330,000; 103,000	9. 72,000 (or 75,600); 790,000
2.	160,000; 103,000	10. 15,000; 72,000
3.	203,000; 800,000	11. 597,000; 30,000
4.	72,000; 568,500	12. 20,000; 221,500
5.	203,000; 597,000	13. 900,000; 72,500; 365 (or 360) days; 12.41
6.	900,000; 790,000	14. 550,000; 160,000; 365 (or 360) days; 3.44
7.	126,000; 6,000	15. 72,000; 30,000
8.	72,000; 900,000	16. 30; 2.40

Approach and Explanation: Write down the components of each ratio to be computed. (Refer to **Illustration 25-1** when needed.) Extract the pertinent data from the financial statements and "additional information."

1. Current ratio: $\dfrac{\text{Current assets}}{\text{Current liabilities}} = \dfrac{\$40,000 + \$35,000 + \$85,000 + \$170,000}{\$95,000 + \$8,000} = 3.20 \text{ times}$

2. Acid-test ratio: $\dfrac{\text{Quick assets}}{\text{Current liabilities}} = \dfrac{\$40,000 + \$35,000 + \$85,000}{\$95,000 + \$8,000} = 1.55 \text{ times}$

3. Debt to total assets: $\dfrac{\text{Total liabilities}}{\text{Total assets}} = \dfrac{\$95,000 + \$8,000 + \$100,000}{\$800,000} = 25.38\%$

4. Rate of return on common stockholders' equity:

$$\frac{\text{Net income}}{\text{Average common stockholders' equity}} = \frac{\$72,000}{1/2(\$597,000 + \$540,000)} = 12.66\%$$

5. Debt to stockholders' equity:

$$\frac{\text{Total debt}}{\text{Total stockholders' equity}} = \frac{\$95,000 + \$8,000 + \$100,000}{\$300,000 + \$297,000} = 34.0\% \text{ or } .34 \text{ to } 1.00$$

6. Asset turnover: $\dfrac{\text{Net sales}}{\text{Average total assets}} = \dfrac{\$900,000}{1/2(\$800,000 + \$780,000)} = 1.14 \text{ times}$

7. Number of times bond interest earned:

$$\frac{\text{Net income + interest + taxes}}{\text{Interest charges}} = \frac{\$72,000 + \$6,000 + \$48,000}{\$6,000} = 21 \text{ times}$$

8. Profit margin on sales: $\dfrac{\text{Net income}}{\text{Net sales}} = \dfrac{\$72,000}{\$900,000} = 8.0\%$

9. Rate of return on assets: $\dfrac{\text{Net income}}{\text{Average total assets}} = \dfrac{\$72,000}{1/2(\$800,000 + \$780,000)} = 9.11\%$

OR

$$\frac{\text{Net income + interest expense} - \text{tax savings}}{\text{Average total assets}} = \frac{\$72,000 + \$6,000 - 40\%*(\$6,000)}{1/2(\$800,000 + \$780,000)} = 9.57\%$$

$$*\text{Tax rate} = \frac{\text{Income tax expense}}{\text{Income before taxes}} = \frac{\$48,000}{\$120,000} = 40\%$$

10. Payout ratio: $\dfrac{\text{Cash dividends}}{\text{Net income}} = \dfrac{\$.50(30,000 \text{ shares}**)}{\$72,000} = 20.83\%$

**Balance of common stock = \$300,000; par = \$10 per share; \$300,000 ÷ \$10 = 30,000 shares issued; there are no treasury shares, so outstanding shares = 30,000 shares.

11. Book value per common share: $\dfrac{\text{Common stockholders' equity}}{\text{Outstanding common shares}} = \dfrac{\$597,000}{30,000**} = \$19.90$

**See #10.

12. Cash debt coverage ratio:

$$\frac{\text{Net cash provided by operating activities}}{\text{Average total liabilities}} = \frac{\$20,000}{1/2(\$240,000*** + \$203,000****)} = .09029$$

*** = \$130,000 + \$10,000 + \$100,000 = \$240,000
**** = \$95,000 + \$8,000 + \$100,000 = \$203,000

13. Receivables turnover:

$$\frac{\text{Net sales}}{\text{Average trade receivables (net)}} = \frac{\$900,000}{1/2(\$85,000 + \$60,000)} = 12.41 \text{ times}$$

Average number of days to collect an account receivable:

$$\frac{365 \text{ days}}{\text{Receivables turnover}} = \frac{365 \text{ days}}{12.41 \text{ times}} = 29.41 \text{ days}$$

14. Inventory turnover: $\dfrac{\text{Cost of goods sold}}{\text{Average inventory}} = \dfrac{\$550,000}{1/2(\$170,000 + \$150,000)} = 3.44 \text{ times}$

Average number of days' sales in inventory:

$$\frac{365 \text{ days}}{\text{Inventory turnover}} = \frac{365 \text{ days}}{3.44 \text{ times}} = 106.10 \text{ days}$$

15. Earnings per share: $\dfrac{\text{Net income minus preferred dividends}}{\text{Weighted shares outstanding}} = \dfrac{\$72,000 - \$0}{30,000} = \$2.40$

16. Price earnings ratio: $\dfrac{\text{Market price of stock}}{\text{Earnings per share}} = \dfrac{\$30.00}{\$2.40} = 12.5 \text{ times}$

(b)   1, 2, 3, 5, 7, 11, and 12.

(c)   4, 6, 8, 9, 10, 13, 14, 15, and 16.

EXERCISE 25-4

Purpose: (L.O.10,11) This exercise points out the effects of various transactions on selected computations and ratios.

The following list of transactions relate to the Huseman Corporation for 1999. You are to analyze the transactions, assuming that on the date when each of the transactions occurred, the corporation's accounts showed only common stock (80,000 shares, $100 par) outstanding, a current ratio of 3.1 to 1 and a substantial net income for the year to date (before giving effect to the transactions concerned). On that date, the book value per share of common stock was $141.24. Each numbered transaction is to be considered completely **independent** of the others, and its related answer should be based on the effect(s) of that transaction alone. Assume all amounts are material and all transactions were recorded in accordance with generally accepted accounting principles.

Instructions

For each of the transactions, indicate the effect (increase, decrease, or no effect) on each of the following:
(a)   The corporation's net income for 1999.
(b)   The corporation's current ratio
(c)   The book value per share of the corporation's common stock.

| | Effect on: | | |
	(a) Net Income 1999	(b) Current Ratio	(c) Book Value Per Share
Transaction			
1. The corporation declared a cash dividend of $1.00 per share.	_____	_____	_____
2. The corporation paid the cash dividend which had been recorded in the accounts at the time of declaration.	_____	_____	_____
3. The corporation purchased 100 shares of treasury stock for $150 per share.	_____	_____	_____
4. The corporation sold 100 shares of treasury stock for $145 per share; the shares had cost $150 per share.	_____	_____	_____
5. Huseman declared and paid a property dividend. The property used was a short-term investment which had a cost of $50,000 and a fair market value of $72,000.	_____	_____	_____
6. A loss of $20,000 was recognized due to an impairment in the value of equipment.	_____	_____	_____
7. Huseman sold a plot of land previously used in operations. The carrying value was $60,000 and the sales price was $50,000.	_____	_____	_____
8. A storm caused damage to a building. Repairs of $40,000 were completed, and payment was made. A pending insurance claim for $30,000 will partially cover the $40,000 loss.	_____	_____	_____
9. The corporation purchased equipment for $40,000 on account.	_____	_____	_____
10. The corporation collected $25,000 from a customer on account.	_____	_____	_____
11. Huseman wrote off a $10,000 account receivable.	_____	_____	_____
12. Huseman purchased short-term investments for $29,000.	_____	_____	_____
13. The corporation exchanged a $10,000 account payable for a $10,000 short-term note payable.	_____	_____	_____

	Effect on:		
	(a)	**(b)**	**(c)**
Transaction	**Net Income 1999**	**Current Ratio**	**Book Value Per Share**
14. Huseman provided services to customers for cash of $400,000.	_____	_____	_____
15. Huseman purchased $15,000 of inventory on account.	_____	_____	_____

Solution to Exercise 25-4

	(a)	(b)	(c)		(a)	(b)	(c)
1.	No Effect	Decrease	Decrease	9. No Effect	Decrease	No Effect
2.	No Effect	Increase	No Effect	10. No Effect	No Effect	No Effect
3.	No Effect	Decrease	Decrease	11. No Effect	No Effect	No Effect
4.	No Effect	Increase	Increase	12. No Effect	No Effect	No Effect
5.	Increase	Decrease	Decrease	13. No Effect	No Effect	No Effect
6.	Decrease	No Effect	Decrease	14. Increase	Increase	Increase
7.	Decrease	Increase	Decrease	15. No Effect	Decrease	No Effect
8.	Decrease	Decrease	Decrease			

Approach and Explanation: Write down the components of net income, the current ratio, and the book value per common share computations. Prepare the journal entry for each transaction. Analyze the accounts in each entry for their effects on the various components of the computations in question.

$$\text{Revenues} - \text{Expenses} = \text{Net income}$$

$$\frac{\text{Current assets}}{\text{Current liabilities}} = \text{Current ratio}$$

$$\frac{\text{Common stockholders' equity}}{\text{Outstanding common shares}} = \text{Book value per common share}$$

1.   Retained Earnings   80,000
         Dividends Payable   80,000
   (a)   Dividends are not a determinant of income; they are a distribution of income.
   (b)   Current liabilities increase so the current ratio decreases.
   (c)   Total stockholders' equity is reduced with no change in the number of shares outstanding; thus, book value per common share decreases.

2.   Dividends Payable 80,000
          Cash...   80,000

    (a)   There is no income statement element affected by this transaction.
    (b)   Anytime the current ratio is greater than 1 to 1, a decrease in current liabilities accompanied by a decrease in current assets of the same magnitude will cause the current ratio to increase.
    (c)   There is no effect on stockholders' equity or the number of shares outstanding.

3.   Treasury Stock.. 15,000
          Cash...   15,000

    (a)   There is no effect on net income.
    (b)   There is a reduction in current assets; hence, the current ratio is reduced.
    (c)   Total stockholders' equity and the total number of shares outstanding are reduced. Because the treasury shares are being purchased at a price ($150.00 per share) that exceeds the book value per share before that purchase ($141.24), the book value per outstanding share will decrease.

4.   Cash 14,500
    Retained Earnings   500
          Treasury Stock..   15,000

    (a)   There is no accounting gain or loss. This is a capital transaction.
    (b)   Current assets are increased; thus, the current ratio is increased.
    (c)   Total stockholders' equity and the total number of shares outstanding increase. Because the treasury shares are being sold at a price ($145.00) that exceeds the book value per share before that purchase ($141.24), the book value per outstanding share will increase.

5.   Short-term Investments.. 22,000
          Gain on Appreciation of Investment   22,000

    Retained Earnings 72,000
          Property Dividend Payable.......................................   72,000

    Property Dividend Payable 72,000
          Short-term Investments   72,000

    (a)   Net income is increased because of the gain of $22,000.
    (b)   There is a net decrease of $50,000 in current assets with no net change in current liabilities. Therefore, the declaration and payment of the property dividend causes a decrease in the current ratio.
    (c)   There is a net decrease of $50,000 in retained earnings and no effect on the number of shares of stock outstanding. Thus, the book value per share outstanding is decreased.

6.   Loss on Impairment of Equipment 20,000
          Accumulated Depreciation   20,000

(a)   Net income is reduced by $20,000.

(b)   The current ratio is not affected.

(c)   All income statement accounts are closed to retained earnings. Retained earnings is reduced; thus, total stockholders' equity is reduced. There is no effect on the number of shares outstanding. Book value per share, therefore, is decreased.

7.	Cash	50,000	
	Loss	10,000	
	Land		60,000

(a)   Net income is decreased because of the loss.

(b)   Current assets are increased; thus, the current ratio is increased.

(c)   Retained earnings are reduced because of the loss. There is no change in the outstanding shares. Book value per share is reduced.

8.	Insurance Claim Receivable	30,000	
	Loss	10,000	
	Cash		40,000

(a)   Net income is decreased by the $10,000 loss.

(b)   The current ratio is decreased because current assets are reduced by a net amount of $10,000.

(c)   The book value per share is reduced because total stockholders' equity is decreased by the amount of loss recognized. There is no change in the number of shares outstanding.

9.	Equipment	40,000	
	Accounts Payable		40,000

(a)   There are no income statement accounts involved.

(b)   The current ratio is reduced because of the increase in current liabilities.

(c)   There is no effect on the elements of the book value per share computation.

10.	Cash	25,000	
	Accounts Receivable		25,000

(a)   There are no income statement accounts involved.

(b)   There is no net change in current assets and no effect on the current ratio.

(c)   There is no effect on the components of the book value per share ratio.

11.	Allowance for Doubtful Accounts	10,000	
	Accounts Receivable		10,000

(a)   There are no income statement accounts in the write-off entry when the allowance method is used to account for bad debts.

(b)   There is no net change in current assets and no effect on the current ratio.

(c)   There is no effect on the components of the book value per share ratio.

12.	Short-term Investments	29,000	
	Cash		29,000

(a)   There are no income statement accounts involved.

(b)   There is no net change in current assets and no effect on the current ratio.

(c)   There is no effect on the components of the book value per share ratio.

13.   Accounts Payable..   10,000
           Short-term Note Payable...   10,000
       (a)   There are no income statement accounts involved.
       (b)   There is no net change in current liabilities and no effect on the current ratio.
       (c)   There is no effect on the components of the book value per share ratio.

14.   Cash   400,000
           Services Revenue..   400,000
       (a)   Net income is increased due to the revenue recognized.
       (b)   Current assets are increased so the current ratio is increased.
       (c)   Total stockholders' equity is increased (due to the increase in retained earnings)
              which will cause the book value per share to increase.

15.   Inventory...   15,000
           Accounts Payable   15,000
       (a)   There is no effect on net income.
       (b)   Current liabilities are increased. Even though current assets increase by the
              same amount, the current ratio will decrease. Anytime the current ratio is greater
              than 1 to 1, an increase in current liabilities accompanied by an increase in
              current assets of the same magnitude will cause a decrease in the current ratio.
       (c)   There is no effect on book value per share.

EXERCISE 25-5

Purpose: (L.O.10,11,13) This exercise will provide you with an example of how to interpret
the meaning of ratios and trends.

Bandy Company is a wholesale distributor of professional exercise equipment and supplies.
The company's sales have averaged about $900,000 annually for the three-year period 1997-
1999. The firm's total assets at the end of 1999 amounted to $850,000. The president of
Bandy Company has asked the controller to prepare a report that summarizes the financial
aspects of the company's operations for the past three years. This report will be presented to
the Board of Directors at their next meeting.

In addition to comparative financial statements, the controller has decided to present a number
of relevant financial ratios which can assist in the identification and interpretation of trends. At
the request of the controller, the accounting staff has calculated the following ratios for the
three-year period 1997-1999:

	1997	**1998**	**1999**
Current ratio	1.80	1.89	1.96
Acid-test (quick) ratio	1.04	0.99	0.87
Accounts receivable turnover	8.75	7.71	6.42
Inventory turnover	4.91	4.32	3.42
Percent of total debt to total assets	51.0%	46.%	41.0%
Percent of long-term debt to total assets	31.0%	27.0%	24.0%
Sales to fixed assets (fixed asset turnover)	1.58	1.69	1.79
Sales as a percent of 1997 sales	1.00	1.03	1.07
Gross margin percentage	36.0	35.1	34.6
Net income to sales	6.9%	7.0%	7.2%
Return on total assets	7.7%	7.7%	7.8%
Return on stockholders' equity	13.6%	13.1%	12.7%

In the preparation of his report, the controller has decided first to examine the financial ratios independently of any other data to determine if the ratios themselves reveal any significant trends over the three-year period.

Instructions

(a)   The current ratio is increasing while the acid-test (quick) ratio is decreasing. Using the ratios provided, identify and explain the contributing factor(s) for this apparently divergent trend.

(b)   In terms of the ratios provided, what conclusion(s) can be drawn regarding the company's use of financial leverage during the 1997-1999 period?

(c)   Using the ratios provided, what conclusion(s) can be drawn regarding the company's net investment in plant and equipment?   (CMA adapted)

Solution to Exercise 25-5

(a)   The acid-test ratio is the current ratio with the subtraction of inventory and prepaid expenses (generally insignificant relative to inventory) from current assets. Any divergence in trend between these two ratios would, therefore, be dependent upon the inventory account. Inventory turnover has declined sharply in the three-year period, from 4.91 to 3.42. During the same period, total sales have increased 7 percent. The decline in the inventory turnover is, therefore, not due to a decline in sales. The apparent cause is that investment in inventory has increased at a faster rate than sales, and this fact accounts for the divergence between the acid-test and current ratios.

(b)   Financial leverage has definitely declined during the three-year period. This is shown by the steady drop in the long-term-debt-to-total-assets ratio and the total-debt-to-total-assets ratio. Apparently the decline of debt as a percentage of this firm's capital structure is accounted for by a reduction in the long-term sector of the firm's indebtedness. This reduction of leverage accounts for the decrease in the return on stockholders' equity ratio. This conclusion is reinforced by the fact that net income to sales and return on total assets have both increased.

(c) Bandy Company's net investment in plant and equipment has decreased during the three-year period 1997-1999. This conclusion is reached by using the sales-to-fixed-assets (fixed asset turnover) and sales-as-a-percent-of-1997-sales ratios.

Because sales have grown each year, the sales-to-fixed-assets could be expected to increase, unless fixed assets grew at a faster rate. The sales-to-fixed-asset ratio increased at a faster rate than the 3 percent annual growth in sales; therefore, net investment in plant and equipment must have declined.

ANALYSIS OF MULTIPLE-CHOICE TYPE QUESTIONS

QUESTION

1. (L.O.2) Which of the following should be disclosed in the summary of significant accounting policies:

	Depreciation Method	Composition of Property, Plant, & Equipment
a.	Yes	Yes
b.	Yes	No
c.	No	Yes
d.	No	No

Explanation: The depreciation method for plant assets is a commonly required disclosure with respect to accounting policies. The composition of plant assets should **not** be in the summary of significant accounting policies because that information is required elsewhere in the statements. The accounting policy disclosures are **not** to duplicate information presented elsewhere in the financial statements.

Examples of accounting policies to be disclosed include:
- a. Consolidation method.
- b. Inventory pricing method.
- c. Depreciation method.
- d. Amortization method.
- e. Method of accounting for long-term contracts.
- f. Method of accounting for franchising and leasing activities.
- g. Criteria for determining which investments are treated as cash equivalents. (Solution = b.)

QUESTION

2. (L.O.3) Nickolodeon Corp. has six operating segments:

Segments	Total Revenue (Unaffiliated)	Operating Profit (Loss)	Identifiable Assets
A	$ 30,000,000	$ 5,250,000	$ 60,000,000
B	24,000,000	4,200,000	52,500,000
C	18,000,000	3,600,000	37,500,000
D	9,000,000	1,650,000	22,500,000
E	12,750,000	2,025,000	21,000,000
F	4,500,000	675,000	9,000,000
	$ 98,250,000	$ 17,400,000	$ 202,500,000

For which of the segments would information have to be disclosed in accordance with generally accepted accounting principles?
a. segments A, B, C, and D
b. segments, A, B, C, and E
c. segments A, B, C, D, and E
d. all six segments
e. none of the segments

Approach and Explanation: Write down the criteria to be applied in determining reportable segments. Test each segment to see if it meets **one** of the criteria.

Criteria applied in determining reportable segments are:
1. Operating segment revenue (from unaffiliated customers and other segments) is ≥ 10% of combined revenue of all operating segments.
2. Operating segment's absolute operating profit/loss is ≥ 10% of the greater, in absolute amount, of:
    (a) Combined operating profit of all operating segments that did not incur a loss, or
    (b) Combined operating losses of all operating segments that did report a loss.
3. Operating segment's identifiable assets are ≥ 10% of the combined identifiable assets of all operating segments.

Segments A, B, C, and E pass the revenue and operating profit tests, but A, B, C, D, and E all pass the identifiable assets test. Since an operating segment only has to pass one of the three 10% tests to be considered a reportable segment, Nickolodeon has five reportable segments—A, B, C, D, and E. (Solution = c.)

QUESTION

3. (L.O.4) Donnegan Manufacturing Company employs a standard cost system. A planned volume variance in the first quarter of 1999, which is expected to be absorbed by the end of the fiscal year, ordinarily should:
   a. be deferred at the end of the first quarter, regardless of whether it is favorable or unfavorable.
   b. never be deferred beyond the quarter in which it occurs.
   c. be deferred at the end of the first quarter if it is favorable; unfavorable variances are to be recognized in the period incurred.
   d. be deferred at the end of the first quarter if it is unfavorable; favorable variances are to be recognized in the period incurred.

Explanation: Companies generally should use the same inventory pricing methods and procedures for interim reports that they use for annual reports. One of a few exceptions, however, is that planned variances under a standard cost system which are expected to be absorbed by year end ordinarily should be deferred. (Solution = a.)

QUESTION

4. (L.O.4) For interim financial reporting, a company's income tax expense for the second quarter should be computed by using the:
   a. statutory tax rate for the year.
   b. effective tax rate expected to be applicable for the second quarter.
   c. effective tax rate expected to be applicable for the full year as estimated at the end of the first quarter.
   d. effective tax rate expected to be applicable for the full year as estimated at the end of the second quarter.

Explanation: *APB Opinion No. 28* requires that, at the end of each interim period, an enterprise make its best estimate of the effective tax rate expected to be applicable for the full fiscal year. That rate should be used to determine income tax expense on a current year-to-date basis. (Solution = d.)

QUESTION

5. (L.O.4) With regard to interim financial statements, the Accounting Principles Board concluded that interim reporting be viewed as:
   a. reporting for a basic accounting period.
   b. reporting for an integral part of an annual period.
   c. a "special" type of reporting that need not conform to generally accepted accounting principles.
   d. requiring a cash basis approach.

Explanation: *APB Opinion No. 28* views each interim period primarily as an integral part of an annual period. Generally, the preparation of interim reports should be based on the same accounting principles the enterprise uses in preparing annual financial statements. However, certain principles and practices used for annual reporting may require modification at interim dates so that interim reports may relate more closely to the results of operations for the annual period. (Solution = b.)

QUESTION

6.   (L.O.4) For interim financial reporting, an extraordinary loss occurring in the second quarter should be:
          a.   disclosed only in the footnotes in the second quarter.
          b.   recognized in the second quarter.
          c.   recognized ratably over the last three quarters.
          d.   recognized ratably over all four quarters, with the first quarter being restated.

Explanation: *APB Opinion No. 28* requires that extraordinary items be disclosed separately and included in the determination of net income in the interim period in which they occur. Gains and losses that would not be deferred at year-end should not be deferred to later interim periods of the same year. Therefore, the extraordinary loss should not be prorated. (Solution = b.)

*TIP: The following two questions are derived from the material in Appendix 25-A in the text.

QUESTION

7.*   (L.O.9) Which of the following is **not** a monetary account?
          a.   Accounts Receivable
          b.   Allowance for Doubtful Accounts
          c.   Discount on Note Receivable
          d.   Investment in Stock

Explanation: Monetary items are contractual claims to receive or pay a fixed amount of cash. Monetary assets include cash, accounts and notes receivable, and investments that will be repaid at a fixed amount. In this context, contra accounts are classified the same as the accounts to which they relate. Thus, both the Allowance for Doubtful Accounts and the Discount on Note Receivable are monetary accounts. The Investment in Stock is a nonmonetary asset account because the investment will **not** be repaid at a fixed amount. (Solution = d.)

QUESTION

8.*   (L.O.9) If inventory was purchased in 1995 for $120,000, when the general price level was 100, and sold at the end of 1999 for $200,000 when the general price level was 150 and the current cost was $190,000, the 1999 income statement prepared on an historical cost/constant dollar basis would report:
          a.   no holding gain or loss.
          b.   a holding gain of $80,000.
          c.   a holding gain of $20,000.
          d.   a holding gain of $10,000.

Explanation: A holding gain or loss is due to the change in the current cost of a nonmonetary item. Holding gains and losses are quantified only when a current cost system is employed. A holding gain of $10,000 [$190,000 - ($120,000 x 150/100) = $10,000] would appear on a **current cost/constant dollar** income statement for 1999. (Solution = a.)

**TIP: The following eleven questions are derived from the material in Appendix 25-B in the text.

QUESTION

9.**   (L.O.11) The current ratio at any given date for a particular company is:
  a.   usually equal to the acid-test ratio at the same date.
  b.   usually smaller than the acid-test ratio at the same date.
  c.   usually larger than the acid-test ratio at the same date.
  d.   computed by dividing current liabilities by current assets.

Approach and Explanation: Write down the formulas for both the current ratio and the acid-test ratio. Notice what is similar and what is different about them. Think about how the difference will affect the relative results. The current ratio is calculated by dividing total current assets by total current liabilities; whereas, the acid-test ratio is calculated by dividing cash plus short-term investments plus current net receivables by total current liabilities. Current assets other than cash and short-term investments and short-term receivables would normally include inventory and prepaid expenses. Because the current ratio would normally have a larger numerator but the same denominator as the acid-test ratio, it would be larger than the acid-test ratio. (Solution = c.)

QUESTION

10.**   (L.O.11) A company has a current ratio of 2:1 at December 31, 1999. Which of the following transactions would increase this ratio?
  a.   purchase of merchandise on account
  b.   sale of bonds payable at a discount
  c.   payment of a 60-day note payable
  d.   collection of an account receivable
  e.   both "b" and "c"

Approach and Explanation: Set up an example of the situation described; assume current assets are $8,000 and current liabilities are $4,000. Prepare the journal entry for each of the transactions (assume the amount involved is $2,000) and analyze the effect of the entry on the components of the current ratio. The journal entries and analyses should appear as follows:

a.   Inventory 2,000
        Accounts Payable 2,000
Current assets and current liabilities both increase by the same amount ($2,000); therefore, the current ratio will decrease. (The new ratio will be $10,000/$6,000, or 1.67:1 in this example.)

b.   Cash 2,000
      Discount on Bonds Payable.................................. 200
        Bonds Payable.. 2,200
Current assets increase with no change in current liabilities; therefore, the current ratio will increase. (The new ratio will be $10,000/$4,000, or 2.5:1 in this example.)

c.   Short-term Note Payable 2,000
         Cash..   2,000
Current assets and current liabilities both decrease by the same amount; therefore, the current ratio will increase because the ratio was something greater than 1:1 before the transaction. (The new ratio will be $6,000/$2,000, or 3:1 in this example.)

d.   Cash 2,000
         Accounts Receivable...   2,000
Total current assets and total current liabilities both remain unchanged; therefore, there is no change in the current ratio.

e.   Both "b" and "c" cause an increase in the current ratio.   (Solution = e.)

QUESTION

11.**   (L.O.11) A company has a current ratio of 2:1 at December 31, 1999. Which of the following transactions will **not** cause a change in the current ratio?
         a.   declaration of a 10% stock dividend
         b.   purchase of short-term investments for cash
         c.   payment of a long-term liability
         d.   declaration of a cash dividend
         e.   Both "a" and "b"
         f.   Both "a" and "d"

Approach and Explanation: Set up an example of the situation described; assume current assets are $8,000 and current liabilities are $4,000. Prepare the journal entry for each of the transactions (assume the amount involved is $2,000) and analyze the effect of the entry on the components of the current ratio. The journal entries and analyses should appear as follows:

a.   Retained Earnings 2,000
         Common Stock Dividend Distributable...........................   500
         Paid-in Capital in Excess of Par......................................   1,500
There is no effect on current assets, current liabilities, or the current ratio. (The par value of the dividend shares is an assumed amount here.)

b.   Short-term Investments... 2,000
         Cash..   2,000
There is no effect on total current assets, current liabilities, or the current ratio.

c.   Long-term Liability... 2,000
         Cash..   2,000
Current assets are reduced and, therefore, the current ratio is decreased. (The new ratio in this example is $6,000/$4,000, or 1.5:1.)

d.   Retained Earnings 2,000
         Dividends Payable   2,000

Current liabilities are increased and, therefore, the current ratio is decreased. (The new ratio in this example is $8,000/$6,000, or 1.33:1.)

e.   Both "a" and "b" have no effect on the current ratio.

f.   Although "a" has no effect on the current ratio, "d" causes a decrease in the current ratio. (Solution = e.)

QUESTION

12.**   (L.O.11) If the debt to stockholders' equity ratio is 150% and total assets are $500,000, which of the following is **false**?

a.   The ratio is favorable for obtaining additional loans because it is greater than 100%.

b.   Stockholders' equity totals $200,000.

c.   The ratio may be expressed as "3 to 2."

d.   The amount of total liabilities is 1.5 times the amount of total stockholders' equity.

e.   All of the above.

Explanation: The debt to stockholders' equity ratio is calculated by dividing total liabilities by total stockholders' equity. If X is total liabilities and Y is total stockholders' equity and X/Y = 150% and X + Y = $500,000, then:

$$\frac{X}{(\$500,000 - X)} = 1.5$$

Solving for X:

X	=	1.5($500,000 - X)
X	=	$750,000 - 1.5X
X + 1.5X	=	$750,000
X	=	$750,000 ÷ 2.5
X	=	$300,000
Y	=	$500,000 - $300,000 = $200,000

Based on these calculations, selections "b," "c," and "d," are true. Selection "a" is false because creditors would rather see a debt to stockholders' equity ratio of less than 100%. Thus, potential creditors would not look favorably at a 150% debt to stockholders' equity ratio. (Solution = a.)

QUESTION

13.**   (L.O.11) A company has total assets of $1,000,000. It has 6% bonds outstanding with a face value of $400,000. Income before income taxes for the current year is $110,000. The income tax rate is 40%. No preferred stock is outstanding. There are no liabilities other than the bonds. Which of the following is **true**?

a.   The rate of return on stockholders' equity exceeds the rate of return on total assets by 2%.

b.   The rate of return on total assets is 13.4%.

c.   The rate of return on stockholders' equity is 9%.

d.   The company is not favorably trading on the equity.

Explanation: Net income equals $110,000 - (40% x $110,000) = $66,000. The rate of return on total assets = net income plus interest expense divided by total assets. In this case, ($66,000 + $24,000) ÷ $1,000,000 = 9%. The rate of return on stockholders' equity equals net income divided by stockholders' equity. In this case, $66,000 ÷ $600,000 = 11%. Selection "a" is, therefore, a true statement, and selections "b" and "c" are not true statements. Selection "d" is not a true statement because the rate of return on stockholders' equity is greater than the return on total assets, which indicates a situation of favorable trading on the equity. (Solution = a.)

QUESTION
14.** (L.O.11) A corporation has two classes of stock outstanding. The return on common stockholders' equity is computed by dividing net income:
- a. minus preferred dividends by the number of common stock shares outstanding at the balance sheet date.
- b. plus interest expense by the average amount of total assets.
- c. by the number of common stock shares outstanding at the balance sheet date.
- d. minus preferred dividends by the average amount of common stock-holders' equity during the period.

Explanation: The return on common stockholders' equity is computed by dividing the amount of earnings applicable to the common stockholders' interest in the company by the average amount of common stockholders' equity during the period. The amount of earnings applicable to the common stockholders is the amount of net income for the period less the dividends declared on preferred stock during the period. (Solution = d.)

QUESTION
15.** (L.O.11) Which of the following items would **not** be used in calculating the working capital ratio?
- a. accounts payable
- b. inventory
- c. accounts receivable
- d. furniture purchased during the current period

Approach and Explanation: Think about the working capital ratio and write down the formula to compute it. Then read the answer selections and determine which selection does not fit into the formula. The **working capital ratio** is another name for the **current ratio**. The current ratio is determined by dividing total current assets by total current liabilities at a point in time. Answer selection "d" would be classified under the property, plant, and equipment classification and would, therefore, not be included in the calculation of the working capital ratio. (Solution = d.)

QUESTION

16.** (L.O.14) The base figure used for vertical analysis of the income statement is:
a. net income.
b. gross profit.
c. income before income taxes.
d. net sales revenue.

Explanation: On an income statement, net sales is the base amount for vertical analysis. All other items are then expressed as a percentage of that base amount. (Solution = d.)

QUESTION

17.** (L.O.14) The base figure used for vertical analysis of a corporate balance sheet is:
a. total assets.
b. current assets.
c. property, plant, and equipment.
d. stockholders' equity.

Explanation: In performing a vertical analysis of the balance sheet, total assets is the base figure. All other amounts are then expressed as a percentage of the total assets amount. (Solution = a.)

QUESTION

18.** (L.O.14) The Goodings Corporation reported sales of $80,000 in 1997, $96,000 in 1998, and $112,000 in 1999. In a trend analysis for these years, where 1997 is used as the base year, the respective sales percentages would be:
a. 100%; 120%; 137%.
b. 100%; 120%; 117%.
c. 100%; 120%; 140%.
d. 80%; 96%; 112%.

Explanation: Trend analysis is a type of horizontal analysis that is prepared for more than two years. In horizontal analysis, a base year (1997 in this case) is selected. Each item being analyzed is then divided by the amount reported for the base year for the same item. Thus, $80,000 is the 100% figure, $96,000 divided by $80,000 = 120%, and $112,000 divided by $80,000 = 140%. (Solution = c.)

QUESTION

19.** (L.O.14) An analyst is examining an income statement that shows only percentages; all items are expressed in terms of a percentage of net sales. This type of analysis is often called:
a. common-size analysis.
b. horizontal analysis.
c. ratio analysis.
d. multiple-step analysis.

Explanation: **Vertical analysis**, sometimes referred to as **common-size analysis**, is a technique for evaluating financial statement data that expresses each item within a financial statement in terms of a percent of a base amount. For an income statement, net sales is used as the base amount. (Solution = a.)

Notes

Notes

Notes

Notes

Notes

Notes